The Uneasy Alliance

Managing the Productivity-Technology Dilemma

Edited by
Kim B. Clark
Robert H. Hayes
Christopher Lorenz

HARVARD BUSINESS SCHOOL PRESS
Boston, Massachusetts

Harvard Business School Press, Boston 02163
© 1985 by the President and Fellows of Harvard College.
All rights reserved.
Printed in the United States of America.

89   88   87   86   85   5   4   3   2   1

Library of Congress Cataloging in Publication Data

The Uneasy alliance.

  Includes index.
  1. Industrial productivity—Addresses, essays,
lectures. 2. Efficiency, Industrial—Addresses, essays,
lectures. 3. Technological innovations—Addresses,
essays, lectures. I. Clark, Kim B. II. Hayes, Robert H.
III. Lorenz, Christopher, 1946–
HD56.U53   1985   658.5   85-8709
ISBN 0-87584-172-4

Harvard Business School

Research Colloquium

CONTRIBUTORS

Lewis M. Branscomb
Alfred D. Chandler, Jr.
Kim B. Clark
John L. Doyle
Gordon E. Forward
J. Richard Hackman
Robert H. Hayes
Anthony G. Hopwood
Ken-ichi Imai
Philip Jarymiszyn
Robert S. Kaplan
Robert B. McKersie
Edwin Mansfield
Richard R. Nelson
Ikujiro Nonaka
Nathan Rosenberg
Richard S. Rosenbloom
Roland W. Schmitt
Wickham Skinner
Lawrence H. Summers
Hirotaka Takeuchi
Richard E. Walton

Contents

Foreword
  John H. McArthur   vii
Preface   ix
Introduction: The Issues in Perspective   1

PART ONE
THE HISTORICAL CONTEXT

Overview   13
  1 The Commercial Exploitation of Science by American Industry
      Nathan Rosenberg   19
      Commentary   From Industrial Laboratories to Departments of
      Research and Development
      Alfred D. Chandler, Jr.   53

  2 The Taming of Lions: How Manufacturing Leadership Evolved,
     1780–1984
      Wickham Skinner   63
      Commentary   Today's Lions in Action
      Gordon E. Forward   111

  3 Chief Executive Background and Firm Performance
      Philip Jarymiszyn, Kim B. Clark, and Lawrence H. Summers   115
      Commentary
      Richard R. Nelson   137

Part One   Discussion Summary   139

PART TWO
PRODUCTIVITY: HARDWARE VERSUS SOFTWARE

Overview   147
  4 Exploring the Sources of Productivity Differences at the Factory Level
      Robert H. Hayes and Kim B. Clark   151
      Commentary   The Micro Approach to Productivity Analysis
      Robert B. McKersie   189

  5 Accounting Lag: The Obsolescence of Cost Accounting Systems
      Robert S. Kaplan   195

Commentary   The Growth of "Worrying" about Management
Accounting
   Anthony G. Hopwood   227

6   From Control to Commitment: Transforming Work Force Management in
the United States
   Richard E. Walton   237
   Commentary   The Commitment Model: From "Whether" to "How"
   J. Richard Hackman   267

Part Two   Discussion Summary   279

PART THREE
TECHNOLOGY: HARNESSING "CREATIVE DESTRUCTION"

Overview   289
7   Managing Technology for the Longer Term: A Managerial Perspective
   Richard S. Rosenbloom   297
   Commentary   Extraordinary Innovation: Experiment,
Organization, and Teamwork
   Roland W. Schmitt   329

8   Managing the New Product Development Process: How Japanese
Companies Learn and Unlearn
   Ken-ichi Imai, Ikujiro Nonaka, and Hirotaka Takeuchi   337
   Commentary   Managing New Product Development:
How Japanese Companies Learn and Unlearn
   John L. Doyle   377

9   Public Policy toward Industrial Innovation: An International Study of
Direct Tax Incentives for Research and Development
   Edwin Mansfield   383
   Commentary   Direct Tax Incentives for R&D: Time to Cut Bait
or to Fish?
   Lewis M. Branscomb   409
   Reply to Lewis M. Branscomb by Edwin Mansfield   423

10   Exploring Factors Affecting Innovation and Productivity Growth within
the Business Unit
   Kim B. Clark and Robert H. Hayes   425

Part Three   Discussion Summary   459

Contributors   467
Index   471

Foreword

Founded in 1908, the Harvard University Graduate School of Business Administration celebrated its seventy-fifth anniversary in the academic year 1983–84. We chose to take this opportunity to involve our faculty in thinking seriously about the challenges and opportunities ahead in important fields of management research and teaching.

Field-based empirical research, within and across organizations, has always been fundamental to Harvard Business School's ability to meet its objectives of educating business managers and helping to improve the practice of management. In some respects, we are creating a distinctive model of research. We have often broken through the bounds of traditional disciplines and methodologies to borrow whatever tools and concepts were needed for a particular inquiry. In addition, we have been less concerned with testing existing theory than with generating new insights. And while we often find ourselves drawn to problems that are broad in scope, we strive for results that are operationally significant to managers.

Because Harvard Business School faculty members are committed to pursuing research on the way business actually *does* function, as well as theoretical explorations of how it perhaps *should* function, they can give students and practitioners a vital perspective on the real world of professional practice. Their continuing close contact with operating businesses keeps Harvard Business School faculty at the frontiers of management practice. Research conducted by the faculty often yields insights that are of considerable practical benefit to managers in both day-to-day operations and longer-range planning.

In sponsoring the colloquium series of 1983–84, we hoped to set the course for research development over the next decade, and in particular to encourage greater emphasis on multiperson, multiyear studies of major issues. The complexity of many issues confronting business today almost requires that academicians find more effective forms of collaboration in doing our research. The problems we study are often beyond the capacity of any individual researchers.

In addition to encouraging a reshaping of researcher's work habits, the conferences promised to help strengthen the ties beween Harvard

Business School and the outside academic and business leadership communities. The series comprised sixteen conferences held at the Harvard Business School campus, each lasting two to five days. Papers were presented by eighty members of the HBS faculty and an approximately equal number of practitioners and academics from other institutions. Altogether, some 450 academics and practitioners were involved as discussants and participants.

Some of these colloquia focused on current research topics, such as U.S. competitiveness in the world economy, productivity and technology, global competition, and world food policy. Others concentrated on establishing agendas for the coming decade's research and course development in a particular field. Clearly, these were not tasks to be attempted in isolation. Rather we wanted to work jointly with others in business, government, and the academic world who could contribute and would themselves gain from the undertaking. The papers presented in this volume have all benefited from the thoughtful discussion they received at the colloquium.

Beyond exploring research findings in particular areas, we hoped that these colloquia would sustain and enliven the continuing dialogue between students and practitioners of management. From that melding of perspectives, we have found, insights emerge that can revitalize the education of future managers and refine current professional practice. In that spirit of cooperative endeavor, I am proud to introduce this collection of essays.

JOHN H. MCARTHUR
Dean of the Faculty
Harvard Business School

Preface

Harvard's decision to sponsor a series of colloquia in commemoration of its seventy-fifth anniversary provided us with an opportunity to do something we had often talked about. Traditional theories of international industrial competition were unable to provide adequate explanations of recent trends. New theories were being proposed, but they had not been validated. There was renewed interest in exploring these issues at the micro level—the individual firm or factory—since the macro perspective based on aggregate data had proven inadequate. It seemed a good time to bring together a group of distinguished business practitioners and academics to review what was going on, to discuss the insights that were emerging from new research (largely based on field research), and to formulate new explanations and prescriptions.

This type of meeting can be somewhat risky. There is always the possibility that practitioners and academics will decide that the other has little of value to contribute. Each group then ends up talking only to itself, reinforced in its view that it alone understands what is going on. Happily, this colloquium was just the opposite. Within an hour or two it was almost impossible to distinguish academics from practitioners as they questioned, supported, and informed one another. The colloquium was not simply a series of papers presented, discussed, and forgotten. It was far more a cumulative examination of fundamental issues in the management of production and technology, in which succeeding presentations added perspective, raised new questions, and provoked insightful debate. The two days we spent together were stimulating and instructive for all. We are grateful for the contribution of the Shell Companies Foundation to this project.

We have tried to capture what transpired during those two days in this book. In doing this, we organized the papers around the three major themes that were addressed—the historical context, productivity, and technology—added commentaries to assist the reader in understanding the context within which various issues were discussed, and summarized some of the specific points that arose during the discussions.

Our late colleague Professor William Abernathy spent most of the last ten years of his life working on the intertwined issues of productivity and technology, and the last two helping to organize this colloquium. In December 1983, three months before the colloquium, he finally lost his long battle against cancer. Although he was not able to be with us in person, the spirit of his work pervaded our meeting and the subsequent preparation of this book. It is therefore with a mixture of pride, appreciation, and sorrow that we dedicate it to his memory.

Kim B. Clark
Robert H. Hayes
Christopher Lorenz

THE UNEASY ALLIANCE

Introduction: The Issues in Perspective

The U.S. Productivity Slowdown

Over the last twenty years there has been an alarming slowdown in the productivity growth of the U.S. economy, while foreign competitors have carved out strong, sometimes leading, positions in technically advanced markets. America is still the most productive of the industrialized economies, and many U.S. firms remain—or have become— vigorous competitors. But, in overall terms, relative positions have changed dramatically.

These changes have attracted widespread attention. Analysts from a variety of disciplines have published numerous studies of productivity trends and the competitive misfortunes of U.S. industries. The two basic questions they have tried to address are straightforward: Why did productivity growth slow down? And why have U.S. firms lost market share to foreign competitors who face similar external pressures? The search for answers to these questions has led to a thorough reexamination of the fundamentals of productivity growth, technological innovation, and competitive behavior.

Much of the research, particularly that done by economists and political scientists, has focused on public policy at the national and industry level. But this approach has yielded few insights into the productivity slowdown. As Edward Dennison, a leading authority on productivity analysis, concluded after a study of seventeen possible causes of the slowdown: "What happened is, to be blunt, a mystery."[1] Some economists have therefore proposed a fundamental reevaluation of their traditional macroeconomic approach.

Just as economic research has failed to unravel the productivity enigma, so has most recent managerial research. As a result, both managers and managerial theorists are beginning to recognize that their conventional "business strategy" and "corporate portfolio" frameworks are unable to explain satisfactorily the dynamics of productivity and competitive behavior at the level of the operating manager.

1

The colloquium on which this book is based was conceived during the period of doubt, frustration, and reflection that followed the apparent breakdown of these traditional models. Academics, government policy-makers, and business leaders have agreed that a continuation of America's comparative slowdown would not only have a major economic impact, but eventually serious social consequences as well. There has been sharp disagreement, however, as to who was to blame for the slowdown, what should be done to correct it, and who should be entrusted with taking action. Unfortunately, in the absence of a credible alternative framework this debate has been largely ideological in nature.

Economic versus Managerial Research

To the extent that traditional economic analysis has focused on the behavior of individual companies, it has done so within a textbook framework in which each firm faces a known set of opportunities and constraints and competes against similar firms primarily on the basis of the cost of its product. Technological change is assumed to originate outside the company and is available to all competitors on an equal footing. No long-term commitments are required; investments are reversible, and the factors of production—including human skills and relationships—can be acquired (and divested) through market transactions. In this environment the firm's only problem is to choose and assemble the combination of factors that will produce the right level of output given the prices it faces.

This stylized model of the firm is used primarily to study entire markets and industries and is not assumed to be an accurate description of what actually happens inside individual companies; it remains, however, a powerful guiding force in economic research. Moreover, traditional economic theory views productivity growth (measured by output per person, or output per unit of total input) as being largely the product of changes in such macro variables as capital investment, demographics, and education, so statistical analyses typically focus on large aggregates (for example, the nation or broad industries), using data collected by government agencies. As a result, few economists have been interested in or have studied closely the impact of specific management activities on firm behavior and performance.

This framework contrasts sharply with that guiding management-oriented research, which assumes that a firm's managers have very poor information about constraints and opportunities. Therefore, coping with and trying to reduce uncertainty is one of their major functions. The products a company produces and the nature of the competition it faces are complex, so there are many ways to compete. It must continually adapt to a changing environment, yet most investment decisions involve commitments that cannot easily be undone. Moreover, some factors of production (for example, certain kinds of knowledge) can only be acquired through internal experience; they are not traded on markets. The manager's task, therefore, is to create order out of this potential chaos, and to create distinctive capabilities within the firm without perfect information about alternatives.

The implications of the contrast between traditional economic models and management-oriented research run deeper than is suggested by this contrast between the behavior of whole industries and what goes on inside firms. Take, for example, the role of a company's history. The economist, steeped in the tradition of the textbook firm, is unlikely even to include this issue in an agenda of important questions. Strictly applied, the textbook theory suggests that the decisions a firm faces at any given moment are independent of the path that it has taken up to that point. In short, history does not matter. For the student of management, however, knowing a firm's history is essential. Within the framework that guides management-oriented research, such a history represents a legacy of decisions that profoundly influence the firm's choices and opportunities. Whereas the first approach denies historical experience a role in competition or in productivity growth, the other treats it as a central issue. We emphasize this centrality by choosing to begin this book with a collection of historical chapters.

Similarly, on a variety of other issues—the possible conflict between the pursuit of production efficiency and the ability to respond to technical change, the value of rapid growth and market share, the relative importance of investment decisions—textbook economics is silent. For students of management who want to understand their influence on innovation and productivity, however, these issues are fundamental.

Toward a New Framework

The failure of traditional macroeconomic models to shed light on the nature and causes of productivity growth and technological change has led to renewed interest in what managers of individual firms and factories do to encourage or retard these changes. This shift of emphasis, by both economists and management researchers, has also been prompted by a growing realization that the success of America's foreign competitors has come not so much from strategic brilliance as from their straightforward ability to improve product quality, reduce costs, and expand their technical capabilities. The problems encountered by firms that espoused "modern management" approaches—with their emphasis on portfolio management, "management by the numbers" within ROI-oriented control systems, strategic planning that considers technology to be available on demand, and so forth—have raised challenging questions about the effectiveness of certain management policies and competitive practices. More important, they have led a number of management experts to extoll the virtues of a new-old approach, sometimes referred to as "back to the basics."

Out of these two contrasting bodies of theory a new framework for research is beginning to emerge. It combines empirical economic analysis with a "managerial" perspective, and it must grapple with the inherent tension between productivity and innovation.

The Productivity-Technology Dilemma

Although most economists have tended to focus on comparative efficiency (the amount of output obtained from existing resources) as the primary dimension of industrial success, a few (notably Schumpeter and Veblen) have highlighted the companion dimension of innovation. Management researchers, on the other hand, generally accept, almost as an axiom, that successful firms must be innovative as well as efficient. Both schools tend to assume, however, that an extraordinarily efficient company need not be especially innovative, while one that is extraordinarily innovative need not be especially efficient. Firms can choose in which way, or mixture of ways, they wish to compete.

Since the mid-1960s, however, there has been increasing understanding that the issue for the manager is more complicated than simply exercising free choice among these two dimensions of competitiveness. Instead, there is growing recognition that efficiency and innovation are fundamentally adversarial in nature. One of the earliest and most persuasive statements of this conflict was made by our late colleague, Professor William Abernathy, in his 1978 book, *The Productivity Dilemma*. Based on an exhaustive historical study of the U.S. automobile industry, he argued: "Stated generally, to achieve gains in productivity there must be attendant losses in innovative capacity; or, conversely, the conditions needed for rapid innovative change are much different from those that support high levels of production efficiency."

The focus of this book is the dilemma that Abernathy articulated. Its title utilizes somewhat more glamorous words—"productivity" for efficiency and "technology" for innovation—but the issue is the same. An industrial firm must be *both* productive in its use of existing resources and knowledge, and capable of technological innovation. Yet it is difficult (and possibly counter-productive) to be both. How can the inherent contradiction between the two be resolved, their uneasy alliance strengthened?

Several of the chapters that follow address this issue directly and serve to sharpen the nature of the conflict between the two concepts. For example, in "Exploring the Sources of Productivity Differences at the Factory Level" (Part Two), Robert H. Hayes and Kim B. Clark found that a major cause of productivity decline in the factories they examined appeared to be due to what they termed "confusion-engendering activities." In addition to such obvious causes of confusion as rapid changes in production schedules, these included Engineering Change Orders (ECOs) and the introduction of new equipment. Both of the latter reflect technological activity. Complementary evidence of the productivity-reducing effect of introducing new equipment into an existing production system is contained in their companion chapter "Exploring Factors Affecting Innovation and Productivity Growth within the Business Unit" (Part Three).

But they also observed evidence that ECOs were not inevitably disruptive. In certain situations it seemed possible to manage them in such a way that the confusion they caused was minimized. The question that is raised by this tantalizing but fragmentary evidence is that if a major part of the Abernathy dilemma is due to the confusion induced by technological change, and if certain forms of managerial behavior can mitigate this confusion, then is it possible that the dilemma can be "managed away"?

Another approach to resolving the contradiction between efficiency and innovation is contained in the concept of "learning" which highlights the dynamic interaction of the two dimensions. The actual level of a firm's productivity is critical to its competitive success at each point in time, but the rate of growth of that productivity is at least as important over the long run. Activities that sacrifice long-term productivity growth (which is, in major part, the result of technological innovation) to improve near-term efficiency are eventually self-defeating.

The measurement of factory learning rates played a major role in the Hayes-Clark chapter mentioned above. They also observed a "steady state mentality," inherently antilearning in nature, in many of the factories they examined. Wickham Skinner, in his chapter "The Taming of Lions" (Part One), also alludes to the static nature of the term "productivity" as it is used by many U.S. manufacturing managers today. He argues that future managers must understand and encourage a more dynamic view of competitive progress if they are to prevail against their foreign adversaries. Finally, in their chapter subtitled "How Japanese Companies Learn and Unlearn" (Part Three), Imai, Nonaka and Takeuchi emphasize the importance of organizational fluidity and learning in new product development.

The Managerial Causes of Economic Decline

Two years after *The Productivity Dilemma* appeared, Abernathy joined Robert Hayes in writing "Managing Our Way to Economic Decline,"[2] an article containing a broad indictment of the management philosophies they asserted were at least partly responsible for American industry's declining competitiveness. Although widely publicized (and almost as widely denounced) at the time of its publication, many of the Hayes-Abernathy assertions no longer appear so heretical. They are summarized in the inset.

THE MANAGERIAL CAUSES OF DECLINE

1. Many important American industries have become dangerously vulnerable to foreign competition;
2. A major reason for this competitive vulnerability has been U.S. companies' decreasing willingness to match their competitors' technological aggressiveness—new products and new production processes;
3. While environmental factors played a part in their comparative decline, many of the same factors affected their foreign competitors; therefore U.S. managers had to shoulder a major share of the blame for their loss of position;
4. One of the major causes of these managers' problems was their increasing unwillingness to sacrifice short-term profitability for long-term, less quantifiable benefits (they noted, for example, a decrease in the rate of investment in capital equipment and R&D, a shift to organizational structures and control systems that induced a "management by the numbers" mentality, and financial markets that encouraged such behavior);
5. Another cause, however, was an imperfect understanding of the impact that certain actions—such as the decision to make rather than buy certain components, or to rely on external equipment suppliers for all of one's manufacturing equipment rather than attempt to develop proprietary processes—had on a firm's long-term technological capability;
6. And both causes were influenced by a management selection and development system that prized impersonal analytical skills and impeded managers from gaining extensive experience in all of their firms' core competitive activities—particularly those pertaining to manufacturing and technological development.

Several of those assertions are tested in this volume. In their chapter "Exploring Factors Affecting Innovation and Productivity Growth within the Business Unit," for example, Clark and Hayes examine the impact of investments in new equipment, in product and process R&D, and in vertical integration, on both new product introduction and total factor productivity. The results they obtain are somewhat ambiguous but generally support the Hayes-Abernathy hypotheses.

In "Chief Executive Background and Firm Performance" (Part One), Jarymiszyn, Clark, and Summers explore the nature and possible effect of the changes in the functional backgrounds of U.S. CEOs over the period 1960–80. They find that in large firms, as Hayes and Abernathy argued, there was a shift away from those with operations backgrounds whereas the percentage of those with marketing and financial backgrounds roughly doubled. This pattern, however, was reversed in smaller firms. Moreover, they detected a shift in both large and small firms to professionally trained (M.B.A. degreed) CEOs.

Skinner's "The Taming of Lions" enriches this statistical analysis with a historical perspective, going back to the 1800s, on the changing nature of the background and characteristics of production managers. His study suggests a much more complex explanation for the behavior patterns of modern U.S. manufacturing firms than can be captured by the indicators used by Jarymiszyn et al. Nor is he very optimistic that such behavior patterns will change for the better in the immediate future if firms continue to monitor and motivate production managers' behavior with their traditional measurement and reward systems.

A number of the chapters that follow emphasize other aspects of the importance of a firm's infrastructure to its dynamic performance. This includes its policies on management selection, development and promotion, its measurement and control systems, its capital budgeting systems, its work-force policies, and its organizational structure. If these infrastructural issues are just as important as structural ones (the location of factories, the age and technology of processing equipment, the amount invested in R&D, and so forth) or if structural decisions must be complemented by appropriate infrastructure activities to be effective, then a company cannot restore its competitive position through structural changes alone.

In other words, it cannot simply spend its way out of a competitive hole. Pouring money into new plants and new equipment is useless if one's workers and managers do not have the skills to run them effectively, or if one's control systems and managerial traditions encourage them to be used improperly. Investing money in research, or in buying new product designs from the outside, will similarly fail if the firm is unable to translate the resulting technologies into well-engineered products, produce such products efficiently in its factories, or sell them effectively through its sales organization.

Robert Kaplan addresses one aspect of this infrastructure in his chapter, "Accounting Lag: The Obsolescence of Cost Accounting Systems" (Part Two). He found that the traditional cost accounting systems used by U.S. manufacturing firms are becoming increasingly inappropriate as new technologies and approaches to production management appear in their factories. Yet most of the companies he examined were much less willing to change their accounting systems—the selection and arrangement of numbers on paper—than they were to make fundamental changes in their manufacturing technologies. Worse, he asserts, unless such changes are made, the effectiveness of the new technologies will be undermined.

Richard Walton in "From Control to Commitment: Transforming Work Force Management in the United States" (Part Two) addresses the same theme in arguing that most American companies will have to make fundamental changes in their work-force policies and worker-manager relationships before they can achieve major improvements in productivity. Similarly, Imai et al. suggest that nontraditional kinds of organizational structures and working relationships seem to be more conducive to new product development in the Japanese companies they studied.

Where Are We Now and Where Are We Headed?

Where are we today, therefore, in terms of our understanding of the sources of industrial success? Based on these chapters, together with related studies going on elsewhere, we are gaining a much richer and more satisfying understanding of the complex nature of the activities that facilitate the interaction of efficiency and innovation, and encourage them both.

The relationship between productivity and technology is far from straightforward. Long-term productivity growth requires more than simply wringing more of the same output from the same inputs. It requires changing the nature of the output, through product innovation, and this in turn is likely to cause shifts in market demand. It also requires changes in the inputs and manufacturing processes.

A company that is highly efficient in producing an obsolete product may find itself out of business despite its high "productivity." On the other hand, the changes in products and processes that are essential to remain competitive in a dynamic market are usually both risky and expensive. The investment needed for such innovation will reduce immediate financial returns to the business, and the disruption of production that is caused by such changes can have a severe impact on productivity.

We now see more clearly than before that such dilemmas cannot be resolved entirely through the kind of structural changes, achieved through capital investment, that preoccupy the senior managers of most American companies. Solutions to deep-seated competitive problems cannot be easily bought or sold. Nor is new technology always the answer; it may cause more problems than it solves. Unless properly conditioned and managed, a firm may reject a new technology (or a new measurement system) just like the human body rejects an organ transplant that is necessary for its survival.

Finally, we are beginning to develop a fuller appreciation—as did the industrial lions of yesteryear—of the dynamic nature of competition. One does not simply make and sell a product, one must build an organization that can continually make ever-better products in ever-better ways. Hence, in the long run it is less important for a firm to attain a certain level of competitiveness, either in efficiency or innovation, than it is to develop the capability continually to improve itself.

We are gradually coming to believe, however, that the traditional "command and control" approach to management (what Walton refers to as the "Control Model") may be inherently static. Within such an organization, productivity and technology may inevitably be in conflict. Resolving this conflict, this productivity-technology dilemma, may be possible only through the development of organizations that learn easily and naturally, and where progress occurs organically rather than as a result of top-down direction. Such firms are likely to require vastly different kinds of infrastructures, different kinds of managers and, more important, a different philosophy of management. In them, the term "productivity" will not have the short-term connotation that it does in most firms today. It will encompass both efficiency and innovation and look to technological innovation as an ally rather than an obstacle in the battle against external competitors.

An Outline and Reading Guide

This description of the environment—both economic and intellectual—against which the colloquium took place is followed by three major parts. Part One contains three of the papers that describe various aspects of the historical background of these issues. Each in its own way underscores the central role that managerial attitudes and practices play in shaping the longer term course of productivity growth and technological development. Part Two is composed of three chapters that focus on some of the subtler, more conceptual aspects of productivity improvement. Their theme is not "how do you make it happen?" but rather "what are the characteristics of organizations in which it seems to happen more naturally?" In Part Three we turn to technology, ranging from macro issues, such as public policy toward R&D, to a micro level discussion of how successful firms manage new product development.

The volume is based on a collection of papers written by different authors and highlights a number of important issues relating to the management of productivity improvement and technological innovation. As with any such collection it does not pretend to be comprehensive. Nor do all papers have a uniform style and approach; indeed, we purposely encouraged a variety of perspectives.

Readers are therefore advised to begin by reading the Overviews of each of the three parts. These provide a conceptual framework for the chapters that follow, as well as specific information about them. Each chapter is generally followed by a commentary, and each part of the book concludes with a summary of the discussion the papers sparked among our participants. Some readers may wish to use this bridging material to help them fashion their own customized reading plan, rather than proceeding through the papers sequentially.

Notes

1. Edward F. Denison, *Accounting for Slower Economic Growth: The United States in the 1970s* (Washington, D.C.: Brookings Institution, 1979, p. 4.)

2. Robert H. Hayes and William J. Abernathy, "Managing Our Way to Economic Decline," *Harvard Business Review*. July-August 1980, pp. 67–77.

Part One

The Historical Context

Overview

History of any kind, be it political, social, economic, or industrial, casts a long and often distorted shadow. Not only is its impact on modern attitudes and behavior frequently underrated, but it tends to be misunderstood, and its lessons misapplied.

So it is with the history of the management of productivity and technology. On the one hand, there is still far from sufficient recognition of how deeply the attitudes, structures, and behavior of American manufacturing firms have become locked by historical influences into a pattern unsuited to today's social and business environment. On the other, those influences tend to be interpreted in a misleading fashion— not only within the corporate world but also at the government level.

Such historical influences and misinterpretations have affected both the structure and strategy of modern corporations. In the particular context of this volume they have affected the relative priority given to the development of new products on the one hand and to the production process on the other—with the latter generally coming off a poor second. Indirectly, they have influenced the way in which the various managerial functions are organized, and the relationships between them.

The chapters in this section of the book deal with two key, interrelated "histories":

- *The way in which American industry began to exploit science on a large scale during the nineteenth century, and how this has been carried through to the present day; and*
- *The way in which the nature of U.S. manufacturing leadership has evolved since the late eighteenth century.*

Focusing on the first, Nathan Rosenberg argues that, for all the general excitement about "frontier-pushing" science and Nobel-Prize winning, the generation of science has been far less important than its application. Contrary to a widespread view in the scientific establishment, in industry, and among government policymakers, he also argues that "new" science has generally taken some considerable time to be applied in industry. Disputing the idea that application occurs in a fairly direct and linear fashion, he demonstrates that various kinds of change in the industrial environment—including factors largely independent of science, and sometimes even of technology—have encouraged the use of "old" scientific knowledge. This has tended to be applied in the form of step-by-step, "incremental" improvements (often embedded in production processes) rather than in the radical product breakthroughs with which most recent innovation literature has been concerned.

Success has gone to those companies and industries that were quickest to spot and exploit relatively straightforward technical opportunities, reports Rosenberg. So, "to a much greater extent than we have been aware," he concludes, "science has become the handmaiden of technology in industrializing societies. If we want to penetrate deeply into . . . productivity growth . . . we must study the multitude of ways, often complex and circuitous, in which industrial technologies have shaped the demand for scientific knowledge."

Rosenberg also charts the consequences of this for business organizations—in particular, the establishment of the first industrial research laboratories. In the three industrial sectors examined in his paper— iron and steel, construction, and processing and packing—U.S. firms achieved large size before their foreign competitors. This not only secured them the advantage of scale, but also forced them to apply new techniques to controlling the quality of their processes and products. Hence the first corporate R&D laboratories—usually integral parts of the factory—were essentially dedicated to testing, measuring, quality control, and standardization. Until World War I, few performed actual research.

In the commentary immediately following Rosenberg's chapter, Alfred D. Chandler, Jr. takes the story forward, examining the impact of the new organizational arrangements for R&D that emerged in the United States and Germany as large firms began to apply the findings of science on a more systematic basis. The R&D lab was now separated off from the factory and the rest of the firm and started to work closely with the university world. The benefits of this coupling were immeasurable, as evidenced by the signal inability of entrepreneurs in Britain, the leading industrialized nation at the time, to secure them. "The failure of the British manufacturers to create the organizational arrangements necessary to exploit the commercial potential of the new science-based industries meant that the nation lost out on many of the fruits of the Second Industrial Revolution," comments Chandler. "It was a failure from which the British never recovered." The British did set up R&D laboratories, but they failed to build the necessary link-ages between "science," technical knowledge, and commercial develop-ment.

This historical episode has immediate relevance for today, Chandler concludes, as the United States and other Western nations rush to try and learn from the success of Japanese organizational strategies and structures.

As these papers make clear, one can learn much from the "old mas-ters," as well as the new. Drawing lessons too glibly from history can be dangerous, however. The very increase in scale and complexity that encouraged U.S. and German firms to reap the benefits of science and technology also led to a distancing between the factory and the labora-tory. Countless companies are now urgently trying to bridge this gulf in their quest for better linkages between development and manufac-ture. (For more about this trend, see both the discussion at the end of this part and the Chapters in Part Three.)

The growth in organizational size and complexity also contributed heavily to the distancing of top management from the factory, which is traced in the paper by Wickham Skinner. His central thesis is that American manufacturing is suffering from a management problem of considerable proportions. This is due in part to a "mind set"—and a reinforcing selection process—that evolved early in the history of pro-duction management and that today is highly dysfunctional. It con-sists of several characteristic tendencies in managerial thinking about factories and how to manage them, principally:

1. *Perceiving and managing the factory largely through financial and narrow efficiency measures, rather than through measures that reflect a broad, long-term view of productivity;*
2. *Looking upon plant managers essentially as custodians, whose basic task is to control and coordinate existing systems rather than design new ones;*
3. *Treating labor as a constraint, rather than as a potential creative resource;*
4. *Pursuing mass production and mechanization whenever econom-ically feasible, regardless of their appropriateness to a firm's com-petitive strategy.*

In the nineteenth century, argues Skinner, top management played the role of manufacturing "architect," making the key production man-agement decisions, including the selection or design of equipment and processes. Such industrialists as Andrew Carnegie and Isaac Singer

were veritable "lions" in their forceful personal investment in the factory and their development of innovative processes and systems. Short-
term operational decisions and labor issues were largely delegated to
powerful, independent foremen.

By 1900, however, industry's growing scale, complexity, and multi-
plant nature caused the need for a middle-level managerial function of
planning, coordination, and control. Hence the creation of the first
production departments and the implementation of the industrial engineering concepts of Frederick Taylor and his followers. From then
on, not only did the foreman's role diminish in importance, but the
function of these "middle managers" became essentially to generate
the best possible financial return from the assets entrusted them. Says
Skinner: "The earlier [top] management emphasis on process innovation got lost in the delegation of manufacturing management . . . to a
secondary position in the firm."

In this way, executives who in the earlier era tended to be formidable, "lion"-like production "architects" became tame, cautious, bureaucratic, conservative "caretakers," looking after immutable production
systems. Given that change and instability are the enemies of efficient
operations, and that most of these production managers were (and are)
measured on their short-term performance, this was entirely sensible
behavior on their part. For several decades, it did not appear to be
harmful to their companies. But caution and aversion to change are
inappropriate and counterproductive today when, as Skinner points
out, "technological change is, more than ever before, the basis of industrial competition."

The chapter concludes with suggestions of how firms can change this
stifling management environment: notably by perceiving the factory,
not as a short-term "productivity machine," but as an institution
"which can create multiple values for its various stakeholders and, in
particular, strategic leverage for the firm." Such an approach is clearly
in place at Chaparral Steel, whose chief executive's commentary on
Skinner's chapter immediately follows it.

Whether the future will mirror the immediate past depends largely
on the character of the next generation of production managers, and
Skinner's chapter includes a study of the attitudes of these "comers."
But for this new generation to have a real impact, it needs support
from top management. To the extent that the support a chief executive
gives his or her manufacturing managers depends on the extent of his
or her own background in operations, the picture is not especially
hopeful. This is one implication of the findings of the final chapter in
this section, by Jarymiszyn, Clark, and Summers, on the functional

background of chief executives since 1960. In larger companies the proportion of new CEOs with an operations background appears to have fallen sharply in the second half of the 1970s, to only 10 percent of the total sample. Even more troubling, by 1980 less than half of the new CEOs in these large companies had backgrounds that can be identified with one of the core functions (marketing, R&D, and operations) of the business. On the other hand, the conventional picture of CEOs indulging in an incessant game of intercompany musical chairs is not borne out by the study; it finds that the vast proportion of firms actually appear to promote from within.

The authors also draw some tentative conclusions about the impact of the changing patterns they observe on certain measures of corporate performance. These sparked a spirited debate among the colloquium participants.

1

The Commercial Exploitation
of Science by American Industry

Nathan Rosenberg

Introduction

A unique feature of twentieth-century industrial economies has been the systematic and widespread application of scientific knowledge and methodologies to the business world. In view of the importance of science in shaping our past, present, and prospective economic performance, it is astonishing that we know so little about the exact nature of the science-industry relationship and the specific historical forces that have shaped the application of science to industrial uses. This surprising lacuna takes on additional significance in view of a widely held belief that America has in the past excelled, not so much in the performance of pure science, as in the sustained application of the findings of science to the diverse needs of an expanding industrial establishment.[1]

This paper attempts to throw some new light upon the historical emergence of science as a productive force in American industry. In dealing with a subject that has been dominated more by sweeping rhetoric than by a precise specification of the actual content of science-industry relationships between science and industry, the paper's perspective is intentionally specialized.

Rather than supporting a common charge against the discipline of economics, that it has reduced the immensely valuable and creative human activity of scientific research to a series of calculations of costs and benefits, I would argue that it has actually *failed* to do so. That is, economists have long been content to treat science as essentially an exogenous variable, an ongoing activity in which resource allocation has not been discernibly connected to calculations of future benefits

The author would like to acknowledge the valuable comments he has received from Moses Abramovitz, Stanley Engerman, Ralph Landau, and David Mowery.

and present costs.[2] It is surprising, in view of the frequency with which economists have been accused of some form of intellectual imperialism in recent years, that they have devoted practically no attention to the search for the economic determinants of scientific activity.[3]

In fact, some important part of scientific research has always been motivated by strong, if imprecise, expectations that research in specific directions would yield large payoffs, private as well as social. But, more significantly for present purposes, an interest in the economic impact of science requires that we focus upon the forces influencing not just the search for new knowledge, but those affecting the applications of that knowledge as well. (The two activities, of course, are not entirely unrelated.)

It is curious that so little attention has been devoted to this question. On the one hand, it seems to be of no particular interest to historians of science, while social scientists seem to have regarded the matter of the application of scientific knowledge as, somehow, so straightforward or self-evident as to require no special attention.

In examining the long sequence of events against the backdrop of the history of industrializing societies, the causal priority of scientific breakthroughs may seem readily apparent. To most observers of what Simon Kuznets has aptly called "The Scientific Epoch,"[4] it has been the cutting edge of newly acquired scientific knowledge that has brought forth entirely new industries and an unprecedented intimacy between scientifically trained personnel and the productive process. Important historical episodes come readily to mind.

Electricity is, of course, the perfect embodiment of such a historical sequence. It was, essentially, an entirely new scientific discipline, one that had only the most meager and tenuous of roots (in experiments involving Leyden jars and kites) until the key discoveries of Galvani and Volta in the closing years of the eighteenth century. The nineteenth and early twentieth centuries display an easily recognizable line of descent in which fundamental scientific breakthroughs in understanding the phenomenon of electricity were translated into novel products of great practical utility—such as radio.

Faraday made the fundamental discovery in 1831 when he provided an experimental demonstration of electro-magnetic induction. Over the next six decades, Maxwell, Hertz, and Marconi all built upon his, and each other's, work. A few years after Marconi achieved the first wireless transmission of telegraphy signals in 1895, speech was being transmitted over considerable distances. With the subsequent invention and improvement of the vacuum tube, the technological basis for radio (and eventually television) broadcasting was established.

Chemistry was the other discipline in which major breakthroughs brought vast new industrial expansion and the large-scale employment of scientifically trained personnel. Indeed, in terms of the number of scientists employed, chemistry has been the dominant discipline over the past century. It was the combined industrial thrust of chemistry, electricity, and the internal combustion engine that generated the so-called "Second Industrial Revolution" around the turn of the century.[5]

Chemistry differed considerably from electricity in that it was a very old discipline, and chemistry-based industries were also very old by the middle of the nineteenth century. Nevertheless, Perkins's accidental synthesis of a brilliant mauve dye from aniline (a coal-tar derivative), in 1856, touched off an expansion of industrial research and innovative activity centered upon a deepening understanding of the structure of the organic molecule.[6] The rise of the industrial research laboratory in the United States, an institutionalization of science that became particularly conspicuous just after the turn of the century, is closely associated with these developments (see *Table 1-1*). It is important to note, however, that a considerable number of research labs—at least 139— had already been established before the turn of the century.

This sketch is perfectly accurate as far as it goes. It is, however, seriously incomplete. This is because the growing impact of science upon industry has been presented as if the causal forces all ran from recent breakthroughs in frontier science to fairly direct "downstream" applications by industry. That this is an important part of the story is not to be doubted, and this is precisely the way the picture is usually painted. But to regard it as the whole story is to present a seriously incomplete, and therefore ultimately seriously distorted, explanation of a much more complex historical process.

Table 1-1
Establishment of Research Labs in American Industry

	Manufacturing	*Resource-based*	*Utilities, etc.*	*Total*
Before 1899	112	0	27	139
1899–1908	182	1	41	224
1909–18	371	2	83	456
1919–28	660	12	141	813
1929–36	590	8	128	726
1937–46	388	6	99	493
	2,303	29	519	2,851

Source: David Mowery, *The Emergence and Growth of Industrial Research in American Manufacturing, 1899–1945* (Stanford University doctoral dissertation, 1981), 51.

Even if we were to make the very extreme and implausible assumption that the production of new scientific knowledge is totally independent of economic forces, the actual industrial *application* of scientific knowledge obviously is not.

Thus, to understand the growing application of science to industry, it is necessary to examine certain ongoing changes in the industrial world that have altered the need, the opportunities, and the technological possibilities for the application of science—in the form of established scientific principles and procedures at least as much as "new science."

For more than a century, there has been an extensive set of changes (a) in the nature of production technologies and inputs generally, and (b) in the composition of industrial output, that have had the effect of raising the payoff to a number of categories of scientific knowledge. The growing proximity of science and industry was intimately bound up with these changes. Thus, this paper may be regarded as an attempt to account for the growing application of science to industry by identifying those forces at work in the industrial sector that generated an increasing demand for scientific knowledge.

The relevant forces were not confined to small sectors of the economy nor embodied in just a couple of distinctive technologies, even though individual technologies were sometimes extremely important, as in electrification. They were, as I will show, pervasive and expressed themselves in the most basic and elemental of economic activities.

They were based, first, upon a metallurgical revolution beginning after the Civil War, a revolution flowing from remarkable reductions in the cost of steel which were made possible by the application of "old" science.

This cheapening of steel made possible an immense increase in its use—its widespread substitution for wood and iron—for example, in machinery and rails. The cheapening of iron and steel was fundamental to the emergence of national markets for branded, packaged products, because such markets required a low-cost transportation system that became available with a dense network of railroads in the closing decades of the nineteenth century. The emergence of that market, in turn, was a critical component in the growth in size and in the functions performed by individual firms—a process that has been so cogently analyzed by Alfred Chandler.[7]

At the same time, the cheapening of steel and the availability of other new materials for construction purposes—for example, reinforced concrete—made possible entirely new techniques of construction that transformed the urban environment in dramatic and tangible ways. This involved building on a vastly larger scale and departing from earlier limitations upon design and construction that were imposed by the nature of available materials. Out of these new possibilities emerged the high-rise living environment of cities, skyscrapers, and suspension bridges across wide rivers and bays.

Finally, the growing productivity of agriculture and the large-scale urbanization of the American population led to a complete restructuring of the production and preparation of food. Agriculture became a much more specialized activity, involving a declining proportion of the labor force and an increasing degree of geographic specialization. As a result, the reorganization of the food supply and its distribution to a geographically widespread but increasingly urbanized population of consumers involved fundamental changes in the technology of food production and its subsequent processing, preservation, and transportation.

While these three sectors—metallurgy (and metal-using industries); construction; and food processing, packing, and canning—are not fully representative of the rest of the economy, they are together a sufficiently large part of the total economy for significant trends within them to be, at the very least, necessarily significant for the economy as a whole.

Important in all three sectors were certain key features of the growing commitment of resources to the research process which deserve a great deal of attention, but which will have to be neglected in the detailed sections of this paper:

1. There was a roughly simultaneous growth in research activity within private industry, the academic community, and the public sector. This suggests that there may have been some common underlying force (or set of forces) accounting for the rising social payoff to research activity. Moreover, that rough simultaneity raises important questions about the relationships of these separate research activities. To what extent, and in precisely what ways, did these activities depend upon, and draw upon, one another? How strong were the complementarities between public and private sector research, or between academic and business-supported research?

2. Within the business community itself, research in the United States had a particular feature that distinguished it, at least in degree, from western European patterns. A much larger fraction of business-supported research was conducted *within* the firm, and not by some form of industrywide association or other arrangement. To a much

greater extent than appears to have been the case, say, in Britain,[8] the growth of research in the United States was directly linked to considerations of business strategy at the level of the individual firm.

3. The diversity of institutional mechanisms that were involved is striking, and the underlying rationale for the particular pattern that emerged requires more scholarly attention. For not only did it include a huge growth of in-house industrial research and university-based research; by the outbreak of the First World War there were also a number of diverse, specialized organizations such as the National Bureau of Standards, the National Advisory Committee on Aeronautics, the Forest Products Laboratory, and the American Society for Testing Materials—the last an interesting example of interfirm cooperation sponsored by a professional engineering society. These organizations obviously provided their members with different agendas and different incentives. Their economic effectiveness for exploiting a growing body of scientific knowledge is still not very well understood.

4. The growing utilization of scientific knowledge and methodology in industry was vastly accelerated by an expanding pool of technically trained personnel—especially engineers. Associated with this expansion was the growth in the number of engineering schools, engineering programs, and engineering subspecialties in the second half of the nineteenth century. The dividing line between science and engineering is always difficult to draw, and doing so inevitably involves introducing rather arbitrary boundary lines across certain continuities in different realms of knowledge. What is clear, and sufficient for my present purposes, is that a considerable part of the training of engineers was a training in the scientific knowledge and scientific methodology of the time. That training was, to be sure, at the more elementary levels and did not prepare engineers for work at the scientific frontier. But it is essential to what follows to realize that it was the larger body of scientific knowledge, and not merely frontier science, that was relevant to the needs of an expanding industrial establishment.[9]

Thus, engineers and other technically trained personnel served as valuable carriers of scientific knowledge. As a result, the number of people bringing the knowledge and methods of science to bear upon industrial problems was vastly greater than the limited number of individuals that society chose to label "scientists" at any particular time. These assertions can be readily confirmed by the most cursory examination of technological innovation within the particular subspecialties of engineering—for example, chemical engineering, mechanical engineering, or aeronautical engineering.

Throughout the sectors examined here, a variety of common forces was at work. In the post–Civil War years the improvements in transportation destroyed the earlier isolation of small local markets that were catered to by small-scale, locally oriented industry, and played a major role in creating a large, internal market of continental scale. This market was also growing rapidly in terms of population, per capita income, and extent of urbanization. For a number of reasons, cultural and social as well as economic, it was a market that was apparently prepared to absorb products of a higher degree of standardization and uniformity than was the case in Europe. At least there seemed to be fewer obvious obstacles. In any case, firms in these industries grew to a larger absolute size, and on the whole attained large size earlier than elsewhere. (In the construction industry, the growth of firm size was particularly conspicuous among the suppliers of construction materials.) Bigness in this respect was critical to the issues at hand because bigness created a vast range of problems, but also opportunities, that required control of inputs and their qualities to a degree that had not previously been nearly so significant.[10]

In addition, larger scale required careful attention to numerous aspects of the new production processes, in which more precise regulation and control were essential to successful performance. This was notoriously the case with the new, large-scale production technologies in metallurgy. Moreover, throughout the sectors under consideration, there were significant changes in the nature of the final product, often involving quite exceptional, or precisely defined, performance characteristics that were essential to economic success. Thus, the baker producing on a larger scale could not make purchases from the miller, the Pennsylvania Railroad could not buy steel products from the rolling mill, nor could the urban construction firm make purchases from the cement manufacturer, without the assurance of certain precise performance or quality specifications for these purchased inputs. Failure to meet precise specifications was likely to be commercially disastrous, but it was increasingly likely to pose a threat to life and limb as well.

The point is that the pattern of industrial development that began to emerge in the late nineteenth century has to be understood not only— and perhaps not even primarily—as the emergence of new bodies of scientific knowledge that were subsequently applied to industry. Rather, the central feature is a rapidly growing and industrializing economy that is encountering all sorts of situations at the level of newly emerging technologies where further improvement and progress required drawing upon the existing fund of scientific knowledge.

As is often pointed out, the earliest industrial research laboratories (say before 1900, or even much later) were not yet performing activities that should be regarded as research. Rather, they were engaged in a variety of routine and elementary tasks such as the grading and testing of materials, assaying, quality control, writing of specifications, and so forth. It is certainly correct that these were the primary uses to which science was first put in an extensive way in the industrial context. Science, when it entered the industrial establishment, came to perform tasks that were elementary *from the point of view of the science content.*

In a volume devoted to the history of science, such activities would properly merit little attention, if any. Very little of the work of scientists in industry before the First World War was of interest to anyone concerned *exclusively* with science and its progress.

From the point of view of industrial growth, however, the work of these scientists was absolutely vital. It is difficult to envision how the emerging industrial technology could have functioned successfully without the vital information that could only be readily supplied by scientifically trained personnel. Competitive success increasingly went to those industrialists who were the quickest to perceive and to exploit these opportunities. Carnegie could not help gloating over the advantages conferred upon him by his decision to employ a trained chemist:

> We found . . . a learned German, Dr. Fricke, and great secrets did the doctor open up to us. (Ore) from mines that had a high reputation was now found to contain ten, fifteen, and even twenty percent less iron than it had been credited with. Mines that hitherto had a poor reputation we found to be now yielding superior ore. The good was bad and the bad was good, and everything was topsy-turvy. Nine-tenths of all the uncertainties of pig iron making were dispelled under the burning sun of chemical knowledge.
>
> What fools we had been! But then there was this consolation: we were not as great fools as our competitors . . . Years after we had taken chemistry to guide us (they) said they could not afford to employ a chemist. Had they known the truth then, they would have known they could not afford to be without one.[11]

The substantive point at issue here goes far beyond that of Carnegie's percipience, or the ability of one firm to derive a competitive advantage in a particular market or industry. The point is much more far-reaching. The industrial growth of the United States coincided with a geographic expansion over a vast continent. It is widely agreed that one of the most distinctive aspects of American industrialization was the extraordinary richness of the natural resource environment within which it took place. Such mundane scientific techniques as chemical analysis, evaluation, and assaying played a crucial role in identifying and providing guidance to the speedy and efficient exploitation of hitherto unexplored and untapped mineral resource deposits.[12]

The ability to grade and sort with a reasonably high degree of precision played, and continues to play, a major role in the way markets for specific products can be organized and operated. Historically, commodity futures markets have been established only for those products that could be well sorted in terms of the needs of the eventual users. For example, even very small differences in coal composition continue to be very important for metallurgical purposes. The Chicago Board of Trade still does not deal in long-term coal contracts because of the difficulty of acceptable, standardized grading of metallurgical coal.

Metallurgy

The spectacular developments in the iron and steel industry beginning in the mid-nineteenth century are a forceful demonstration that the new directions—including the very transformation of the industry from an iron industry into a steel industry—did not originate in advances in new scientific knowledge.

In the case of the three great innovations in the steel industry in the second half of the nineteenth century—the Bessemer Converter, Siemens's open-hearth method, and the Gilchrist-Thomas basic lining that made possible the exploitation of high phosphorus ores—none of the major innovators drew upon chemical knowledge that was not already available before the end of the eighteenth century.[13] Siemens was the only member of the trio with a university education. Although Sidney Gilchrist-Thomas (a clerk in a London police court with only the smattering of chemical knowledge that he managed to acquire in evening classes) had to solicit the help of a cousin who was indeed a trained chemist, he did so only long after his correct fundamental insight into the requirements for a solution to the high phosphorus problem.

The spectacular growth in steel production that was set in motion by the Bessemer process was not due to some recent increment in scientific knowledge, because there had been no such recent increment. However, after the major technological innovations in steelmaking were installed, they raised immensely the *payoff* to the use of existing science in this industry, and to the development of new science. This became apparent immediately with the introduction and rapid diffusion of the Bessemer process.

The very success of the Bessemer process in cheapening the price of steel and in introducing steel to a rapidly expanding array of new uses made it necessary to subject the inputs of the process to quantitative chemical analysis. This was because, as was quickly discovered, the quality of the output was highly sensitive to even minute variations in the composition of the inputs. Sulfur and phosphorus content had an immediate and very deleterious effect upon the quality of the final product. Even the addition of very small quantitites of nitrogen from the air during the course of the blast eventually led to serious and unexpected deterioration in the performance of the metal, although this causal relationship was not established until many years later.

The first Bessemer steel produced in the United States was made in Wyandotte, Michigan, in 1864. In anticipation of the problems associated with chemical variations in inputs, a chemical laboratory was established at Wyandotte in 1863. This was the first chemical laboratory established in the metallurgical sector of the United States, as well as one of the first laboratories attached to any industrial firm.[14]

Similarly, large *users* of Bessemer steel were likely to set up testing laboratories to assure that the steel met appropriate specifications. Such was the case of the railroads, where the larger companies established their own central testing laboratories—as did the Burlington in 1876 when it adopted the steel rail,[15] and the Pennsylvania Railroad which established a chemical laboratory at Altoona, Pennsylvania, in 1874.[16]

The new uses to which cheaper steel was introduced defy brief summarization. It was employed in a wide range of machines in which cast iron or wood had been used before. As a result, the machines could now be made of larger size, greater strength, higher speeds, and improved performance generally. Steel played a major role in agriculture, as a bewildering number of machines were introduced that had the effect of raising the acreage that could be cultivated by a single farmer. It was increasingly employed in mining machinery.

It was also a vital part of the transportation revolution, as it became a basic material input in the structure of ocean-going vessels and in the rapidly expanding network of railroads. At the outbreak of the Civil War, rails were made of iron which wore out in a couple years and which could support rolling stock of only about eight tons. By 1905, steel rails might last as long as ten years and they could support rolling stock of seventy tons. The railroad network was now able to exploit steel bridges of far greater span and capacity than previous materials would have permitted.[17]

With the introduction of the automobile in the opening years of the century, there was a huge increase in the demand for steel but also for a large number of specialty steels with many different kinds of high-performance characteristics. Alloy steels began to be developed before the turn of the century, but their use was mostly limited to armor and ordnance until after the First World War. In the 1920s the rapid growth of the automobile, airplane, and petroleum refining brought rapid increases in demand.[18] In cities, the availability of steel as a structural material made possible the construction of skyscrapers (that is, high-rise buildings with no dependence upon masonry) beginning in Chicago and New York in the early 1890s.[19] A series of other major innovations each exploited the properties of steel in important ways—sewing machines, bicycles, typewriters, barbed wire, and so forth.

Thus, the manufacturer of steel confronted an increasingly stringent set of requirements for steel imposed upon him by a widening set of customers. Each one was likely to be interested in a different property or, more likely, in different combinations of properties. Steel requirements in the electrical industries might revolve around conductivity, machine tool manufacturers required steel that retained its cutting edge at very high temperatures, manufacturers of steam engine boilers sought corrosion resistance, army ordnance increasing strength and hardness, and so forth.

The ability to deliver steel according to the precise specifications required by different classes of final users was substantially improved by two developments. First was the emerging dominance of the open-hearth process. Although it was the Bessemer process that first made cheap steel possible, it was also a technology that had not permitted really precise control over quality, partly because of the sheer speed of the process. The open-hearth process, by contrast, did permit such control (in addition to being able to exploit a wider range of ores than the Bessemer process).[20] Second, the development of new steel alloys, especially those involving nickel, chromium, and tungsten, brought an immense improvement in the ability of metallurgists to manufacture steel according to precisely designed quality characteristics, such as toughness and hardness.[21]

In effect, therefore, the manufacturer of steel may be said to have had both an internal and external motivation to assert a precise, more scientific control over his manufacturing process. Internally, the manufacture of steel involved elaborate chemical transformations in which such control enabled the manufacturer to minimize the cost of producing any given output mix and to assure quality control. Externally, a critical aspect of the competitive process was to develop new products that optimally achieved the specific combination of performance requirements of a growing number of specialist users of steel. These production requirements brought trained chemists and metallurgists into the industry in increasing numbers.

Thus, the increasing dependence upon science in metallurgy was a consequence of two sets of prior and ongoing changes: in production technology, largely thanks to "old" science; and in the peculiarities and special performance requirements of new products.

As the new production technologies made steel cheaper, its widening diffusion and application to new uses strengthened the economic importance of understanding its characteristics and performance properties. In this respect, developments in the late nineteenth and early twentieth centuries strengthened a concern over metallurgical phenomena that had become central to machinery designers and engineers during the "first" industrial revolution. The capacity to sustain higher temperatures and pressures, for example, had been a continuing preoccupation since the invention of the steam engine in the eighteenth century.

It became an increasing concern with the introduction of locomotives, steamboats, and steamships, which attached much greater importance to fuel efficiency (as evidenced by the introduction of the compound engine) as well as safety. With the introduction of electricity and steam turbine generators, the diesel engine, the automobile, the modern oil refinery, and eventually the airplane, the capacity to sustain very high temperatures and pressures, and therefore to understand the metallurgical conditions that would make them possible, increased incessantly.[22]

Wherever steel was used as a structural material, as well as in the emerging, mass production metal-fabricating industries generally, similar tensions arose. It was not enough to be able to produce steel cheaply. In both the construction and the manufacture of increasingly complex products, the metal inputs needed to be produced to a high degree of uniformity and predictable reliability. Such conditions were essential to the possibility of designing and manufacturing high-performance products. Failure to achive such reliability could, under certain circumstances, be disastrous, as was obviously the case with respect to large gun forgings, steam turbines aboard oceangoing vessels, or the structural members of large-span bridges.

As steel became cheaper, it not only served as a substitute for iron in many established structural uses; it also provided the possibility for far more audacious construction designs. But, here again, as a material was pushed to new and previously unexplored limits by skyscrapers and large-span bridges, the ability to predict its performance limits with a high degree of accuracy became indispensable.[23] Furthermore, even the mere substitution of steel for iron in a product of more conventional design called for a thorough exploration of its performance possibilities. For, without that information, excessive amounts of steel were likely to be committed to any given purpose, with consequent waste and inefficiency.

The economic importance of these relationships between cheaper metal and its more intensive utilization would eventually play a significant role in expanding the frontiers of metallurgical science. Their shorter-run and more pervasive effect was to increase the industrial payoff to a wider application of the existing body of scientific knowledge.

The innovative activity that led to the production of cheap steel, and the resulting substitution of steel for iron, calls attention to a phenomenon of pervasive economic importance in the twentieth century. It was to occur over and over with respect to a widening range of materials exploited by industrializing societies. That is, the growth of knowledge with respect to the behavior of materials was to lead, in a myriad of ways, to a prolongation of the useful lives of the products made of these materials. This has been one of the most decisive impacts of the expanding body of useful knowledge—and also an impact that is, by its very nature, undramatic and not readily observable.

A large part of the history of alloys is the development of new materials with a number of more useful properties, or combinations of properties—one of which was commonly greater strength and durability and a longer life expectancy than the simpler metal that it replaced. Similarly, an increase in the potential useful life of all products of the construction industry, to which we now turn, flowed from this kind of deepening understanding of the whole range of material inputs.

Construction

Construction has already received frequent mention in the discussion of metallurgy, because steel had become a major construction material in the late nineteenth century. Construction nevertheless warrants further consideration, because at a time when its materials were far from standardized, it became an important focal point for the introduction of trained scientists into industry quite independently of the increasing reliance upon structural members made of metal.

Concrete has an unusually long history going back to the ancient Romans who had even discovered how to prepare a cement that would harden under water. But its use as a construction material bears some striking parallels to that of steel. Like steel, it was not extensively used as a building material until late in the nineteenth century. Like steel, its large-scale use came after the introduction of a new European technology—in this case, the rotary kiln, which had been invented in England in 1873.[24] Like the earliest British experience with the Bessemer process, its introduction was beset by difficulties that were ultimately traceable to the failure to exercise sufficient chemical control over the composition of the raw material inputs. As in the case of steel, its eventual performance was extremely sensitive to variations in the processing as well as to variations in the quality and composition of the inputs, since the transformation of a wet plastic into a rigid material involves some complex chemical reactions.

In addition to its low cost as a building material, concrete has great compressive strength and durability and can be made to assume an unlimited number of possible structural shapes. When supplemented by its reinforced and prestressed forms,[25] concrete came to far exceed (by weight) the use of steel for structural purposes in the course of the twentieth century.

These achievements were made possible by the systematic application of chemical analysis to the raw materials employed in the manufacture of concrete—lime, silica, alumina, iron oxide, and associated impurities.[26] The first major step was identification of the aluminum and silicon oxides as the active ingredients in the production of hydraulic lime, even though ". . . the full understanding of the chemical reactions that occur in the setting of concrete was not to come until well into the twentieth century."[27]

The fact that cement would be required to function for long periods of time in very different kinds of environments meant that exhaustive chemical studies were necessary to develop a cement that behaved appropriately in each of those environments. Whether a process worked or not, and whether the cement eventually behaved as expected, might depend upon very small variations in the chemical components or in timing, the percentage of specific impurities and the specific forms of chemical compounding in the raw materials, the degree of fineness to which the raw materials were ground, and so forth. Separate studies were necessary to examine instances of failure and their causes, or of insufficient stability over time. From this chemical analysis has emerged a body of knowledge that was eventually capable of "designing" different kinds of cement to suit each of a wide range of eventual end uses.[28]

In its reinforced and, more recently, prestressed form, concrete has become the predominant twentieth century building material. Its performance characteristics came to be gradually established through patient, sustained empirical analysis, usually without the benefit of a larger theoretical framework to provide specific guidance to the research process.[29] Indeed, here too, as in metallurgy, the actual practices, structural achievements as well as problems and failures of the users of the material, provided the intellectual challenge for the deeper scientific understanding that eventually followed practice rather than preceded it. Although the work of trained chemists in all this would provide only occasional footnotes in a history of science, the economic importance of their achievements may be encapsulated in the observation that a larger quantity of concrete by weight is currently embodied in American construction than all other building materials combined.

Concrete was not the only example of scientists being drawn into work for the construction industry by the growing use of a material. Scientific knowledge (primarily chemical) also came to be applied to the industrial uses of wood. This took place at several levels. The Department of Agriculture had long included a Division of Forestry that had emphasized the use of scientific principles (or what they thought were scientific principles) in growing timber as a crop ("silviculture"). However, the problems confronted by industrial users of wood went far beyond the application of such principles. This was recognized by the establishment of a federally financed Forest Products Laboratory at the University of Wisconsin in Madison, Wisconsin. This laboratory, which opened in 1910, provided for the centralization of research on all questions pertaining to the use of woods for industrial purposes.[30]

The prominent role played by the railroads is again noteworthy. Even though the railroads gave up the use of wood as a fuel in the post-Civil War years, it is estimated that they accounted for between 20–25 percent of the country's annual timber consumption between 1870 and 1900.[31] The largest single use was for crossties.

The economic benefits flowing from the systematic chemical testing, grading, and classifying of the woods of the immense and heterogeneous forest lands of the United States were very great. A more exact determination of the composition of woods, and the linking of composition to performance characteristics, made it possible to utilize resources far more efficiently. One immediate result of chemical testing was to establish that some tree species were far more useful than previously believed. Although white oak was strongly preferred for the making of crossties before 1890, subsequent research revealed that chestnut oak and post oak were "perfectly interchangeable" with white oak.[32] Similarly, ". . . studies of southern pines demonstrated that bleeding trees for turpentine in no way damaged the strength of the timber. Trees that had been bled for many years were therefore no longer excluded from the bridge timber market."[33]

More significantly, the research that led to important improvements in techniques of wood preservation by chemical treatment eventually made it possible to make routine use of wood that was abundant in many regions and that was unsuitable for use on crossties in an untreated condition.[34] Far and away the most important chemical treatment was impregnation with creosote, a coal-tar derivative. Treatment with creosote rendered "inferior" woods usable and substantially prolonged the useful life of the better woods. The proportion of crossties treated with chemical preservatives rose to over 20 percent in 1910, over 75 percent in 1930, and over 95 percent by 1950. The number of wood-preserving plants in the United States increased from 14 in 1900 to more than 70 in 1907, to 102 in 1915.[35]

Finally, chemical and physical testing identified the precise performance requirements of each end use so that a finer matching of specific end use with specific wood input became possible. With such information, the high quality woods were used only where they were needed, and cheaper, lower quality woods were introduced wherever higher quality wood could be dispensed with.

> About 1908–1910 the Santa Fe, Pennsylvania, Northern Pacific, and Burlington, among others, established definite systems of geographical distribution in track for ties of several species and treatments. Hardwood ties were reserved for curves and grades, softwood ties for tangent track. The untreated white oak was reserved for steep grades, sharp curves, and heavy traffic zones where it would wear out before decay destroyed it. The treated species, if given such punishment, would have worn out before their added life could be realized because many of the new timbers were softer. The cellular structures that made them absorb preservatives readily also gave them less desirable mechanical properties. Ties treated with zinc chloride were placed in arid districts, while those treated with creosote or zinc chloride and creosote were reserved for the wet areas. The same principle of careful allocation was also applied to larger timber structure. The soft shortleaf and loblolly pines were utilized for temporary structures (falsework), and the denser, harder, and stronger pieces and longleaf pine were treated and reserved for permanent structures.[36]

Thus, a detailed knowledge of physical properties made possible a more efficient matching of specific grades of wood to the wide range of possible end uses.

Materials Testing

There is an important common denominator running through much of the discussion of metallurgy and construction so far: Commercial as well as technological success was coming to be increasingly dependent upon the ability to predict performance of both inputs and outputs with a high degree of accuracy. The growth of mass production metal-using industries and the remarkable new feats of construction all relied upon the ability to push materials to new limits and to predict the performance of these materials with a high degree of confidence. This involved bringing together in a systematized way the knowledge of the behavior of materials that had been gleaned from the work of scientists and engineers working on these materials in innumerable industrial contexts. These activities were crystallized in the formation, in May 1902, of the American Society for Testing Materials.[37]

The charter of the A.S.T.M. states that ". . . the corporation is formed for the Promotion of Knowledge of the Materials of Engineering, and the Standardization of Specifications and the Methods of Testing." The kinds of concerns that led to the new organization are well summarized by the topics that were proposed for the Paris meeting of the International Association for Testing Materials in 1900. "Of the nineteen problems to be considered by the nineteen international committees, six are on iron and steel, one on stone and slate, eight on mortars, one on tile pipe, one on paints, one on lubricants, and one on the dry rot of wood."[38] By 1908 the members of the American Society were being presented, in their annual proceedings, with a wide range of reports dealing with the behavior of metals and building materials. Steel rails were still a major topic—including "Some Results of the Tests of Steel Rails in Progress at Watertown Arsenal," "A Microscopic Investigation of Broken Steel Rails: Manganese Sulphide as a Source of Danger," "Rail Failures, Mashed and Split Heads." Tests and standards for road-building materials, fireproofing, waterproofing, and boilers were also prominent. But so also were papers discussing equipment and methods for testing.[39]

This was an inevitable outgrowth of the attempt to set objective standards. For, assuming one could demonstrate the relevance of given standards in quantitative terms, such standards were of limited usefulness unless tests and instruments could be developed that predicted reasonably well the actual performance in service,[40] and unless these tests and instruments yielded at least roughly uniform results in different places and in different hands. This codification of knowledge concerning the performance of materials formed the basis for writing of specifications over a large part of the economy. It provided a scientific basis, in terms of uniformity and reliability of materials, for the efficient performance of complex capital goods, and for the design and manufacture of high performance consumer durable goods that have played such a great role in the economic history of the twentieth century.

Food Processing, Packing, and Canning

Although it is possible to label a particular aggregation of industries as "food processing," it is obvious that such a classification includes a very diverse collection of industries. Nevertheless, these industries have shared a common shift in the locus of the preparation of food products after they have left the farm. That shift has been from preparation (including preservation) in individual households or by small-scale entrepreneurs catering to local markets, to factory processing on a much larger scale, involving a high degree of regional specialization in production and with products prepared for eventual distribution over a vast geographic region, perhaps even the entire nation.

This transformation was set in motion by specific economic, social, and technical forces quite independent of science. None of these major transformations was *initiated* by a scientific breakthrough. Nevertheless, at critical junctures in the transition to large-scale factory production, scientific knowledge and analytical procedures had to be invoked, because the new, larger-scale production technologies, or the nationwide distribution of perishable products, encountered problems or constraints that could be much more effectively dealt with by scientifically trained personnel.

Although the biological nature of the raw materials and therefore their high degree of variability presented certain unique difficulties that distinguished them from steel or concrete, much of what food processing required from science was strikingly similar to the role of science in metallurgy and construction. This included, above all, a detailed understanding of the composition of inputs, because that composition was highly relevant to the success of certain subsequent large-scale production technologies, and also because the highly specific needs of purchasers of intermediate inputs required both precise predictability and uniformity of composition.[41] Thus, along with the new technologies, markets were becoming increasingly sensitive to even small variations in taste, texture, and size, and the development of national markets, national distribution networks, advertising and brand names, and trademarks intensified these trends.[42]

Canning. The preservation of food by canning began in the first decade of the nineteenth century. In fact, the term "canning" is a misnomer with respect to the original process. Nicolas Appert, a Parisian confectioner, managed to preserve certain foods by placing them in glass bottles that had been immersed in boiling water. He published his findings in a treatise in 1810 bearing the title *L'art de conserver, pendant plusiers années, toutes les substances animales et vegetales.*[43] No one could explain exactly how this heat sterilization process, and subsequent airtight sealing, prevented food deterioration. Indeed, the process did not work with complete reliability. Spoilage was to remain the great nemesis of the canning industry for a century or more. Nevertheless, the industry grew. Tin-coated steel cans were introduced in the 1830s, and the autoclave, offering higher and more precise temperature control, was adapted to canning in 1852. Pasteur discovered the role played by microorganisms in food spoilage in 1873, effectively establishing the new science of bacteriology. (This seminal contribution to pure science, it should be noted, emerged out of Pasteur's very practical concern with the deterioration of food.) Nevertheless, spoilage persisted as a major problem for several decades more, as chemists and bacteriologists wrestled with the particularities of individual food products and the specific roles, not only of microorganisms, but of oxidation, dehydration, and enzyme action as well. "The form of spoilage to which a food is susceptible depends on its composition, structure, specific micro-organisms, and storage conditions. Micro-organisms themselves are affected by temperature, moisture, oxygen concentration, available nutrients, degree of contamination with spoilage organisms, and the presence or absence of growth inhibitors."[44]

Chemists, biochemists, and bacteriologists thus spent much time identifying the role played by each of a large number of variables in food spoilage and how they interacted in the case of each canned product. Chemists gradually established the connections between temperature, length of cooking time, and desirable food characteristics such as flavor, aroma, and texture. Careful bacteria counts established how it was possible to attain acceptable bacterial levels and more attractive food properties by shorter periods of cooking at higher temperatures. Out of this came the precise, food-specific information upon which the control over the preservation technologies was dependent, as well as a gradual expansion of the varieties of fruits and vegetables that could be successfully canned. This increasingly effective knowledge led also to greater discrimination in the selection of crops for canning and to greater geographic localization as knowledge of optimal soil and climatic conditions was also established.

Eventually, the needs of the canners, as well as other food processors, were to exercise a great deal of influence upon the work of geneticists and plant breeders. Twentieth-century science was able to move from the passive selection activities of earlier scientists to the active shaping of plant varieties that conformed better to the needs of the food processors: fruit and vegetable varieties that yielded more uniform size, ripened simultaneously, and resisted the bruising effects of mechanical picking.

Milling. The technological changes that occurred in milling beginning in the 1870s serve to highlight in a forceful way the subtle relationship between technology and natural resources, on the one hand, and the changing economic role of science, on the other. Although milling technology became very complex, involving the use of a large number of specialized machines, two basic innovations (plus, of course, the availability of new power sources) dominated the transition from the local, small-scale grist mill to the large-scale, mass production technology catering to huge and distant urban markets. The first was the replacement of millstones by a system of rollers. These rollers had a capacity many times greater than technologies based upon mill stones.[45] The second major innovation was the introduction of a technique exploiting air currents to separate the flour from the bran. The older method had relied exclusively upon sifting. Both of these techniques were of European origin—the rollers having been developed mainly in the Danubian basin and the air separation technique (purifier) in France. By the time these two innovations had been thoroughly assimilated in the United States in the early twentieth century, the milling capacity of the United States was concentrated in ten or twelve cities in close proximity to the major wheat-growing areas of the Midwest.[46]

The impact of this new technology cannot be expressed simply in terms of conventional measures of productivity improvement. Such measures are too static to encompass the effects of the new milling methods. Prior to their introduction, there was a strong preference for flour made from winter wheat, a preference reflected in a higher price. Spring wheat had a variety of inferior milling qualities.

> Its kernel was rich in gluten, but very hard. To grind it satisfactorily it was necessary to run the millstones with a great pressure and at high speed. The heat thus generated tended to discolor the flour, and also injured its keeping qualities. Moreover, the husk of the spring-wheat kernel was thin and brittle; hence, it tended to crumble into fine particles which it was difficult to sift from the flour. Winter wheat, on the contrary, had a thick, tough bran which in milling, was more likely to separate from the kernel in large flakes which could be easily sifted out. Winter wheat was softer and so ground more easily. There was not the same pressure and speed of stones with resulting heating and discoloration. Winter wheat flour was therefore whiter, stronger, and less likely to spoil; hence it was everywhere preferred and this preference was extended to the winter wheat.[47]

As a result, only small quantities of it were produced before the advent of the new milling techniques, and wheat growing was therefore largely confined to those regions that were well suited to the cultivation of winter wheat. The new technology, however, could produce a quality of flour from spring wheat as good as the flour from winter wheat. Consequently, wheat with good milling quality (the new techniques had redefined "good milling quality") could now be grown for the first time across a vast land area where *only* spring wheat could be grown—Minnesota, the Dakotas, and Montana. It was these developments that made Minneapolis the leading flour milling city of the world in the course of the 1880s. But, more importantly, they expanded immensely the land area over which a basic cereal crop could be grown.

The conditions of the new milling technology created a number of difficulties not encountered under the older technological regime. There is considerable variation among different types of wheats, variations that require somewhat different methods of processing.[48] As mills became larger and made use of wheats from an increasing number of locations, the flour could exhibit wide variations in strength and quality. The new markets for flour, however, demanded an increasing degree of uniformity for each of various types of flour that were utilized for specific purposes within bakeries or households. A high degree of predictability in the properties of the flour was essential in making breads, pastries, crackers, biscuits, and baking powders that were produced and marketed on a large scale. Large bakeries operate with formulas that require gluten measurements. Any deviation is unacceptable. "[A] big baker would have just as little use for a batch of flour of slightly higher gluten content as for one that was slightly deficient—both would disturb his formulas."[49] Furthermore, the internal requirements of the new milling process itself demanded more precise measurement and control to attain the important goal of uniform grinding characteristics.[50]

All of this required chemical analysis and control, and the new technology therefore brought with it the establishment of laboratories for testing the wheat and the flour to establish their precise chemical composition—protein content, gluten content, moisture, ash, and so forth.[51] Chemistry soon discovered that criteria formerly in use were misleading—in this respect performing an invaluable service exactly analogous to Carnegie's chemist who subjected different ore supplies to the hard light of chemical analysis. "The great difficulty is that the system of wheat-grading now in use emphasizes certain external factors, such as hardness, plumpness of kernel, color, and weight, which do not always correlate closely with milling quality. This the cereal chemists have shown is largely dependent on the chemical composition of the wheat; its protein content and the quantity and quality of the gluten it contains."[52]

Finally, the use of rollers, together with other improvements, gave the miller a much greater degree of control over the grinding process than was previously possible. It thereby offered him an enhanced capacity for making more exacting choices. The miller could, by incurring an additional cost, increase the proportion of high grade to low grade flour. But, to determine the optimum composition of output it was essential to be able to measure a number of relevant magnitudes with greater accuracy than was previously attainable, and to exercise a more informed control over each stage of the milling process.[53]

Meatpacking. The meatpacking industry was the product of two innovations—the railroad and the expansion of the railroad network throughout the Midwest, and the introduction of mechanical refrigeration. Before the 1870s, meatpacking was primarily a local business confined to pork products and the dominant preservative techniques were salting and smoking. Cattle were necessarily slaughtered near the place of final consumption. Within a couple of decades meatpacking had become a national, year-round industry, no longer merely seasonal in nature, highly concentrated in Chicago and a few other midwestern livestock centers, and providing beef as well as pork to a rapidly growing and rapidly urbanizing population.[54]

Some winter shipments of dressed beef to eastern cities were made in the late 1860s, but artificial refrigeration was not successfully introduced until the mid-1870s. In short order the major packers—Swift, Hammond, Armour, and others—entered the refrigerated beef trade, and by 1890 a national distribution system was firmly in place. In that year also a federal meat inspection system was introduced.

The employment of scientists (mainly chemists and bacteriologists) in meatpacking involved certain functions basically analogous to those in canning.[55] Refrigeration as a technique of food preservation involved a distinctive set of problems of its own. Full-time chemists began to be employed in the industry in the second half of the 1880s.[56] Chemical control of meatpacking production involved the setting of numerous chemical standards and extensive sampling procedures in fulfilling criteria that were relevant to health, taste, and appearance. Specific agents entering into the various meat-curing processes were analyzed for uniformity and quality, and then the curing process itself was monitored. Chemical analysis was eventually extended to provide rigorous guidance from the initial purchase of livestock to the eventual flow of finished products.

What was most distinctive about the role of science in meatpacking, however, was not its control over the preservation processes or the assurance of uniformity of quality in the final product. Rather, it was the part played in the development of by-products. Indeed, if the term "by-product" is defined to include everything other than edible meat, then it constituted almost one half of the weight of the live animal. In the early days of the industry before refrigeration, when slaughter houses and packing plants were separate establishments, most of the nonedible portions of the animal were dumped into a convenient waterway, or even buried.[57] The rendering of lard was only a partial exception, because lard was made primarily from portions of the hog that would not be thrown away. Whether the pork was packed or rendered into lard depended upon the relative prices of pork and lard. When lard prices were high, a larger fraction of the hog was converted into lard.[58]

The development of the by-products industries in the 1880s and after is a remarkable story of the creative use of techniques of chemical analysis to transform an enormous quantity of meatpacking-house waste materials into a very long list of valuable products. Although the nearby glue factory indeed antedated the chemical laboratory in the packing industry, the by-products industry was basically an outgrowth of the huge increase in scale of plant that accompanied the introduction of the railroad and refrigeration. These two innovations made much larger markets accessible to the packer (who also absorbed the activities of the slaughterhouse) and led directly to a high degree of geographic concentration and a large scale of operation of individual plants. The large scale of operation in turn made possible the diverse range of highly specialized activities exploiting what had formerly been mainly waste materials.

Although the earliest work of chemists focused upon food products such as oleomargarine and beef extract,[59] before the turn of the century the chemists' attention also turned to more distant fields that were to experience an extensive proliferation in the early decades of the twentieth century: pharmaceuticals,[60] commercial fertilizers, soap, explosives, lubrication oils, cosmetics, and so forth. The development of these by-products involved systematic chemical analysis to determine the exact chemical composition of former waste materials. But, in addition, the new markets that were being targeted often required a high degree of uniformity in the final product. In pharmaceuticals it turned out that ". . . the products being manufactured in the pharmaceutical department were by no means standard and that uniform results were not being obtained by physicians in prescribing and using those compounds, due to the variation of the content of the active principle. The laboratory was asked to develop standards for all of the medicinal products and to undertake to check each day's product against these standards, so that an absolutely uniform medicine would be produced."[61]

Even for an older and more traditional product such as beef extract, however, better chemical analysis played an essential role in achieving a marketable product.

> For many years beef extract had been one of the standard by-products of the packing industry. It was known that various batches apparently handled in the same manner differed widely as to color, odor and taste. Nothing was known, however, of the nutritive value; nothing was known as to the actual reasons for the above mentioned variations. This problem was put up to the laboratory and it was discovered that certain minor changes in the methods of making beef extract and certain separations of raw materials would enable the factory to produce a uniform product of standard nutritive value.[62]

By-products Other than Meatpacking. Although the issue has not been explicitly formulated in such terms, our discussion has several times disclosed how sensitive the concept of an economic resource is to the progress of technological knowledge. In fact, the waste materials of one generation have become the valued by-products of the next. This transformation of waste materials into valuable resources has been one of the most pervasive of all the effects of the application of science to industry. It is widely observable throughout the sectors that we have been considering but it has been by no means confined to them. We have seen, over and over, how elementary scientific knowledge, often only the most basic tools of analytical chemistry, has provided essential information that has raised the efficiency of resources (often including the initial selection process), product design, and materials processing.

Although the exploitation of by-products involved scientific techniques very similar to those we have been considering, they involved some other basic economic considerations as well. One of these is, of course, relative prices. Whether or not it pays to utilize a previous waste material depends upon its price and the price of the products for which it may be a close substitute. Indeed, what is a product and what is a by-product (or potential by-product) depends upon the cost of bringing it to market, upon the prices of other products for which it is a potential substitute, and upon the level of technological and scientific knowledge. Although the hide of a cow and the tallow were regarded as valuable by-products of the meatpacking industry in Chicago, on the Argentine pampas earlier in the nineteenth century cattle were slaughtered merely for their hide or tallow—as Marx indignantly observed in *Capital*.[63] More recently, natural gas, a high-quality fuel, was flared for many years because of the absence of satisfactory techniques of pipe manufacture.

In the early history of petroleum, everything aside from kerosene (which was highly desired as an illuminant) was considered to be a by-product. Petroleum was not regarded as an energy source. Subsequent technological change in the form of internal combustion and diesel engines changed all that.

The ability and the financial incentive to exploit waste materials depended, in addition to the availability of scientific knowledge, upon a central trend in the process of industrial development: the growth in scale of a productive operation. Marx saw this clearly in the last years of his life (he died in 1883).[64] Indeed, in the history of individual industries we find case after case in which the increasing scale of productive operations eventually gave rise to an awareness that certain materials of great potential usefulness were being discarded in large quantities. Since techniques for utilizing these materials did not yet exist, it was this awareness that often gave rise to the necessary research activities, sometimes to the original establishment of a research laboratory. Thus, growth in scale commonly had the effect of raising the private financial returns to investment in research, leading to the acquisition of new techniques for the utilization of by-products.

Such developments were particularly common in the growth of chemical processing industries, such as petroleum refining. The origin of the central research laboratory for the Royal Dutch Shell Oil Company's American subsidiary has been characterized as ". . . an attempt to make profitable uses of the tremendous amounts of oilfield and refinery gases which had up to then been flared into the air or, at best, burned for boiler fuel." The importance of developing a research thrust to utilize these by-products was closely linked to the growth in scale of plant: "The quantities of these gases were at first insignificant, but with rapid expansion of cracking facilities in the second half of the Twenties, the volume of cracking gases became enormous."[65]

Nevertheless, although the search for by-products led to systematic laboratory research in the twentieth century, the earlier search for petroleum by-products in the nineteenth century was the work of practical people or those with only a smattering of chemical training.[66] Before the turn of the twentieth century the value of these "by-products" (gasoline, naphtha, paraffin, petroleum jelly, and lubricants) was equal to the value of the main product—illuminating oil.[67]

The point is, of course, as the last sentence suggests, that historically a great deal of innovation has been conducted under the guise of by-product exploitation. Indeed, the exploratory and information-collecting activities that are involved in the search for by-products necessarily overlap very heavily into other kinds of innovative activity: product improvement, new product development, and the discovery of potential new uses for both product and by-product.

Conclusion

Most R&D even today is not of a knowledge-creating nature, if by knowledge one means new *scientific* knowledge. Some two-thirds of research and development, in recent years, has been development, and only about one-twelfth has been basic research. Similarly, the work of most scientifically trained people, historically, has been, in this sense, knowledge-applying and not knowledge-creating. In addition, economically valuable knowledge has been, to a much greater extent than is generally recognized, old, not new, scientific knowledge.

These facts and their implications have been neglected because of the preoccupation with the generation of new knowledge, a preoccupation that, perhaps understandably, has been especially strong in the academic world. Obviously, in the sufficiently long run, if no new knowledge is created, the application process will eventually fall to very low levels as the returns to the application of older knowledge decline, as they certainly will. Nevertheless, it is essential, in order to understand science as a social phenomenon, that attention be devoted to the entire system of component activities, and not just to single, isolated parts.

The economics of science necessarily involves a study of both the relationships and the incentives that lead to the production of new knowledge and the relationships and the incentives that are responsible for the *application* of that knowledge. The central thrust of this chapter has been to show how the application of scientific knowledge has been shaped by the peculiar needs and special problems confronting the production technologies of a rapidly expanding industrial economy. Over the past century there has been an extensive set of changes in production technologies and the inputs employed in productive activities, and there have been major associated changes in the nature and composition of industrial output. These changes were critical in raising the payoff to scientific knowledge. As a result, science has provided its economic benefits through a number of channels, but most commonly by assisting in the exploitation of innovations that did not have their origins in recent science. Thus, to a much greater degree than we have been aware, science has become the handmaiden of technology in industrializing societies, at least for the kinds of phenomena that are of central importance to economists.

Even if economists were content to treat scientific progress as an exogenous variable (which they should not be), the industrial *applications* of science need to be accounted for by developments at the technological level that shape the industrial demand for scientific knowledge. Without a serious examination of these determinants of industrial demand, statements concerning the commercial exploitation of science will remain either highly abstract or merely platitudinous.

How, for example, can we account for the particular *distribution* of scientists among industries at any given time or—a closely related phenomenon—the industrial distribution of R&D? In the United States for many years almost two-thirds of private industrial R&D has been concentrated in five industrial sectors, and these same five sectors—aerospace, electrical and electronics, instruments, computers, and chemicals and allied products—accounted for over 70 percent of total industrial R&D.[68] These figures reflect powerful economic (as well as, of course, military and strategic) determinants.

Thus a central conclusion of this chapter is that, if we want to penetrate deeply into the functioning of "the scientific epoch," and the productivity growth that has been associated with it, we must study the multitude of ways, often complex and circuitous, in which industrial technologies have shaped the demand for scientific knowledge.

Notes

1. For some perceptive observations on international differences in the capacity to apply scientific knowledge to useful ends, see Joseph Ben-David, *Fundamental Research and the Universities* (Paris: Organisation for Economic Co-operation and Development, 1968). The view that America's distinctive strength lies in the application of science, rather than in pure science, goes back at least as far as de Tocqueville. "In America, the purely practical part of science is admirably understood and careful attention is paid to the theoretical portion, which is immediately requisite to application. On this head, the Americans always display a clear, free, original, and inventive power of mind. But hardly any one in the United States devotes himself to the essentially theoretical and abstract portion of human knowledge . . . every new method which leads by a shorter road to wealth, every machine which spares labor, every instrument which diminishes the cost of production, every discovery which facilitates pleasures or augments them, seems [to such people] to be the grandest effort of the human intellect. It is chiefly from these motives that a democratic people addicts itself to scientific pursuits . . . In a community thus organized, it may easily be conceived that the human mind may be led insensibly to the neglect of theory; and that it is urged, on the contrary, with unparalleled energy, to the applications of science, or at least to that portion of

theoretical science which is necessary to those who make such applications." Alexis de Tocqueville, *Democracy in America* (New York: The Century Company, 1898), 2:48, 52–53.

2. See "How Exogenous is Science?" chapter 7 in Nathan Rosenberg, *Inside the Black Box* (Cambridge: Cambridge University Press, 1982).

3. For a partial exception, see Jacob Schmookler, "Catastrophe and Utilitarianism in the Development of Basic Science," in *The Economics of R and D*, ed. Richard A. Tybout (Columbus: Ohio State University Press, 1965).

4. "If economic growth of nations within the last two hundred years represents a process within the framework of a new economic epoch, what is the epochal innovation that is being exploited? . . . . The extended application of science to problems of economic production." Simon Kuznets, *Modern Economic Growth* (New Haven: Yale University Press, 1966), 8–9.

5. David Landes, *The Unbound Prometheus* (Cambridge: Cambridge University Press, 1969).

6. The leadership in these developments for many years was in Germany. For a good concise account, see J. J. Beer, *The Emergence of the German Dye Industry* (Urbana: University of Illinois Press, 1959).

7. Alfred D. Chandler, Jr., *The Visible Hand* (Cambridge, Mass.: Harvard University Press, 1977).

8. David Mowery, "British and American Industrial Research: A Comparison, 1900–1950," (Paper presented at the Anglo-American Conference on the Decline of the British Economy, Boston University, 1 October 1983).

9. Moreover, to a much greater extent in the United States than elsewhere, technically trained engineers moved into positions of industrial leadership. See Alfred D. Chandler, Jr., *Strategy and Structure: Chapters in the History of Industrial Enterprise* (Cambridge, Mass.: M.I.T. Press, 1962), 317.

10. This discussion does not require growth in size of firm to the extent of involving a significant degree of market concentration, although this kind of growth did indeed frequently occur.

11. Quoted in H. Livesay, *Andrew Carnegie* (Boston: Little, Brown and Company, 1975), 114.

12. Useful entry into this history may be found in Harold Williamson ed., *Growth of the American Economy* (New York: Prentice-Hall, Inc., 1951), chapters 23 and 24.

13. J. D. Bernal, *Science and Industry in the 19th Century* (London: Routledge & Kegan Paul, 1953), 110.

14. Victor S. Clark, *History of Manufactures in the United States* (New York: McGraw-Hill Book Company, 1929), 2:70, 78.

15. Sherry Olson, *The Depletion Myth* (Cambridge, Mass.: Harvard University Press, 1971), 45. "Railroad men used and developed chemical analysis, microscopic study, physical tests, and statistical methods in their attempt to obtain longer lasting rail. They devised laboratory and manufacturing tests that would identify defective rails before they were put in track." Ibid., 46.

16. See *The Life and Life-Work of Charles B. Dudley, 1842–1909* (Philadelphia: American Society for Testing Materials, n.d.). Dudley was a leading figure in the field of materials testing, and was subsequently first president of the American Society for Testing Materials, as well as president of the American Chemical Society. By the end of the First World War, the Altoona laboratory had a staff of more than 600 men, ". . . half of whom are engaged in inspection work." See also Arthur M. Greene, "Conditions of Research in U.S.," *Mechanical Engineering*, July 1919, 588.

17. American builders had shown remarkable daring and ingenuity in constructing even quite large railroad bridges out of timber. Nevertheless, the

increase in the weight and speed of locomotives had earlier made the transition to iron, with its far greater tensile strength and rigidity, inevitable. Thus, many steel bridges were constructed as replacements for iron ones. See Carl Condit, *American Building* (Chicago: University of Chicago Press, 1968), chapter 8.

18. Bartlett points out that the output of alloy steels grew from 570,000 tons in 1910 to about 4 million tons in 1930. Howard R. Bartlett, *Research—A National Resource*. II. *Industrial Research* (Washington, D.C.: Resources Planning Board 1941), 161.

19. "Skyscraper construction . . . began in 1891, when the Columbia Iron and Steel Company, of Uniontown, Pennsylvania, was awarded the contract for supplying the structural steel for the new Masonic Temple in Chicago. This building, twenty stories high and at the time the loftiest business structure in the world, required between 3,500 and 4,000 tons of steel for its skeleton frame. As in the case of bridges, each piece was exactly fitted, holes drilled, connections dove-tailed, and all connections adjusted for ultimate use before leaving the factory." Clark, *History of Manufactures*, 2:345.

20. Bessemer steel output reached its all-time peak in the United States in the first decade of the twentieth century, after which the long dominance of the open-hearth method asserted itself.

21. Clark, *History of Manufactures,* 3:80–81; Bartlett, *Research,* 168.

22. Clark, *History of Manufactures,* 3:150–53.

23. "Without the development of a science of structure and materials, construction in iron and steel could never have been accomplished on the scale necessary to modern urban life. As the engineer was faced with constantly increasing demands for higher buildings and heavier, longer bridges, he was increasingly compelled to turn to science in order to solve the structural problems thrust upon him. Building could no longer be treated as an art or a craft; it had to become a branch of theoretical and applied science." Condit, *American Building,* 76–77.

24. Although the rotary kiln was of European origin, it is interesting to note that the smaller-scale vertical kiln is still used by European manufacturers, whereas, "cement plants in the United States have used the rotary kiln almost exclusively since its invention in 1873." David Huettner, *Plant Size, Technological Change and Investment Requirements* (New York: Praeger, 1974), 101. See also Clark, *History of Manufactures,* 253–256.

25. There is a further interesting link between concrete and metallurgy. For prestressed concrete to perform properly, ". . . the cable wire must be made of high quality steel so that it will maintain its tension throughout the life of the structure. The success of pre-stressing thus depended as much on progress in the metallurgy of steel as in the technology of concrete construction." Condit, *American Building,* 248.

26. "The major structural innovations of the twentieth century have been the products of concrete technology, and many of these have led to radical changes in the form and action of structural systems. No building material was treated to a more scientific investigation than concrete, with the consequence that by mid-century its chemistry, its internal structure, and its behavior under every condition are as well understood as the properties of familiar metals. Indeed, the engineers regard it as the most scientific material, one that allows the closest approach to the organic ideal, in which structural form exactly corresponds to the pattern of internal stresses." Condit, *American Building,* 240.

27. Ibid., 158.

28. "Out of this research work has come the ability of the cement chemist to

produce products with special properties, such as high-early strength for concrete that must be put into service quickly; low-heat cement that hardens slowly but develops less heat during hydration in large masses of concrete; sulphate-resistant cement, which is free from the disintegrating action of sulphate soils or waters; and special oil well cements able to withstand very high temperatures and pressures before the mixture of cement and water can be placed around the casing in the bottom of oil wells from ten to fifteen thousand feet in depth." John Glover and William Cornell, *The Development of American Industries* (New York: Prentice-Hall, Inc., 1951), 629. Cf. also Clark, *History of Manufactures*, 3:253–56.

29. "Because concrete by itself can work only in compression, it will quickly fail if it is used for members subject to high bending forces, such as beams and floor slabs. If it is reinforced with iron or steel bars, however, the elastic metal will take the tensile and shearing stresses, and the rigid concrete will sustain the compressive forces. Exactly why this nice division of labor occurs is not entirely understood, but it can be made exact if the metal is concentrated in the region of maximum tension." Condit, *American Building*, 168.

30. For a detailed institutional history, see C. A. Nelson, *A History of the Forest Products Laboratory* (Ph.D. dissertation, University of Wisconsin, 1964). It is worth mentioning that, in the year 1910, the lumber industry was, by a wide margin, the largest single industrial employer in the United States with 700,000 workers. Bureau of the Census, *Census of the United States: 1910*, (Washington, D.C., 1913), 8:40.

31. Sherry Olson, *The Depletion Myth* (Cambridge, Mass.: Harvard University Press, 1971), 11–14.

32. Ibid., 17.

33. Ibid., 50.

34. "Wood preservation enlarged the supply of timbers suitable for crossties. The 'inferior species,' that is, the cheaper kinds of wood that if untreated decayed rapidly, were treated and substituted for the relatively durable white oak. The red oaks were abundant in the same regions as the white oaks, and their use increased. Treated hemlock and tamarack entered production in large volumes in the states bordering on the Great Lakes, nearly five million ties in 1905. The use of cedar began to decline, displaced by treated timbers. Durable foreign woods from Japan, Hawaii, and Australia were tested and found more expensive than the treated 'inferior species.'" Olson, *Depletion Myth*, 110. See also p. 186.

35. Ibid., 104, 111.

36. Ibid., 110–12. See also p. 119. In the pulp and paper industry, research conducted at the Forest Products Laboratory laid the technical basis for the southern pulp and paper industries that emerged during the 1930s by making possible new uses for previously "inferior" woods. "Previously Southern pines had been used to make 'kraft' paper, a strong, brown paper, useful for wrapping exclusively. During the 1920s the FPL experts discovered a modified sulfate process which, in combination with a new two-stage bleaching process, permitted the manufacture of strong, white paper from Southern pines good for book and magazine paper. The so-called 'semichemical' process, which ranks among the most outstanding of the many FPL accomplishments, was also developed at FPL during the 1920s. This process featured a combination of the chemical and mechanical pulping methods of reducing wood substance to fiber form. The process revolutionized the pulp and paper industry by providing a method for the successful pulping of hitherto useless hardwoods." Nelson, *History of Forest Products*, 223.

37. The Society was an outgrowth of the American Section of the International Association for Testing Materials that had been organized in June 1898.

38. International Association for Testing Materials, American Section, *Bulletin* no. 4, September 1899, 22.

39. American Society for Testing Materials, *Proceedings*, 1908, vol. 8, see table of contents.

40. In his presidential address to the Society in 1911, Henry Howe stated: "The shakiness of our foundations is only too evident. In order to determine whether a given steel is fitted for a given use, for instance for rails, we prescribe certain reception tests, the conditions of which are very far removed from the conditions under which that steel is to do its work. The results of these tests are not quantitatively convertible into terms of service usefulness." American Society for Testing Materials, *Proceedings*, 1911, 24.

41. Consider the Babcock test, an extremely simple way of measuring the butterfat content of milk. All that is required is a small amount of sulphuric acid, a properly graduated container, and a sample of the milk. The test was introduced by Professor S. M. Babcock of the University of Wisconsin in 1890. Its use made it possible for dairy processors (creamery men, cheese makers, etc.) to make more informed purchasing decisions and to control their own production processes more effectively; it provided farmers with a means of measuring the productivity of their dairy cows in a more economically significant fashion than was possible before. More than incidentally, it also discouraged the adulteration of milk.

42. Chandler, *The Visible Hand.*

43. Appert's method secured for him a prize of 10,000 francs that had been offered in 1797 by Napoleon's Society for the Encouragement of Industry for the development of a technique of food preservation that could be used by the military.

44. *Encyclopaedia Britannica*, 15th ed., s.v. "Food Preservation."

45. "The size of American mills was increasing in all sections of the country, but nowhere more rapidly than in Minneapolis, where the average daily capacity per mill, which had been 25 barrels in 1860, rose to 1,837 barrels in 1890 and reached 3,623 barrels thirty years later." John Storck and Walter Teague, *Flour for Man's Bread* (Minneapolis: University of Minnesota Press, 1952), 210.

46. For a detailed, meticulous rendering of changes in milling technology, see Storck and Teague, *Flour for Man's Bread.*

47. Charles Kuhlmann, *The Development of the Flour-Milling Industry in the U.S.* (Boston: Houghton Mifflin Company, 1929), 114. See also Temporary National Economic Committee, monograph no. 35, *Large-Scale Organization in the Food Industries* (Washington, D.C., 1940), 135–38.

48. ". . . different varieties of wheat are quite unlike in their characteristics, the same wheats will vary considerably from season to season and from district to district, and bulk grain comes to the mill mixed with all manner of alien substances—tiny sticks and stones, wire and mud and dust, other seeds and spores, excess moisture, parasitic infestations, and a thousand unsuspected surprises. As little as 0.2 percent of fine outside dirt can discolor a straight flour. If badly stored, wheats go through a change known as sweating. In a modern mill, the storage of wheats, their cleaning and preparation for grinding, and their reduction demand constant vigilance and an instant resourcefulness." Storck and Teague, *Flour for Man's Bread*, 199.

49. Storck and Teague, *Flour for Man's Bread*, 312.

50. Ibid., 232.

51. "The need for quality control along scientific rather than merely empirical lines was felt at least as early as 1886, when A. W. Howard founded a commercial testing laboratory at Minneapolis to which millers sent their flours for baking tests and for analyses of their contents. Stimulated by Jago's work on the chemistry of flour, the Washburn Crosby Co. set up a testing room in 1893—the first such step to be taken by an American miller. Today every large miller determines precise quality standards for his products, of whatever kind, and bends every effort to see that they are maintained." Storck and Teague, *Flour for Man's Bread*, 315. See also Kuhlmann, *Flour-Milling Industry*, 231.

52. Kuhlmann, *Flour-Milling Industry*, 231.

53. Storck and Teague, *Flour for Man's Bread*, 237–38, 286–87.

54. "In 1890, according to the census, meat packing establishments located in five cities—Chicago, Kansas City, Omaha, St. Joseph and St. Louis—accounted for 69 percent of the total domestic cattle slaughtered, 49 percent of the hogs and 52 percent of the sheep. Chicago alone contributed 30 percent of the cattle slaughter, 23 percent of the hogs and 30 percent of the sheep." *Encyclopedia of the Social Sciences* (New York: The Macmillan Company, 1933) s.v. "Meat Packing and Slaughtering."

55. Some meat was, of course, preserved by canning. Here, too, changes initiated by trained scientists played a very significant role, in spite of (because of?) the extreme simplicity of their suggested innovations. "A change in the process of canning, which consisted in precooking the meat before it went into the container and in making the latter wedge-shaped so the contents could be removed in a loaf, eliminated the disagreeable taste and appearance of meats cooked in the can and packed floating in their juices, and thus gave a great impetus to this form of food preparation." Clark, *History of Manufactures*, 2:507.

56. Charles MacDowell, "The Chemist in the Packing and Allied Industries," *Chemical Age* 29, no. 6, June 1921, 217–20; Rudolph Clemen, *American Livestock and Meat Industry* (New York: The Ronald Press Company, 1923), see Chapter 16.

57. "As long as the slaughtering was done at an establishment which was conducted independently of the packing plants, the offal, head, internal organs, blood, hair, and other trimmings of the slaughtered animals were considered a part of the waste material which the slaughterer must dispose of. The packer did not want to be bothered with it, and for that matter, neither did the slaughterer. In fact, at Cincinnati all this material was dumped into the Ohio River, and since the current was swift enough to carry it away that proved to be an easy method of getting rid of it." Clemen, *American Livestock*, 127. See also Philip Armour, "The Packing Industry," in *One Hundred Years of American Commerce*, ed. Chauncey M. Depew (New York: D. O. Hayes and Co. 1895), 388.

58. Clemen, *American Livestock*, 129.

59. Ibid., 360–62.

60. Writing in the early 1920s, Clemen stated: "At present, for the medical profession only, 48 pharmaceutical preparations are made, glands and membranes being utilized, while fresh, in the plant laboratories. Among the most important medical agents produced in the packinghouse laboratories are pepsin, pancreatin, thyroids, rennet, benzoinated lard, suprarenals, and pituitary liquids." Ibid., 370.

61. MacDowell, "The Chemist," 218.

62. Ibid. Products such as fertilizers were usually sold with guarantees to

the buyer concerning composition, strength, and so forth. In this respect, the guarantees were similar to those available for flour and steel products.

63. "While simple cooperation leaves the mode of working by the individual for the most part unchanged, manufacture thoroughly revolutionises it, and seizes labour-power by its very roots. It converts the labourer into a crippled monstrosity, by forcing his detail dexterity at the expense of a world of productive capabilities and instincts; just as in the States of La Plata they butcher a whole beast for the sake of his hide or his tallow." Karl Marx, *Capital* (New York: The Modern Library, 1936), Modern Library Edition, 396.

64. Production on a large scale, Marx pointed out, offers certain decisive advantages. Among them: "We refer to the reconversion of the excretions of production, the so-called waste, into new elements of production, either of the same, or of some other line of industry; to the processes by which this so-called excretion is thrown back into the cycle of production and, consequently, consumption, whether productive or individual. This line of savings . . . is . . . the result of large-scale social labour. It is the attendant abundance of this waste which renders it available again for commerce and thereby turns it into new elements of production. It is only as waste of combined production, therefore of large-scale production, that it becomes important to the production process and remains a bearer of exchange-value . . . In the chemical industry, for instance, excretions of production are such by-products as are wasted in production on a smaller scale; iron filings accumulating in the manufacture of machinery and returning into the production of iron as raw materials, etc." Karl Marx, *Capital* (Moscow: Foreign Languages Publishing House, 1959), 3:79, 100.

65. K. Beaton, *Enterprise in Oil: A History of Shell in the United States* (New York: Appleton-Century-Crofts, 1957), 502–03. As quoted in David Mowery, *The Emergence and Growth of Industrial Research in American Manufacturing, 1899–1945* (Ph.D. dissertation, Stanford University, 1981), 123.

66. This was true only of the early search for by-products. "Most improvements in the refining process were the work of practical refiners rather than trained chemists. The most serious chemical problem facing refiners before the end of the century, the sulfur content of crude from the Lima, Ohio, fields, was solved by Herman Frasch, a German-born technician with only minimal formal training in chemistry." Kendall Birr, "Science in American Industry," in *Science and Society in the U.S.*, ed. David Van Tassel and Michael Hall (Homewood, Ill.: The Dorsey Press, 1966), 61. Birr points out that Standard Oil Co. had begun hiring trained chemists in 1882 ". . . primarily for analytical and control purposes."

67. Clark, *History of Manufactures*, 2:519.

68. National Science Board, *Science Indicators, 1982* (Washington, D.C., 1983), appendix tables 1-10, 1-11.

Commentary
From Industrial Laboratories to Departments of Research and Development

Alfred D. Chandler, Jr.

This commentary looks beyond the creation of the industrial laboratory—the historical phase described in Professor Rosenberg's paper—to the subsequent building of a larger organization responsible for systematic development of product and process.

Rosenberg describes in detail the reasons for the initial use of the laboratory in American industry. He shows how the needs to test and measure in the production process, to assure quality control, to standardize both product and process, and probably most important of all, to meet the precise specifications of customers, led to the founding of the industrial laboratory and the employment of trained chemists, metallurgists, mechanical and electrical engineers. He demonstrates convincingly the profound impact this new development had on the productivity of specific industries and, indeed, on that of national economies. He points out, too, that the laboratories were established within the large firm, within the universities, and by the federal government. He might have added that such laboratories also appeared as commercial enterprises. A. D. Little, Stone and Webster, the Mellon Institute, and the Battelle Institute carried on testing, standardizing, and similar functions for profit.

At the end of his paper, Rosenberg describes still another function carried out by the new industrial laboratory. This was the conversion of by-products or even waste products into valuable goods with major markets of their own. For example, the by-products of meat packing— fertilizers, soap, and pharmaceuticals—became major sources of income to the large packing companies; and before the turn of the century, the by-products of kerosene refining came to provide more income than the main product to the oil companies.

This development of improved and new products seems to be a second stage in the emergence of science as a productive force in industry. Here, the activities of the industrial laboratory move beyond testing, standardizing, and quality control. Focusing on this second stage—one that involves the systematic application of the findings of science to process as well as product development—not only links Rosenberg's historical paper to others in this volume that deal with more current technological changes; it also emphasizes even more dramatically the importance of industrial research to the continuing productivity and growth of industrial enterprises, of major industries, and even of national economies.

Critical to this second stage was a separation of the testing, standardizing, and quality control functions from those of product and process development. This separation involved, first, the creation of a laboratory physically separate and usually geographically distant from the factory or factories of the enterprise. Of even more importance, it called for the creation of a separate, specialized organization to exploit the laboratory's activities. This organization usually took the form of a department separate from those responsible for production, distribution, and purchasing activities of the enterprise. The new department's objective was to define programs for the laboratory by monitoring both market and technological opportunities. Its most critical task was to integrate the activities of the research personnel with those of university professors working closer to the sources of scientific knowledge and with those of managers in the company's design, manufacturing, and marketing offices.

The primary function of the new department was then, and as papers in this volume suggest is still today, not basic research, but the commercial development of product and process. Its task was in providing the all-important linkage between science, technology, production, and marketing—a linkage that was critical to increased productivity within the firm, within industries, and within countries.

Quite understandably, the new departments of research and development, and with them, scientifically trained industrial personnel, have been concentrated in those industries where the potential for the application of science to industrial products and processes has been the greatest.

The concentration of individual R&D in a few sectors, to which Professor Rosenberg refers, has always existed. As my *Table C1-1*, taken from David Mowery's dissertation,[1] indicates, in 1921—the first year for which we have data—over half the scientific personnel employed in nongovernmental research was concentrated in industries dependent

Table C1-1

1921 Survey, Total Employment, Scientific Personnel, Research Intensity, and Employment Concentration

	Staff (% of total)	Scientific Personnel (% of total)	Research Intensity[a]	% of Scientific Personnel in Bottom 10% of Laboratories	% of Scientific Personnel in Top 10% of Laboratories
Food/beverages	204 (3.0)	116 (3.2)	.19	2.5	24.2
Tobacco	—	—	—	—	—
Textiles	16 (.23)	15 (.41)	.015	—	—
Apparel	—	—	—	—	—
Lumber products	70 (1.0)	30 (.83)	.043	—	—
Furniture	—	—	—	—	—
Paper	115 (1.7)	89 (2.5)	.49	1.2	38.1
Publishing	—	—	—	—	—
Chemicals	1,627 (24.3)	1,102 (30.4)	5.2	1.4	44.8
Petroleum	246 (3.7)	159 (4.4)	1.83	1.8	49.1
Rubber products	522 (7.8)	207 (5.7)	2.04	0.5	49.8
Leather	29 (0.4)	25 (0.7)	.09	4.0	40.0
Stone/clay/glass	146 (2.2)	96 (2.6)	.38	2.1	50.0
Primary metals	592 (8.8)	297 (8.2)	.78	1.0	47.0
Fabricated metal products	185 (2.8)	103 (2.8)	.27	2.9	41.7
Nonelectric machinery	148 (2.2)	127 (3.5)	.25	2.4	36.2
Electrical machinery	2,049 (30.6)	199 (7.2)	1.11	1.6	53
Transportation equipment	464 (6.9)	83 (2.3)	.204	2.4	51.8
Instruments	238 (3.5)	127 (2.5)	.396	1.6	52.0
Total mfg.	6,693	2,775	.56	1.1	47.4

a. Defined as scientific and engineering personnel in research laboratories per 1,000 workers.

on the sciences of chemistry and physics. *Tables C1-2* and *C1-3* show that the concentration increased as time passed, with a pronounced shift from scientific personnel employed in the chemical-based industries to those based on physics. In 1921, 40 percent of the scientific personnel was located in chemical, petroleum, and rubber industries, and just under 10 percent more in electrical machinery and instruments. By 1933 the figures were 45 percent for the first and over 18 percent for the second, and they remained in about the same proportion until after World War II. In the postwar years, the communication revolution and military needs—through the emphasis on electronics, computers, and jet planes—further changed the ratio from a concentration of those industries based on chemistry to those relying on physics.

From the beginning, the impact of the application of the findings of chemistry and physics was pervasive and profound. As Rosenberg points out, it was at the core of what historians have come to call the Second Industrial Revolution. The broad range of new chemical products, particularly the new synthetics—the synthetic fabrics, plastics, and other materials, the synthetic dyes, pharmaceuticals, detergents, insecticides, nitrates, and many others—the new broad range of household appliances, x-rays, vacuum tubes, radio, and television generated by the makers of electrical equipment; and the new electrochemical techniques used in the production of metals and chemicals transformed industry after industry, sector after sector, and economy after economy. With the coming of the new, mass-produced machinery, produced through the fabricating and assembling of interchangeable parts, they also revolutionized transportation, agriculture, medicine, and nearly every aspect of modern living.

From the start, the coordination between science, technology, product design, production, and distribution so essential to increased productivity of the science-based industries was carried out primarily within the large industrial firm. At the turn of the century, such American enterprises as General Electric, Du Pont, and Eastman Kodak had built their general research laboratories and created their development departments to monitor and integrate the laboratory's activities. Soon, Westinghouse, the predecessors of Allied Chemical and Union Carbide, as well as American Telephone & Telegraph, followed suit. In the same years, and sometimes even earlier, the new giant German chemical and electrical enterprises built comparable organizational structures.

This growth in industrial research, in turn, fostered the formation of industry and nationwide research organizations. In Germany, the

Table C1-2

1933 Survey, Total Employment, Scientific Personnel, Research Intensity, and Employment Concentration

	Staff (% of total)	Scientific Personnel (% of total)	Research Intensity[a]	% of Scientific Personnel in Bottom 10% of Laboratories	% of Scientific Personnel in Top 10% of Laboratories
Food/beverages	839 (4.29)	651 (5.96)	0.973	2.2	31.5
Tobacco	21 (0.11)	17 (0.16)	0.19	—	—
Textiles	185 (0.95)	149 (1.36)	0.15	2.7	29.5
Apparel	—	—	—	—	—
Lumber products	93 (0.48)	65 (0.59)	0.22	3.2	22.6
Furniture	9 (0.05)	5 (0.05)	0.041	—	—
Paper	461 (2.36)	302 (2.76)	1.54	1.8	32.7
Publishing	4 (0.02)	4 (0.04)	0.015	—	—
Chemicals	5,239 (26.8)	3,255 (29.79)	12.81	1.1	48.2
Petroleum	2,809 (14.37)	994 (9.1)	11.04	0.7	51.7
Rubber products	1,434 (7.34)	564 (5.16)	5.65	1.5	48.0
Leather	80 (0.41)	67 (0.61)	0.24	1.6	25.4
Stone/clay/glass	889 (4.55)	569 (5.21)	3.25	1.8	37.5
Primary metals	1,356 (6.94)	850 (7.78)	2.00	1.1	41.6
Fabricated metal products	777 (3.97)	500 (4.58)	1.53	2.0	27.0
Nonelectric machinery	1,484 (7.59)	629 (5.76)	1.68	2.2	29.5
Electrical machinery	2,340 (11.97)	1,322 (12.1)	8.06	1.5	44.7
Transportation equipment	858 (4.39)	394 (3.61)	1.28	1.3	47.5
Instruments	657 (3.36)	581 (5.32)	2.69	1.1	60.1
Total mfg.	19,548	10,927	1.93	1.3	47.7

a. Defined as scientific and engineering personnel in research laboratories per 1,000 workers.

Table C1-3
1946 Survey, Total Employment, Scientific Personnel, Research Intensity, and Employment Concentration

	Staff (% of total)	Scientific Personnel (% of total)	Research Intensity[a]	% of Scientific Personnel in Bottom 10% of Laboratories	% of Scientific Personnel in Top 10% of Laboratories
Food/beverages	5,308 (4.5)	2,510 (5.46)	2.26	1.6	41.4
Tobacco	108 (0.09)	67 (0.15)	0.65	2.2	57.8
Textiles	1,229 (1.04)	434 (0.94)	0.38	2.6	22.4
Apparel	55 (0.05)	25 (0.05)	0.026	—	—
Lumber products	359 (0.31)	187 (0.41)	0.31	1.9	41.5
Furniture	53 (0.05)	19 (0.04)	0.068	—	—
Paper	1,764 (1.5)	770 (1.68)	1.96	1.7	38.3
Publishing	48 (0.04)	28 (0.06)	0.064	—	—
Chemicals	32,560 (27.67)	14,066 (30.62)	30.31	1.1	51.9
Petroleum	12,412 (10.55)	4,750 (10.34)	28.79	0.6	52.4
Rubber products	2,418 (2.06)	1,069 (2.33)	5.20	0.7	40.5
Leather	174 (0.15)	86 (0.19)	0.25	2.1	18.7
Stone/clay/glass	3,692 (3.14)	1,508 (3.28)	3.72	1.3	47.9
Primary metals	5,539 (4.71)	2,460 (5.35)	2.39	1.2	42.3
Fabricated metal products	3,355 (2.85)	1,489 (3.24)	1.81	1.1	37.3
Nonelectric machinery	8,261 (7.02)	2,743 (5.97)	2.20	1.5	38.9
Electrical machinery	18,421 (15.66)	6,993 (15.22)	11.01	1.1	53.0
Transportation equipment	14,897 (12.66)	4,491 (9.78)	4.58	0.9	42.3
Instruments	7,007 (5.96)	2,246 (4.89)	3.81	1.0	55.9
Total mfg.	117,660	45,941	3.98	1.0	61.1

a. Defined as scientific and engineering personnel in research laboratories per 1,000 workers.

most famous institute for chemical research, the Kaiser Wilhelm Society (later named the Max Planck Institute) was established in 1910 at the instigation of successful chemical manufacturers who saw as their model the National-Physical-Technical Institute set up by Werner von Siemens in 1883 from the profits of his electrical manufacturing enterprise.[2] Both institutes soon had their galaxies of Nobel Prize winners in chemistry and physics. In the United States similiar, though less prestigious, research institutes were also fathered by chemists, chemical and electrical engineers working in private industrial enterprises.

As I have already suggested, the new research and development departments were not only critical to the rapid growth of the science-based industries and to the development of a wide variety of new materials, machines, and processes, but they profoundly affected the health and wealth of nations. In those years in which the American and German industrialists were creating their new organizational structures, British manufacturers did little. They continued to operate enterprises in the new technologies as they had in those using the old, that is through personal and family management. With very few exceptions they did not create departments of research and development managed by scientifically informed personnel. The results were disastrous.

The dye industry provides a striking example.[3] As Rosenberg points out, an Englishman, William H. Perkin, invented the new synthetic azure dye. These dyes were produced from coal tar and Britain had a plethora of coal. Indeed, the first German dye manufacturers imported their raw materials from Britain. Most important of all, the British textile industry was, by far, the largest market in the world for dyes. Yet it was German, not British, entrepreneurs who first created organizations to manage large-scale production of dyes, who first built international sales forces to market in volume, and who set up the industry's first research and development departments. Until World War I, German firms totally dominated the British market for dyes; and quickly recaptured it in the 1920s.

The pattern was much the same in the production of electrical equipment. In 1912, two-thirds of the electrical equipment produced *within* Britain was manufactured by the subsidiaries of General Electric, Westinghouse, and Siemens.[4] Not surprisingly, the new London subway system was equipped by General Electric. A similar story occurred in the production and distribution of mass-produced machinery, a sector in which American enterprises in Britain were particularly strong. The failure of the British manufacturers to create the organizational arrangements necessary to exploit the commercial potentials of the new science-based industries meant that that nation lost out on many of the fruits of the Second Industrial Revolution. It was a failure from which Britain never recovered.

The lesson of this historical story is not, it needs to be stressed, that British scientists and manufacturers did not see the potential of science-based technology. Although they relied, as Rosenberg indicates, more on government-supported research and joint interindustry cooperation than did the Americans and Germans, many of their leading enterprises did set up laboratories separated from their factories. They failed, not in research, but in development. They failed because they did not create the critical organizational linkages. They failed to build the organization, hire the personnel, and set up the facilities so central to the development of new processes and products. They failed to carry out the developmental processes that are so much more costly in manpower and money than basic research. In particular, they failed to forge the linkages between research, design, production, and marketing so critical to rapid and effective development of new products.

This lesson has relevance for today. The Japanese challenge has not been, at least until very recently, one of research. The Japanese success has been one of development. They acquired nearly all their basic technology from the West; but they then substantially improved both the borrowed processes and the borrowed products. As Hirschmeier and Yui noted in their *Development of Japanese Business*:

> Between 1950 and 1967, Japanese industry set records of technological transfers. A total of 4,135 licenses were purchased by Japanese industry, mainly from the U.S.A., over half in the field of machinery construction and about 20% in the field of chemical industries. During the same time, exports of licenses amounted to only about one percent of the money spent on imports of patents and licenses.[5]

By the 1980s, the tide had turned. However, much of the turnaround appears to be improved processes and products, and in ways to introduce them more rapidly and effectively, rather than in more fundamental technological innovations. In any case, the industrial histories of Britain and Japan help to make clear the importance of that distinction between research and development in product and process invention, innovation, and application.

This addendum to Rosenberg's historical introduction emphasizes the importance of organizational arrangements in the effective application of the findings of science to the improvement of industrial productivity, and with it, industrial competitiveness in international markets.

The first major stage in the emergence of science as a productive force in industry involved the formation of laboratories employing technically trained scientific personnel, either within the firm—and usually within the factory—or as central units in industrywide or national organizations whose functions were to test, to standardize, to assure quality, and to meet precise customer specifications. The second stage—that of applying science to the development of specific processes and products—brought a separation of the laboratories carrying out these two different functions and demanded that the latter function be integrated systematically with university science and industrial production and distribution.

This historical background prompts two sets of questions. First, about the relationship between Stage One and Stage Two. What, precisely, are the differences between the functions of testing, quality control, and standardization, and those of product and process development? Are there other functions involved in the application of science to industrial production? What types of organizational or institutional forms are best suited to carrying out each of these different activities? Second, how precisely do the functions of research differ from those of development, and how have the integrative linkages between the two been improved, or become less effective in recent years?

Notes

1. David Mowery, "The Emergence and Growth of Industrial Research in American Manufacturing, 1899–1945" (Ph.D. dissertation, Stanford University, 1981).

2. See L. F. Haber, *The Chemical Industry, 1900–1930* (Oxford: Oxford University Press, 1971), 49; and Segfrid von Weiner, *Werner von Siemens* (Gottingen: Musterschmidt, 1975), 73–74.

3. Haber, *Chemical Industry*, chapters 5–6. In 1913, eight German firms produced 140,000 tons of dyes out of a total world output of 160,000 tons, p. 121. British production in 1913 was 4,100 tons, consisting "predominantly of the simpler and cheaper colors," p. 145.

4. I. C. R. Byatt, *The British Electrical Industry, 1875–1914* (Oxford: Oxford University Press, 1979), 150.

5. Johannes Hirschmeier and Tsunehiko Yui, *The Development of Japanese Business, 1600–1973* (Cambridge: Harvard University Press, 1975), 258.

2

The Taming of Lions: How Manufacturing Leadership Evolved, 1780–1984

Wickham Skinner

Introduction

Recent competitive events remind us with great force of the necessity for excellence in manufacturing. Starting from a position of American dominance of many industries in the fifties, we look back now on two decades of declines in world market share. This steady deterioration raises questions about that former dominance and our vaunted manufacturing leadership.

Was our former high level of manufacturing performance due to our proficiency in the management of manufacturing rather than the fact of limited competition? And are the inefficiencies and fundamental structural problems (Abernathy, 1977) that have surfaced over these two troubled decades new, or have they been there all along, hidden by easy success?

The central thesis of this chapter is that we have a management problem in American manufacturing today which is due to a "mind set" of mistaken premises and implicit objectives which are rooted in the history of production management and are now inappropriate and dysfunctional. In its first 160 years American manufacturing leadership developed skills, techniques, concepts, and patterns of thinking, a paradigm for a profession that appeared enormously successful. Now many conditions have changed. Worldwide industrial competition and

This paper has benefited from the generous efforts and thoughtful comments of many colleagues, particularly Alice Amsden, Alfred Chandler, Jr., E. Raymond Corey, Robert Hayes, Alan Kantrow, George C. Lodge, and W. Earl Sasser, of the Harvard Business School; Anne Firor Scott of Duke University; and Virginia C. Welles, whose able work as research associate is much appreciated.

changing technology are among the many factors that have rewritten the rulebook and changed the game (Abernathy, Clark, and Kantrow, 1981). Meanwhile we think about the factory institution and make manufacturing decisions in much the same way as sixty years ago. Our premises and perceptions and even our objectives do not always fit reality. The resulting "wrong thinking" got us into trouble and keeps us there. The question today is not whether, but how, the manufacturing management profession must change its ways of thinking.

But what are "its ways of thinking"? How and in what patterns did they develop? Analysis of American industrial history suggests five traditional characteristics of American manufacturing leadership that are now holding back industrial performance. These characteristic tendencies are:

1. Accepting that the performance of the factory and its management is principally measured by financial yardsticks (such as cost reduction, return on investment, and efficiency).
2. Accepting a secondary role in the firm as custodians of fixed assets.
3. Perceiving the keys to managerial success as achieving maximum production and minimum cost by excellence in controlling and coordinating, while stabilizing the factory in every way possible against external changes.
4. Perceiving the work force as an annoying and potentially destabilizing, frequently pernicious factor of production to be handled by simultaneously delegating work force management to first-level supervision and minimizing the involvement and preoccupation of top-level management (Clawson, 1980).
5. As a consequence of these four tendencies, seeking the maximum degree of process mechanization and high volume—mass production—continuous flow processes permitted by production economics.

These characteristics are rooted in history and they persist today. They are the way the profession evolved during the nineteenth century. Such managerial behavior was reinforced and rewarded with successful careers, and it contributed to American industry's 180-year climb to a peak of industrial success about 1960.

But after 1960 these premises appear to have been dysfunctional. The new industrial competition has proved to be technology-based, with processes, products, and information systems changing with accelerating rapidity, requiring a different, more flexible, and aggressive kind of manufacturing management. To compete in 1984 it appears that the thinking and premises of American manufacturing leadership may have to be almost diametrically opposed to the five characteristics developed in history. The characteristics of thought that seem needed now are something like this:

1. Seeing the factory as a resource that can be used to create competitive advantage and leadership, rather than just as a financial investment.
2. Carrying out a primary role in the corporation as the architect and builder of new manufacturing systems structured to provide competitive and strategic advantage, rather than acting as custodian and housekeeper.
3. Emphasizing as key skills those of managing technological and product change and building flexible, learning organizations, rather than acting as coordinator and stabilizer.
4. Becoming involved with and gaining the support and commitment of the work force, rather than considering labor as a cost and a disturbing element to be managed well down the organization.
5. Seeking maximum flexibility for product and volume change by choosing technology appropriate for the competitive market, rather than generally seeking maximum mechanization and the use of mass-production processes.

This chapter traces the antecedents of the outmoded characteristics from our industrial history and describes how they have continued as a dominant paradigm, becoming increasingly ineffective in the past twenty years. It then describes ongoing field research based on interviews with forty-six "fast-track comers," directed toward the question: Will the next generation of manufacturing managers, developed under adversity and new, more demanding competitive conditions, have the same or different characteristics?

The main conclusion is that, although one can see many encouraging signs about these "comers," the picture is not altogether optimistic. For the hand of history is heavy and, while the next generation appears to think more broadly and to demonstrate more of a general management focus in skills and outlook, most of its members still function as "custodians" and "housekeepers" rather than determined "architects." Though the competitive world is changing its demands, a profession steeped in the values and traditions of a century apparently cannot make such basic changes in one short generation.

More optimistically, the history of manufacturing leadership shows that basic changes in management focus and characteristics were brought about by major developments in technology and markets, the transitions requiring about twenty to thirty years, the equivalent of two or three generations of top manufacturing leadership. Today we are already influenced by the very ingredients history seems to require for change: new economics, in the form of severe competition, and major innovations in process technology (Toynbee, 1884; Skinner, 1984a). In many industries technology offers the greatest changes in a century, such as microprocessor based computer-aided design and manufacturing (CAD/CAM), robotics, computer integrated manufacturing (CIM), and flexible machining centers. Taken together these revolutionary factors may be powerful enough to eventually sweep away worn-out paradigms of manufacturing leadership and bring on something new.

The Evolution of Manufacturing Management

Five periods of industrial history stand out in the development of dominant characteristics of manufacturing management:

1780–1850   Manufacturing leaders as technological capitalists
1850–1890   Manufacturing leaders as architects of mass production
1890–1920   Manufacturing management moves down in the organization
1920–1960   Manufacturing management refines its skills in controlling and stabilizing
1960–1980   Shaking the foundations of industrial management

Manufacturing Leaders as Technological Capitalists, 1780–1850

New technology first allowed production to begin to shift from the traditional enterprise of low-volume artisans shops to capital-intensive use of machinery. The harnessing of water and steam energy to power machinery was combined with new machines and equipment using recently engineered mechanisms for power transmission and mechanization of hand-performed operations. Shafting, gears, bearings, and ingenious mechanical movements added the ability to eliminate many manual operations. The shift was limited as well as triggered by technological factors, for there were as yet inadequate means of transporting coal, of producing strong and nonbrittle metals, and, equally detrimental, limited means of communication and only slow, small-scale transportation—all of which kept markets small and local and power supplied by man, animal, or flow of water. As a result the industrial "revolution" was slow in developing in all but textile production (Chandler 1977), some metalworking and machine-making facilities, and modest agricultural processing plants such as grain mills.

In America the first water-powered mill was developed by a partnership between a Samuel Slater and four Brown brothers, the former being a skilled mechanic and the latter, wealthy merchants (Chandler 1983). The first integrated textile mill was built by Francis Cabot Lowell, "an able self-taught engineer" as well as a merchant, and he "recognized the primary of technological problems" (Douglass 1971). These operations built up to unprecedented scale and degree of integration.

While the management of the large, integrated textile mills was something that had never been done before, it was still basically not complex (Chandler 1977, 246). Because of equipment constraints and lack of flexibility, each mill had a relatively small range of product. The equipment was essentially balanced and integrated around that product range (Nelson 1975, 18).

The main tasks of management—after the mill was engineered and built, with power shafting and belting installed and machinery purchased and set up by a technologically oriented and mechanically assisted top management—were delegated to the "overseers," one on each floor. Overseers reported to the owner's "agent" who more or less singlehandedly (and often from a distance) ran the mill. Profits were calculated twice a year, accounting was by the mercantile system with no product costing. The agent's chief specialized knowledge and competence was also essentially technical. He focused on the machinery and equipment and performed the calculations needed for setting up spinning ratios and cloth balances (Chandler 1977, 68–72).

As this early factory period moved along in time, large increases in productivity came about as technological changes took place in spinning, metalworking machinery improved, and continuous processes were developed for the milling of grains.

In metalworking, and parts and assembly industries such as riflemaking, a major innovation late in this period (Chandler 1977, 72) was the shift from individual parts and unique products to making interchangeable parts, and products that could be readily repaired later by substituting new parts. This "American factory system" required fixtures and gauges and more complex measuring and inspection equipment and procedures. It also required a standard method of manufacture and therefore worker discipline and supervisory surveillance (Smith 1977). At the Springfield Armory, for example, where guaranteed markets based on annual production contracts allowed large batches to be made and hence standardized, the use of the interchangeable parts philosophy induced standardization of processes, specialized jobs (making a few parts rather than a whole or major assembly of the rifle), and finally, the beginning of detailed accounts to provide management with cost information (Chandler 1977, 72).

The management of manufacturing was relatively simple and performed by the owner's agent. After the system was started up by the technologically competent owners, they were much less involved. The most demanding aspect of plant operation was technological, centering around the engineering of the plant, the mechanics of machinery operation, and instructing overseers on each floor. The overseer took entire responsibility for every aspect of the employee and employment arrangements. Even the agent was often remote.

From the outset an unmistakable characteristic of the early factory period was worker resistance and unrest, the formation of unions, and occasional sabotage (Rosenbloom 1984). This seems surprising at first, for the factory system had many advantages for employees. The pay and working conditions were far superior to farm and physical labor. Further, the work was light and easy in comparison to tasks not performed by a machine powered by coal or water. The hours were long but not at all unusual for those times. There were opportunities for advancement and, for some, the challenge of machinery. The tasks of coordinating materials and products were simple but provided an opportunity for pleasurable social interaction, and the support and warmth of friendly and cooperative associations at work (Ure 1835, 277–373).

For some, of course, this was enough. Satisfying economic, physical, and social needs, the factory was a good place to spend one's working life. For apparently many others, however, the factory was an alien environment for a human being (Thompson 1967). It required strict self-discipline to get to work on time, the work was performed in accordance with prescribed methods; starting and stopping work was not a matter of personal choice but was ordered by a preemptory bell or whistle; the pace, often driven by machine and overseer, could feel relentless (Gutman 1977, 14). There was an overseer on each floor who had total authority to hire, fire, discipline, and use physical punishment if he chose. The factory may have been warm and dry and even relatively clean, but it was generally noisy, frequently the belt-driven machinery was dangerous, and the work was sometimes monotonous. The transition to industrial society "entailed a severe restructuring of working habits—new disciplines, new incentives, and a new human nature upon which these incentives could bite effectively" (Nelson 1975, 55).

In 1887 Arnold Toynbee wrote of the early factories in England:

> When huge factories were established there could no longer be a close tie between the master and his men; the workman hated his employer and the employer looked on his workmen simply as hands. From 1800 to 1843 their mutual relations, as was admitted by both parties, were as bad as they could be. There could be no union, said employees, between classes whose interests were so different. . . . Trade-unions, too, have done much to sever what was left of the old ties. Workmen are obliged, in self-defense, to act in bodies (132).
>
> Between the individual workman and the capitalist who employed hundreds of hands a wide gulf opened. The workman . . . became the living tool of whom the employer knew less than he did of his steam engine. The breach was admitted by the employer who declared it to be impossible. "It is as impossible," said one, "to effect a union between the high and low classes of society as to mix oil and water. There can be no union between employer and employed because it is the interest of the employer to get as much work as he can done for the smallest sum possible" (206).

So there was "the labor problem"[1] from the very beginning. People did not easily adjust to factory life. "Subordination is the very essence of the factory system" (R. Taylor 1891, 441). Those who were willing to take factory jobs tended, therefore, to be from the lower rungs of society. Each wave of farm immigrants and immigrants brought in ultimately provided the labor source for the insatiable, growing factory system. These workers generally had the least education, were not acculturated to the United States, or often spoke little or no English. But they were cheap and they were willing to work. Management had no reason or need to associate with them and for over a century this area of management was simply delegated and ignored.

Worker assignments, discipline, and compensations were handled by the overseers, and families and relatives often worked together. Even this support system was frequently inadequate to cushion the shock of a restricted, constrained life in the factory. As a result, from the beginning of industrial society, there were strikes, unions, and occasional violence and sabotage. "Thus gloomily amid tumult, fear and suffering was the modern factory system introduced" wrote R. W. C. Taylor concerning the resistance of workers to the factory (R. Taylor 1886, 429).

In sum, the early factory period saw a genuine revolution in how products were made and how large numbers of workers worked. Its concepts and its factories began to change Western civilization. Its leadership came from technologically competent entrepreneurs, investing in new labor saving equipment to gain an economic return. Aside from ownership and mechanics it required little management and only the simplest management hierarchy (Chandler 1977, 14). Nevertheless, the seeds of mass production—capital invested in equipment and process technology, the use of a central power source, the producing of standardized products, the use of interchangeable parts and repetitive operations (Rosenberg 1969), a few isolated experiments in accounting as a control mechanism, and the employment of large numbers of workers on machine-controlled jobs—had been sown (Fong 1930). But the owners were not much involved with the workers. In 1891 looking back at the short history of the factory system R. W. C. Taylor wrote:

> [The captain of industry] has not played that splendid part in industry which was assigned to him [operatives were dependent on him for present support and future progress]. He has been content with the far more vulgar one of a more or less successful trader (438).

A big revolution had occurred—on a small scale—and a real industrial revolution awaited further key technological breakthroughs in power, transportation, communications, and equipment and process technologies.

Manufacturing Leaders as Architects of Mass Production, 1850–1890

The real industrial revolution which took place during the next forty years was one of the most massive, powerful, and rapid changes in economic history. What took place was not only nearly total change in how most products were made but a large scale-up in industrial employment, in industrial output, and a total revolution in the sophistication, penetration, and contribution of equipment and process technology.

What made all this possible was what Chandler called "the end of technological constraints" (Chandler 1977, 75), in particular the limitations of water power. With the advent of newly dug canals in the United States (and subsequently railroads), coal could now be transported in bulk to sites where raw materials could also be gathered, closer to sources of employees and markets. With coal and new developments in iron and steel metallurgy, machinery progress accelerated, including great improvements in the efficiency, safety, and versatility of steam power. All of this led to new locations for plants, and when this was accompanied by scientific and engineering progress in heat-using industries such as chemicals, chinaware, metals production, glass, rubber, paper, sugar, and distilleries, industrial growth was

rapid. The American factory system expanded from the notion of interchangeable parts to high-volume, continuous processes of identical
products called mass production.

The revolution was fueled not only by the ending of technological
constraints but by increases in population and markets and by vast
increases in the speed of production. Its manufacturing leadership was
provided from the top down by owner-investor-capitalists who were
technologically competent. For the new processes required bold investments in equipment that had never been tried on massive scales. The
manufacturing manager had to be closely enough involved in the design and structuring of manufacturing on unprecedented scales to assure himself that it would work and produce sufficiently low costs and
high volumes. During the forty years after 1850, mass production with
such leadership found its way into the processing of liquids such as
sugar and beer and whiskey, and next in the continuous processing of
agricultural products such as wheat and other grains. In metalmaking
and metalworking mass production came later, held back by the need
for advances in metallurgy, a science more sophisticated than that
required for most liquids and agricultural products processing (Glover
1936).

Increases in speed of production and volumes of production attended
by lower prices, more uniform quality, and population growth resulted
in much larger productive units. Through economies of scale, an increase in plant size often permitted more fully integrated facilities.
Single plants began to include more of the processing stages from raw
material to finished product.

For these reasons after about 1850 the task of management of manufacturing began to involve plant design and system economics while
continuing to delegate work-force management to powerful overseers
or foremen. Bigger, integrated plants required coordination skills and
techniques to balance and match inputs and outputs at varying levels
and stages of production. This coordination had to be handled by foremen for there was no one else to do it. (Technicians, clerks, and staff
specialists were unknown until the late nineteenth century factory.)
As "undisputed rulers," (Nelson 1975, 42) foremen had complete
charge of their departments, often, in fact, acting as contractors to the
owner. They bought material and supplies, hired workers, and produced the product at a contract price. With such command and control
when the plants were one-product and single-unit production facilities,
coordination-type management tasks in manufacturing could be handled by the foremen in spite of the increasing size.

There were no personnel officers, and virtually none of what would today be called "staff." Even material handling was generally performed by production workers. The foreman and production workers set up, maintained, and changed over the machinery with occasional specialized help from a "master mechanic" as needed.

The foreman had a virtual empire. He hired, fired, assigned jobs, exerted discipline, established individual wages, trained, promoted, and often procured the necessary materials. "The foremen's authority derived from the fact that technical skills were the key to power" (Nelson 1975).

In the mechanical industries this forty-year period saw rapid technological advances early on but then a leveling out. In textiles the major technical advances in carding, spinning, and weaving were largely accomplished by the 1850s (Chandler 1977, 247). In other mechanical industries this rate of technological advance also slowed after earlier breakthroughs. In other industries such as cigarette making, matches, and food processing, new process technologies developed and allowed for more continuous processing (Glover 1936). This in turn simplified the tasks of management. Similarly, in chemical process industries such as soap, dyes, rubber, and basic chemicals, new processes allowed substantial improvement in both product quality and product variety. In these "process"-type industries there was an especially close collaboration between top management and production process developers and great technological innovation resulted.

Mass production had largely arrived by 1890; the American factory system was well established. While management of factories remained both relatively technical and simple, manufacturing leadership remained at the top, with owner-investors playing a substantial role in the technological and economic concepts underlying the operation (Hammond 1941). Since competitive advantage was created by investment of capital in mass-production equipment and processes, this was the critical decision. Running the plant hard, driving foremen for output—while they, in turn, drove the workers—then made the formula successful. Since workers were generally immigrants with little education who were accustomed to hard work and considered themselves fortunate to have a job, foremen handled everything down in the plant, from worker discipline to coordination. But as Abernathy and Corcoran stated "the standard of excellence that emerged in American industry during the nineteenth century owed much to the fact that there existed a broad class of "industrial entrepreneurs—men who made continuous efforts to develop and refine process equipment internally, and to exploit outside sources in unrelated industries" (Abernathy and Corcoran 1983, 158).

Manufacturing Management Moves Down in the Organization, 1890–1920

By the decade 1880–1890 the American factory system was flourishing. New industrial technologies, the railroad, the telegraph, coal-steam power, large-scale immigration, and expanding markets had provided the impetus for this remarkable system. But the next forty years saw it multiply tenfold in output, employment, and complexity.

The history of manufacturing management until 1890 saw leadership held at the top of the organization by top officers generally involved in key choices of equipment and process technology. Of course, there was a factory, equipment, and workers and all had to be "managed." But the economics and the equipment and facilities were engineered, designed, and constructed by technical people working with top officers heavily involved, delegating work-force management to the foremen. The foremen had to keep the materials moving on the floor between operations so as to keep expensive machines producing. But this was not very complicated as long as the firm had few plants and few products.

After 1890, however, the growth of corporations, sales volumes, and multiunit, multiproduct enterprise led to the need for systematic controls, and this evolved into "scientific management." The new complexity came about through more of the same growth in markets that forced expansion of facilities and multiple plant sites, and through improved process technologies that increased productive capacities and speeds of output. But a great deal more happened as well. There was growth within companies. There was a profusion of new products, new industries, and new modes of power, construction, transportation, and communication. Business and industry exploded in size, variety, complexity, and diversity (Chandler 1977, 249).

Companies such as Du Pont, General Electric, Westinghouse, and dozens of others began to expand product lines, cross over into new industries, market nationally rather than regionally, and manufacture in more than one location (Glover 1936). New products proliferated, many—such as electric motors, lights, and the telephone—based on the use of electricity, proliferated. In the early 1880s electric lights began to be used in the factories. Ten years later electric motors were applied for the first time to run individual machines. Gone was the necessity for power mechanically transferred through shafts and belts from a central point all over a factory. And the use of reinforced concrete in construction allowed buildings to be higher and larger with wider spacing between columns. Factories could now be bigger, and with size came additional economics of scale, savings in purchasing and transportation by making more and buying less, centralizing and integrating whole manufacturing systems under one roof or in one large complex.

With all these growth-inducing factors came "model factories" such as those set up by Westinghouse in 1895, National Cash Register in 1896, Allis in 1902, United Shoe Machinery in 1904, plants of a size that had never been built before. These plants became much more of a complex challenge to manage. Gone were the days of only small plants, producing a few products for only regional markets. But the modern multiunit, multiproduct industrial enterprise produced a whole new set of tasks for management.

As a result, the "foreman's empire" and the "contracting system," which delegated decisions to first-line supervision, were simply overpowered when product varieties and volumes proliferated, and schedules changed under conditions of rapid growth (Chandler 1977, 274). The increased uncertainty and instability that derive from multiunit enterprises with departments transshipping to each other across the web of supply points inherent in integrated production systems produced unprecedented and complex coordination demands.

As technologies allowed for faster production, and innovations in telephone and telegraph communication reduced the long delays previously involved in placing orders and changing schedules, industrial management had to devise entirely new forms of organization and concepts and techniques with which to handle mounting problems of coordination and complexity (Bernard 1971). Clerks and expediters, accountants, schedulers, method and procedures planners, and purchasing departments were added and became necessary overheads. And as many employees had to specialize more and the facts of growth and size raised issues of employee equity (especially around compensation), the first personnel officers were established. The foreman's empire began to decline as his range of clear-cut, accountable authority was eroded by these new managerial functionaries (Pollard 1965).

Of course all this overhead creation did not take place without considerable internal controversy. It was sheer cost and accountants called it "burden" with some justification. It was justified partly by necessity, for without coordination and control the wrong things were produced at the wrong time in the wrong amount. And delays, scrap, rework, excessive lead time, and inventories were the result. Men like Frederick Taylor tried to prove that a dollar spent for staff people would save two dollars in direct labor. Middle managers were needed. Four staff departments began to be common: (1) the personnel department, (2) plant facilities and equipment planning, (3) materials control, and (4) methods and procedures department (Chandler 1977, 277). Indeed, all of management had to become more systematic to make the system work at all.

In this way, this period saw the rise and development of the first systematic efforts to plan, coordinate, and control manufacturing. The foreman declined in influence as he was increasingly directed by staff departments as to whom he could employ, how much they were to be paid, what work was to be done each week or day, detailed priorities for production, the methods and processes to be used, the product specifications to be met, the costs that were acceptable, and in-process inventories allowable (Wells 1890).

Size, volume, speed, variety, and integration brought about such control and coordination problems. But management techniques and methods and systems for handling these problems were nonexistent before 1890. Into this vacuum entered the pioneers of industrial engineering, Taylor, Gilbreth, Cooke, Barth, and others. They were not only reformers who endeavored to bring system and planning to chaotic factories, they were also creators of totally new management concepts. As Nelson put it, there was no management literature before 1880 (Nelson 1975, 49) and these men began to write it in the 1890s (F. Taylor 1895).

Taylor and his followers founded the school of "scientific management." It was probably more "systematic" than "scientific." Its principal notion was that any operation involving people and/or materials could be made more efficient by analysis of a breakdown of the operation into its components, measuring those components, and diagnosing where waste occurred and could be eliminated. A great burst of energy and activity followed Taylor and his disciples' early work. By his death in 1915, a new profession had been created—industrial engineering.

Industrial engineering introduced a totally new point of view about manufacturing: Factories must be not only engineered and staffed, but also managed. Until 1890 management of industry took place at only two levels: top management and the plant floor. The top management allocated capital to equipment and processes they generally had engineered personally or closely monitored. The plant operation was entirely delegated to first-line supervision who controlled the workers and pushed out the production. Swiftly in the thirty-year period from 1890 to 1920 a new management function, demanded by the physical realities of growth, size, and complexity, led to development of the production department and a production manager whose responsibility it was to tie together and coordinate all the elements of manufacturing into a working, functioning, and economically efficient system. That was a whole new idea and it was in place by 1920. It added the functions of planning, analysis, operation, improvements, coordination, control, and personnel management, bringing the function elaboration and a conceptual base, and shifting nearly all the scope and power of manufacturing management from the president-foremen team to a middle level in the organization.

This was the first major drastic change in the prior smooth evolution of manufacturing management. It shattered a century-old pattern of technological innovation and investment decisions involving management at the top and the heretofore total, comfortable delegation of work force management and daily production problems to be handled at the bottom. Henceforth, the "production department" was to manage both.

First, the foreman's power demise: In the 1890–1920 period, the impact of the worker on efficiency and productivity was realized so their jobs were engineered, simplified, standardized, and thereby controlled without the prior total dependence on supervision. The foreman's authority and scope was reduced in other aspects as well by the coming of scientific management. No longer was the foreman solely in charge of the department. Planners took over scheduling, expediting, dispatching, and materials handling; inspectors took over quality control; and method engineers developed the engineered methods and process techniques, specifying the tooling and equipment to be used for each step in the process. The foreman's job has never been the same since 1920—his scope and authority were drastically reduced over three decades by clerks and staff.

More serious for the foreman and production management as a whole, the job became ambiguous in its authority, responsibility, and accountability. What was he really responsible for now? Productivity? No, not without methods and process control and scheduling latitude. Morale and worker commitment and competency? No, not without authority to define job content. Schedule completion? Only partially, for the dispatching and expediting staff took over the responsibility for setting priorities and told the foremen what to run first. With this ambiguity, the foreman's empire had fallen.

The new allocation of manufacturing leadership began to develop a whole new bureaucracy, the production department. Until 1890 corporate management consisted largely of manufacturing management. Industrial entrepreneurs were technologist-capitalist-investors. They invested in new equipment and processes based on technology and economics they knew intimately. The Du Ponts, the founders of Brown and Sharpe, Andrew Carnegie and Alexander Lyman Holley for the steel industry, and George Pullman were men who created mass-production, process-type industries through a combination of technological and entrepreneurial innovation. Manufacturing leadership was technological leadership and that could create the whole essence of a firm and its competitive advantage. The rest of management could be delegated to the plant floor.

The new bureaucracy of a production department, created only to handle complicated coordination problems, soon became the custodian of the whole manufacturing investment. Held responsible for the production function of the firm, it was its job to make it work and to answer for the financial investment in fixed assets with adequate returns.

In this way the factory came to be seen by top management in largely financial terms. For if the production manager was to be granted funds for new production equipment, he had to assure the owners of a good economic return on investment. He typically was custodian of 70–85 percent of a firm's assets. The name of the game was "efficiency" for profit, year by year. The process of management of course became more bureaucratic with size and complexity. Coordination and control and stabilization of the productive unit became of increasing concern, since changes upset the smooth flows that were key to efficiency, volume, and profitable operation.

This revolutionary period also saw two other major developments. One was the explosion of the automobile industry early in the century. It grew so quickly that by 1908 Ford built a superbly modern auto plant at Highland Park and in 1913 began to produce using a new technique—the moving assembly line. The auto industry spawned dozens of subsidiary industries, its products revolutionized transportation and further created markets and the need for more geographically decentralized multiunit enterprises serving the nation.

A second powerful factor was the massive impact on industrial development furnished by World War I. The "Great War" provided step-function impetus to industrial production and induced the initiation of many new technologies, processes, products, and markets. By 1920 modern industry as we know it today, with immense productive facilities, multiunit, multiproduct, line and staff management, paperwork planning, scheduling, accounting, and controlling, was a flourishing reality. And it was managed by a new and flourishing bureaucracy of staff specialists with a growing sense of becoming a group of professions, under a rubric called "production management." Manufacturing leadership had been moved down in the organization.

Manufacturing Management Refines Its Skills in Controlling and Stabilizing, 1920–1960

The forty years following World War I saw further growth in the American industrial system with attendant geometrical increases in the scope and complexity of production management problems of controlling and stabilizing. As a consequence, it also spurred a spontaneous eruption in the form of the dynamic creation of management tools and techniques which built on the early efforts of "systematic management" and "scientific management" but led into vast new arenas of management, spawning an entirely new era of professional management.

Marred by serious labor problems and held back in the 1930s by economic depression, these four decades nevertheless have become in retrospect a kind of golden age for American industrial managers and their body of knowledge. By 1960 the dominance of U.S. industry in many world markets was supreme.

Employment grew 109 percent from 1920 to 1960, manufacturing output by a factor of three, productivity at an average annual rate of 3 percent, and the domestic market share of U.S. manufactured goods reached 97 percent. The logistics and supply for the biggest war in history were carried out with astonishing success. U.S. companies continued the tradition begun in the 1880s of producing abroad, in particular in Europe, and over 2,000 U.S. factories were established outside the United States. American products and manufacturing proficiency resulted in worldwide domination of giant industries: automobiles, trucks, construction equipment, office equipment and business machines, household appliances, industrial machinery and equipment, textile machinery, shoe machinery, communications equipment, pharmaceuticals, personal consumer goods, electrical machinery and equipment, power plants and generators, and more.

In top management councils, manufacturing executives played key roles. They were responsible for contributing to the P&L statement the difference between sales and costs of goods sold, the cash flow vital for R&D, engineering, marketing, and sales. As a source of corporate presidents, the production department was the largest of any functional group (Hayes and Abernathy 1980).

It was in production as a body of knowledge and a discipline that the energetic power of this era is most clear. The flow of new ideas and techniques and the honing of older ones suggests an extraordinary vitality and motivation of the managers, engineers, and academics who worked on the management tools to support the American industrial machine.

The scope and volume of this outpouring of managerial science and technology is impressive. Beginning where Taylor and his followers had left off in the field of time study and improving work methods, a great deal more was accomplished in refining time-study techniques, including the use of microfilming, and the setting of standards for wages and control purposes. This led to the development and extensive use of predetermined standards which could be built up from data banks of standard motions and operations. Standards came to be nearly universal in use, frequently for incentive wage rates but even more typically for what came to be known as "measured day-work." In the early 1950s, Alan Mogenson pioneered in making widespread the knowledge and practical techniques for "work simplification," a technique that managers and workers could use to analyze and improve their jobs.

The focus of much of the industrial engineering work in this period continued where it had started, on the direct labor worker. Meanwhile, however, with all the staff/burden/overhead expense, concerns arose as to how to control indirect labor. A new technique, "work sampling," which was based on statistics, became a useful tool for analyzing the efficiency of such workers as materials handlers, tool and die workers, and inspectors.

A flood of other new concepts and techniques came into being as responses to the complexity and coordination problems of size and multiunits which had been increasing since the century began. The first was simply a projection of schedules of parts needs using lead times and bills of materials to create parts and materials requirements and after deducting inventories, to result in shop orders. This was in effect a computerless form of modern MRP (Materials Requirements Planning), with the calculation done by the business machines of the 1920s and 1930s.

The eternal dilemma of how much to produce was apparently "solved" by the Economic Order Quantity (EOQ) formula which balanced inventory carrying costs with setup costs to minimize total costs. More refinements in Production Planning and Control (PPC) came along fast in the 1940s and 1950s, including the use of probabilistic statistics with improved forecasting methods. The concept of the "learning curve" emerged from aircraft buildups in World War II and predicted the improvements in cost that tend to accompany the accumulation of production experience.

The war and pressures for unhead-of volumes of production in new products and high technology brought into being many other techniques in production control and project planning. These included PERT and CPM (Project Evaluation and Review Technique and Critical Path Method), techniques extremely useful in construction, new product development, and other projectlike production tasks. The LOB (Line of Balance) technique was another effective technique developed for controlling major production buildups and taking action to prevent shortages when sufficient time for overcoming the problem was still available.

Success to the production manager meant profit, and that meant "coordination" above all else. Management's most difficult job in the volume explosion of 1920–1960 was principally that of coordinating between sales, customers' requirements, and the factors of capital, engineering, equipment, materials, and labor resources required. Its objectives were the utmost in efficiency, or "productivity" as it is now called. It is a difficult function, indeed an impossible one. Manufacturing managers are constantly pressed to produce a good return on capital invested and achieve ever better productivity. But the worst enemy of efficiency and profit is change. And every factor of production is subject to change. Products, sales rates, engineering product design, specifications, materials needed: all change in kind, rate, and quantity. Scientific managements attempt to measure, predict, schedule, rationalize, and control all these elements.

The great burst of management concepts and techniques during the decades from 1920 to 1960 were directed toward closer and better control of all these nasty fluctuating variables. The most basic nature of the profession of production management from its start in 1890 has been the attempt to stabilize, systematize, simplify, and control every ingredient (Adams 1983).

Many other new techniques for control and reduction of uncertainty came out of a new science that developed between 1947 and 1960: "operations research" (OR). OR came into being to help handle the increasingly complex problems of forecasting, coordinating, and controlling large manufacturing operations with an ever-growing product mix, geographical decentralization, shorter life cycles, internationally located facilities, and considerable vertical integration. OR is simply the application of mathematics and modeling combined with computer science to production management. It found its usefulness in job shop scheduling, inventory management, logistics, quality control, work sampling, MRP, and linear programming. It used modeling and simulation techniques to predict and minimize queues and inventories, improve quality, shorten lead times, and plan optimal capacity levels under conditions of uncertainty.

The period also featured modest step-by-step improvements in equipment and process technologies. While the word "automation" became popular, there was little of it accomplished outside the process industries. But there were gradual process improvements in electronics and servo-mechanisms, which were driven by wartime. As such, they came on the scene after the war and accelerated in the late 1950s with the first stages of "automation," with servo-controlled feedback loops, advanced instrumentation, transfer machines (which transferred parts from one machine to another), allowing continuous operations free from the need of machine operators.

Process industries such as chemicals, paper, glass, and rubber benefited early from electronic automatic process controls which started to remove much of the manual "art" and human guesswork from industrial processes. The parts-making and assembly industries were more difficult to mechanize. But linked machines using transfer mechanisms and semiautomatic processes such as in electroplating, paint spraying, and welding began to be used in functional departments in these industries, mechanizing where repetition made it possible.

The numerically controlled machine tool (NC) was a major breakthrough in the parts-making/assembly industries. Operated first by punched cards and later by computer control, these machines increased precision and quality output, allowed for short runs via automatic tool changing and minimal fixturing, and reduced lead times by combining in one "machining center" operations previously requiring parts moved to several machine departments. Since their costs were astronomical by comparison to standard machine tools and they eliminated old skills and demanded many new ones, their penetration, in spite of their enormous advantages, was slow (Skinner 1968). The NC took thirty years to become the dominant technology in metalworking.

This buoyant forty years in industry was marred by a long depression and a more or less continuous rumbling of labor unrest. The Depression was a positive factor in one sense, namely that it promoted industrial efficiency. Depression engendered price cutting, furthered the importance of effective industrial engineering, cost reduction, productivity improvements, and aggressive industrial management. Production executives were corporate kings for much of this forty-year period—for ten years when survival depended on becoming a low-cost producer; five years of wartime production, and three years of unfilled demand which followed the war. Manufacturing leaders were in the "catbird seat"—at the very top—in corporate management.

But the labor situation was another story. In this otherwise golden age of industrial management, while new administrative concepts, tools and techniques were mushrooming yearly, there boiled to the surface strident discontent. There was tragic physical violence and a series of battles over the unionization of millions of noncraft workers. The rising power of organized labor was strong during these four decades as the percentage of unionized workers rose from 6.8 percent in 1930 to 23.6 percent in 1960 (Department of Labor). In nearly every industry, strikes at contract time were common and the union strategy of isolating a company as a target, shutting it down with a strike, winning a favorable settlement, and using it as a pattern for the rest of the industry drove up wages far faster than productivity.

But even plush, popular wage and benefit settlements seldom seemed to lead to contented and committed workers. The problem was impossible to ignore. The realization that workers were generally not committed to their employer and the company's growth and prosperity, that morale was frequently poor, that adversarial relationships benefited neither party, that employees pegged production and withheld ideas and full-out enthusiasm—all became more clear.

A positive feature of this otherwise discordant period of industrial history was the continuous efforts on many fronts to improve labor relations. For example, in this period grievance procedures were much improved, along with better pensions and health insurance, safety and accident prevention procedures, workers' compensation, and the emergence of a more professional industrial relations and personnel department.

Academics began to try to understand human relations better. Elton Mayo and Fritz Roethlisberger researched these issues. The famous Hawthorne experiments demonstrated that working conditions may be important but social expectations and personal feelings are even more so. Worker counseling, foreman training, human relations training for managers, sensitivity training, worker participation plans, profit sharing, gainsharing plans (such as the Scanlon Plan) were given time, money, and hope. Experiments of many types were tried in the late 1950s, often featuring such heresy as nonsupervised work groups and off-plant sessions with third parties to surface feelings and promote better understanding. Whether or not this wave of experimental concepts of human resource management actually worked is less the question than the fact that for the first time long-smoldering serious labor problems were seen in terms other than adversarial or paternal. Corporate managers and academics had finally begun to invest in experimentation in radically new solutions.

In total, 1920–60 was a period of progress largely focused on improving controls and coordination mechanisms but with modest technological accomplishments as well. Manufacturing managers were riding high but at least in some quarters they also finally began to face their heritage of employee disaffection and to support isolated but determinedly optimistic efforts to improve industrial society. At the end of President Eisenhower's second term, American industry had grown to a position of overtowering financial, technological, and managerial strength. It looked unbeatable.

Shaking the Foundations of Industrial Management, 1960–1980

During the next twenty years the American self-concept of industrial leadership was severely shaken, first by a growing inability to compete in the steel and auto industries and the resulting flood of imports, then by similar catastrophes in dozens of other industries led by the electrical machinery, machine tools, textile equipment, and consumer electronics industries.

By 1980 there were many indications that nationwide confidence in manufacturing leadership had largely collapsed. The business periodicals ran countless articles on our "industrial malaise," "the loss of the work ethic," and the need for "reindustrialization" (*Business Week* 1980). Industrial analysts and managers returned from Japan to report that we were outthought and outclassed in every area of production management (Baranson; Marsland and Beer; Schonberger). The turnabout in results was only outleveraged by the total cave-in of pride in U.S. industrial might, matched, in some instances, with scathing criticism of the people who had managed "our way to industrial decline" (Hayes and Abernathy 1980, National Academy of Engineering).

From Japan, Germany, Switzerland, Korea, Singapore, and Taiwan, came shiploads of imports of goods, many of which formerly would have been labeled "made in U.S.A." Worse, the Japanese and many other foreign managements were seen as beating us not just with cheaper labor—that would have been easy to understand—but with better worker effort and cooperation. They had better management systems for scheduling and production control; made better use of both old and new process technologies; had infinitely better quality systems, procedures, and attitudes; better internal management communications and group problem solving; better financial controls; a massive outpouring of suggestions and ideas from employees; and more committed and better trained workers (Schonberger 1982). They had imaginative use of the computer, excellent application of operations research techniques, disciplined preventive maintenance systems, outstanding employee benefits and job security, unbelievably low work-in-process inventories, consistent support and cooperation from vendors, and so on.

They had beaten us, it seemed, at every single one of our vaunted industrial management techniques. Either they took what we had and did it better, as in statistical quality control and the use of engineered standards, or they took what we had and threw it out, as in our traditional heavy use of work-in-process inventories for buffering variable rates of production between operations (versus Japanese "just-in-time," Kanban systems) (Hayes 1981). In either case, it was devastating to any lingering beliefs that American manufacturing management know-how was still an outstanding competitive weapon on the world scene.

Quite the contrary, the results suggested that 200 years of the evolution of manufacturing management knowledge and wisdom had led us to something that only *seemed* to work quite well. For when competitive pressures finally came along, it was revealed to be not very good at all. How could we have so deluded ourselves? It seemed so good. It made our workers the world's most productive people. It helped to produce the world's best living standards and the richest consumer economy. Yet in twenty years we came to realize that by comparison, maybe it was only "grade B," not the most productive, and in many industries competitively deficient.

Was something wrong with manufacturing leadership's thinking that not only made our manufacturing systems grade B, but blinded them to it? Certainly the prior lack of international competition made for complacency. Being number one carries its penalty along with its rewards. In fairness to the production managers of 1900–1960, they had been pressured for volume and growth in all but ten of those years and had been extremely successful. Further, history shows that since 1900 they have been placed in a secondary role in the corporate scheme with contradictory and nearly insurmountable, paradoxical objectives, creating dilemmas that catapulted them from "catbird seat" to a certain oblivion.

Summary: Impacts from History

This history suggests that leadership of American manufacturing which was provided at the top of the corporation for nearly a century was steadily delegated to a lower level beginning in the 1890s. There are two periods, therefore, in which the management responsibilities for manufacturing were handled distinctly differently.

Prior to the turn of the century, the technically competent industrial-entrepreneur developed the economic and technological concepts, procurred the equipment and facilities, supervised its installation and startup, and delegated the work force management to overseers or foremen. There was no production staff. After about 1900 the requirements of size and product, process, and physical complexities brought about the creation of a production department and production management with specialized staff groups and responsibilities.

The characteristics of modern production management and its managers were much more influenced by twentieth-century industrial history than by what went on before—with one major exception—the labor problem. That problem, as stated earlier, has always been delegated to establish the greatest distance between management leadership and the source of annoying disturbances—the worker. After 1900 the delegation was even more complete—for the foreman's power was becoming decimated in every respect, including authority over the worker, which was now ambiguously shared with personnel and labor relations departments. So in one respect it was delegated to no single accountable manager, into a vacuum.

The delegation of manufacturing leadership in the twentieth century to the new production department resulted in a kind of bureaucratization of the function and its relationship with top management, for example:

- Growing specialization and professionalization of staff experts
- Innovation of imaginative and creative control and coordination techniques
- An implicit contract between top management and production managers which read something like this:

Top Management Demands	*Production Management Responses*
• We entrust dollars of fixed assets to you.	• We accept that custody.
• You must earn a good return on that investment for the investors of that capital.	• We accept that reality.
• You will be measured on that return.	• We must keep volume high and costs low.
• To receive more assets you must project a good financial return.	• We must be careful not to choose equipment that does not work out well.

- You must deliver the right product at the right time and these will change.
- Your job is to coordinate the whole works, that is why we pay you well.
- Productivity is what counts in the end. Mass production and automation have been the best way since the Industrial Revolution.

- Of course. But product and schedule changes always hurt.
- Our only hope is to coordinate, stabilize, placate workers, satisfy customers.
- The fewer workers and coordination problems the better. That means mechanization— wherever we can justify it.

This contract is implicit in the nature of the production function, once it is necessarily delegated to the department level. It develops because:

- Delegation requires performance evaluation.
- Production requires substantial assets.
- Investors must have adequate returns.
- For a given production system, the return is enhanced by volume production, continuous steady output, mechanization, stability of products, technology, volume reliability of the work force.
- But all these factors change and keep changing.
- Cost performance is important but customers want quality and on-time reliable delivery, marketers want new products, engineers want design improvements, treasurers want low investment in facilities and inventories.

These trade-offs and conflicting demands are the very reality of the dilemma of manufacturing managers. Were there the same dilemmas before 1900 when top management ran manufacturing? The problems were there, though to a lesser extent because businesses were smaller, more single-unit, single-product entities. But the problems did not create dilemmas because trade-offs are only a dilemma to managers with superiors to whom they must answer for conflicting demands. So the act of delegation that created the production department also made for the dilemmas of trade-offs and a virtually no-win set of responsibilities.

In this way history has planted the deep roots of present-day management thinking. Manufacturing managers are custodians of assets, and in this secondary role they must focus on productivity, control, coordination, and stabilization, and mechanize to the utmost for simplicity and cost reduction. This combination produces a grade-B industrial establishment.

It is frequently grade B and competitively deficient because production managers on the defensive are forced to become careful and protective. They know only too well that production systems are complex and fragile and, like a freeway at rush hour when one thing goes wrong, disasters ensue one after another. They become experts at control, stabilization, and industrial engineering techniques, the ample use of buffer inventories, and concentrate on meeting weekly schedules. They are so vulnerable to criticism that they must focus on the short term, be systematic, detailed, and pedestrian in their thinking, and exert unceasing control over the work force.

There is one other element that is just as serious in the scenario of production management which emerged after 1900 when top management delegated manufacturing dealership to a newly formed management department: Technological innovation of processes got lost in nonaccountable bureaucracy.

Prior to 1900 top management—which built the first factories before 1850 and the mass-production systems by 1890, and then moved into the modern complex industrial corporation—more often than not were technologically competent and often brilliantly so. As entrepreneurs building enterprises, those men seized upon process innovation possibilities and developed or selected the latest in equipment and process technology. After 1900 who was to do it?

Not corporate heads, for after the turn of the century top management typically focused on new complexities of finance and corporate structure, sales in the 1930s, marketing in the 1950s, financial maneuvers in the 1960s, and government and legal complexities in the 1970s. Nor was the new bureaucracy of production management well fitted to meet the challenge of giving a lead in technological innovation and the architecture of manufacturing systems.

There it has stayed and decayed—or at least has been frequently managed with an absence of the verve and daring of top managers in the nineteenth century. This, of course, should be no surprise. Docility in this function is a natural response with the realities of vulnerability to criticisms on conflicting criteria that are built into the job.

Technological innovation and system architectural change introduces the maximum of risk and the minimum of stability. Productivity enhancement may be the long-range objective but it is apt to be the short-range victim. New equipment and major changes in system structure—such as new plants, locations, and improved infrastructures—all take years to work out and are personally risky ventures for any manager caught in the corporate bureaucracy. So the habitual response to technological innovation is usually "be careful." Get your boss and boss's boss involved. Don't try to be a hero. Let someone else go first.

Table 2-1 attempts to portray the results of the massive organizational change in American industry at the turn of the century. Its significance is that

1. Work force management has never had top priority and since 1900 has been considered mostly a labor relations staff function.
2. The production manager's original role as a custodian who was held responsible for financial performance of hard-to-manage assets and who had to meet contradictory performance criteria shifted in the twentieth century to be that of mainly coordinating and controlling.
3. Equipment and process technology and system architecture were handled actively and aggressively before 1900 and not thereafter.
4. After 1900 the development and innovation of equipment and process technologies and the architecture of production systems were no longer principal foci of top management, and typically they were not picked up aggressively by the production department. Hence major system innovations were left dependent on the initiatives of vendors and the R&D departments.[2]

Table 2-2 summarizes some impacts of these facts and constraints as they influenced the development of the role of the manufacturing manager over the years.

Table 2-1
Manufacturing Responsibilities at the End of the Century

Organizational Level	Before 1900				After 1900			
	Labor	EPT[a]	System Structure	Coordination and Control	Labor	EPT	System Structure	Coordination and Control
Top management	U	F	F	U	U	U	U	U
Production department	Did not exist				C	C	C	F
Plant level - FLS[b]	F	U	U	F	C	U	U	C

U = generally uninvolved
F = fully and actively pursued
C = cautiously pursued or abdicated
a. Equipment and process technology.
b. First-level supervision.

Table 2-2

The Historical Process by Which Manufacturing Managers' Thinking Developed

Our mission from top management is	Therefore we need	But we operate in much uncertainty	So we learned that certain practices work best	And we developed ten good success rules
—Meet customer needs —Produce a good return on investment	—Low costs —Low investment —High efficiency	—Equipment does not always work —Subquality production —Costs change —Schedules change —Parts get lost or rejected —Vendors miss deliveries —Designs change —Specifications change —Jobs change —Too few/many workers —Workers unhappy, not competent, not committed	—Maximum scale of production —Continuous process —Tool for volume —Freeze designs —Standardize —Good forecasts —Measure —Stabilize schedules —Schedule and control every element —Control systems —Mature, proven technologies —Short job cycles —Engineer processes —Simplify jobs —Delegate worker responsibility to FLS & personnel —Close inspection of production —Ample buffer inventories	1. Meet customer schedules 2. Minimize costs 3. Maximize productivity 4. Mechanize processes for volume, repetitive, mass continuous production, so as to have the fewest possible workers and least problems of coordination 5. Control and direct the work force via industrial engineering, supervision, and the personnel department 6. Focus on the short term, be systematic, detailed, precise, and accurate 7. Follow the accounting and financial rules handed down by management 8. Seek maximal simplicity, stability and close managerial controls 9. Minimize risks by minimizing changes 10. Manage pressures for change from engineers, salespeople, and marketeers

Under pressure as custodians of capital assets and needing to demonstrate productivity in their use, bedeviled by their often seemingly uncooperative and obstinate labor forces, with efficiency requiring stable, long runs and resource stability, but every resource essentially unstable and changing—production managers became masters of coordination and control. The game was one of minimizing changes and uncertainty, and maximizing control to achieve economic success. Nearly every manufacturing management concept and technique has had those objectives (Hayes 1981).[3]

In this way history and the realities of what production is all about have produced eight or ten generations of manufacturing leaders who see their roles as keeping a complex mix of people, machines, and materials working at full productivity. It is a coordinating, operating point of view which produces extraordinarily competent skills in getting things done, adjusting, reacting, and rolling with the punches. Manufacturing managers are the infantry who fight in the trenches with the nasty facts and unpleasant realities of engineering and schedule changes. They are constantly vulnerable to criticism for failure to deliver, or poor quality, high costs, or excessive inventories, or taking too long to produce a new product. Their every instinct—since they must react and respond to change—is toward stabilization and protection of their system from the ravages of change. Operate it but don't change it.

Internally, they use authority to control and direct whatever they can. Externally, they respect authority, keep their place, and are somewhat in awe of an outside world they cannot fully control, direct, or even communicate with. They are "lions" in the factory, but many are "pussycats" when they go up to the executive offices where they are regularly overpowered with the undeniable but unfamiliar logic of markets, customers, financial models, and grand issues of corporate strategy.

The impact of these patterns on the characteristics of manufacturing leadership and its thinking is shown in *Table 2-3*. Manufacturing managers learned to adapt, survive, and succeed by accepting the financial performance requisites, mechanizing to the utmost, keeping labor at arm's length, fighting for stability and steady schedules, and developing complex and ingenious mechanisms for coordination and control.

The end result of this historical process is a paradigm of thinking that conceptualizes the factory as a "productivity machine," the overriding goal as a maximized short-term profit, labor as a troublesome cost, change as an expensive intrusion, and the mass-production technology of volume production using mechanized equipment as the

Table 2-3
Typical Characteristics of Manufacturing Leadership

Skills	Instincts	Beliefs/Wisdom	Cognitive Style
—Coordination	—Self-protection	—Hedge with	—Systematic
—Operations	—Avoid change	inventories	—Detailed
Control	—products	—Workers need	(Rather than
—Mass produc-	—processes	much supervi-	conceptual and
tion processes	—schedules	sion	intuitive)
—Continuous	—Control the	—Productivity	—Short-term
processes	environment	via	orientation
—High volume	—Keep workers	—volume	—Preoccupation
tooling	at a distance	equipment	with issues
—Orderly de-	—Control/direct	—repetition	within our
tailed think-	—process	—large runs	purview
ing	—logistics	—Distrust of im-	*Executive Style*
—Simplify	—workers	practicality of	—direct
—Standardize	—Theory X/	managers not	—outspoken
—Rationalize	mechanistic	in pdn	—short-term
—Trouble-shoot-	—Avoid ambi-	—Limit plant	urgency
ing in produc-	guity in or-	capacity	—cautious
tion	ganization and	—Keep job con-	—safe
	assignments	tent simple	—conservative
	—Make the best	—Authority of	—protective
	of what you	management	—paternal
	are given	—The big deci-	—use of au-
		sions are out	thority
		of my control	—respectful of
		—Our job is to	authority
		respond	
		—Economies of	
		scale	
		—Spread over-	
		heads	
		—Machines con-	
		trol better	
		than people	
		—Accountability	

smoothest road to productivity. This is the "mind set" that character-ized American manufacturing management thinking at the peak of its success in 1960 and, as we shall see, is still affecting production managers today.

Manufacturing Leadership in the 1980s and Beyond

In the 1960s and 1970s manufacturing in the United States lost market share in many industries. When competition became severe and foreign competitors built products at less cost and higher quality, many manufacturing leaders did not seem to recognize that the problem was not caused only by low-cost foreign labor. Effective corrective action was not taken. Finally, not much before 1979–80 the problem was recognized sufficiently to arouse an energetic and determined response. This recognition only came about after widespread analysis of Japanese manufacturing techniques that demonstrated some comparative inadequacies of American manufacturing management (Hayes 1981; Wheelwright 1981; Baranson 1981; Schonberger 1982; Marsland and Beer 1983).

The nature of the response is important. For the most part it took a form that focused around "productivity," questioning why our productivity growth—labor productivity, that is—had declined and what could be done to get us back on the track again. Companies set up productivity committees, productivity czars and corporatewide productivity coordinators, and even productivity departments, laboratories, and centers. Three national productivity institutions were formed and dozens of articles about productivity and its various ingredients began to appear in business and economic journals (Deutsch 1980).

Within firms it was back to fundamentals. Industrial engineering departments were restaffed and standards reset, jobs and layouts studied and improved, materials handling methods streamlined, and all forms of waste and inefficiency scrutinized. It was back to fundamentals, too, in quality with the old tools of statistical quality control, process and control charts and quality assurance dusted off and newly reinvigorated with the ceremonial blessings of top management. Companies were advised that "high investment is the result rather than the cause of productivity growth" (Grayson 1982). In other words, don't try to invest your way to productivity. Get back to basics first.

These responses were as vigorous and energetic as they were desperate. And they were nationwide and industrywide in their scope. It is early to judge whether they have been effective. Some competitive erosion may have been stopped.[4] And, as always, a resurgence in the industrial sector automatically makes the government productivity data look better (Kearney 1982).[5] Nevertheless, to date little has been accomplished to restore lost competitive edge.

It is clear that what U.S. industry has done is to revert to its customary and long-standing know-how in the crisis. Back to the old game plan! And the old game plan seems to be to try to maximize efficiency through the use of industrial engineering concepts and techniques of coordination and control, just as it worked so well in the forty-year golden age that ran out in 1960.

The premise is that rationalization, standardization, high volume, stability, large-scale production, and strict coordination and controls will restore healthy industrial productivity and growth and that that will recreate the former competitive edge and bring about a genuine industrial renaissance (Abernathy, Clark, and Kantrow 1981). This premise is very debatable (Kanter 1983). It sounds like "business as usual," and, "We're sorry we got sloppy. We only got sloppy because management would not pay us the attention we should have had and used to have."

Clearly, we need better productivity. The question is how to get it and whether "productivity" is all we need (Skinner 1984a, 1984b). A frontal attack on waste and inefficiency—standard productivity doctrine—is fine if it hasn't been done recently. But its potential results are modest in the face of 85-cent Korean labor, for example. So it seems doubtful that productivity medicine and basics and good disciplined control of details is a sufficient prescription.

Such a prescription does not deal with the fact that our capital equipment is typically old, that we have failed to boldly invest, experiment, or take advantage of the new manufacturing technology. Nor does it deal with the fact that diffusion of that new technology is proceeding very slowly (Skinner 1980). Focusing on the productivity solution alone does not deal with the powerful changes going on in markets and technology as evidenced by shorter product life cycles, more customer specials, shorter runs, an accelerated pace of technological innovations in products and processes, and the rapid growth in the cost of capital equipment. Nor does it deal with ongoing problems in the work force.

The curious, but not so surprising fact is that in crisis manufacturing management has reverted to its old paradigm. When it came into being, production management's first role was that of exercising control and coordination essential for efficiency. The choice of roles remains unchanged. It is an adaptive function. The job is to react to changes in technology, customer demand, product specifications, and processes made available by engineers, costs, and materials. The objective was productivity—an economic measure derived from the concept that maximum output per person produces maximum return per machine, and a maximum return to owners pays back invested capital faster. The thinking is based on a valid financial model, but its use as the only dominating objective turns manufacturing managers into custodians of capital assets, whose sole overriding purpose is to return capital to owners.

In retrospect, therefore, the failures of the years since 1960 are not hard to understand. What hit was the competition from cheap labor combined with rapid technological change and previously unseen quality levels (Leonard and Satser 1982; Garvin 1983). What was necessary to survive these new rules was rapid change in products, processes, cost mix, the use of new technologies (Flaherty 1982), strategic thinking with great imagination and innovation—in total, restructuring manufacturing to become a competitive weapon. But the production managers as careful, conservative coordinators, controllers, and commanders were unable to play by the new rules.

We needed aggressive leadership to take charge of massive overhaul and change. Instead, their instincts took them pell-mell back to "productivity," efficiency, and a short-term adaptive, operations focus. Their instincts were 180 degrees out of phase with the new rules (Jaikumar and Bohn 1983). Their thinking and executive styles seemed unable to cope with the rapid overhauls necessary— particularly an inability to provide the ideas and convincing leadership top management needed to make large new investments in newly structured manufacturing systems, under duress and uncertainty (Lawrence and Dyer 1983). Even their accounting tools no longer gave them control information so badly needed (Kaplan 1983a, 1983b). Rip van Winkle had awakened at last, only to find himself in a world in which what he had learned before he went to sleep was no longer of much use on its own. It was a world in which his traditional responses could not cope.

The question for today is whether the harsh environment of the last twenty-plus years is bringing about a new generation of manufacturing managers who will cope better. Is a "new breed" evolving under the duress of the new industrial competition which is surviving by being the fittest and is thereby moving up into leadership? That new breed, it might be hypothesized, would be moving up because its members are successful at bringing about change, introducing new products and technology, managing the work force with less use of authority, more participation, team building, and involvement. If this is true we could expect to look forward soon to a major role change in manufacturing leadership, the first real shift since 1900.

A countertheory would be that, no, the "comers" are apt to be molded in the images of their bosses, the present generation in power, and hence, will not be very different, have been promoted because they are similar to their superiors, and no new leadership is on the way. History moves but the movement is glacial.

In fact, there are some hopeful indications, as evidenced by research carried out for this chapter. The "comers" in a sample of sixty managers from six large manufacturing companies have a broader view than the executives currently in high-level positions (the "incumbents"). They are more outspoken, more zealous, more participative, like to be team builders, have more education but less engineering, and are more strategically oriented (McCaskey 1982). They are more critical of their superiors, better adjusted and at ease with outsiders, and more comfortable when dealing with upper echelons of management. So it begins to look as if the difficult experiences of U.S. industry in the last twenty-five years could be starting to produce a "new breed." But the "comers" do feel constrained by the culture around them: to be effective, they need support from the top, in action as well as words. (The research results are described in detail in the *Appendix*.)

Conclusion: Persistent Signals from Industrial History

History of the manufacturing institution features several dominant themes. The first is of the relentless pursuit and actual accomplishment of ever-rising productivity to meet economic goals. The second is that of the equally relentless protests and dissatisfactions of manufacturing workers. The third is that of the role and locus of manufacturing leadership: before 1900 as top level technological entrepreneur, and after that as department coordinator, adaptor, and stabilizer. When the nineteenth century ended, the production department began, not as an initiator or shaper of production systems, but as custodian of assets. In contrast to their forefathers, production department employees have been "housekeepers," often bureaucratic, and seldom "architects."

At the end of the 1960s American industrial leadership was considered the world's best. By 1980 this had been severely opened to question. Just a few years beyond 1980, it has become evident that apart from exceptional companies (Peters and Waterman 1982) and certain industries, in many important respects manufacturing has not been "led" for many decades.

In spite of its success in 1940–1960, the burst of wartime and postwar production, there were a number of persistent signals of weakness. From the very start of industrialization, the system had seldom worked well for the work force, at least in its opinion. The generally negative feelings of its members, lukewarm loyalty, and low commitment levels surfaced repeatedly for two centuries (Federal Writers Project). After 1900 the newly developed management concepts, techniques, and practices focused on operating the system rather than educating and appropriately restructuring it. The production department was required to be short-term oriented and efficiency-focused by the overriding demand for investment returns, rather than pluralistic in its objectives in a way that would have matched its success criteria to its actual strategic needs.

The techniques and concepts of industrial management show this single-minded quest for system, rationalization, simplicity, certainty, efficiency, and stability amidst a constantly changing environment (Farnham 1921). When the foremen's empires were not coping with scheduling, inventories, costs, and product changes, Taylor and his followers established the fundamental concepts and techniques of a body of knowledge for manufacturing management. Its precepts were straightforward and its thinking linear: measure, analyze, rationalize, command, and control. In the period 1920–1960 these themes were carried out in depth and infinite detail—from micromotion to predetermined standards to EOQ, MRP, and the giant, dream showplace plants of Appliance Park, Sparrows Point, and Lordstown.

Maximal production per labor hour and per machine hour was the logical, straightforward approach to the industrial engineer—streamline, standardize, simplify. Go for long runs, few changeovers, stability in every possible dimension. Select processes from the mass production commodity, process-type technologies. Design jobs so as to be minimal in job content, maximize repetition, minimize learning, engineer every micromotion for minimal waste, tell the foremen and their workers how to perform their jobs, set standards to measure and control each person's daily output, pay good wages to attract the better workers, and keep them happy with money. We have dreamed an impossible dream of stable markets, giant plants, economies of scale, docile work forces, and mature technologies.

For the industrial manager, the servant of investors-owners, the old premises provided the only way to succeed. Success was measured by economics—profit-and-loss statements—and success was achieved by high volume, ever higher productivity, and consistent quality of product. And to do it with ever restless workers, salespeople who would not or could not forecast, new processes that never worked well at first—they turned instinctively to the same rules. The name of the game was "productivity" and it was best won by observing three rules:

1. Use mass production processes to the maximum extent.
2. Rationalize, standardize, coordinate, simplify, stabilize.
3. Direct and control subordinates and employees.

The paradigm was remarkably simple. It was essentially a financially based model of the basis of good industrial management. It was single-minded and nearly obsessive in its theme that the best factory was the most productive factory.

Even today, it is natural to say, "Well, what's wrong with that? Surely we can't have successful factories if they are less than optimally productive, can we?"

The trouble is, it was precisely these productivity premises that led to failure in the 1960s and 1970s. They led to satisfaction only as long as markets grew, immigrants immigrated, and the United States had the only show in town.

But there are new rules now and "productivity" can no longer be the only name of the game. In fact, it never should have been. It only worked in times of expanding markets and limited competition. It failed under international competitive pressures because treating the factory as a financial model, labor as a cost, change as something to be avoided, the proper leadership role as one of coordinating, and mass production/high volume/continuous processes as the ideal is inappropriate and insufficient in the 1980s. To succeed today the factory must now be not just an investment; it must be a competitive resource. Labor can now be seen as a source of energy and imagination, and change as something to be taken advantage of, leadership as aggressive and technologically competent, and processes flexible for a stream of product and volume changes. Why have the rules for success changed so dramatically?

It happened simply because the requirements for success have drastically altered the manufacturing manager's world and thereby the rules that determine who wins the race (Davidson 1984). Some of the key rules changes are the following:

- There is more competition, internationally and domestically.
- Product life cycles are shorter.
- New product development cycles are shortening.
- Product volumes are apt to be smaller.
- Product variety is apt to be greater.
- New product technologies are proliferating.
- New process technologies, especially microprocessor based, are accelerating.
- Worker culture, demographics, and the sociology of work is vastly different than in 1960 (Lodge, McCormick, and Zuboff 1983).
- Government exerts more control and influence.
- Product quality, service, delivery, and reliability are generally increasing in importance.
- The mix of costs is shifting, with overheads, materials, and energy costs rising and direct labor declining (Kaplan 1983b).

The new rules demand a concept for the factory that is entirely different from the old financial model. First of all, it must now be an institution that can tolerate and handle pluralistic values and measures for its success. There are at least five stakeholders now, many values to be created besides profits, and at least seven measures of success (Lodge 1980). (See *Table 2-4*.)

The new rules require new players, or at least, players with different skills, attitudes, and beliefs. Manufacturing leadership, it appears, will be more successful if it can let go of its heritage of a unidimensional framework of productivity and standardization and see the factory as an instrument for competitive success, handling a continuous shifting of manufacturing tasks as they are presented by the changes in technology, the competitive situation, and the firm's competitive strategy. More often than not managers will have to develop structures that can handle a great deal of product change and variety, technological innovation, and organizational learning.

Seen this way, what is needed is a new ideology, or as George Lodge writes, a new "collection of ideas through which we translate values into action" (Lodge 1982). The old notions of a factory and the old rules of manufacturing leadership are worn out.

Before 1900, despite its weaknesses in effective management of workers, manufacturing leadership was well provided by top management. They were technological entrepreneurs, architects of productive systems, vertiable lions of industry. But when they delegated their

Table 2-4
A New Concept of the Factory as a Competitive Resource

Stakeholders		Institution	Values			Competitive Success Measures
Owners	INVEST	in the	WHICH MAY	more quickly	WHICH	cost/efficiency
Managers		factory	PRODUCE	more reliably	CREATE	delivery cycles
Employees				fine products	COMPETI-	delivery reli-
Community				profits	TIVE AD-	ability
Government				meaningful	VANTAGE	quality
				careers		minimal in-
				satisfying		vestment
				jobs		flexibility for
				community		volume
				health		change
				national		products
				progress		change
						technologi-
						cal
						change

production responsibilities to a second-level department, the factory institution never recovered its vitality. The lion was tamed. Its management systems became protective and generally were neither entrepreneurial nor strategic. Production managers since then have typically had little to do with initiating substantially new process technology—in contrast to their predecessors before 1900.

In contrast, a new and more useful, effective paradigm perceives manufacturing as designers of production systems that include people and technology, organizing factories to manage a great deal of change and learning, and structuring manufacturing to perform as a strategic resource for the firm.

We now return briefly to the starting point of this paper. We have suggested the mechanisms and antecedents in history that have produced a "mind set" among manufacturing leaders, and have proposed that events beginning about 1960 made anachronistic and ineffective most of the paradigms of industrial leadership that had evolved after 1900, sadly bringing about the taming of the lion of American industrial leadership.

The next question and the final one for this paper is, will the next generation of manufacturing leadership, those people who will be our manufacturing leaders in the 1990s, evolve a new and more effective paradigm, an ideology for the factory, and concepts and techniques that will displace the mind set and premises and skills that appear outmoded today?

The "comers" in our research are promising in their broadened skills, energetic attitudes, wider knowledge, and zealous, independent spirits. But to restore competitive strength will require a degree of imaginative leadership and basically new concepts that we did not discern other than in a few rare instances. Do they see the factory in pluralistic, multidimensional, strategic, and stakeholder vision, rather than in strictly economic terms? They are starting to see labor not as a cost but as a potential resource of powerful dimensions, and that is encouraging. But do they see the manager as not merely a coordinator and "housekeeper," but as responsible for a creative architectural design of a formidable competitive resource, and of a factory that will attract the best of human resources in our society? Are they technologically competent and imbued with a powerful zeal to be industrial change agents? Are they educated and fully prepared to be effective in top executive councils, "lions," rather than "pussycats"?

The answer to these questions is a careful no. We did not meet more than a handful of such people in our comers. Nor is the data in the *Appendix* exhibits encouraging as it regards technical knowledge, use of time, focus of time, company focus, and focus within management. The comers are different and show many good signs, but they do not as yet seem a new breed.

A change in the mind set and the premises of any set of functional managers is certainly a tall order. It is much more a question of a major shift in ideology than a modest shift to new skills or insights. So it is probably unrealistic to expect that a "new breed" could or would grow biologically from within the ongoing structure in only one or two generations, even under the adverse and demanding conditions of the last twenty years. Any new breed is systematically discouraged by the corporate bureaucracy of short-term reward structures and penalties for taking risks that fail. The intermediate value systems discourage and the old values prevail.

The notion of a factory as a competitive resource and a learning and growing and living working place, and of manufacturing leadership as architect rather than housekeeper, is very different from the prevailing pattern of twentieth-century industrial thinking. In the nineteenth century, however, the owner-managers managed manufacturing and were architects of production systems and innovative process technologies. Will competitive demands for more new products and the advantages of new microprocessor-based technologies combine to vault manufacturing managers again into a leadership role? And will top management lend its support by recovering its lost involvement with technology and the factory, and become again a "visible hand" in manufacturing management?

Far from patiently waiting for evolution to do the job, manufacturing leadership needs to be aggressive. To summarize the recommendations made earlier, I have suggested that competitive advantages will be created by changing how the corporation perceives its factories, by modifying reward systems to focus less on productivity and more on process innovation and on building manufacturing structures that develop strategic leverage; by conceiving of employees as a potential creative resource; and by changing practices in the selection and development of manufacturing leaders to attract the best talent in the corporation and develop that needed new generation of managers.

History is on the side of the impatient today. Breaking old patterns and setting new ones in their place is a process that will be speeded by the impacts of major new technologies, continued severe competition, and perhaps a different mode of aggressive process innovation to replace the nineteenth-century pattern of top management as technological innovators. But this will surely come to pass, and indeed it will probably come soon. For one lesson of this history is that while old ideologies and managerial habits are powerful and enduring, new economics and technology eventually have their way.

Notes

1. F. W. Taylor, 1895. Frederick Taylor referred to "The Labor Problem" half a century later than Toynbee's reference.

2. These comments apply better to the fabricate and assemble industries than to many process type industries, such as chemicals where product and process innovations are developed simultaneously, with the principal responsibilities typically located outside the production department.

3. For example, the American factory system began early to use "buffer inventories" and "safety stocks" to cushion the impact of the uncertainties of the factors of production to insure smooth flows and continuous operations. In contrast, the Japanese minimize inventories and seek to prevent changes from the outside, as well as maintenance, scrap, or other discontinuities from the inside. (See Chapter 4 this volume.)

4. *Fortune*, 23 January 1984.

5. *Business Week*, 23 January 1984.

Appendix

Researching the "Comers": A Source of New Lions?

Six large manufacturing companies in the electronics, metalworking, electrical equipment, and heavy defense industries were invited to participate in a research project in which the companies identified promising future manufacturing managers who were then interviewed by a researcher from the Harvard Business School. Sixty interviews were conducted, including forty-six "fast-track" managers ("comers") and fourteen executives presently in high-level manufacturing positions ("incumbents"). A description of the research methodology and questionnaire is available from the author.

Research Results

The comers in relation to the incumbents were found to be:

- More college educated
- Broader in manufacturing skills and focus
- More participative and interested in team building and collaboration
- More zealous, driving, independent, and confident
- More intuitive and conceptual
- Faster moving careerwise than the incumbents
- More staff experience than the incumbents
- Less loyal
- More critical of their superiors

- Better balanced vis-à-vis workaholic tendencies
- More achievement oriented
- More perfectionist than the nonperfectionist incumbents
- More comfortable at tolerating ambiguity
- Critical of the company's lack of communication
- More supportive of the company's direction
- Equally (and positively) supportive of the company's "management style"
- Fewer engineering degrees; more M.B.A.s and other nonengineering degrees

Somewhat surprisingly, the comers were sure that in-depth technical knowledge was not necessary or important for them as managers. It was disappointing that—to their frustration—they were being constrained to share the short-term time focus of the incumbents, and that they were also generally functionally focused on departmental rather than on companywide or strategic issues.

Exhibit A2-1 shows the comers to be about fifteen years younger than the incumbents. The comers had worked about fifteen years and the incumbents twenty-eight. But already the comers had worked for

Exhibit A2-1
Career Questionnaire Data (expressed in averages)

	Comers N = 46	Incumbents N = 14
Age	37.8	53.3
Number of jobs	7.7	8.3
No. of companies worked for	2.5	2.1
Years per company	6.2	16.0
Jobs held per company	3.1	4.0
Years per job	2.0	3.3
Line jobs in manufacturing	2.7	4.6
Staff jobs in manufacturing	3.6	3.0
Jobs outside manufacturing	1.4	0.8
Breakdown of jobs outside:		
Engineering	0.7	0.8
Marketing/sales	0.3	0
Finance/accounting	0.4	0
Years in manufacturing in line positions	5.7	15.8
Years outside manufacturing	3.2	1.1
Breakdown of years outside:		
Engineering	2.3	1.1
Marketing/sales	0.4	0
Finance/accounting	0.5	0

more companies on average than the incumbents. Each had held seven or eight jobs on the average and the comers had 20 percent of their jobs outside manufacturing while the incumbents had only 10 percent. The comers had worked six years per company and the incumbents sixteen. For the incumbents all the outside jobs had been in engineering, while some comers had worked in engineering, finance and accounting, marketing, and personnel.

Exhibit A2-2 shows that the bulk of time of both groups is spent on scheduling, delivery, and coordination. About half the comers' time is devoted to those traditional, largely short-term focused activities and 39 percent of the incumbents'. (The data suggest that as the executive advances he or she spends a little more time on work-force issues and equipment and process technology.)

While the incumbents were generally satisfied with their allocations of time, the comers showed a strong desire to spend more time on new products and technologies. *Exhibits A2-3* and *A2-4* compare the comers and incumbents on various factors.

From these findings some hopeful indications emerge. The comers are broader, more outspoken, more zealous, more participative, like to be team builders, have more education but less engineering, and are more strategically oriented (McCaskey 1982). They were more critical of their superiors, better adjusted and at ease with the interviewer, and indicated more comfort in dealing with upper echelons of management. It begins to look as if the difficult experiences of U.S. industry in the last twenty-five years may be producing a "new breed" (Stevenson 1983).

Before yielding to the temptation of predicting a turnaround led by a magnificent "new breed," we must introduce a number of warnings:

1. The sample size for this research is small, especially the incumbents, of whom there were only fourteen. While the inferences are very interesting and suggestive, a sample of this size does not prove very much.

Exhibit A2-2
Allocation of Time—Percent Spent on Various Kinds of Decisions

	Control and Coordination[a]	*Maintenance and Impacts of Engineering Changes*[b]	*Work Force*[c]	*Other*
Comers	47	30	16	7
Incumbents	38	36	20	6

a. Responses A C E from questionnaire question on time allocations.
b. Responses B D F H.
c. Responses G.

Exhibit A2-3
Characteristics and Attributes of Comers and Incumbents

Career Data	Low (few, slow)	Medium	High (many, fast)

Rate of career progression
Formal education level
Nonengineering under-
  graduate degrees
Jobs outside production/manu-
  facturing
Staff (vs. line) experience

Breadth of Focus

On company (vs. solely department)
Includes manufacturing strategy (vs. limited to productivity)
Includes long term (vs. limited
  to short term)

Managerial Tendencies

Team building
Participative
Likes collaboration
Amount of communication de-
  sired

Personal Attributes

Skill/knowledge re manufac-
  turing strategy
Technical knowledge
Belief that technical knowl-
  edge is not important to
  managers
Vision/drive
Independence
Conceptual skills
Intuitive (vs. detailed, system-
  atic)
Achievement motivation
Work ethic
Mobility—companies worked
  for
Self-confidence
Tolerance for ambiguity
Perfectionist tendencies
Social ease in interview
Ease with superiors
Critical of company's manage-
  ment style
Support of company's direction

Key: ○———— Comers ————○

  □———— Incumbents ————□

Exhibit A2-4
Characteristics and Attributes of Comers and Incumbents

Factor	Range Low	Range High	C	I	C	I	Interpretation— Comers Are:
Manufacturing focus	"Efficiency" to	"strategic"	43	21			More broad in
			57	79			spite of lower positions
Manufacturing skills	Operating to strategy				65	36	More broad in
					35	64	spite of lower positions
Management of subordinates	Orders to team building		93	57			Much more participation
			7	43			
Management of employees	Control to participation				85	57	Seeking more participation
					15	43	
Company focus	Production to strategic		20	21			Equally functionally focused
			80	79			
Time focus	1 month to beyond 2 years				27	27	Equally short-term focused
					73	73	
Vision and drive	Satisfied to insistent		85	57			Show more zeal
			15	43			
Independence	Captive to independent				89	50	Much more independent
					11	50	
Cognitive style	Detailed to conceptual		76	43			More intuitive
			24	57			
Cognitive style	Systematic to intuitive				64	43	More conceptual
					36	87	
Career progression	Slow to fast		76	7			Moving much faster
			24	93			
Line vs. staff	Line only to staff only				73	36	Getting more staff experience
					27	64	
Career scope	Prod. only to general mgr.		17	7			Equally limited to production
			83	93			
Education level	High school to doctorate				87	64	More educated
					13	36	
Undergraduate degree	Engineering to other		41	20			Fewer with engineering education
			59	80			
Job level	Foreman to general manager				15	75	In lower-level jobs, of course
					85	25	
Social ease	Uncomfortable to excessively candid		78	50			More at ease socially
			22	20			
As collaborator	Dislikes to highly collaborative				70	36	More collaborative
					36	64	
Ease with superiors	Uncomfortable to arrogant		91	50			Nearly arrogant
			9	50			
Loyalty to company	Loyal to mobile				48	21	Not as loyal
					52	79	
Technical knowledge	Little to much		30	33			Equally lack technical knowledge of processes
			70	67			
Importance of technical knowledge	Unnecessary to necessary				13	50	More sure it is unnecessary
					87	50	
Work ethic	Relaxed to workaholic		52	29			Fewer workaholics
			48	71			

Exhibit A2-4 *(continued)*
Characteristics and Attributes of Comers and Incumbents

Factor	Range — Low	High	Scores*	Interpretation— Comers Are:
Achievement orientation	Low to high		85 | 29 / 15 | 72	Very achievement oriented
Perfectionist tendencies	Low to high	43 | 16 / 57 | 86		More but not very perfectionistic
Self-confidence	Low to overly confident		74 | 21 / 26 | 79	Much more confident
Tolerance for ambiguity	Low to high	78 | 29 / 22 | 71		Much better at tolerating ambiguity
Appraisal of company's communication	Too much to too little		96 | 67 / 4 | 33	Strongly anxious for more communication
Appraisal of company's management style	Critical to supportive	61 | 67 / 39 | 33		Equally supportive
Appraisal of company's direction	Wrong to excellent		80 | 67 / 20 | 33	More supportive of company's direction

Key C = Comers   I = Incumbents

*Sample:

	C	I	
High	70	45	Each four-way box is set up as the sample on the left.
Low	30	55	

2. There could be a bias from the interviewer, that is, the interviewer knew in advance whether the company had classified the subject as incumbent or comer and therefore may have been subtly or overtly influenced by this knowledge in rating the subject on the judgmental factors. Such a bias could probably have been discerned by the researcher in reading the interview summaries and checking the factor ratings and no bias appeared to exist. Nevertheless it remains a possibility.
3. The data may be influenced by the choice of companies and industries, the executives selecting the comers, and so forth.
4. Due to age differences between comers and incumbents, and job-level differences, responsibility differences, and experience differences, it could be expected that the comers' and incumbents' scores would naturally be different, and the contrasts found therefore, would be less significant.
5. Similarly, it may be that time and the natural pressures of responsibility plus maturation and the inevitable levelling off of most executive careers may change the comers so that in ten years they could look just like the incumbents.

One final set of impressions of the comers by the interviewer may be significant. She felt that they are chafing at the bureaucratic jungle in which they feel themselves to be caught (Blau 1965). They are highly critical of their superiors, concerned about how the whole corporation is being run, and almost arrogant at times in their opinions of what is needed. They show consistent zeal and insistence for change, and they want their companies to be more open and communicative with all employees. Although most comers indicated that technical knowledge was not essential in their managerial roles, they believe that the adaptation and use of new technologies is essential for the future success of their manufacturing operations.

More educated and with more breadth in their education, the comers feel more mobile, more confident, and less willing to just wait for the next promotion. They feel less company loyalty, move between jobs more often than the incumbents, and move more often between companies. In spite of their success and position as comers in their companies, they are restless and show impatience and even a tinge of anger at the "no-win" dilemmas many manufacturing managers feel are part of their jobs. They are being evaluated as are their superiors by the same melange of performance criteria in use for eighty years. They are still coordinators and their bottom line is still more often than not efficiency and productivity.

The comers are a fast-track group and they want to move even faster. But is it realistic to expect that they will grow to do what their elders, the incumbents, and several generations before them, have not been able to do while still being measured and evaluated by the same yardsticks as before? Can they and will they be the ones to supply the manufacturing leadership necessary to begin to restore the American competitive edge? Surely it will not come about readily unless management development practices and programs focus on the problem.

References

Abernathy, William J. *The Productivity Dilemma*. Baltimore: Johns Hopkins Press, 1977.

Abernathy, William J., Kim B. Clark, and Alan M. Kantrow. *Industrial Renaissance*. New York: Basic Books, Inc., 1983.

———. "The New Industrial Competition." *Harvard Business Review*, September-October 1981, 68–81.

Abernathy, William J., and John E. Corcoran. "Relearning from the Old Masters: Lessons of the American System of Manufacturing." *Journal of Operations Management* 3, no. 4 (August 1983): pp. 155–167.

Adam, Everett E., Jr. "Towards a Typology of Production and Operations Management Systems," *Academy of Management Review* 8, no. 3 (1983): 365–75.

Baranson, Jack. *The Japanese Challenge to U.S. Industry*. Lexington, Mass.: Lexington Books, 1981.

Bernard, J. E. "Science in History." vol. 2, *The Scientific and Industrial Revolutions*. Cambridge, Mass.: MIT Press, 1971.

Blau, Peter M. *The Dynamics of Bureaucracy*. Chicago: University of Chicago Press, 1965.
———. *Bureaucracy and Modern Society*. New York: Random House, 1956.
Business Week. "The Revival of Productivity." 13 January 1984, 92–100.
———. "The Reindustrialization of America." 30 June 1980, 56–142.
Chandler, Alfred D., Jr. *The Visible Hand*. Cambridge, Mass.: Belknap Press of Harvard University Press, 1977.
———. "Samuel Slater, Francis Cabot Lowell, and the Beginnings of the Factory System in the United States." Harvard Business School Case No. 9-377-222, 1983.
Clawson, Dan. "Bureaucracy and the Labor Process—The Transformation of U.S. Industry, 1860–1920." *Monthly Business Review*, January 1980.
Davidson, William H. *The Amazing Race: Winning the Technorivalry with Japan*. New York: John Wiley & Sons, 1984.
Department of Labor, Series D946–951.
Deutsch, Claudia H. "Productivity: The Difficulty of Even Defining the Problem." *Business Week*, 9 June 1980, 52–53.
Douglas, Elisha P. *The Coming of Age of American Business*. Chapel Hill: University of North Carolina Press, 1971.
Farnham, Dwight. *America vs. Europe in Industry*. New York: Ronald Press Co., 1921.
Federal Writers' Project. WPA. *These Are Our Lives*. New York: W. W. Norton and Company, 1939.
Flaherty, M. T. "Market Share, Technology Leadership and Competition in International Semiconductor Markets." In *Research in Technological Innovation Management and Policy,* vol. 1. Edited by R. S. Rosenbloom. Greenwich, Conn.: JAI Press, 1982.
Fong, Hsien-T'ing. *The Triumph of the Factory System in England*. Philadelphia, Penn.: Porcupine Press, 1930.
Garvin, David. "Quality on the Line." *Harvard Business Review,* September-October 1983, 64–75.
Glover, John G., and William B. Corvell. *The Development of American Industries*. New York: Prentice Hall, Inc., 1936.
Grayson, C. Jackson. "Emphasizing Capital Investment is a Mistake." *Wall Street Journal,* Manager's Journal, 11 October 1982.
Gutman, Herbert G. *Work, Culture and Society in Industrializing America*. New York: Random House, 1977.
Hammond, John Winthrop. *Men and Volts in the Story of General Electric*. Philadelphia: J. B. Lippcott Co., 1941.
Hayes, Robert, and William Abernathy. "Managing Our Way to Economic Decline." *Harvard Business Review,* July-August 1980, 67–77.
Hayes, Robert. "Why Japanese Factories Work." *Harvard Business Review,* July-August 1981, 56–66.
Jaikumar, Ramchandran, and Roger Bohn. *Some New Approaches to Production Management*. Discussion draft. Harvard Business School, 1983.
Kanter, Rosabeth. *The Change Masters*. New York: Simon & Shuster, 1983.
Kaplan, Robert S. "The Evolution of Management Accounting." Address to American Accounting Association. New Orleans, 23 August 1983a.
———. "Measuring Manufacturing Performance: A New Challenge for Managerial Accounting Research." *The Accounting Review* 58, no. 4 (October 1983b): pp. 686–705.
Kearney. *Managing for Excellence: A research study of the state-of-the-art of productivity programs in the United States*. Chicago: A. T. Kearney & Co., 1982.

Lansburgh, Richard H. *Industrial Management*. New York: John Wiley & Sons, Inc., 1928.

Lawrence, Paul R., and Davis Dyer. *Renewing American Industry*. New York: Free Press, 1983.

Leonard, Frank and W. Earl Sasser. "The Incline of Quality." *Harvard Business Review*, September-October 1982, 163–171.

Lodge, George C. *The New American Ideology*. New York: Alfred A. Knopf, 1980.

———. *The Uses of Ideology for Managers*. Harvard Business School Case No. 9-380-021, 1982.

Lodge, George C., Janice McCormick, and Shoshana Zuboff. *Sources and Patterns of Management Authority*. Harvard Business School Case No. 0-484-039, 1983.

Lodge, George C. "Ideological Implications of Changes in Human Resource Management." Drawn from *The American Disease*. New York: Alfred Knopf, 1984.

Manufacturing Technology. *Dun's Business Month*, February 1984, 26.

Marsland, Stephen and Michael Beer. "The Evolution of Japanese Management: Lessons for U.S. Managers." *Organizational Dynamics,* Winter 1983, 49–67.

McCaskey, Michael B. *The Executive Challenge: Managing Change and Ambiguity*. Boston: Pitman Publishing, Inc., 1982.

National Academy of Engineering. *U.S. Leadership in Manufacturing*. Washington, D.C.: National Academy Press, 1983.

Nelson, Daniel. *Managers and Workers: Origins of the New Factory System in the United States, 1880–1920*. Madison, Wisc.: University of Wisconsin Press, 1975.

Peters, Thomas J., and Robert H. Waterman, Jr. *In Search of Excellence*. New York: Harper and Row, 1982.

Pollard, Sidney. *The Genesis of Modern Management*. Cambridge: Harvard University Press, 1965.

Rosenberg, Nathan, ed. *The American System of Manufacturing*. Edinburgh: Edinburgh University Press, 1969.

Rosenbloom, Richard S. "Men and Machines: Some 19th-Century Analyses of Mechanization." *Technology and Culture* 5 no. 4 (Fall 1984): 502.

Schonberger, Richard J. *Japanese Manufacturing Techniques*. New York: Free Press, 1982.

Skinner, Wickham. *The Stubborn Infrastructure of the Factory*. Harvard Business School Working Paper, 1968.

———. "The Factory of The Future: Always in the Future?" in *Towards the Factory in the Future*. Edited by L. Kops. Chicago: American Society of Mechanical Engineers, 1980.

———. "Getting Physical: New Strategic Leverage from Operations." *Journal of Business Strategy* 3, no. 4 (Spring 1984a): 74–79.

———. "The Productivity Disease" in *The Princeton Papers*. Missassagua, Ontario: Northern Telecom Ltd., 1984b.

———. "Reinventing the Factory: A Manufacturing Strategy Response to Industrial Malaise" in *The Latest Advances in Strategic Management*. Edited by R. Lamb. Englewood Cliffs, N.J.: Prentice-Hall, Inc., 1984c.

Smith, Meritt Roe. *Harpers Ferry Armory and the New Technology*. Ithaca, N.Y.: Cornell University Press, 1977.

Stevenson, Howard. *A New Paradigm for Entrepreneurial Management*. Harvard Business School Working Paper, 1983.

Stobaugh, R., and P. Telesio. "Match Manufacturing Policies and Product Strategy." *Harvard Business Review,* March-April 1983, 113–20.

Taylor, Frederick B. *A Piece Rate System: A Step Toward Partial Solution of the Labor Problem*. ASME Transactions 16 (1895): 856–93.

Taylor, R. Whately Cooke. *Introduction to a History of the Factory System*. London: Richard Bentley & Son, 1886.

———. *The Modern Factory System*. London: Kegan Paul Trench Trubner & Co., Ltd., 1891.

Thompson, E. P. *The Making of the English Working Class*. New York: Random House, 1963.

———. *Time, Work, Discipline and Industrial Capitalism*. New York: Panther Press, 1967.

Toynbee, Arnold. *The Industrial Revolution of the Eighteenth Century in England*. London: Longmars, Green & Co., Ltd., 1972, first ed., 1884.

Ure, Andrew. *The Philosophy and Manufactures or An Exposition of the Scientific, Moral, and Commercial Economy of the Factory System of Great Britain*. London: Charles Knight, 2d ed., 1835.

Wells, David A. *Recent Changes*. New York: D. Appleton & Co., 1890.

Wheelwright, S. C. "Japan—Where Operations Really are Strategic," *Harvard Business Review*, July-August 1981, pp. 67–74.

Commentary
Today's Lions in Action

Gordon E. Forward

The themes of productivity, labor relations, and innovation will be at the forefront of world attention during the next decade; Professor Skinner's conclusions concerning these issues track closely with my own management experience. Those points raised that were of particular interest to me were the following:

1. The authority of the foreman has declined over the last eighty years.
2. Top management has ignored labor by delegating it's management to mid-level managers.
3. Staff functions have grown.
4. The manager is or has been a custodian of assets and not the architect of change.
5. American business has ignored international competition.

There is, however, a light at the end of the tunnel—we must hope it is the way out and not an onrushing train—in the new breed of managers that Skinner calls "comers."

While my own experience coincides with many of the paper's conclusions (see Chapter 2 *Appendix.*), one should note that the research sample was based upon interviews with a relatively small number of managers (sixty-three) employed by six companies, which were described as large manufacturing companies. It would be useful to expand the research to include more managers, and more important, to expand the list of companies to include small- and mid-sized companies.

This paper has benefited from the efforts of Dennis E. Beach, vice president personnel, Chaparral Steel Company, Midlothian, Texas; and the comments of Gerald R. Heffernan, chairman, Co-Steel International, Limited, Toronto, Canada; and Robert D. Rogers, president, Texas Industries, Inc., Dallas, Texas.

It is my firm but unsubstantiated belief that there is a new breed of manager; these managers, however, may not stay in large manufacturing companies through their mid-30s. I believe that fast-track managers may have gone to (or formed) smaller companies that give them the opportunity to flex their entrepreneurial muscles.

Some of the research results seem somewhat contradictory in that comers are supportive of management style and company direction and at the same time critical of their superiors. If one looks at the way time is spent by the comers, they demonstrate caretaker roles. As an engineer, I am uneasy that few comers are engineers; and I am not sure that having an M.B.A. is necessarily useful to a comer.

I am also concerned that Skinner's paper might be construed as downplaying the role of productivity. Among other remarks, he says, "There are new rules now and 'productivity' can no longer be the name of the game. In fact, it never should have been." I suggest that one basic rule still exists; that if we are to survive in a world market, then we must be low-cost producers of comparable products, and thus the productivity "focus" is vital. In the case of my own company, Chaparral Steel, high productivity has led to greater flexibility, more products, shorter production runs, and better quality.

Chaparral Steel is a greenfield plant established in 1974 to produce hot-rolled carbon bars and shapes. It now employs 850 highly motivated people in steelmaking and produces at the rate of one million tons of steel annually, which at 1.8 man-hours per ton, makes us one of the most productive steel mills in the world. We produce 350 different products, which are marketed in forty states, and feel we are a low-cost producer of steel products worldwide. The plant is one of the most modern and technically advanced in the world. The flexibility of Chaparral was developed through productivity improvements and can be demonstrated by the following examples. A few years ago, we developed a new method of rolling which quadrupled the production rate of a particular product. The time saved has allowed us to roll new products in the same mill. Also, new electronic controls just installed in this mill not only added 15 percent capacity but resulted in vastly improved product quality.

Skinner's paper goes on to make other points on which I am in total agreement. As he notes, prior to the 1970s, the lack of international competition led to complacency in our major industries and management in this environment took on the role of housekeeper. When faced with international competition in the seventies, they attempted to get things in order through industrial engineering techniques and coordination and control. The real problem, of course, was that their equipment, methods, and in some cases, products were outdated and the industries now needed architects, not caretakers to survive.

Manufacturing leadership has changed during the last 300 years and I believe it will continue to evolve at an even faster rate in the future. To support Alvin Toffler's view of the future rate of change (Toffler 1970, 1980), consider what changes a manager has experienced in only the last ten years in the fields of communication, transportation, and the arena in which the manager does business. It is now a world market and the best place for the entire world to sell something is here in the United States. If managers want to survive, they should consider the world as their marketplace and, more important, should learn to manage and anticipate change. Corporate planning is too important to be left to corporate planners.

The successful manager will certainly be more concerned with labor relations in the future, although it almost seems we are going full circle. In the 1780s we had a shallow organization coupled with cottage industry and in the 1980s Chaparral has built a small plant with a shallow organization (not quite a cottage industry but, when compared to some large steel companies, it might qualify), with only four layers of management between the chief executive and the production worker. We have in our labor relations returned the authority to the foreman. For instance, he does his own hiring and firing; he represents Chaparral Steel to the employee he supervises. This time there is a difference. Everyone in the company is considered a resource, not a cost.

We have very few staff personnel at Chaparral Steel. To be sure, we have a personnel department of three people whose focus is on pre-screening applicants and keeping us out of jail. We have engineering and accounting departments, but they are responsible for record keeping and implementing decisions made by the production units. We have no industrial engineers, and quality in our product is the responsibility of the production department, as is safety and productivity. We have no research and development department (I consider the whole plant a laboratory), and all levels of employees, including production and maintenance employees, have traveled the world in search of new technology. Everyone in the company is considered to be a member of the sales department.

The management of Chaparral firmly believes in participative management, but a decision maker is clearly defined. If we were to give credit to anyone for our style of management, it would be three behaviorists: Maslow and his hierarchy of needs, McGregor's theory X and Y, and Herzberg's hygiene factors and participative management (Maslow 1983; McGregor 1983; Herzberg 1966, 1959).

The purpose of participative management that pushes decision making down to the lowest competent level in the company is not altruistic. It is geared to tap that vast resource—employees' minds. If you involve everyone's ego in making the company successful, you can be a low-cost producer in the world, you can be a leader in innovation, and you can be technically advanced. We think of our plant as a resource that employs 850 bright people who know a lot about their job and can master new skills quickly. Therefore, change is sought after and not looked upon as a threat to security.

Future management leaders or comers will be those who will create an environment that will utilize our greatest natural resource—our people. They will develop lean, technically advanced, action-oriented, "people" organizations—and it will be the innovative nature of these organizations that allows them to continue to compete in ever-changing world markets.

References

Abernathy, William J., Kim B. Clark, and Alan M. Kantrow. *Industrial Renaissance*. New York: Basic Books, Inc., 1983.

Herzberg, Frederick. *Work and the Nature of Man*. Cleveland: World Publishing, 1966.

Herzberg, Frederick, B. Mausner, and B. B. Snyderman. *The Motivation to Work*. New York: John Wiley and Sons, Inc., 1959.

Kanter, Rosabeth Moss. *The Changing Masters*. New York: Simon and Schuster, 1983.

Maslow, Abraham H. *Motivation and Personality*. New York: Harper & Row, 1983.

McGregor, Douglas. *The Human Side of Enterprise*. New York: McGraw-Hill, 1983.

Toffler, Alvin. *Future Shock*. New York: Random House, 1970.

———. *The Third Wave*. New York: Morrow, 1980.

Townsend, Robert. *Further Up the Organization*. New York: Random House, 1984.

3
Chief Executive Background and Firm Performance

Philip Jarymiszyn

Kim B. Clark

Lawrence H. Summers

Introduction

The competitive difficulties of prominent U.S. firms and industries in recent years have focused attention on the role of management, and in particular, on certain managerial concepts and practices that have become the rule in many U.S. firms since World War II. The selection and the career paths of senior executives have been singled out for special scrutiny. Hayes and Abernathy, for example, have argued that managers' typical career paths fail to provide future top executives with the kind of in-depth understanding of technology, operations, and customers that effective strategic direction demands.[1] A number of observers have decried the practice of drawing chief executives from the ranks of financial control and legal specialists, while managers experienced in production and technology play secondary roles. Further, the mobility of executives in the United States, both within and across firms, has been cited as a systemic weakness that promotes short-term thinking and uninformed action.

The manager's "path to the top" criticized in these arguments is configured around a background in financial control, law, or planning; jobs in several different companies and industries; and often begins with an M.B.A. In contrast, the career path these critics favor includes a background in several core functional areas—operations, marketing, and R&D —long experience in the firm, and a technical background appropriate to the firm and its industry. Despite the prominence given this contrast in career paths in the business and popular press, there is little empirical evidence for its validity. The changing background of

CEOs and other senior executives, in terms of their functional special-ization, education, or experience in the firm, has not been closely ex-amined to date. Moreover, little systematic evidence that illustrates the effect of executive background on firm performance has been pro-duced.

This chapter presents the results of our analysis of the changing patterns of executive background over the period 1960–1980. Using information on the work experience and education of the chief execu-tive officers of over 600 corporations, we examine the relationship be-tween the CEO's background and the firm's productivity and profitability. The data allow us to study the executive's functional specialization, years of experience inside the firm, and major field of study.

It is important to emphasize that these results are preliminary; we have used only very simple methods of analysis and have not ad-dressed a number of important substantive and methodological issues. Our findings, however, underscore the potential value in pursuing fur-ther work on these problems. The results suggest that the "path to the top" has changed over the last twenty years, but in ways that differ somewhat from the stereotypes noted above. We find that in this period the great majority of new CEOs have been promoted from within and have long years of experience in the firm. It also appears that while marketing and finance have become more important functional sources for CEOs in large companies, an operations background has increasingly characterized the top managers in smaller firms. Size differences among firms also figure in the relationship between CEOs' background and their firm's performance. We find, for example, that marketing experience is particularly valuable in small firms, but has no significant relationship to performance in large firms.

The chapter is divided into four sections. The first section presents a brief discussion of the conceptual framework that guides our empirical work. Here we indicate why background might affect performance and indicate under what circumstances experience in the firm, and in what we call the "core" of the business, is likely to be linked to performance. The second part presents the data, including a description of the sources of information on background and performance, the definitions of the variables we use, and summary measures of the changes in background characteristics of new CEOs from 1960–1980. The third section presents statistical evidence on the relationship between back-ground and performance, and the chapter concludes with a brief sum-mary and a description of our plans for further work.

Executive Experience and Competitive Performance

Traditionally economists have modeled productivity as a function of the factor inputs chosen by firms. A static production function expresses the maximum output obtainable from any combination of factor inputs. The role of management is rarely discussed explicitly. Managers are implicitly considered a form of labor input whose function is to ensure that the firm reaches the frontier of its production capability. Neoclassical economic theory provides a clear justification for this approach; since managerial compensation represents a trivial fraction of firms' costs, it must be a relatively unimportant input. But these standard approaches do not allow for the impact that managers can have on firm productivity.

Neoclassical views about productivity have recently come under attack from a number of sources. Most dramatic has been the failure of the "growth accounting" methodology employed by neoclassical economists to explain the dramatic productivity slowdown observed around the world in the last decade.[2] Careful microeconometric work surveyed by Nelson has shown that identical plants with similar labor forces have dramatically differing productivity records.[3] Perhaps most importantly, advances in economic theory have called into question the plausibility of the neoclassical framework as a guide to firm behavior in complex environments.

CEO Background and Behavior of the Firm

The notion that the background of the chief executive may influence the performance of the firm, as presented in the business history and management theory literature, rests on a set of assumptions about the nature of managerial work and how its effectiveness is related to skill and knowledge. In the first place, the CEO's role is not fully defined or understood, especially the cause-effect impact of his relationships with other individuals and institutions. Moreover, the CEO must exercise leadership through other individuals and through decisions that are not routine. Substantial historical and psychological evidence suggests that accumulated experience is likely to influence an individual's behavior decisively.[4] Previous experience establishes an interpretive framework through which managers filter information and select among alternative courses of action. Moreover, even where the task of a CEO is fairly well defined, differences in the skill with which he carries it out may be important. And such skills may depend on the nature of prior experience. For these reasons and others discussed in the literature, previous experience may influence the CEO's choice of priorities, interpretation of events, style of operation, areas of emphasis, and blind spots.

The fundamental notion that background does matter is well established in the literature on management. But recent work on this subject has argued that a specific kind of CEO background is more conducive to a firm's competitive success. It is this hypothesis that we wish to examine. Although not all authors state the issues in the same way, the following propositions about success in management and excellence in competitive performance reflect their common themes. Success is more likely when:

1. The CEO has long experience in the firm;
2. The CEO has broad experience in the "core" functions of the business, those that directly involve the design, manufacture, and marketing of the product;
3. The CEO has "line" experience in the basic technologies and production operations of the business.

The characteristics that hurt a CEO's competitive effectiveness (that is, when he is hired from outside, when his experience is concentrated in staff functions like finance, when he has no direct experience with product or process technology) highlight the importance of education. The stereotype of the "professional manager," trained in a graduate school of business and ready (in the words of Hayes and Abernathy) to "step into an unfamiliar company and run it successfully . . . ," fits the hypothetical low-performance CEO. As the "professional manager" career path has come under condemnation, business school training has been criticized, sometimes implicitly, sometimes directly.[5] Conversely, it is implied that an educational background in science or engineering would be a useful complement, if not a prerequisite, to "hands on" experience in production and technology. We shall examine the effect of formal business training in our empirical work.

The criticism of the so-called "professional manager" assumes that the skills and knowledge essential to effective executive performance can come only through firsthand experience. This implies that the critical managerial knowledge has not been codified; that there is a high degree of idiosyncrasy in the management of specific firms; and that experience in the firm's industry is not a close substitute for experience in the firm itself.

Measuring Firm Performance

Up to this point we have discussed CEO background in terms of its impact on a general concept of competitive success. A sharper definition of "firm performance" and "competitive success" is essential to further analysis. Hayes and Abernathy, for example, are concerned with a firm's record of productivity and technological progress over the long term. This focuses on the firm's enduring capabilities in comparison with its competitors; their standard is the extent to which the firm creates economic value. Although they leave specific measures implicit, these seem to include growth, market share, and long-term profitability. Clearly the measure of success is not this quarter's (or even this year's) profits. The Hayes-Abernathy focus on the long term and on economic value is consistent with the approach taken by Peters and Waterman in their definition of excellent companies; they too deal with long-term profitability, growth, and economic value.[6] These authors and others also use direct measures of innovative capability to portray the long-term technological progress of the firm.

In our study of CEO background and firm performance we use the ratio of the market value of the firm to its replacement value as our indicator of long-term competitive success, while data on annual sales, employment, and capital stock are used to construct a rough indicator of productivity. We present productivity results only, although this measure is not very satisfactory because of product mix changes, inflation, and an absence of materials data. We hope to remedy some of these deficiencies in subsequent work, where we will also look at indicators such as data on firms' patents and market share.

Of all the measures available to us at present, the one most closely related to the concepts of performance stressed by Hayes and Abernathy, Peters and Waterman, and others is "Tobin's q"—the ratio of market value to replacement value of the firm's assets.[7] This concept is closely related to the "market to book ratio" of accounting parlance, but it differs from that in two ways. First, the capital stock is valued at replacement cost rather than historic cost. Second, the numerator and denominator refer to total firm value rather than just the value of equity.

There are three important advantages of using q as a dependent variable in a study of this type. First, we assume rationality on the part of participants in financial markets; therefore the stock market provides a forward-looking measure of performance. The market's assessment of managerial capability matters, not only to current performance, but to a rational expectation of future performance. This is likely to be captured by a q ratio. Firms with good prospects will have high ratios of market value to replacement costs of capital, because the market will include in its current evaluation the expectation of future profits to be earned. Second, the value of a firm is, apart from issues of accounting measurement definition, an objectively measurable concept. Presumably, it is what managers ultimately seek to maximize. As Fisher and McGowan have recently shown, comparisons of performance based on measures of profitability are very suspect, given the inherent ambiguities in depreciation accounting.[8] Third, the q ratio circumvents problems of risk measurement. Standard capital market theories suggest that firms can improve expected performance by taking on a more risky portfolio of investment projects. Because of the social costs of risk bearing this does not entail any gain in economic efficiency but it might show up as higher profits or productivity. In contrast, the q ratio reflects the market's valuation of future income streams, which is directly influenced by their risk characteristics.

Needless to say, the q ratio is not a perfect measure of performance. Perhaps its most important drawback is that it takes no account of intangible capital. This means that companies that invest heavily in product development or advertising will tend artificially to look good; the market will value the potential income stream from the intangible capital, but the measure does not include the value of the intangible capital when estimating the replacement value of the firm's assets.

Models and Interpretations

Empirical analysis of CEO background and firm performance raises several problems of interpretation. Foremost among them is the likelihood that the selection of a CEO may be affected by firm performance, or other firm characteristics. One way to deal with this problem is to build a structural model of firm performance and CEO selection. Given the model and appropriate statistical techniques, we could estimate structural parameters that would allow us to draw inferences about cause and effect relationships. Moreover, by specifying how the CEO might influence other determinants of performance, we could trace the channels through which the CEO's background might emerge. This is a likely goal of our future work. In this paper we have adopted a more modest agenda. We postulate a model that treats firm performance as a function of CEO background, industry characteristics, and time. More formally, we can define the basic model as shown below:

$$q_{it} = f(C_{it,} \ Ind_{it,} \ [Time]) + e_{it}$$

Where q_{it} is Tobin's q for the ith firm at time t, f is a linear function, C_{it} is a vector of CEO background characteristics, Ind_{it} represents a set of dummy variables indicating the firm's 2-digit SIC category, Time is the year, and e is an error term.

The definitions and sources of the variables are discussed in the next section. Here it is sufficient to identify three kinds of background variables: (1) functional work experience (areas of experience in the firm— marketing, finance, production, and so forth); (2) age and years of experience in the firm and in the CEO position; and (3) educational background (major field of study and highest level of degree received). The model is in simplified form; we do not identify the channels through which CEO background works, but rather its overall net effect. The industry characteristics control for differences in technology and market conditions, while the time variable reflects trends in the data.

The model provides us with information on patterns of association in the data. But the estimates may not reliably indicate the causal links between CEO background and firm performance. We have already noted the problem of reverse causality. A further problem is that firms may groom potential CEOs to perpetuate the character and personality of the organization. This process may occur after the manager has undergone a program of management development that would effectively eliminate any relationship between CEO background and observed firm performance. In effect, anyone who gets to be CEO of company X would have the characteristics of a company X CEO, independent of his own background. There are two further reasons why we may observe no clear relationship between firm performance and CEO background. In the first place, the CEO may choose subordinates who compensate for his lack of experience or knowledge. This highlights one of the problems encountered when focusing on the CEO as the indicator of managerial background in the firm. The arguments of Hayes and Abernathy pertain to the "executive suite," or small cadre of senior managers who govern the firm. If the significant relationship is between the background of the "executive suite" as a whole and the firm's performance, and if CEO background is not a good surrogate for it, then our estimates may convey little information about the true connection between background and performance.

The second problem with observed background-performance connections is the possibility that the market for executives would attenuate, if not eliminate, any relationship. That is, executives with valuable characteristics would earn higher rates of compensation which would offset improved performance. The force of this argument is limited to

Table 3-1

A Comparison of the Compustat, Dunn and Bradstreet Match Sample and
Compustat Research File

		Minimum	*Maximum*	*Mean*	*Standard Deviation*	*# Observations*
Sales ($ mil.)	M	11	103,143	2,077	6,243	637
	C	0	103,143	1,071	4,461	1,907
Employees (000s)	M	0.2	746	21	44	637
	C	0.1	746	10.7	33	1,834
Gross Plant ($mil.)	M	2.0	46,437	1,095	3,307	637
	C	0.1	46,437	562	2,427	1,906
(Inc. bef. tax)						
Sales (%)	M	− 19	39	11	6.6	637
	C	− 1,200	57	9	34	1,907
R&D						
Sales (%)	M	0	9	1.7	1.9	500
	C	0	833	3	24	1,370

Source: 1980 Compustat Research File, Standard and Poor's
Note: The matched sample used the 1980 Compustat industrial file which includes only 1,200 of the 1,900 firms in the research file, therefore, some of the comparisons in this table may be inaccurate.
M—The Compustat, Dunn and Bradstreet matched sample used in this study
C—Manufacturing firms in the 1980 Compustat file

the extent that firms do a good deal of internal training and develop their senior executives from within. Further, this argument applies to profitability, but not to real measures of efficiency or innovation.

The Data: Sources, Definitions, and Patterns

The sample of companies and managers examined in this study was defined by matching the manufacturing companies in the 1980 Compustat File (the source for financial and operating statistics) with the companies contained in Dun and Bradstreet's Reference Guide to Corporate Management (RGCM, the source for biographical data on chief executives). The Compustat file contained data describing large- and medium-sized publicly traded companies, while RGCM contained a sample of public and private companies with annual sales greater than $1 million. This created a sample of 637 companies. A comparison of mean operating statistics for the main Compustat source and our sample is presented in *Table 3-1*. Companies in the combined sample were twice as large, on average, as companies in the Compustat file. They were also slightly more profitable while spending less on research and development.

Biographical Data on the Chief Executive

Biographical data on chief executives was collected from RGCM, a compendium on the senior executives of an extensive sample of U.S. companies. Each company entry contained the resumes (as edited by Dun and Bradstreet) of the firm's senior officers. The chief executive was usually labeled; when he was not, we used other sources (such as Standard and Poor's index and annual reports) to identify him. Still other sources verified the accuracy of Dun and Bradstreet's CEO labels. Information was collected on the CEO of each company as far back in history as the RGCM would permit. In the empirical work we have used information from the period 1960–1980. From each chief executive's resume, we transcribed and machine-coded the following information:

1. CEO's name
2. Company name
3. CEO's date of birth
4. Some indication if the individual was the company's founder or a member of its founding family
5. A list of degrees earned
6. A list of jobs held, including: title, date job was assumed, date job was left, company name.

For the analysis reported in this study we defined a set of variables describing the CEO's education, dominant area of work experience, and tenure within the company. The data can be used to define additional variables (for example, years of experience in each functional area) that we plan to use in subsequent work.

The variables are defined as follows:

Education: A system of dummy variables was constructed to describe each degree reported by a CEO according to major field of study (liberal arts, engineering, science, law, military) and highest degree completed (associate, bachelor's, M.B.A., non-M.B.A. master's, doctorate).

Dominant Functional Area: The list of titles held by all managers in the sample was used to create a set of eleven dummy variables, seven business functions (administration, operations, marketing, finance, research and development, legal affairs, and consulting), and three nonbusiness functions (academics, government affairs, and other, such as professional athletics, charitable foundations, and so forth). The amount of time an individual spent in each of these categories was measured and recorded, and the area of expertise or dominant experience was defined as the category in which he spent the most time.

Pre-CEO Tenure (TEN): This is the number of years that the manager spent as an employee of the firm prior to becoming its chief executive.

Internal Promotion (PR): Given a chronological listing of a manager's work history, it was possible to define the dummy variable PR that indicates whether a CEO was promoted from within (PR = 1), or hired from another firm.

Tenure as CEO (CEOTEN): This figure was simply the current year (per observation) minus the year a manager became chief executive.

Age at time of selection (AGE): Current year (per observation) minus year of birth.

Founding Family (FF): This is a dummy variable equal to 1 if the Dunn and Bradstreet source indicated that the CEO was the founder or a member of the founder's family and 0 otherwise; occasionally we used common knowledge to define this variable (as in the case of Henry Ford II).

Trends in Functional Background

Table 3-2 presents data on the functional background of new chief executives in the period 1960–1980. The entries in the table are the percentage of the newly installed CEOs in a given time period (for example, 1960–1965) who have a given area of specialization. The data represent the total sample, broken into large and small firms. Thus, for example, 9.8 percent of the new CEOs in small companies in the 1960–1965 period had operations as their dominant functional area. Much of the recent literature on management background and firm performance has focused explicitly on larger firms; our distinction between large and small thus provides a useful perspective on the validity of hypotheses in the literature. Furthermore, substantial evidence suggests that size affects the structure of organizations, including the degree of centralization, the importance of specialization of tasks, and the formality of relationships and communication. The remainder of this section deals with differences in trends in CEO background in large and small firms; the next section examines whether the size of the firm affects the background-performance relationship.

The data on trends in functional background reveal some important changes in the functional experience of CEOs in the last twenty years. Looking first at the overall sample, we find a sharp decline in the

Table 3-2

Functional Experience of New CEOs, 1960–1980 by Size of Company
(% distribution by period)

Period by Size of Company	Functional Area										
	Consult.	Admin.	Ops.	Mkt.	Fin.	R&D	Legal	Multi.	Acdmc.	Other	Govt.
Total											
1960–65	0.3	30	13	14	17	11	5.5	1.4	0.6	0.9	5.8
1966–70	1.9	30	14	17	14	10	6.3	1.4	1.9	0.0	3.7
1971–75	1.5	20	21	16	20	9.6	4.6	1.8	0.4	0.4	5.0
1976–80	1.6	17	16	24	22	7.3	5.2	2.3	1.0	0.0	3.6
Small											
1960–65	0.6	24	9.8	17	21	12	4.6	0.4	1.2	1.2	6.9
1966–70	1.6	29	12	18	16	10	5.6	0.0	4.0	0.0	3.2
1971–75	2.8	19	21	18	16	8.5	6.6	0.9	0.0	0.9	6.6
1976–80	1.2	21	23	26	18	2.4	2.4	2.1	1.2	0.0	2.4
Large											
1960–65	0.0	35	16	11	13	11	6.4	2.6	0.0	0.6	4.7
1966–70	2.1	31	15	15	13	10	6.9	2.6	0.0	0.0	4.2
1971–75	0.6	20	21	15	22	10	3.2	2.5	0.6	0.0	3.9
1976–80	1.8	14	10	23	25	11	7.3	2.5	0.9	0.0	4.6

importance of the administration category, while the percentage of CEOs coming from marketing and finance backgrounds has increased over the period. From a share of 14 percent in 1960–1965, marketing rose to a share of 24 percent in the last half of the 1970s. In this sample, marketing has replaced administration as the leading functional source of CEOs, with finance a close second. Operations emerged with a share of 21 percent in the early 1970s, but declined to 16 percent in the last half of the decade.

The growing importance of finance and marketing as sources of new CEOs confirms the arguments advanced by Hayes and Abernathy and others. Some of these arguments were largely based on data developed by Golightly and Co. International, which showed strong growth in the number of CEOs with finance and legal backgrounds. The Golightly data reflected the experience of the 100 largest U.S. companies, and the data on large companies in our sample further confirms the growing role of CEOs with financial experience. However, we find quite different trends in the smaller firms.

Among large firms in our sample, the share of CEOs with marketing and finance backgrounds doubled from the early 1960s to the late 1970s, while the share with an operations focus fell sharply (21 percent to 10 percent) from 1970 to 1980. In small firms, however, the share of operations backgrounds more than doubled, while finance fell from 21 percent to 18 percent. As in large firms, marketing became more important, rising from 17 percent in 1960–1965 to 26 percent at the end of the seventies.

The evidence thus confirms the growing importance of finance and marketing backgrounds in big firms but highlights a different pattern of CEO development in smaller companies. This focus on specific function, and the apparent diversity of background, however, may obscure the dichotomy between experience in the core of the business and experience in staff or support functions. By combining functional areas into "core" (operations, marketing, and R&D), "staff" (finance, administration, legal, and consulting), and "others" (government, academic, multis, and other), we find that in the 1976–1980 period, 44 percent of the new CEOs in large firms came out of the core, while 52 percent came out of the staff. These percentages were 38 and 55 in the 1960–1965 period. Although there has been an increase in the share of CEOs from the core, it is striking that over 50 percent of new CEOs in large companies have spent the dominant portion of their functional experience outside the core of the business.

The picture is somewhat different among small firms, but a staff-oriented career looms large there as well. From 1960 to 1980, the share of the core areas rose from 38 percent to 51 percent in small firms, while the share of the staff fell from 50 percent to 42 percent. This still implies that almost 50 percent of the new chief executives of smaller firms bring to the job a background of experience outside the firm or the core of its business.

Age and Tenure

As noted in the introduction, much has been made of the apparently high level of mobility of senior executives in the U.S. economy. The following quotation from Hayes and Abernathy sums up the issue quite well:

> . . . Companies are increasingly choosing to fill new top management posts from outside their own ranks. In the opinion of foreign observers, who are still accustomed to long-term careers in the same company or division, "High level American executives . . . seem to come and go and switch around as if playing a game of musical chairs at an Alice in Wonderland tea party."[9]

Table 3-3 addresses the question of the mobility of CEOs with data on age at the time of selection, tenure with the company, percent promoted from within the firm, and percentage who were members of

Table 3-3
Age and Years of Experience of New CEOs, 1960–1980:
Mean Values by Size of Company

Year by Size	Age at Time of Selection	Tenure with Company at Time of Selection	Percent Promoted from Within	Percent Member of Founding Family
Total				
1960–65	46.6	15.5	78.8%	19.6%
1966–70	51.2	16.5	84.1	7.2
1971–75	51.9	17.1	85.5	6.1
1976–80	52.5	16.8	82.6	4.7
Small				
1960–65	43.0	11.1	67.8	26.9
1966–70	49.9	14.5	76.8	10.1
1971–75	50.6	15.1	78.4	9.5
1976–80	50.9	14.2	72.8	6.5
Large				
1960–65	49.7	19.5	88.5	1.3
1966–70	52.3	18.3	90.8	4.6
1971–75	52.8	18.5	90.1	3.7
1976–80	53.7	18.8	90.1	3.3

the founding family. This evidence makes it clear that the image of the CEO labor market as a game of musical chairs is simply wrong. The turnover rate for CEOs in the sample fell from approximately 8.5 percent in the mid-1970s to 5.5 percent in 1980 (changes in sample size prevent us from comparing turnover rates calculated on data from earlier periods), with a concomitant increase in the average CEO's tenure in office from 8.3 years (71 to 75 average) to 10.8 years (76 to 80 average). The great majority of new CEOs are hired from within the firm; this has been true over the last twenty years, and it is not a phenomenon limited to small companies. Indeed, internal promotion is more prevalent in the larger firms, where 90 percent of new CEOs come from within.

Those promoted from within assume their new position with a long record of experience inside the firm. In the larger firms, the average tenure with the firm for a new CEO is nineteen years. Since those promoted from outside are likely to have little or no tenure, the data imply that CEOs promoted within the firm have more than twenty years of experience. The same is true for smaller firms, although because of the greater prevalence of outside hiring, the average years of tenure are somewhat fewer.

Table 3-4
College Background of New CEOs, 1960–1980

Year by Size of Company	Field of Concentration[b]						Highest Level of College Completed[b]					No College
	Liberal Arts (%)	Science (%)	Engi- neering (%)	Busi- ness (%)	Law (%)	Military (%)	Associate (%)	Bach- elor (%)	M.B.A. (%)	Master's (%)	Doctorate (%)	Education[a] (%)
All Firms												
1960–65	27.7	34.3	13.6	15.4	7.8	1.2	0	68.4	8.4	17.8	5.4	28
1966–70	28.3	26.9	17.1	21.3	5.2	1.0	0.7	65.7	14.7	15.0	3.8	21
1971–75	24.2	22.9	15.8	28.3	7.7	1.0	0	64.3	17.8	14.5	3.4	18
1976–80	24.5	23.7	16.5	30.9	4.0	0.4	1.2	62.2	20.1	13.3	3.2	16
Small Firms												
1960–65	17.8	36.2	18.4	19.6	6.1	1.8	0	65.6	9.8	18.4	6.1	32
1966–70	27.0	28.6	16.7	22.2	5.6	0	0	62.7	17.5	16.7	3.2	25
1971–75	25.9	21.3	20.4	25.0	4.6	2.8	0	69.4	16.7	10.2	3.7	21
1976–80	29.8	13.5	22.1	29.8	3.9	1.0	1.9	61.5	21.2	13.5	1.9	17
Large Firms												
1960–65	37.3	32.5	8.9	11.2	9.5	0.6	0	71.0	7.1	17.2	4.7	22
1966–70	29.4	25.6	17.5	20.6	5.0	1.9	1.3	68.1	12.5	13.8	4.4	17
1971–75	23.3	23.8	13.2	30.2	9.5	0	0	61.4	18.5	16.9	3.2	16
1976–80	20.7	31.0	12.4	31.7	4.1	0	0.7	62.8	19.3	13.1	4.1	16

a. The data in this column reflect the fraction of the *total sample that did not go to college.*
b. The data in these columns reflect the appropriate fraction of the *subset of the sample that went to college.*

At one level, these data dispel the notion of rampant hiring of CEOs from outside the firm. But they also confirm the importance of executive mobility at lower levels. The evidence on age and tenure implies that the average new CEO of a large firm assumes that position at about age fifty-four with about twenty years' experience in the firm. If we assume that the average new CEO spent four years in college, we can estimate he had ten to twelve years of work experience outside the firm. Thus, while most CEOs possess many years of firm experience, most have worked for several years in other firms.

Educational Background

Discussion of managers' education and firm performance in the popular literature focuses on the growing importance of M.B.A. degrees and the concomitant rise of what Hayes and Abernathy have called the "professional manager." The data on degrees and field of study presented in *Table 3-4* confirm these hypotheses for large firms, disclose a more complicated story for small firms, and reveal that almost one-fifth of all chief executives have not received or completed a college education. In 1960, 28 percent of all newly hired CEOs did not go to college. More of these individuals were managing small firms (32 percent of new CEOs with no college degree) than large ones (22 percent of new CEOs with no college degree). Between 1960 and 1980 the general level of education of all CEOs rose; and it rose faster in small firms. In 1980 the gap between CEO education in small and large firms disappeared, with approximately 16 percent of all CEOs having no college degrees.

Differences in fields of concentration between large and small firms are sharp. As popularly described, the share of new CEOs in large firms who studied business tripled, absorbing most of the increase in educational attainment while the share of liberal arts majors decreased. In small firms, the percentages of CEOs with business and liberal arts degrees both increased by 50 percent. These increases came from rise in college attendance and a sharp decrease in the study of science among newly hired CEOs.

The data on the level of educational attainment provide further support for the notion that U.S. managers are becoming increasingly "professionalized," especially in large firms. There is solid evidence of the emerging importance of the M.B.A. degree. From 8 percent in 1960–1965, the share of new CEOs with an M.B.A. degree rose to 20 percent in the late seventies. Large and small firms differ little in the importance accorded the M.B.A.; in both groups the share has risen sharply over the period and was close to 20 percent by 1980. Given the large number of people who entered the labor market with an M.B.A. in the 1960s and 1970s, we would expect to see the share of new CEOs with that degree increase in the future.

Impact on Firm Performance—Empirical Results

This section presents some preliminary results of our statistical analysis of the relationship between the attributes of CEOs and firm performance. As we have already emphasized, the results are tentative. We have not used sophisticated econometric techniques which could exploit the longitudinal character of our data. Nor have we attempted to address the fundamental selection biases that may affect our results. Differing assessments of the business environment may lead firms to choose differing types of leadership. Our analysis may reflect the effects of the differing environments that lead to CEO selection.

Table 3-5 presents the results of estimating the basic model relating Tobin's q to three types of CEO attributes and a variety of control variables; we also present results on productivity. The control variables are included to hold constant industry, time, and size in examining the effect of CEO attributes on performance. The three CEO attri-

Table 3-5
Firm Performance and CEO Background

Background Variables	Performance Measures	
	q	*Productivity*
Age and Tenure		
Tenure of CEO	.019	−.009
	(.004)	(.002)
CEO tenure, squared	−.0003	.0002
	(.0001)	(.0001)
Years with firm	.006	−.001
	(.001)	(.001)
Internal promotion	−.002	−.097
	(.037)	(.019)
Age	−.001	.006
	(.002)	(.001)
Selected Functional Areas		
Government	.124	.171
	(.078)	(.040)
Other	−.368	−.272
	(.245)	(.122)
Academic	−.316	−.529
	(.210)	(.106)
Legal	.008	.051
	(.074)	(.037)
R&D	−.018	.064
	(.051)	(.026)
Finance	−.015	−.055
	(.039)	(.020)
Marketing	.112	.029
	(.038)	(.020)
Operations	.197	.008
	(.042)	(.021)
No history	−.013	−.027
	(.038)	(.020)
Consulting	.070	−.028
	(.120)	(.060)
Multi	−.280	−.053
	(.093)	(.047)
Educational Background		
Law	−.049	−.007
	(.067)	(.034)
Science	.025	−.029
	(.031)	(.016)
Engineering	.048	−.092
	(.039)	(.020)
Business	.124	−.062
	(.049)	(.025)

Table 3-5 (*continued*)

Background Variables	Performance Measures	
	q	*Productivity*
M.B.A.	−.063	.071
	(.056)	(.028)
Doctorate	−.193	−.141
	(.068)	(.034)
Associate	.185	.079
	(.228)	(.115)
Master's	.125	.010
	(.046)	(.023)
SEE	.833	.421
R²	.285	.605
d.f.	5,725	5,724

Note: Each regression includes two-digit SIC industry dummies, a time trend, and the log of employment to control for size. The productivity regression includes the log of the capital-labor ratio.

butes refer to the CEO's age and experience, both as a CEO and within the firm; his functional background; and his educational background. The results suggest that all three attributes have an impact on firm performance.

While both the productivity and q equations suggest that managerial experience has an important impact, they tell rather different stories. The q equation implies that, other things being equal, a CEO's extra year of experience in that position raises a firm's market value by almost 2 percent, while an extra year of pre-CEO experience with the firm raises its market value by just over half a percent. This finding underscores the importance of experience within the firm and supports the emphasis on executive turnover in the management literature. We should note, however, that the productivity equation suggests that experience has a negative impact on performance. We are puzzled by this discrepancy. One possible hypothesis is that senior managers are found in firms that have focused on sources of economic value that may conflict with current productivity. This may involve, for example, investments in new products and new technologies that provide future growth options but may hurt today's productivity.

The evidence on q and functional background reveals positive sizable coefficients in the core areas of marketing and operations, while a multifunction background has a decidedly negative effect. (The coefficients in the table indicate performance relative to the performance of managers with a specialization in administration.) On the productivity side, managers with backgrounds in R&D and government do somewhat better than those with backgrounds in administration, while those with miscellaneous and academic backgrounds appear to perform dismally.

Finally, the results on educational background are puzzling. No clear patterns emerge. For example, it appears that managers with undergraduate business majors raise profits and reduce productivity when compared with those without specialized bachelor's degrees. This might be taken as evidence for the Hayes-Abernathy view. However, exactly the opposite results obtain for M.B.A.s who appear to raise productivity but reduce q. The results also suggest that managers with Ph.D.s perform poorly both in terms of productivity and profitability.

The Background-Performance Connection and Firm Size

We noted earlier that much of the discussion of CEO background and performance focuses on large firms. It thus seems useful to examine the relationship between our measures of prior experience and the long-term performance of the firm in a sample broken down by size. In addition, there are well-established differences between large and small organizations that may influence the background-performance connection. The literature on organization structure suggests that the extent to which technology influences the characteristics of the organization depend on the size of the enterprise. In the language of the organization theorist, the technology of production is likely to impinge on the specialization of work, the importance of formal and standardized procedures, and the degree of centralization in small organizations.[10] This implies that managers of small firms are more likely to be less insulated from the technological core of the firm irrespective of their functional area. Furthermore, the evidence on size and structure suggests that in small organizations, jobs are less specialized and staff personnel play a less important role in controlling the organization.

The size-technology-organization structure nexus has implications for the effect of functional background on firm performance. Because managers outside of operations are likely to be less insulated from technology in small firms, the absence of operations experience may be less detrimental than the Hayes-Abernathy hypothesis suggests.

This conclusion is reinforced by the lower degree of job specialization in smaller organizations. The implication is that an operations background may have more value in large firms. General experience, however, may be of more value in the small firm, since it may provide the individual with a broader basis for decision and action.

The distinction between large and small firms can perhaps be carried too far. The small firms in our sample (less than $200 million in sales) are relatively large as organizations go and may therefore have the characteristics of the large organizations studied in the organization structure literature. However, given the emphasis on large firms in the management literature, and given the clear differences in trends in CEO background in our data, it seems useful to examine whether or not size makes a difference in the background-performance connection.

In *Table 3-6*, we report estimates of the relationship between attributes and performance for both small and large firms. The sample was divided on the basis of sales to achieve this breakdown. Two major differences emerge. First, a background in the technical core of a firm—operations and R&D—appears to be much more conducive to success in large firms; in small firms the coefficient of operations is positive but half as large, while the effect of R&D is negative. This finding is consistent with the notion that the core technology is generally more influential in small firms. Second, managers of large firms tend to benefit from legal and financial backgrounds suggesting that the staff of a large organization may play a more central role in performance. In small firms, legal and financial backgrounds appear to be liabilities. Finally, we note that the M.B.A. appears to be a substantial liability for the managers of large firms, while it is a small asset for managers of smaller companies.

Table 3-6

Tobin's q and CEO Background in Small and Large Firms

Background Characteristics	Large Firms	Small Firms
Age and Tenure		
Tenure of CEO	.010	.028
	(.005)	(.006)
CEO tenure, squared	.0000	−.001
	(.0001)	(.0002)
Years with firm	.004	.010
	(.002)	(.0001)
Internal promotion	.114	−.268
	(.050)	(.058)
Age	.006	−.005
	(.002)	(.003)

Table 3-6 (*continued*)

Background Characteristics	Large Firms	Small Firms
Functional Areas		
Government	−.142	.166
	(.111)	(.109)
Academic	−.477	.661
	(.235)	(.475)
Legal	.413	−.196
	(.135)	(.088)
R&D	.158	−.079
	(.076)	(.067)
Finance	.151	−.148
	(.058)	(.052)
Marketing	.011	.212
	(.056)	(.053)
Operations	.255	.127
	(.063)	(.055)
No history	−.081	.073
	(.050)	(.059)
Consulting	.273	−.055
	(.153)	(.117)
Multi	−.485	−.105
	(.152)	(.117)
Educational Background		
Law	−.133	−.197
	(.118)	(.084)
Science	.142	−.065
	(.050)	(.042)
Engineering	.006	.101
	(.053)	(.057)
Business	.477	−.147
	(.074)	(.063)
M.B.A.	−.342	.121
	(.085)	(.074)
Doctorate	−.016	−.280
	(.093)	(.100)
Associate	.003	.262
	(.427)	(.261)
Master's	.076	.322
	(.064)	(.065)
SEE	.823	.784
R^2	.280	.384
d.f.	2,869	2,810

Note: Each regression includes 2-digit sic dummies, a time trend, and log of employment to control for size of firm.

Notes

1. Robert H. Hayes and William J. Abernathy, "Managing Our Way to Economic Decline," *Harvard Business Review,* July-August 1980, 67–77. See also, chapter 1 in Robert H. Hayes and Steven C. Wheelwright, *Regaining Our Competitive Edge: Competing Through Manufacturing* (New York: Wiley and Sons, 1984).

2. For an example of growth accounting and its recent inability to explain fully the changes in productivity see Edward F. Dennison, *Accounting for Slower Economic Growth: The United States in the 1970's* (Washington D.C.: Brookings Institution, 1979).

3. Richard R. Nelson, "Research on Productivity Growth and Productivity Differences: Dead Ends and New Departures," *Journal of Economic Literature* 29 (September 1981): 1029–64.

4. This has been an important theme, for example, in the work of Hedberg, Nystrom, and Starbuck. See Bo Hedberg, "How Organizations Learn and Unlearn" in *Handbook of Organization Design,* vol. 1, ed. Paul Nystrom and William Starbuck (Oxford: Oxford University Press, 1981).

5. Thomas J. Peters and Robert H. Waterman, *In Search of Excellence* (New York: Harper and Row, 1982), 35–36.

6. Peters and Waterman, for example, use asset and equity growth, the market-to-book value ratio, and returns on capital, equity, and sales. See Peters and Waterman, *In Search of Excellence,* 22–23.

7. For a discussion of Tobin's q and its method of calculation, see Michael Salinger and Lawrence H. Summers, "Tax Reform and Corporate Investment: A Microeconometric Simulation Study" in *Behavioral Simulation Methods in Tax Policy Analysis* (Chicago: University of Chicago Press, 1983).

8. Franklin M. Fisher and John J. McGowan, "On the Misuse of Accounting Rates of Return to Infer Monopoly Profits," *American Economic Review,* March 1983, 82–97.

9. Hayes and Abernathy, "Managing Our Way to Economic Decline," 74.

10. See Henry Mintzberg, *The Structuring of Organizations* (Englewood Cliffs, N.J.: Prentice Hall, 1979), chapter 13, for a review of the literature on size and organization structure.

References

Dennison, Edward F. *Accounting for Slower Economic Growth: The United States in the 1970's.* Washington, D.C.: Brookings Institution, 1979.

Fisher, Franklin, M., and John J. McGowan. "On the Misuse of Accounting Rates of Return to Infer Monopoly Profits." *American Economic Review,* March 1983, 82–97.

Hayes, Robert H., and William J. Abernathy. "Managing Our Way to Economic Decline." *Harvard Business Review,* July-August 1980, 67–77.

Hayes, Robert H., and Steven C. Wheelwright. *Regaining Our Competitive Edge: Competing Through Manufacturing.* New York: Wiley and Sons, 1984.

Mintzberg, Henry. *The Structuring of Organizations.* Englewood Cliffs, N.J.: Prentice Hall, 1979.

Nystrom, Paul, and William Starbuck, eds. *Handbook of Organization Design,* vol. 1. Oxford: Oxford University Press, 1981.

Nelson, Richard R. "Research on Productivity Growth and Productivity Differences: Dead Ends and New Departures." *Journal of Economic Literature* 29 (September 1981): 1029–64.

Peters, Thomas J., and Robert H. Waterman. *In Search of Excellence.* New York: Harper and Row, 1982.

Salinger, Michael A., and Lawrence H. Summers. "Tax Reform & Corporate Investment: A Microeconometric Simulation Study" in *Behavioral Simulation Methods in Tax Policy Analysis.* Chicago: University of Chicago Press, 1983.

Commentary

Richard R. Nelson

The authors of this chapter have provided an early window into a fascinating new study of how the characteristics of a company's chief executive officer (CEO) affect a company's performance. The data clearly contain a lot of information; however, as the authors recognize, the causal connections among the variables are complex, nonlinear, multidimensional, and difficult to identify.

Most of this chapter is concerned with identifying the characteristics of new chief executive officers in large companies and small companies, and in assessing the match of the actual patterns with various statements or conjectures that have been made about the matter. This is an endeavor that is important in its own right. It has its own difficulties, but these seem an order of magnitude simpler than those involved in trying to relate CEO characteristics to firm performance. Yet the authors do not explore the issues here widely or deeply enough.

The patterns they depict in CEOs are fascinating and raise a number of interesting questions. The rise in the relative importance of CEOs with backgrounds in marketing and finance is interesting and confirms various conjectures about that that have been put forth. But just why did this development take place? It occurred mostly in large firms and at the expense of CEOs from administration and operations. Why? The authors' data reveal a sharp drop in the fraction of CEOs in small firms that have come from R&D. Why? Does this reflect a decline in the relative number of small firms that are science based, or the maturation and changing of the guard in the small science-based firms of the sixties, or what? Why has there been an increase in the fraction of small firms' CEOs who come from operations? Why does this pattern differ from that in large firms?

The authors note that there has been a steady increase over time in the educational attainments of CEOs, and a striking increase in the fraction of CEOs who have M.B.A.s. Neither of these facts is surprising, although it is good to have confirming evidence. The first might be simply ascribed to the growing educational attainments of the relevant cohort. It would be interesting to know if the educational attainments of CEOs have increased more than, or only about the same as, educational attainments of the work force in general. But why the demand for M.B.A.s? Has there always been excess demand for M.B.A.s, and does the phenomenon largely reflect increasing supply brought about in response? Or has there been a change in judgment at the level of those who decide who should be CEOs about the importance of having a person with an M.B.A.? Or is it that the business world has changed so that the skills imparted by an M.B.A. are now deemed more important? Or have M.B.A.s who have been brought into companies at lower levels simply done very well and thus become obvious candidates for positions as CEOs? All these are different propositions that seem worthy of exploration in some detail.

Considerably more material might well be introduced exploring the reasons behind the observed shifts in the characteristics of CEOs. On the other hand, the last few pages of the chapter, which are concerned with a first cut at the connections between CEO characteristics and firm performance, are not particularly helpful at this stage. While the former question is interesting in its own right, the latter is difficult; even results that are explicitly labeled as preliminary will gain much more attention than they warrant, and this may be dangerous.

The authors have gathered a considerable body of material both on CEO characteristics and on various measures of firm performance. On the one hand, one can see this data as a field to be mined carefully and thoughtfully. From another point of view, it is a minefield.

The authors clearly state that the relations they have estimated in this chapter are reduced forms, not structural equations. But it is too easy to interpret them as the latter, and the authors themselves, in a number of places, have fallen into causal language. They recognize that the selection of a CEO may have something to do with the characteristics of, and performance of, firms, but they do not dwell sufficiently on these matters. It seems important to understand the kinds of CEO shifts induced by firms in trouble. Do firms that are not in trouble tend to stay with their prevailing CEOs, unless retirement hits? If forced to change by retirement, do they try to get more of the same? Or what?

The authors divide their sample into large and small firms. But there must be many more dimensions of firm characteristics that influence the kind of CEO who will be effective. Is the same CEO background appropriate for a company producing semiconductors for the Air Force as for TV games? For computer companies? Soap for a mass consumer market? Surely there are many variables that are characteristic of the firm in question, and of the markets where the firm is operating. They need to be included in an analysis that attempts to explain the role of CEOs' backgrounds.

Part One
Discussion Summary

The Need for a New Manufacturing "Architecture"

A recognition that manufacturing prowess is central to the success of an industrial firm has, until recently, escaped many American managers. Yet that recognition drives the best industrial Japanese companies. Hence, according to Dr. Lewis Branscomb, vice president and chief scientist at IBM, Japan's "greatest technological strength" vis-à-vis the United States is "the speed with which developments are translated into improved products and processes. What they do with manufacturing engineers, we do with development engineers, and that gives them a quicker turnaround."

This picture of American competitive shortcomings synthesizes the key issues raised in an intense debate on the chapters in this section:

- The need for U.S. industry to study the management practices both of its current competitors and its own "old masters," as well as today's avant-garde small firms;
- The recognition that production-oriented research and development is at least as important to the firm as R&D for new products;
- The need for a new breed of executive "lions" at various levels through the manufacturing organization;
- The need for top and middle management, in close alliance, to create a new manufacturing "architecture," instead of continuing to carry out mere "caretaking" on their existing systems;
- The need for the interfaces between research, development, engineering, and production to be better understood and more closely coordinated;
- And, by implication, whether all this is likely to be achieved in a company whose chief executive has a narrow functional grounding.

In Search of Architects

According to Alfred D. Chandler, Jr. (professor, Harvard Business School), someone like Chaparral Steel's Gordon E. Forward could be seen as a latter-day Andrew Carnegie—the iron and steel baron who in the nineteenth century epitomized so many of the traditional virtues of American industrial leadership. Himself a manufacturing "architect," he placed central reliance on the quality of his technical team and delegated far-reaching powers of management to his foremen. So far, at least, Chaparral has avoided matching its growth with the creation of a stifling corporate bureaucracy, in which many former line responsibilities are expropriated into staff functions and committees. As in many Japanese and German companies, technical expertise and functions are heavily shared down the organization.

The advantage that small firms gain from having chief executives with a manufacturing background was underlined by several participants. In the case of large companies, by contrast, there was considerable skepticism about whether a chief executive's functional background (see the paper by Jarymiszyn, Clark, and Summers) was critical to the firm's success, not only on the grounds that "background is less important than attitude" (Frank Pipp, corporate group vice president, Xerox Corporation), but that the background of the top management team was a more meaningful factor than that of any individual manager.

Yet there was little disagreement with the concern expressed by Robert Hayes (professor, Harvard Business School) that the paper's data on the functional experience of CEOs could have serious implications for the many large firms that are facing increasing technological challenges: Taking the classifications "operations" and "R&D" together, the proportion of CEOs with strong technical experience appears to have fallen sharply since 1975, particularly in large firms.

A further doubt was raised about whether companies in this situation are likely to encourage the emergence of a new breed of "lions" among their manufacturing managers. As Harold Edmondson (vice president–manufacturing of Hewlett Packard) warned, before they emerge and become effective, they will need to feel that the new approaches they espouse can have some effect on the company—and for that "they need help."

As to the likely source of these new lions, James Bakken (vice president, Ford Motor Company) argued that "they are already out there— they will emerge when senior corporate management is sufficiently threatened by eroding competitiveness and encourages massive struc-

tural change." Drawing on the results of Skinner's survey of "comers," however, many other participants suggested looking to new sources of management talent, just as we did in the nineteenth century, when many U.S. industries looked for management talent in railroads and steel. Subsequently they turned to the auto industry, as well as to such individual companies as National Cash Register.

For Dale Hartman (director of manufacturing technology, Hughes Aircraft), the "lions of tomorrow will not come from the existing young managers in large organizations, but from the combined engineering-management degree courses that are being established at various colleges and universities." Given rotating assignments by their employers, they could then develop the necessary cross-cultural expertise, suggested Robert Kaplan (professor, Harvard Business School).

But to John Doyle (vice president of research and development, Hewlett Packard) there was some hope of short circuiting this process by finding multidisciplinary "comers" currently employed in such fields as microelectronics manufacturing, where, as he put it, "product and process are inextricably interwoven. It's almost a process industry, but not quite."

Dismantling Functional Barriers

The multidisciplinary microelectronics engineer, in fact, might well serve as a model for education and recruitment in a wide range of manufacturing industries. "We don't want to train people for traditional types of functions—manufacturing departments, for example, may well disappear" (possibly merging with R&D), argued Frank Pipp (Xerox). Many companies were already moving substantial numbers of people across the boundaries between design, development, program management, and manufacturing, he said.

The separation of R&D from the factory in the early 1900s had been "a watershed," argued Jeffrey Miller (professor, Boston University). This was originally seen as an advantage, as the work of the industrial laboratory moved away from testing, standardization, and quality control toward product and process development, and as links with universities became of greater importance (see the Rosenberg and Chandler papers). "Many companies are now trying to reverse that, and to push development and manufacturing people together," reported Miller.

Participants saw the need for such a coalescence arising from a combination of factors. Both in industrial R&D and in the universities there was an excessive bias toward the product and away from the production process, argued Branscomb (IBM): "The universities have made very little in the way of contribution to the production process, with the exception of chemical engineering. Chemical engineering is the only discipline taught in our engineering schools in which most of the students are given the impression that their career is going to be in production." This situation "really needs fixing. . . . The universities are an enormous resource, but the engineering schools first must be given the opportunity to turn their attention to the production function as a respectable technological career for bright people."

Within the firm, and among economists, better understanding was also needed of the R&D process itself, in the opinion of many participants. Economists have a very limited conceptualization of the process, complained Rosenberg. "In the academic world, when we talk about R&D we're usually talking only about R—the D is frequently ignored."

Geoffrey Place (vice president–research and development, Procter & Gamble) divided the R&D process into three parts: (1) The "traditional research function" of understanding the physical sciences; (2) The (generally neglected) process of understanding how an industry might be redefined through product or process innovation; and (3) Development. Until World War II, for example, Britain had been good at (2), but very poor at (3), whereas today's Japan is good at both.

A fourth category, the transition from development to production, was spotlighted by Bob Slade (advisor, manufacturing technology, IBM). "It's something that industry ignores to an increasing degree. It's a transition that requires a tremendous degree of technical sophistication because it deals with physical science and processes, and with how subtle changes are made from the development lab to the production floor. If the Japanese had accomplished that transition successfully, it was probably "because of their emphasis on manufacturing as a science." If the United States did not learn to master that transition, "our productivity is going to be limited."

The Industry-Government-University Complex

In the converse direction, virtually the only U.S. advantage over Japan identified by the participants was the possession of a highly developed research infrastructure. Hitherto, argued Ken-ichi Imai (professor, Hitotsubashi University), Japan's success had been critically dependent on applying existing scientific and technological knowledge—the relationship described in Rosenberg's paper on the exploitation of science by U.S industry in the nineteenth century.

But recently, reported Imai, bottlenecks had been developing because of the lack of an infrastructure of basic research—hence the relative weakness, for example, of Japanese aircraft design. The Japanese government responded by spending heavily on mission-oriented basic research, but Imai considered the probability of success to be quite small because of the lack of previous accumulated research. In other words, there was a gap between the creation of knowledge and its application to industry.

"This is the United States' only hope," responded several participants. Drawing lessons from history, Chandler emphasized that the close relationship of General Electric and Du Pont with the Massachusetts Institute of Technology dated back to the 1890s. This, he reiterated, was the sort of connection that German industry made so successfully with the academic world in the late nineteenth century, but which British industry failed to establish—with serious consequences for its future health.

Warning against complacency, James Utterback (director—industrial liaison program, Massachusetts Institute of Technology) said that Japanese industry is already tied into the U.S. academic infrastructure. MIT has over 500 Japanese alumni, and about a quarter of the formal visits from industry to MIT are now from Japan. Japanese financial support of MIT research programs is still only a fraction of the U.S. level at present but is rising dramatically.

Questioning the value of past national or industrywide R&D programs in the West, Chandler argued that they had never worked as effectively as those within large firms in those industries where the exploitation of the economies of scale and scope gave the firm a competitive advantage. But Donald Wingard (partner, Arthur Andersen & Co.) pointed to positive impacts of the U.S. government's space program and of university work in biotechnology.

In a macroeconomic sense, government spending on space and defense R&D had raised the cost of all R&D in the rest of the economy, especially its personnel costs, argued Rosenberg. The lack of such government "crowding out" was one of the great hidden advantages of the Japanese economy, he felt.

Part Two

Productivity: Hardware versus Software

Overview

Toward a Better Infrastructure

Little more than fifteen years ago computers were evaluated almost exclusively in terms of their hardware capabilities. The more powerful the machine, the more likely it was to sell. The trouble was, the software necessary to make such hardware work effectively was often inadequate. As a result, many well-engineered computers performed far below expectations.

So it is today in manufacturing. The vast sums being invested in the hardware of new process technology and product development are likely to be wasted if the organizational and human software are neglected. Just as the computer industry has learned that it is essential to provide software that meshes with and reinforces the capabilities of its hardware, so must manufacturing managers.

The inadequacy of the software infrastructure in much of American manufacturing, together with suggestions for improvement, is the subject of the three chapters in this section. They focus on:

- Why productivity (defined broadly) varies so much between similar factories, and why many supposedly productivity-enhancing investments produce disappointing results;
- Whether existing cost accounting systems are appropriate to today's manufacturing organizations, and what changes might be needed;
- Whether a deep-seated shift in organizational relationships is needed to achieve major improvements in productivity.

Why Are Some Factories More Productive than Others?

In the first chapter, Professors Robert Hayes and Kim Clark (Harvard Business School) explore the sources of differences, over an extended period of time, in the total factor productivity (TFP) of twelve plants belonging to three different companies. They then relate the behavior of each factory's TFP to various types of managerial policies: equipment policies (purchase and maintenance); inventory and quality

control policies; work-force policies; and policies affecting complexity
and "confusion" in the factory. They find that several of these variables
have quite a strong impact on a plant's productivity, but that the
relationships often are quite different for factories in fabrication/
assembly businesses than for process or high technology plants.

One of the strongest relationships observed, and one of the few that
holds true in all three companies, is between TFP and work-in-process
inventory: Reductions in WIP inventory seem to cause improvements
in TFP that exceed those that would be expected from simply reducing
the capital invested in inventory. Common management practices that
increase the level of "confusion" in a factory are also found to be a key
factor. These include rapid changes in the production rate from month
to month, attempting to introduce large and fluctuating numbers of
engineering changes, and adding new equipment.

These last two findings have some disturbing implications, since
they suggest that product and process changes cost much more in
terms of lost productivity than is generally thought. The discussion of
these results (summarized at the end of this section) identifies three
key contributory factors behind the disappointing impact of capital
investment: Capital is frequently misinvested; even if the right investment decision is made, not enough attention usually is paid to preparing for and managing the inevitable confusion wrought by adding any
sort of new equipment; and new capital increasingly embodies new
technologies that cause an unexpected degree of further disruption,
often over lengthy periods. In short, confusion breeds further confusion.

Accounting Obsolescence

In his chapter "Accounting Lag–The Obsolescence of Cost Accounting Systems," Professor Robert Kaplan (Harvard Business School)
finds that, rather than reacting to the dramatic changes that are now
taking place in the manufacturing environment, companies are still
using their traditional cost accounting and management control systems. Intellectually rooted in the scientific management movement
that emerged in the late 1800s, they treat efficiency in the use of direct
labor as the key to productivity. So, even though variable labor costs
are becoming a very small part of most companies' manufacturing
costs, firms are still allocating costs on the basis of the direct labor
content of their products.

In an environment where short-term profits may not reflect a firm's
long-term competitiveness, companies are also continuing to place un-
due reliance on such financial criteria as return on investment. They
are disregarding a host of other criteria that, Kaplan argues, could be

*used to reflect such factors as product and process improvements, hu-
man capital development, the length of product development cycles,
levels of product quality and work-in-process, set-up times, and speed
of delivery. Many firms do not even measure some of the basic physical
inputs to productivity, such as materials and energy consumption.
They remain almost entirely focused on aggregate and largely abstract
financial summaries. These not only fail to capture what actually goes
on inside the firm but heavily influence the objectives and behavior of
its managers.*

*Why should companies have such trouble creating measures of this
kind and using at least some of them in their top management reporting systems? This ought to be relatively easy to achieve compared with
the far more complex business of altering the manufacturing process
itself. One of Kaplan's explanations is the lack of progressive corporate
role models. Another is that the leading accounting firms are not providing tested alternative approaches to measurement. Nor does he
observe the academic world injecting new ideas.*

*The advent of personal computers raises his hope that local plant
controllers and accountants will begin to experiment with new measures and reporting formats. Companies must realize, he argues, that
it is they, not the Securities and Exchange Commission or any other
body, that dictate their own internal measurement and accounting
system. A very dependable producer of high-quality, reliable products,
for example, needs a different type of system from that which is appropriate for a firm emphasizing rapid product innovation. In either case,
the system should be designed to support its firm's particular strategy.
Neither is likely to be identical with the traditional cost accounting
systems found in most U.S. factories today.*

Work Force "Commitment" or "Control"?

*In his chapter on the emerging "commitment" model of U.S. work-
force management, Professor Richard Walton (Harvard Business
School) argues that in the past the major premise underlying work-
force management practices has been the need to impose control to
achieve efficiency. This traditional control model evolved over the first
half of this century but began to break down in the late 1960s and
early 1970s. In certain instances it has produced dramatically
counterproductive behavior. As a result, about twenty years ago many
managers began a process of fundamental rethinking, and union
officials have become increasingly involved. Conviction grew, Walton
reports, that the control model would be inadequate to the new,
significantly higher standards of performance required by the interna-*

tional competitive environment of the late 1970s and early 1980s. He argues that it now appears essential to elicit employee commitment to achieve major improvements in results.

As Walton points out, the commitment model represents a new departure in several respects: Jobs are defined more broadly; management is leaner and more flexible; ambitious and dynamic performance expectations replace minimum work standards; compensation systems place more emphasis on learning and collaboration; employees are expected to contribute ideas for improvement; union-management relations stress their common interests; and job security assumes a higher priority.

While the broad outline of the new approach has emerged, certain policy areas remain unresolved. For example, how can managers simultaneously share power and still be leaders? What level of employment assurance is desirable and feasible, and what forms will such assurances take? What compensation policies will reinforce the other elements of the commitment model—in particular, what should be the relative emphasis on individual performance versus group sharing of productivity gains? How far will unions and managements go in replacing adversarial bargaining and unilateral management action with mutual planning and problem solving? Will the "commitment" model be more or less suited than the control model to managing the innovation process? Will it, in terms of the Hayes-Clark chapter, create more or less "confusion" in the production environment?

Walton concludes that the commitment model, if properly implemented, produces superior results: higher productivity, better utilization of new technology, and greater human development and satisfaction. He argues that it also accords more legitimacy to the management of the enterprise.

Several participants in the discussion questioned the validity of the model, however, arguing that well-managed "control" organizations—as opposed to poorly run organizations—can produce equally good results, and that it is premature to predict that the commitment model will be resilient and enduring over time. Walton's view is that, while only a small fraction of U.S. workplaces today are managed in accordance with a comprehensive commitment model (although a number are in a transitional stage), the rate of transformation continues to accelerate, embracing offices as well as plants. He argues that those companies that experimented with the model at an early stage and are now applying it across their organizations appear to be well satisfied that—at least in terms of human organization—they have found a superior software system that enhances their hardware strategy.

4

Exploring the Sources of Productivity Differences at the Factory Level

Robert H. Hayes and Kim B. Clark

Introduction

The apparent failure of economists, using their traditional models of production, to explain the slowdown in the growth rate of U.S. productivity over the past fifteen to twenty years has led to a serious questioning of the models themselves (Nelson 1981). These questions, in turn, have focused renewed interest on the factors that affect productivity at the micro (individual factory) level: If macro variables, estimated using aggregate data, are unable to provide an adequate explanation of the productivity slowdown, perhaps it is because the macro analysis is based on an inadequate microeconomic foundation. This is the motivation that led us to conduct a direct analysis of the decision patterns of factory managers in order to better understand the impact their activities might have on productivity growth (Hayes and Abernathy 1980; Abernathy, Clark, and Kantrow 1983 provide further background).

Understanding the factors that influence productivity at the firm or individual operating unit level, however, is comparable in difficulty to understanding them at the national level and requires a large amount of detailed data. In fact, measuring productivity at the factory level, and explaining productivity changes, is usually difficult even for the manager who has access to such data. Within the same company, several factories—all making essentially the same products using essentially the same manufacturing process—often show widely differing levels of productivity, productivity growth, and/or profitability. How can one explain such differences?

We want to acknowledge the tremendous contribution that Paul Adler, Bruce Chew, and Russell Radford made to the preparation of this paper. They took the leading role in both the collection of data and their analysis.

Some of the possible explanatory factors are "structural" in nature, in that they are out of the direct control of a factory's management. Examples include the age of the factory (or the average age of the equipment in it), its size, its location, and whether its work force is unionized. Other factors are much more under the control of local management, such as equipment policies, materials control policies, and work-force policies. We term these "managerial" factors. How is a firm's senior management to fairly assess the performance of its factory managers, or decide how to deal with a productivity "problem," unless it can somehow disentangle those factors that are within their control from those that are outside? Yet such evaluations are routinely made, and factory managers are routinely rewarded or punished on their basis, using only senior managers' subjective judgment to make the separation.

In this paper we present the first results of a field study of twelve factories which seeks to measure directly the impact of managerial policies on factory productivity. Our hope is that, by helping to clarify some of the variables that influence productivity growth at the micro level, we can provide insights about effective production management, as well as begin to identify some of the linkages between micro and macro phenomena.

The twelve factories belong to three different companies. One of them employs a manufacturing process that is highly connected and automated. On the continuum from "job shop" to "continuous process" (see Hirschman 1958; Hayes and Wheelwright 1979) it is closest to the latter; therefore we refer to it as the *process* company. Another employs a batch manufacturing process based on a disconnected line-flow work organization; we refer to it as the *fab* (fabrication)/*assembly* company. The third company produces electronic equipment using a manufacturing process that is separable into four stages, ranging along the continuum from process to fab/assembly; we refer to it as our *hi-tech* company. All of the five factories of the process company and three of the four factories of the fab/assembly company are in the United States (the fourth is just across the border in Canada). Of the three factories belonging to the high tech company, one is in the United States, one in Europe, and one in Asia.

We developed measures of each factory's total factor productivity on a monthly basis (this calculation will be described in the next section) for at least one-and-a-half years and usually more than five. In several cases it was possible to track performance over a nine-year period, and in more than half the cases our data go back to the factory's start up. We then attempted to relate the behavior of each factory's total factor productivity to various types of managerial behavior. To our knowledge this is the first attempt to explore in depth a wide range of factors affecting productivity growth at the factory level in the United States, and the data base we have developed is the most comprehensive yet compiled.

Data Collection

We developed a measure of each factory's monthly total factor productivity (TFP) by dividing an estimate of its "output" each month by the sum of four inputs: labor, materials, capital, and energy. We also estimated its (partial factor) labor productivity by dividing the estimated output by the labor input alone, so as to allow us to compare changes in labor productivity with concurrent changes in TFP. This TFP value was then compared with a variety of managerially influenced variables (described in *Table 4-1*) in an attempt to identify relationships over time within the same factory. Some attempt was also made to sort out relationships across factories within the same company, but this analysis is still in a very early stage and is not reported here.

The situation at each of the three companies was somewhat different, as described below. As a result, we were often forced to use slightly different approaches for estimating the values of different variables. (See Kendrick and Vaccara 1975 for a more complete discussion of productivity measurement and analysis.)

Output

The intent is simple: we calculate a factory's total monthly output by multiplying the number of each of the products it makes in any month by that product's 1982 standard cost. This calculation was complicated by certain problems at various sites, however. For example, one company's accounting system did not measure output directly; only actual transactions were recorded, so we had to estimate output by adjusting reported monthly shipments to reflect inventory changes. We also had to guard against confusing changes in product quality or in the product mix—from labor-intensive to capital-intensive products, for example—with productivity changes. Finally, we had to accommodate changes in the standard costs of different products over the time period encompassed by our study.

One can choose among several alternative methods for dealing with such changes in standard costs. The Laspeyres approach, for example, normalizes the output calculation by using the costs that were in use during the initial period of observation. The Paasche approach, on the other hand, normalizes by using latest period costs.[1] We chose the Paasche approach (based on 1982 costs) for the process and fab/assembly companies for two reasons. First, it is linked directly to the actual cost of the output of the most recent production period, which made it more meaningful to the managers we were working with. Second, to the extent that "learning" is taking place (that is, partial factor productivities are improving as cumulative volume increases), the Paasche calculation of output is based on the most efficient stage of the production process.

The hi-tech company presented us with a more complicated problem. The components under study were associated with a product launched in 1981. Rapid growth of output permitted rapid "learning" and unit cost decreases. Rather than arbitrarily choosing a particular point in time as our reference point, as in the other two cases, we used projections prepared by that company's cost engineers of the estimated potential unit cost that could be achieved within the next two years. These ultimate (that is, mature or post rapid-learning) costs were used to convert unit output to a constant dollar figure.

We were able to avoid problems associated with product mix changes by confining our attention to factories that produced relatively narrow product lines. In those cases where there was considerable diversity, individual products were generally produced by separable production units or stages, and we were able to gather data within each of these subunits.

Inputs

Labor. Each month we estimated the total hours worked by each major employee classification (for example, hourly worker, maintenance worker, indirect manufacturing worker, and so forth). To aggregate these various categories we multiplied their hours by that classification's end-1982 wage (including benefits). The units of measurement and the labor classifications differed slightly across firms but were generally very similar.

Materials. The measurement of materials consumption generally presented a much more difficult problem because, while most companies keep fairly good records of materials purchases, many do not record the material actually consumed during a month. Instead, they estimate material consumption by multiplying a product's standard material cost (which itself implies an assumption that the usage of materials is constant) by its unit output. Periodically (typically every year or half-year) this estimated consumption is reconciled with actual material usage, based on a physical count.

Measurement is further complicated by the fact that even when actual (rather than standard) materials transactions are recorded, they are typically recorded in dollar, rather than physical, terms. Therefore, changes in the costs of materials (caused either by inflation or learning effects) that are not reflected in the standard costs described above can distort estimates of material productivity. Finally, little attempt is generally made to measure the physical consumption of indirect materials; they are usually incorporated into a manufacturing overhead account that is periodically adjusted to reflect the changes in a variety of indirect expense categories.

These problems affected our collection of data in the three companies in different ways. The hi-tech company, for example, kept good records of the purchase cost of the materials actually consumed in any given month but made no attempt at all to estimate the effect of material price inflation, which is necessary for calculating the actual physical usage of materials. This lack of concern is perplexing given that materials costs, averaging about 50 percent of total manufacturing cost, were sometimes over five times the cost of direct labor (about which the company collected very detailed information). It was therefore necessary for us to get management personnel to estimate the average plantwide material price inflation that occurred during each year of our study. We then used straight line interpolation to translate that annual figure into monthly inflation rates that could be used to estimate monthly material consumption.

In the case of the fab/assembly company, on the other hand, material consumption was estimated by multiplying the standard material cost by unit output and adjusting the resulting figure by the reported material cost variance reported each month; indirect material purchases were then added. This aggregate value was then deflated by a price index based on the annual price inflation estimated by plant management for certain major categories of material.

The surprising lack of attention paid to materials usage is also reflected in the productivity measures chosen by many American companies. Typically they are based on value added per employee (or value added as a multiple of wage expenses). This completely neglects materials cost and thereby deflects attention from approaches for improving overall productivity that seek to use materials more efficiently. Perhaps this is because, as Davidson (1976) has suggested, the United States has historically had ample materials but scarce labor. As a result, management attention has been directed primarily at finding ways to increase labor productivity.

Energy. Measuring energy consumption was much more straightforward, because the rapid increase in energy prices after 1973 had caused two of the three companies to keep good records of energy consumption and cost. It is noteworthy that these two companies placed much more attention on keeping accurate records of various categories of energy consumption than of material consumption, even though total energy costs were typically on the order of one-tenth of total material costs. In fact, energy productivity grew much faster than all other partial factor productivity ratios in the fab/assembly company (this was also true in all but one of the process plants) largely, we suspect, because of the attention placed on it since the oil shocks of 1974 and 1979. The third company did not record manufacturing's energy consumption at all, even though it apparently represented about 3 percent of total manufacturing costs.

Capital. The measurement of capital presented some of the trickier problems faced in our study. Our difficulty was largely due to the aforementioned preoccupation of factory accounting systems with transactions (for example, equipment purchase) rather than usage, and with nominal, rather than constant, dollars. To compensate for the impact of price inflation, equipment price indices were used (where appropriate) to translate the fixed asset base existing at the time our study began, and all equipment purchases since then, into 1982 dollars. The capital charges—straight line depreciation plus the real (adjusted for inflation) interest cost—applied to the gross book values of various categories of assets were chosen, after careful consultation with each firm, to reflect its particular situation (length of useful equipment life, rate of obsolescence, and so forth).

Process. The most complete data were available in the process company, where monthly transactions (additions to and deletions from capital stock) were recorded by department in each factory. The following (annualized) capital service rates were employed: manufacturing equipment (6 percent), buildings (2.5 percent), other processing equipment (9 percent), inventories (15 percent).

Fab/assembly. Just as at the process company, plant level transactions data were converted to constant (1982) dollars and the following total annualized capital service charges were applied to Gross Book Value: buildings (5 percent), machinery (10 percent), inventory (9 percent).

Hi tech. The capital invested in equipment was estimated by first estimating the maximum feasible daily-going-rate machine capacity. This unit capacity was converted into a dollar value by multiplying it by a rate reflecting the end-1982 cost per unit of that category of asset. The following annualized capital charges were then applied: machinery and equipment (22 percent), facilities (12 percent), and inventory (10 percent).

Once these estimates of output and input were obtained, a factory's TFP in a given month was then calculated by dividing its total output that month, expressed in terms of 1982 standard costs, by the sum of that month's labor, material, energy, and capital inputs, again expressed in 1982 costs.[2]

Adjustment for Capacity Utilization

Because of the large fixed component in capital cost, as well as (to a lesser degree) that in labor cost, each factory's estimated total factor productivity is quite sensitive to changes in its production volume and to the timing of major capital investments. In the attempt to separate the movements in TFP that are due to changes in production capacity and operating rates from those that are due to efficiency changes—the focus of our study—an estimate of capacity utilization was included as one of the terms in all regression analyses of the raw data.

Unfortunately, none of the three firms was able to provide us with a reliable measure of its capacity utilization. In the absence of internal measures we were forced to develop our own. We used the output values actually achieved during successive peaks of monthly production as estimates of a plant's capacity at those times, and then estimated its capacity during other periods by interpolating linearly between those peaks of actual output. We did not take into account the timing of actual facility expansions on the assumption that production capacity added far ahead of its actual usage was not necessarily a poorly used resource, but simply reflected a desire to maintain a certain capacity cushion and/or the economies associated with adding large blocks of capacity at one time. Graphs of the resulting adjusted TFPs for selected factories in each of the three companies are provided in *Figures 4-1, 4-2,* and *4-3.*

Once these TFPs were graphed, each factory's results were discussed with its management in an attempt to understand the causes of interesting patterns in the data (for example, trends, trend reversals, and cyclical behavior) and apparent major anomalies. Some of these anomalies were found to be due to errors in the data provided us; these were corrected. Others were explicable in terms of identifiable events that occurred that month (the advent of the deer hunting season, for example, was clearly apparent in the data describing one of the factories,

Figure 4-1
Total Factor Productivity, Hi Tech (European plant, Product G)

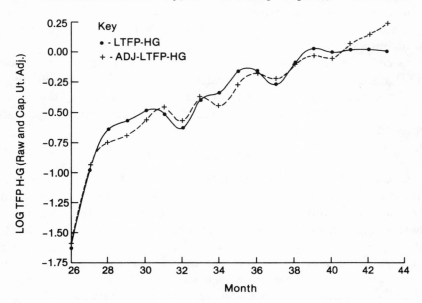

Figure 4-2
Total Factor Productivity, Fab/Assembly Plant 3

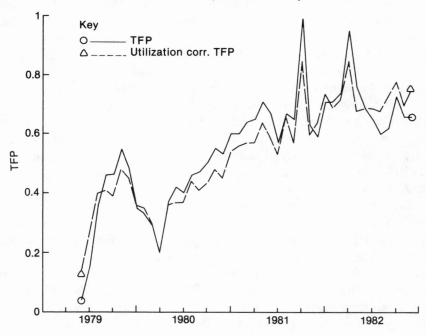

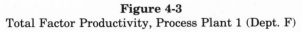

Figure 4-3
Total Factor Productivity, Process Plant 1 (Dept. F)

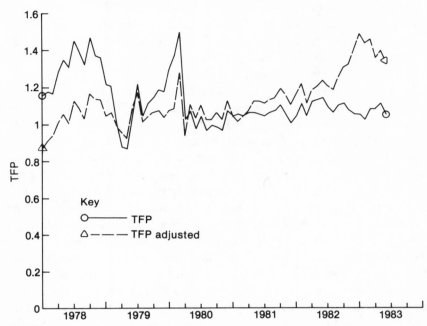

as was a year-end peak in purchased materials that was observed when that plant sought to use up its annual budget for indirect materials). We did not attempt to relate our estimates of monthly TFP to managerial variables until each factory's managers understood how its productivity had been calculated and agreed that the resulting pattern of TFP over time fairly represented their factory's behavior.

General Comments about the Methodology Used

Our discussions with various factory management groups not only helped us improve our measurement approach, they also revealed the potential value of such measurements to practicing managers. Many of these managers felt that their usual periodic profit and loss statements did not provide adequate up-to-date information about their factory's actual efficiency (in converting inputs into outputs) in any given month because of the artificial decompositions and smoothing associated with traditional cost accounting systems. Each month these people received a blizzard of variance reports but no overall measure of efficiency. The TFP data that we developed generally appeared to be quite credible to them and provided a fairer representation of their factory's performance than the standard profit and variance reports. Some managers, in fact, began calling us up at the end of each month to get the latest information about their factory's TFP.

There were two aspects of our TFP data that appeared to be particularly appealing to these managers. First, we presented data in constant dollar terms. Most accounting systems collect and report current dollars, which leads to distortions during periods of high inflation (such as the late 1970s and early 1980s). When we eliminated these distortions, we provided them data that were regarded as being more plausible and intuitively appealing than the usual reports they received. Second, our TFP data were presented in such a way that it was possible to gain a perspective on a factory's behavior over a period of several years. Few managers are able to develop this kind of perspective, both because their own internal reporting systems are geared to one-year budgets and because their own tenure in a particular job or location is generally restricted to two or three years. As a result, there tends to be little collective "memory" at the plant-manager level.

We have come to the conclusion that the traditional organizational structures and control systems found in most U.S. manufacturing companies tend to encourage a "steady-state mentality," in that plants are expected to stay within rather tight operating ranges that are specified by standard costs, delivery schedules, and annual budgets. Within such a constrained environment there is little flexibility for experimentation or incentive for continual improvement. Our TFP measure, on the other hand, provided a more dynamic perspective on the manufacturing managers' mission; it gave them a sense of where their operation had come from, where it was, and where it was going.

One of the companies, which had begun a simple productivity measurement program before we began our project, decided our approach was better and changed theirs to be more like ours. Another was motivated by our study to begin the development of a productivity measurement program modeled on ours.

Defining Managerial Variables

The development of credible TFP estimates was the first step in our empirical analysis; the second was the identification and measurement of various managerial policies that we felt might have an impact on TFP. In *Table 4-1* we have organized these policies into five groups (not all of the variables listed in *Table 4-1* were measurable in all companies) and described the specific measures we used to capture them. The first four groups of managerial policies are relatively well-

Table 4-1

Managerial Policies: Categories and Indicators

Policy Category	*Indicators Used*
1. Equipment policies	a. Average age of equipment
	b. Average maintenance expense as a percent of equipment book value
2. Quality policies	a. Process waste; yield as a percent of total input materials
	b. Intermediate and final reject rates
	c. Customer return rates
3. Inventory policies	a. WIP as a percent of total materials or production cost
4. Work force policies	a. Average age and education of workers
	b. Hours of overtime per week
	c. Absenteeism rate
	d. Hiring and layoff rates
	e. Average hours of training per employee
5. Policies affecting confusion	a. Fluctuations in production volume
	b. Number of product types produced
	c. Number of production orders scheduled
	d. Number of schedule changes as a percent of (c)
	e. Number and type of engineering change orders (ECOs)
	f. Introduction of new processing equipment

known and straightforward in interpretation. In the course of collecting the data, however, we saw evidence that some of the most critical management activities were those that affected the level of confusion in a factory. Therefore our fifth group attempts to measure the degree of such confusion-engendering activities as disruptions in production schedules (product changes, volume changes, expediting), engineering changes, and the installation of new equipment.

Data Analysis

In analyzing our data we first attempted to estimate the longitudinal relationships between managerial decisions and productivity; that is, we examined the impact of these management policy variables on TFP within the same factory over time. The analytical approach we used was multiple linear regression analysis; a more complete description of it is contained in the *Appendix* at the end of this chapter.

Our early exploration of this data, coupled with discussions with a number of managers (and some reflection), suggested that the simple ratios and averages that we used initially to measure the various management policies described in *Table 4-1* were often not able to capture adequately the phenomena we were trying to understand. For example, many managerial actions (among them, investing in new equipment or overhauling older equipment, training workers, and implementing an engineering change order) have similar characteristics as investments; that is, they might be expected to cause inefficiencies in the period in which they are instituted but are expected to lead to higher levels of efficiency in later periods. To test the long-term effects of such actions, we included lagged variables into our equation in these cases; this allowed us to estimate the effect on TFP of management actions taken in previous months, as well as those taken in the current month.

There are still other management activities that might not be expected to have any real impact on productivity unless they are held at a certain level for several months. Increasing the amount spent maintaining equipment, for example, might have little impact if done during one month only. To properly assess the impact of an increased level of certain activities, therefore, we looked at the relationship between productivity and the five-month moving averages of these activities.

Still other activities might not be expected to have much effect unless they are characterized by some consistency. A major change in the rate of production, in an otherwise smooth monthly production schedule, for example, might be expected to have one kind of impact on productivity in that (or a later) month, whereas a *pattern* of widely fluctuating scheduled rates of production might be expected to have a different impact. In the case of certain variables, therefore, we examined the relationship between TFP and that variable's average absolute deviation (using the five-month moving average as the estimated mean value for the variable).

Even after incorporating these additional variables we confronted problems of interpretation, particularly in connection with issues of timing and causality. For example, before beginning the study we expected to find that equipment maintenance and work force training were positively related to productivity growth. Our belief in the value of both activities had been based on observing a number of successful "turnaround" situations, where a new management group had been able to make a major change in a factory's effectiveness. Almost invariably one of the new management's first actions was to increase dramatically expenditures on equipment maintenance and worker training. Our observation of high levels of maintenance and worker training in well-run Japanese companies appeared to reinforce the importance of such activities.

Our analysis of the correlations between TFP and both training and equipment maintenance in this data, however, led to consistently negative relationships: High expenditures on maintenance and training, even in lagged forms, generally were associated with *low* TFP. In discussing this result with the managers involved, we discovered that in all three of our companies maintenance and training were used as *corrective* activities. That is, maintenance was increased in response to machine problems—and such problems usually caused reduced productivity. There were no records that would allow us to separate corrective from preventive maintenance, or even from the costs of rebuilding equipment.

Similarly, training was typically increased in response to specific worker or operating problems. In one company the amount of worker training scheduled was in direct proportion to the number of Engineering Change Orders (ECOs) scheduled (because ECOs typically necessitated different processing steps or approaches). And a high rate of ECOs, as we shall later see, can have a strong negative impact on productivity.

As another example, a strong positive correlation was observed between productivity and absenteeism in one of our companies; that is, high absenteeism was associated with high productivity. This relationship was much stronger than would have occurred if the remaining workers had simply increased their level of effort so as to fill the gaps left by their absent colleagues. It was as if when the tenth worker was absent the remaining nine did the work of 10.5 workers! It turned out that this behavior actually reflected the high morale in the company: when processing problems were being encountered (leading to low productivity) everybody chipped in to solve them. Absenteeism was very low during such periods. Once these problems had been solved (high productivity periods), people took a little "well deserved time off."

These examples suggest the need for care when interpreting the relationships uncovered in a statistical analysis of behavior within an operating unit over time. They also underscore the importance of combining a quantitative analysis of this sort with ongoing field research: communicating the preliminary results obtained to those directly involved and asking for their help in interpreting and clarifying them. Each type of research informs and guides the other.

Our analysis of the data we have collected is still in progress, and the statistical results we present in the next section should be viewed only as preliminary. It has uncovered, however, a number of interesting and provocative relationships. Before presenting specific results we should note that many of the most significant findings we describe were those observed in connection with the fab/assembly company. The relationships that emerged between managerial variables and production performance were much weaker and were characterized by erratic sign changes, in the process and hi tech companies. We offer the following hypotheses in explanation.

First, the production histories obtained from the hi tech company were much shorter than those available from the other two companies. This resulted from our focus on a relatively new product. Hi tech therefore experienced rapid improvements in manufacturing performance as products moved down the learning curve. The learning phenomenon simultaneously affected many variables: Process yields improved, labor productivity increased, work-in-process inventories fell, product designs stabilized, and so on. The straightforward use of a linear regression technique can provide some insight into the different patterns of learning that are observed in various plants and firms. Disentangling the effects of different management policies, however, will probably require more sophisticated techniques (and perhaps additional data). This is a focus for future work.

The process company presented a different challenge. Its production process was largely dominated by the equipment used and the relatively inflexible operating procedures that had been developed to facilitate smooth operations. The imperatives of continuous processing necessarily limited the range of variation of most of the managerial variables whose impact we were seeking to understand: Inventories, wastage and product changes, among other key variables, were carefully maintained within rather narrow ranges. Developing appropriate measures of inputs and outputs was also complicated by the sequential nature of much of the materials processing. Materials flowed from one department to the next, and sometimes from one plant to another, and this often obscured the observation of when certain costs were actually incurred.[3] Although we collected cost and other information about management variables by stage of the process, the interrelatedness of these stages made it difficult to separate joint costs and shared resources—not to mention causes and effects. Certain relationships did emerge with some clarity from our longitudinal analysis, however. Further progress is likely when we conduct a cross-sectional analysis: looking across plants or departments within the same company at the same point in time.

Productivity and "Learning"

Most of our factories exhibited a gradually increasing TFP over the time period tested. The growth rate was strongest in the hi tech company and weakest in the process company. One of the first issues we explored was the extent to which this growth was better modeled as a trend over time or as the result of the accumulation of cumulative production volume (the typical "learning curve" assumption). The regression coefficients, their statistical significance, and the coefficients of multiple regression (describing the percent of the total variation in productivity that was explained by learning) are provided in *Table 4-2*. As can be seen, the strength of the relationship between learning and TFP is often very high: cumulative volume (or time) and capacity utilization often explain over 90 percent of the variance in TFP. The three negative coefficients associated with capacity utilization in the hi tech company (bottom three cases) may reflect the strong collinearity observed there between cumulative output, capacity utilization, and productivity. Such collinearity often obscures underlying relationships and results in erratic signs.

It is also important to note that the regression coefficients describing the rates of learning vary considerably across factories, as do those attached to capacity utilization. The same variety was observed in connection with all other managerial variables. This implies that the level and behavior of a factory's TFP are not determined primarily by its ownership by a particular company, or by its product and process technology. If it were, then all the factories belonging to the same company should exhibit roughly similar relationships. The specifics of each plant's situation—and particularly its management—appear to have a profound effect on its performance. While this observation is intuitively plausible to most managers, it is at odds with much current economic theory.

Generally we found that cumulative volume was a slightly better estimator of TFP than time for the fab/assembly company and for the less capital-intensive stages of the hi tech company. Such cumulative volume-based learning appeared to be most active, however, during the start-up of a factory or process. No records of cumulative volume were available in the process plants and one of the fab/assembly plants, so we were forced to restrict our attention in these cases to time effects only.

Productivity and Shared Experience

In the case of the hi tech company it was possible to compare the rates of learning (TFP as a function of cumulative volume) of the same

Table 4-2
Basic Model Relating TFP to Cumulative Output (or Time)
and Capacity Utilization

Model A: Log (TFP) = B_0 + B_1 log (cum. output) + B_2 log (cap. util.)

Co./Plant (dept./prod.)	B_1	B_2	R^2 of Model (A)	(B)†
Fab/assembly				
1	(cum. output not available)		—	.505
2	.108**	.483**	.826	.762
3	.221**	.384**	.877	.914
4	.080#	.549**	.433	.431
Hi tech				
United States (G)	.491**	.521**	.981	.982
Europe (G)	.264**	.666**	.935	.868
Asia (G)	.391**	.273*	.951	.945
United States (C)	.508**	1.024**	.933	.942
Europe (C)	.500**	.734**	.927	.941
United States (E)	.287**	[−.267]	.812	.636
Europe (E)	[.075]	−.744@	.092	.087
United States (A)	.597**	−.383@	.791	.777

Model B: Log (TFP) = B_0 + B_1 (month) + B_2 log (cap. util.)

Process (companywide process aggregations)				
(M)	−.002**	.731**	—	.313
(F)	.001**	.063*	—	.025
(D)	.002**	.197**	—	.387
(H)	.466**	−.211**	—	.120

†The regression coefficients for this model are available from the authors on request.
Note: The level of statistical significance of each estimate is indicated by the following notation:
** = Highly significant (the probability that B has the opposite sign is less than 0.5 percent)
 * = Significant (probability between 0.5–1 percent)
 # = Moderately significant (probability between 1–5 percent)
 @ = Possibly significant (probability between 5–10 percent)
 [] = Not significant (probability greater than 10 percent)

product produced at different factories in different countries. In the case of product G, for example, the U.S. plant exhibited the highest rate of TFP learning, while the Asian plant was second and the European plant third. For product C, both the U.S. and European plants displayed about the same rate of TFP growth; and for product E the European plant displayed a higher rate of learning.

Hi tech's *labor* productivity, on the other hand, showed a very different pattern: The U.S. plant consistently exhibited the slowest rate of labor productivity growth. In the one case where all three plants produced the same product G, the Asian plant showed the highest rate of labor productivity growth and the European plant was second. The European factory also eventually attained a higher rate of labor productivity growth than the U.S. factory in two products (C and E), after a rather extended period of debugging the process. The overall superior performance of the U.S. factory, in terms of TFP, when producing product G was due largely to its more rapid growth rate in material and capital productivity. It should be noted, however, that the European plant developed some of its own processing equipment for product C, and in that case its total factor productivity growth rate was roughly equal to that of the U.S plant (as noted before, its labor productivity growth rate was higher).

Since the production of all three products began in the United States and was later shifted to offshore plants, we were able to estimate the "shared learning" that took place during these transfers (see *Table 4-3*).[4]

These values of B_0 suggest that the offshore plants generally benefited greatly from the prior experience of the U.S. plant. One measure of the amount of this shared learning is the implied proportion of the prime facility's experience that is transferred to the new facility at its start-up. For example, in the case of product G, we can use the value of B_0 (-5.79) to estimate the level of TFP at the start-up of the European plant. This same level of TFP had been achieved by the U.S. plant some time earlier, when its cumulative output was only 68 percent of its level at the time of the European start-up. On the other hand, the Asian plant, newer to such technically advanced processes, could only share 51 percent of the U.S. experience when it started up two months later.

Table 4-3
Hi Tech: Shared Learning between Factories

	Product G			Product C		Product E	
	U.S.	Europe	Asia	U.S.	Europe	U.S.	Europe
B_0	-10.7**	-5.79**	-6.80**	-12.73**	-7.57**	-4.03**	2.24@
B_1	0.49**	0.26**	0.39**	0.51**	0.50**	0.29**	[0.08]
R^2	0.981	0.933	0.951	0.933	0.927	0.812	0.092

Note: The level of statistical significance of each estimate is indicated by the following notation:
** = Highly significant (the probability that B has the opposite sign is less than 0.5 percent)
@ = Possibly significant (probability between 5 percent and 10 percent)
[] = Not significant (probably greater than 10 percent)

As a result of this shared experience, together with the comparable growth rates of TFP they generally achieved, these offshore plants usually were able to outperform the U.S. plant, in terms of their actual TFP levels, at equivalent months after start-up. In the case of product G, the Asian plant was marginally superior to the European plant, which was considerably superior to the U.S. plant for the same number of months after start-up. These relationships held for most of the partial factor productivity measures as well. Similarly, the European plant tended to dominate the U.S. plant in all partial factor productivities associated with products C and E.

Despite this evidence of experience sharing during the start-up of a new plant, the continuing differences in the growth rates of TFP after start-up (together with the fact that the TFPs of the different factories did not eventually converge) suggest that this sharing of production expertise soon dwindled. In fact, plants developed considerable rivalry as time passed. The transfer of relevant information appeared to be limited by the organizational difficulties associated with coordinating and communicating engineering knowledge, by the desire of each plant to protect its proprietary knowledge, and by each plant's reluctance to assimilate superior techniques developed at other plants—the so-called "not invented here" syndrome. The seriousness of these problems has led the hi tech company to undertake significant organizational changes. Interplant coordination has been made the responsibility of product managers, and attempts are being made to channel plant rivalries into constructive directions by designating different plans as "centers of competence" in particular areas of technical expertise.

This phenomenon was not confined to the transfers of information across national borders. Evidence of the same behavior was uncovered in the plants belonging to the process company. One, in particular, appeared at one time to have cut itself off from its sister plants. The parent company is now encouraging more interplant communication and coordination by sponsoring biannual meetings of the department superintendents from all the plants. One person comments, however, "That plant's psyche balks at the thought that others might be able to do it better." Not surprisingly, this plant's TFP performance is consistently below that of the other process plants.

Productivity and Equipment Policies

It is widely believed—by economists, public policymakers, and managers (including most of those in our study)—that using newer equipment facilitates higher productivity. Yet our longitudinal analyses of all three companies found no discernible relationship between equipment age and TFP, after correcting for the impact of cumulative output and capacity utilization. In the case of the fab/assembly and hi tech companies this result may reflect problems in the data, since most of their plants started with new equipment. The average age of this equipment thereafter increased by somewhat less than one year during each year of our study. During this period the TFPs and cumulative outputs of these factories rose steadily, so perhaps this explains why we failed to observe the anticipated negative relationship between the aging of equipment and TFP. Similar findings, however, are reported in the paper by Clark and Hayes and in an unpublished paper by Cook and Schmenner (1983).

We have already mentioned the negative relationship we observed between TFP and maintenance spending, which appeared to be due to the fact that variations in the maintenance levels at both the fab/assembly and process companies were largely reactive in nature—a response to machine problems that led to low productivity. As a result, the signs of the coefficients relating maintenance hours (or total dollars expended) to TFP were consistently negative and statistically significant.

The most interesting finding in our study of the effect of equipment policies was the magnitude of the indirect cost associated with introducing new equipment into a factory. Again and again we found evidence that the cost, in terms of lost productivity, of a change in the process far exceeded the actual cost of the equipment itself. Moreover, unambiguous negative aftereffects often persisted for up to a year (beyond that point the regression coefficients were not statistically significant). We will return to this issue later in this paper when we discuss the effect of various "confusion" variables.

Productivity and Reject Rates

Recent years have produced increasing evidence that there is an inverse relationship between material wastage (or defect rates) and total factor productivity that seems to go well beyond the direct effect on material productivity. Studies of a number of Japanese firms (see, for example, Abernathy, Clark, and Kantrow 1983) indicated that success in lowering their defect rates well below those that had previously been considered "acceptable" had led to a reduction in their total manufacturing cost. These findings triggered a close examination of the experience of several U.S. firms where the same phenomenon was observed. Therefore, we expected to find a negative correlation between waste rates (or percent rejects) and productivity in our data sample.

This expected relationship was observed in the hi tech company, where both TFP and process yield rose dramatically during the period following the start-up of production. It was impossible, however, to separate the impact of improved yield on productivity from the effects of the several other variables that were changing as cumulative volume increased.

Data from the process company, on the other hand, made it possible to examine this relationship under more steady-state conditions. Its material processing technology is relatively mature, and the waste that is produced is routinely salvaged and reprocessed. Moreover, its operating procedures are designed to accommodate a certain level of waste, and its control system attempts to ensure that waste stays within a rather narrow range around this acceptable level. Small variations within this range can be handled easily, and should not be expected to cause much change in overall production efficiency.

The evidence presented in *Table 4-4*, however, suggests that changes in the waste rate (in this case measured by the ratio of waste material to total cost, expressed as a percentage) can have a profound effect on TFP. The regression coefficients for eleven of the fourteen processes are negative and generally statistically significant. In some cases they suggest the possibility of dramatic operating improvements. For example, consider product group D in plant number 4: Reducing waste by 10 percent from its mean value (from 9.34 percent to 8.41 percent of total materials consumption, or less than 0.5 percent of total manufacturing costs) in that product appears to be accompanied by a 3 percent improvement in total factor productivity. Discussions with plant managers suggest that these estimates may even understate the ultimate impact of changes in equipment and operating procedures that are designed to reduce waste significantly.

The strength of this relationship is more surprising when it is taken into account that in process factories the proportion of waste generally increases with the speed of the process. Therefore, a decision to increase the production throughput rate (which might be expected to cause TFP to increase because of the large fixed components in labor and capital costs) would tend to be associated with higher waste ratios. This should weaken estimates of the impact of waste on productivity. Our results suggest the importance of examining further this relationship. We need to understand better both the coefficients themselves and the managerial activities that lead to differences in waste rates across plants.

Productivity and Work-in-Process Inventory

Work-in-process (WIP) inventory was one of the strongest and most consistent explanatory variables that we examined. Both the fab/

Table 4-4
Relationship between Waste and TFP

Model: Log (TFP) $= B_0 + B_1$ (time) $+ B_2$ (cap. util.) $+ B_3$ (waste %)

Co./Dept. (plant)	B_3	R^2	% Waste, Average Value¶
Process			
M-1	[.0129]	.781	6.87%
M-2	−.0245**	.563	5.42
M-3	−.0071@	.694	9.05
M-4	−.0080#	.467	9.55
M-5	−.0180**	.473	9.41
F-1	—	—	—
F-2	−.0129@	.423	4.18
F-3	[−.0059]	.274	7.20
F-4	.0089@	.195	6.51
F-5	[.0047]	.456	3.14
D-1	−.0108*	.828	11.23
D-2	−.0145**	.688	12.42
D-3	−.0157**	.607	12.71
D-4	−.0325**	.505	9.34
D-5	−.0095*	.808	8.22

¶These values have been disguised by multiplying them by a constant. This preserved the ratios between the values at different plants, while obscuring the values themselves.
Note: The level of statistical significance of each estimate is indicated by the following:
** = Highly significant (the probability that B has the opposite sign is less than 0.5 percent)
 * = Significant (probability between 0.5–1 percent)
 # = Moderately significant (probability between 1–5 percent)
 @ = Possibly significant (probability between 5–10 percent)
 [] = Not significant (probability greater than 10 percent)

assembly and process companies exhibited strong and statistically significant negative relationships between work-in-process (measured in a variety of ways) and TFP. Adding this variable to our basic regression model for the fab/assembly plants, for example, reduced the unexplained variation $(1-R^2)$ by from 10 percent to 45 percent. Lowering work-in-process inventory, in fact, appeared to be one of the major contributors to higher TFP as a plant's cumulative volume increased. This is another link in a growing body of empirical evidence that suggests that the emphasis placed on reducing WIP inventory by Japanese manufacturing companies is justified. Clearly more research into this important topic needs to be done.

The same strong negative relationship was observed in the one department in each of the process company's plants that kept records of

Table 4-5

Relationship between TFP and Work-in-Process Inventory

Log (TFP) = B_0 + B_1 log (cum. output or time) + B_2 log (cap. util.) + B_3 (avg. WIP/Prod.)

Co./Plant/Dept.	B_3	R^2	Effect on TFP of a 10% Increase in WIP
Fab/assembly			
1	−.2235**	.560	−2.86%
2	−.0616**	.893	−1.14
3	−.2320**	.900	−3.59
Process			
HHP-1	−.1565**	.433	−1.63
HHP-2	−.4290**	.672	−4.01
HHP-3	−.4412**	.439	−4.65
HHP-4	−.6342**	.644	−3.52
HHP-5	−.4490**	.730	−3.84
Hi tech			
United States-G	[−.0089]	.982	−1.28
United States-C	[−.0543]	.940	−3.41
United States-E	[−.0378]	.816	−2.02
United States-A	−.0792#	.755	−5.02
Europe-G	−.0755**	.970	−4.79
Europe-C	[−.0082]	.925	−0.86
Europe-E	[.1054]	.537	1.59
Asia-G	[.0049]	.951	0.07

** = Highly significant (the probability that B has the opposite sign is less than 0.5 percent)

\# = Moderately significant (probability between 1–5 percent)

[] = Not significant (probability greater than 10 percent)

work-in-process inventory. The relationship observed in the hi tech company was much less convincing, although on balance increases in work-in-process inventory generally were associated with decreases in TFP. These data are summarized in *Table 4-5*.

Work-in-process as a percent of total production was averaged over five months, centered on the current month. The relationships observed in all three companies were about the same no matter how we defined this variable and had a greater impact on TFP than would have resulted simply from changing the amount of capital invested in WIP. This suggests that what we are picking up is not a spurious relationship reflecting the way we chose to define the WIP variable.

Productivity and Work Force Policies

Our analysis of the various work force variables described in *Table 4-1* was complicated by the fact that two of the companies did not keep adequate records of many of the variables we were interested in. We also had to sort our way through situations where, as noted earlier, both training and absenteeism behaved more like effects rather than causes in certain plants.

Some fairly clear and provocative relationships emerged, however, when we studied the interaction between productivity, absenteeism, grievance rates, and the prolonged use of overtime. For example, in the one unionized plant of the fab/assembly company, which was the only factory in that company to keep monthly records of grievances filed and absenteeism, we found strong negative relationships between TFP and both grievances per worker and absenteeism (each averaged over five months). When we regressed labor productivity alone against these variables, the relationship was even more strongly negative, and generally more statistically significant. When this relationship was described to the manager of this plant, his response was, "I'm not surprised. I've always felt that nine out of ten grievances had nothing to do with the issue grieved. When people are unhappy, they start looking for things to grieve about." (That general worker morale does appear to be important is suggested by the fact that the regression coefficients resulting from regressing productivity against five month average grievance rates were greater than those obtained when single month grievance rates were used.) These relationships are summarized in *Table 4-6*, and are similar to those reported in Katz, et al. (1983) and Ichinowski (1983). They imply that reducing the grievance rate by 10 percent in this factory might be expected to be accompanied

Table 4-6

Relationship between Productivity and Grievances in the Unionized Plant of the Fab/Assembly Company

Total: Log (TFP) = Basic Model + B_3 (5-mo. avg. grievances/worker)
Labor: Log (Lab. Prod.) = Basic Model + B_3 (5-mo. avg. grievances/worker)

Grievances	B_3	R^2	*Grievances Avg. value¶* *(per worker/month)*
Total	−123.4**	.544	.00695
Labor	−172.1**	.681	.00695

¶These values have been disguised by multiplying them by a constant. This preserved the ratios between the values at different plants, while obscuring the values themselves.
** = Highly significant (the probability that B has the opposite sign is less than 0.5 percent)

by an increase in labor productivity of about 10 percent, and in TFP of about 8 percent.

No statistically significant longitudinal relationships were observed between productivity and absenteeism or grievances in any of the process company's plants. We suspect that the capital intensity of its manufacturing process, together with its dependency on equipment operating rates rather than operator work rates, clouded these relationships. Ichinowski's study involved a company using a somewhat similar process, however, so we were somewhat surprised not to find any variables reflecting worker morale that clearly appeared to affect either the labor productivity or the total factor productivity of the process company's plants. In two of the hi tech plants, on the other hand, we observed evidence of the reverse causality behavior described earlier: Absenteeism tended to increase when productivity increased. No other data that might reflect employee morale was collected in its plants. The data describing the relationships between TFP and absenteeism for the fab/assembly and hi tech companies are summarized in *Table 4-7.*

Some provocative relationships between overtime and productivity were observed in the fab/assembly and hi tech plants. In the fab/assembly company the regression coefficients were generally negative (although sometimes not very significant statistically) and stronger for labor productivity than for TFP. Moreover, the coefficients on overtime were generally more negative when we regressed productivity against the average overtime of the two previous months. In the hi tech company the regression coefficients were more erratic. Upon investigation it appeared that a quadratic relationship fit the data somewhat better: TFP tended to increase for small increases in overtime (evidently due to the fixed components of labor and capital costs) and then to decrease beyond that point. Again, no stable or significant relationships were observed in the process company. These results are summarized in *Table 4-8.*

No clear relationships were observed between productivity (either total factor or labor) and worker age, education, or job tenure at any of the companies. The erratic signs and low statistical significance of the regression coefficients we observed may be explained by the number of "special situations" that existed in various plants. For example, employment in one fab/assembly plant has been dropping over several years. Because layoffs have been made on the basis of seniority, the average age and job tenure in this plant have been increasing, but productivity understandably fell during much of this period of contraction.

Table 4-7
Relationship between Productivity and Absenteeism

Total: Log (TFP) = Basic Model + B_3 (absenteeism %)
Labor: Lob (Lab. prod.) = Basic Model + B_3 (absenteeism %)

	B_3	R^2	Absenteeism %, Average Value¶
Fab/assembly			
Total	$-.0394$**	.571	5.5%
Labor	$-.0569$**	.773	5.5
Hi tech (total)			
United States (G)	.0239@	.982	5.8
United States (C)	$-.0691$@	.937	4.9
United States (E)	[.0287]	.815	7.6
United States (A)	[$-.0216$]	.935	4.1
Europe (G)	.0303#	.955	9.6
Europe (C)	.0732**	.951	6.9
Europe (E)	.0339@	.177	11.3
Asia (G)	(no information, reportedly because absenteeism does not occur)		

¶These values have been disguised by multiplying them by a constant. This preserved the ratios between the values at different plants, while obscuring the values themselves.
** = Highly significant (the probability that B has the opposite sign is less than 0.5 percent)
# = Moderately significant (probability between 1–5 percent)
@ = Possibly significant (probability between 5–10 percent)
[] = Not significant (probability greater than 10 percent)

Nor were we able to uncover the positive relationship between productivity growth and worker training that we expected to find. In most cases (training data was not reported in any fab/assembly plants) we observed the opposite relationship: pulling workers off their jobs for training reduced productivity. Moreover, we were unable, using a longitudinal analysis, to detect any evidence that this lost current productivity was made up for by increased future productivity. This may be due partly to the fact, mentioned earlier, that training in these companies was often used as a corrective measure: It was applied only when processing problems were being encountered (although some of this effect should have been picked up by our lagged variables).

The director of worker training in the hi tech company's U.S. plant, it should be noted, has been highly critical of the way training has been conducted in his plant. He felt that it has been poorly planned,

Table 4-8

Relationship between Overtime Hours per Worker/Month and Productivity

A. Fab/assembly Company
UNLAG: Log (Lab. Prod.) = Basic Model + B_3 (OT)
LAGGED: Log (Lab. Prod.) = Basic Model + B_3 (avg. OT, 2 prior mos.)

Model	B_3	R^2
Unlag		
Plant 1	−.0016@	.566
2	−.0054**	.724
3	[.0005]	.653
4	[−.0025]	.672
Lagged		
Plant 1	−.0042**	.587
2	−.0057**	.706
3	[−.0013]	.654
4	[−.0003]	.661

Note: The number of times that overtime was required in two consecutive months was on the order of five times greater in plants 1 and 2 than in plants 3 and 4.

B. Hi tech Company
Log (TFP) = Basic Model + B_3 (OT) + B_4 (OT^2)

Plant (prod.)	B_3	B_4	R^2
US (G)	.1185*	−.0059#	.984
US (C)	[.0732]	[−.0053]	.936
US (E)	[.0677]	[−.0032]	.818
US (A)	[.0188]	[−.0005]	.953
Eur (G)	[.0249]	[.0008]	.945
Eur (C)	.2431@	−.0490@	.939
Eur (E)	[−.2359]	[.0272]	.158
Asia (G)	[−.0119]	[.0002]	.953

Note: The level of statistical significance of each estimate is indicated by the following notation:
** = Highly significant (the probability that B has the opposite sign is less than 0.5 percent)
 * = Significant (probability between 0.5–1 percent)
 # = Moderately significant (probability between 1–5 percent)
 @ = Possibly significant (probability between 5–10 percent)
 [] = Not significant (probability greater than 10 percent)

poorly supervised, and poorly documented, and he personally estimated that better training would boost yields (and therefore productivity) by 10 percent. Similar sentiments were expressed by both line management and staff process specialists in the process company, which reported surprisingly little on-the-job training. Therefore, the problem may well be that what we are observing is not the effect of training on productivity, but the impact of spotty and poorly conducted training.

In none of the companies did changes in the employment level (hires/layoffs) appear to have much effect on TFP, after correcting for the effect of capacity utilization. Nor did fluctuations in the employment level, as measured by their average absolute deviation over five months, appear to be important. As we explored this issue with plant managers, we became persuaded that local culture and management were able to dilute, even overcome, whatever effect that changes in the work force might have. We observed instances, for example, where a layoff resulted in an *increase* in TFP. The timing of the layoff and the way it was presented to the people in the plant, or (in the case of an increase in the work force) the selection and training of new workers— all appeared to be more important than the action itself.

We had an opportunity in two of the companies to examine the impact of unionization on plant performance. Unfortunately, other concurrent interplant differences confounded our analysis (for example, the one unionized fab/assembly plant was also its oldest and largest one, and the one whose work force had undergone the most reduction over the past ten years). Therefore, we can only provide informal evidence to support our conjecture that the existence of a union also is less important than the way the union and the labor-management relationship is managed. Three vignettes illustrate this point.

In the late 1970s the unionized fab/assembly plant experienced a rapid rise in absenteeism and grievances shortly after the election of a new group of union leaders. This group, referred to as "the radicals" by current plant managers, was vocally antimanagement. When it, in turn, was voted out of office a few years later and a new, more cooperative, union leadership took its place, grievances and absenteeism fell and TFP began increasing again after several years of decline.

On the other hand, a decline in TFP at one of the nonunionized fab/assembly plants was originally attributed by its plant managers to a unionization drive that had eventually failed. Subsequent examination showed that the union drive had ended the quarter *before* the TFP decline occurred. The plant's productivity at the time of the union vote was actually at its highest level prior to that point in time; in fact, this level was not attained again for over eighteen months. Plant management evidently mistook contention for low productivity, even though the two are not inseparable.

Finally, although the level of TFP at the process company's unionized plants was marginally lower than in its nonunion plants, the *rate of growth* of TFP was essentially the same in all plants.

Productivity and Confusion

The terms complexity and confusion describe two somewhat distinct phenomena. A factory's task typically becomes more complex as it becomes larger, as more and different processing technologies and products are added to it and as the number and variety of production orders it must accommodate increases. It is the opposite of what Skinner (1974) and others refer to as "focus."

We were unable to investigate adequately the impact of *complexity* on plant performance because, paradoxically, the factories belonging to the process company were too similar in their complexity (similar sizes, products, production processes, and order mix), while those belonging to the fab/assembly company were too dissimilar. In the first case the range of variation was too narrow, while in the second there was no base of reference. Given this caveat we can report some evidence that increasing the number of products (and grade changes) produced on each machine during a month appeared to reduce TFP in the process factories.

Confusion, on the other hand, refers to managerial actions that disrupt the stability of the factory's operation. It can be caused by, for example, varying the rate of production or changing a production schedule once it has been established, expediting certain orders, changing the crews (or the workers on a specific crew) assigned to a given machine or part of the process, adding new products or changing the specifications of an existing product through an engineering change order, or changing the process itself by adding or altering the equipment used.

We obtained strong evidence that many of these actions have a negative impact on TFP and, particularly, labor productivity. The impact of adding or overhauling equipment was particularly striking in both the fab/assembly and process companies (adding new equipment was a continuous process in the high growth hi tech company, however), and clear evidence of the negative impact of changes in product specifications was observed in both the fab/assembly and hi tech companies. Equipment specifications are so attuned to product specifications in the process company, on the other hand, that none of the latter were observed there.

Output Variation

We measured output variation by the five-month average of the absolute value of the percentage change in month-to-month output. TFP, corrected for cumulative volume and capacity utilization, was negatively affected by increases in this average variability in three of the four fab/assembly plants. The negative effect of output variation became even more pronounced, and the statistical significance of these signs increased when we regressed TFP against average output deviation without correcting for cumulative volume or time. By itself, in fact, this variable explained from about 15 percent to 30 percent of the total variation in TFP in the fab/assembly factories. It is impossible to attribute a causal relationship on the basis of such an analysis, of course, but it suggests to us that one of the major sources of improved efficiency that occurs in these plants over time is learning how (or becoming more able) to control the causes of such variation. These results are summarized in *Table 4-9.*

The process factories did not display the same sensitivity to output variation. Possibly this is because the high fixed costs associated with the operation of a heavily capital-intensive process dilute whatever labor and material inefficiencies arise from changes in the production rate. Therefore the increases in TFP that occur with a given increase in the production rate are essentially balanced out by the decreases in TFP that accompany a similar decrease in production.

Another kind of confusion, however, appeared to be deleterious in the process company. All its plants shifted individuals between manufacturing processes so as to accommodate personal preferences and work imbalances. Such shifting is generally on a small scale and appears to be handled well. Within one department in one plant, however, people were moved frequently—and somewhat haphazardly—from machine to machine and from crew leader to crew leader. Individual workers have therefore been thwarted in developing stable working relationships with a fixed team, and from learning the subtle idiosyncracies of each machine. This department has a markedly lower TFP growth rate than corresponding departments in the other process plants.

Table 4-9
Effect of Variation in Fab/Assembly Production Rate on TFP

Model A: Log (TFP) = Basic Model + B_3 (5-mo. avg. change output/output$_{t-1}$)

Plant	B_3	R^2	Avg. Dev.¶
1	−.3128@	.512	.167
2	−.1833@	.837	.080
3	+.2890**	.807	.373
4	[−.0809]	.505	.398

Model B: Log (TFP) = B_0 + B_1 log (cap. util.) + B_2 (5-mo. avg. change output/output$_{t-1}$)

Plant	B_2	R^2
1	−.2379@	.467
2	−.3565#	.541
3	−.2457#	.313
4	−.4883@	.419

¶These values have been disguised by multiplying them by a constant. This preserved the ratios between the values at different plants, while obscuring the values themselves. Note: The level of statistical significance of each estimate is indicated by the following notation:
** = Highly significant (the probability that B has the opposite sign is less than 0.5 percent)
# = Moderately significant (probability between 1–5 percent)
@ = Possibly significant (probability between 5–10 percent)
[] = Not significant (probability greater than 10 percent)

Engineering Change Orders

Engineering change orders (ECOs) typically specify a change in either the materials to be used in producing a product, the manufacturing process employed, or the specifications in the product itself. One might expect that such changes would reduce TFP in the short run but lead to increased TFP in the long run. We found clear evidence of the expected short-term effect in the fab/assembly plants, but were surprised to see that the debilitating effects of ECOs persisted for up to a year. Since ECOs should be one of the major means for increasing productivity over the long run, this finding deserves further investigation. A few of our results are summarized in *Table 4-10,* in which we also correct for changes in the WIP inventory ratio.

At hi tech, on the other hand, the effect of ECOs was very different between plants. Since the U.S. facility was the prime facility and had the responsibility for developing and debugging ECOs, ECO activity had a negative immediate impact on productivity in most instances. In

Table 4-10

Effect of ECOs on TFP, Adjusted for WIP changes, in Fab/Assembly Plants

Model A: Log (TFP) = Basic Model + B_3 (number of ECOs)

Plant	B_3	R^2	Average ECOs[¶]
1	−.0028#	.593	16.5
2	−.0046**	.835	12.2
3	−.0166#	.887	7.0
4	na		

Model B: Log (TFP) = Basic Model + B_3 (number ECOs$_t$) + B_4 (number ECOs$_{t-1}$) + B_5 (number ECOs$_{t-2}$) + B_6 (number ECOs$_{t-3}$)

Plant	B_3	B_4	B_5	B_6	R^2
1	−.0032*	[+.0004]	−.0027#	−.0044**	.635
2	−.0064*	[+.0019]	[−.0011]	[+.0024]	.822
3	−.0179#	−.0146#	−.0190#	−.0181#	.918
4	na				

Model C: Log (TFP) = Basic Model + B_3 (avg. WIP ratio) + B_4 (number ECOs)

Plant	B_4	R^2
1	−.0023#	.627
2	−.0027*	.887
3	−.0168#	.911
4	na	

[¶]These values have been disguised by multiplying them by a constant. This preserved the ratios between the values at different plants, while obscuring the values themselves.
Notes: The level of statistical significance of each estimate is indicated by the following notation:
** = Highly significant (the probability that B has the opposite sign is less than 0.5 percent)
 * = Significant (probability between 0.5–1 percent)
 # = Moderately significant (probability between 1–5 percent)
[] = Not significant (probability greater than 10 percent)

the European plant, which mainly implemented U.S. ECOs rather than developing its own, ECO activity had a positive immediate impact.

In seeking to understand what was causing the negative effect at fab/assembly, and how it might be influenced by management, we investigated a variety of possible hypotheses. Two are worth comment. One is that not only the average level of the number of ECOs implemented in a given month, but also their variation, are detrimental to TFP. The other is that the manner in which ECOs are implemented

Table 4-11

Effect of Average Level and Variation in ECOs on TFP in Fab/Assembly
Plants

Model: Log (TFP) = Basic Model + B_3 (Avg. ECOs) + B_4 [Avg. Abs. Dev.:
(ECOs-Avg.)/Avg.]

Plant	B_3	B_4	R^2	Average ECOs
1	−.0087**	+.1497#	.622	16.5
2	−.0050**	−.4072**	.841	12.2
3	[−.0235]	−.8523*	.919	7.0
4	na			

Notes: The level of statistical significance of each estimate is indicated by the following notation:

** = Highly significant (the probability that B has the opposite sign is less than 0.5 percent)

 * = Significant (probability between 0.5–1 percent)

 # = Moderately significant (probability between 1–5 percent)

 [] = Not significant (probability greater than 10 percent)

also affects their impact on TFP. *Table 4-11* summarizes the first effect. Variable 4 is the average ECO level over five months, while variable 5 is the average absolute deviation of the ratio of these ECOs to this average level.

The implication of this tentative finding (assuming that increasing the rate of ECOs does not allow the company to increase the prices charged for its products) is that such a company might be advised to reduce the average number of ECOs to which its plants must respond in a given period of time. This might be accomplished, for example, by exercising discipline on its engineering and marketing people to focus their attention only on the most important changes, and/or to "design it right the first time." Moreover, these ECOs should be released in a controlled, steady fashion rather than in bunches.

A provocative secondary finding is triggered by the observation in *Table 4-11* that the plant whose average ECO level was the lowest had the strongest negative response to percentage variations in ECOs from month to month, while the plant with the highest average level of ECOs seemed to be least affected by such variations. A high average level of ECOs may actually improve a plant's tolerance to changes in the number from one month to another.

Even more intriguing, we discovered that in the one plant that divided ECOs into categories reflecting their cost ("major" denoting the most expensive ECOs to implement), it appeared that minor ECOs had the greatest negative effect on TFP while major ECOs actually had a *positive* effect. Investigating further, we discovered that plants or departments typically had advance warning of impending major ECOs. Recognizing that they were potentially disruptive, managers saw to it that careful preparation preceded their implementation: Supervisors were warned, workers were given training, and engineers were asked to assist. Minor ECOs, on the other hand, were simply "dumped" on the factory. Preparation seems to be rewarded. We conclude that the average number of ECOs, their variability from month to month, and the way they are managed all have a measurable effect on TFP.

Adding Equipment

As in the case of ECOs, adding new equipment (or extensively modifying old equipment) should lead to a long-run improvement in productivity—albeit probably at the cost of some initial loss of efficiency while the equipment is installed and workers learn to use it effectively. But again we were surprised at the magnitude of this initial negative impact—as was Ichinowski (1983, 167)—and at the length of time required before it dissipated. As before, the fab/assembly factories provided the most conclusive data, but the process factories appeared to corroborate these results.

As shown in *Table 4-12*, after correcting for cumulative output (or time) and capacity utilization, the initial (same month) impact of a percentage increase in a factory's capital equipment on TFP is strongly and statistically compelling in three of the four fab/assembly plants.

Table 4-12
Effect of New Equipment on TFP in Fab/Assembly Factories

Model A: Log (TFP) = Basic Model + B_3 (additions in equipment investment as a ratio of existing base)

Plant	B_3	R^2	New Equipment/Equipment Base Average Ratio
1	−3.507**	.541	.008
2	−1.299**	.847	.013
3	[−0.1772]	.740	.041
4	−1.544#	.566	.044

Note: The level of statistical significance of each estimate is indicated by the following notation:
** = Highly significant (the probability that B has the opposite sign is less than 0.5 percent)
\# = Moderately significant (probability between 1–5 percent)
[] = Not significant (probability greater than 10 percent)

In the fourth plant the sign is also negative but not statistically significant. (This plant, started up within the past five years, was adding new equipment rather continuously during its first three years. During this time the elimination of start-up problems and increasing rates of production caused its TFP to increase rapidly, which may have obscured the relationship.) Moreover, negative (and statistically significant) signs persisted for up to a year after the introduction of new equipment. A similar long-term deleterious effect was observed in process factories. In most cases the additional cost, over several months, of adding new equipment (in terms of lost labor productivity, increased waste, equipment idle time, and so forth) appeared to be greater than the cost of the equipment itself.

Summary and Next Steps

The preceding description of our preliminary investigations should be regarded only as a first cut through this data—akin to the exploratory trench that archaeologists dig through the site of a newly discovered ancient settlement. The tests performed thus far are crude; they need to be formulated and carried out more carefully. Yet this trench has also uncovered several provocative findings and triggered a number of hypotheses and research directions that we propose to explore more thoroughly.

Table 4-13 provides a more complete picture of the interesting relationships that await investigation. It contains the full regressions of TFP against the most important managerial variables in all four fab/assembly factories. As can be seen, incorporating additional variables does not change significantly the relationships uncovered during our one-at-a-time analysis.

Reducing work-in-process inventories, for example, seems to lead to improvements in productivity that surpass those associated with simply reducing the capital invested—a finding that a number of U.S. firms have recently corroborated when they followed the example set by their Japanese competitors. We need to investigate this phenomenon more thoroughly.

Second, much of the variation in the TFPs of the different factories we studied seems to be a function of the amount of confusion (or, more precisely, the extent of the confusion-engendering activities) observed in them. Although we have treated rejects (waste), work-in-process inventory, and confusion separately in this paper, they share certain common roots. Work-in-process is often at least partially a function of the amount of unpredictable variation in the reject rate (necessitating

Table 4-13
Complete Regression Analyses for Fab/Assembly Factories
(employing all variables discussed in text)

Variable		PLANT A Regr. Coeff.	PLANT A Pr. (opp. sign)	PLANT B Regr. Coeff.	PLANT B Pr. (opp. sign)	PLANT C Regr. Coeff.	PLANT C Pr. (opp. sign)	PLANT D Regr. Coeff.	PLANT D Pr. (opp. sign)
1.	Constant term	.1713	.014	−1.615	.000	−3.621	.000	−2.273	.010
2a.	Month from start up of plant	−.001629	.025						
b.	Log (cumulative production)			.08345	.000	.2225	.000	.1627	.005
3.	Log (capacity utilization)	.1640	.013	.3131	.000	.4436	.001	.7782	.000
4.	WIP/total cost of production (5 mo. avg.)	−.09071	.112	−.06199	.000	−.2993	.000	—	—
5.	Absenteeism (as % of work force)	−.01044	.152	—	—	—	—	—	—
6.	Grievances filed per worker (5 mo. avg.)	−48.14	.178	—	—	—	—	—	—
7.	New plant and equipment (as % of existing P&E)	−1.360	.123	−.1713	.325	.1253	.410	−1.493	.028
8.	Changes in monthly production (5 mo. avg. abs. deviation)	−.2200	.098	.03604	.351	.2881	.000	.2517	.249
9.	Overtime hours per worker (during month)	.004430	.006	−.002144	.006	−.002174	.219	−.005460	.031
10.	Overtime hours per worker (2 mo. avg.)	−.006403	.007	.001558	.121	.001951	.323	.006453	.082
11.	Engineering Change Orders implemented	−.001862	.087	.002478	.011	−.01158	.062	—	—
R^2		.653		.896		.877		.617	

back-up materials in case the expected amount of good output is not produced). Similarly, work-in-process inventory is both the result of disruptions (confusion) in the plant and the cause of confusion in itself. One of the most important tasks of factory management, it appears from this data, is to prevent confusion and/or to mitigate the potentially damaging effects of confusion-causing activities. We need to explore how these confusion effects can be managed more effectively.

It is unlikely, however, that this can be done adequately just by observing normal plant operating behavior. At some point some simple experiments probably need to be conducted within an actual factory setting. This will not be easy, of course, because factories like to stay within rather rigid operating ranges—both because of their internal technologies and their external reporting and control systems—and they are expected to be continuously profitable. But there is an unprecedented amount of experimentation going on today in American factories, so perhaps the time is right to begin preparing for this eventual stage in our research.

Little mention has been made in this paper about all the things we have learned informally about factory behavior in conducting this study, or about the problems involved in collecting data from them.

Nor have we passed along all the vignettes that were related to us in the course of exploring some of the patterns observed in our data. These often illuminated and broadened our understanding of factory management more than the tedious data-grinding that triggered them.

In the process of collecting and analyzing these data, we have gained a deep appreciation of the remarkable complexity of factory management. While acknowledging the enormous problems that must be overcome in using formal statistical procedures to study them, we would like to encourage others to extend and test our findings through their own field studies. Getting into factories and studying their behavior first hand is important for the same reason Willy Sutton robbed banks: "That's where the money is."

Notes

1. Another approach, the so-called Divisia method, would have constrained us to working only with rates of growth of productivity. Experimentation with all three alternative weighting schemes suggests that our conclusions are little affected by our decision to adopt the Paasche approach.
2. This makes the implicit assumption that any changes in the quality of a product will be reflected in its standard cost.
3. Robert Kaplan expands on this issue in chapter 5.
4. The measurement used was the intercept (B_0) of the basic equation:

$$\text{Log (TFP)} = B_0 + B_1 \log (\text{cum. output}) + B_2 \log (\text{cap. util.}).$$

The smaller (or more negative) the value of B_0, the lower the TFP when cumulative output is small.

Appendix

As described in the text, most of the results reported in this chapter were obtained through longitudinal analyses: trying to relate changes in managerial policies over time to changes in a factory's TFP. In modelling these relationships we decided that they were more likely to be nonlinear than linear, and multiplicative rather than additive (which implies that a particularly disasterous policy affecting one aspect of the factory's operation—its quality policies, say—would have repercussions throughout the organization that could not be erased by outstanding performance in other dimensions).

More formally, we hypothesized the following functional relationship between TFP and the set of independent variables $[X_1, X_2, \ldots X_k]$ representing various factory characteristics or management policies (these X_j may vary depending on the issue under examination and the factory involved):

$$\text{TFP } (i,n) = \exp \{ \beta_0 + \beta_1 X_{1,i,n} + \ldots + \beta_k X_{k,i,n} + e_{i,n} \}.$$

Taking logarithms of both sides resulted in the equation that we examined statistically, using multiple regression analysis:

$$\text{LOG } [\text{TFP}(i,n)] = \beta_0 + \beta_1 X_{1,i,n} + \ldots + \beta_k X_{k,i,n} + e_{i,n},$$

with the error term $e_{i,n}$ governed by the usual assumptions.

The regression coefficients β_i resulting from this analysis therefore depict the estimated effect on TFP of changes in their respective X_j variables, assuming all other X variables stay the same. The errors, $e_{i,n}$, represent the differences between the observed values of TFP and the values estimated by applying the estimated β_i to the observed values of the variables. The value R^2 that is reported in connection with each of the analyses measures the explanatory power of the X_j variables: If they have no detectable relationship with the values of TFP, the variance of the estimated error terms will be equal to the variance of the observed values of TFP and R^2 will be 0. If, on the other hand, the values of TFP estimated through the regression equation are exactly equal to the observed values (all $e_{i,n} = 0$), then $R^2 = 1.0$.

References

Abernathy, William J., Kim B. Clark, and Alan M. Kantrow. *Industrial Renaissance*. New York: Basic Books, 1983.

Cook, Randall L., and Roger W. Schmenner. "Explaining Productivity Differences in North Carolina Factories." Paper, Fuqua School of Business, Duke University, September 1983.

Davidson, William. "Patterns of Factor-Saving Innovation in the Industrialized World," *European Economic Review* 8 (1976): 207–17.

Dogramaci, Ali, and Nabil R. Adam, eds. *Aggregate and Industry-Level Productivity Analysis*. Vol. 2, Studies in Productivity Analysis. Hingham, Mass.: Martinus Nijhoff, 1981.

Hayes, Robert H., and William J. Abernathy. "Managing Our Way to Economic Decline." *Harvard Business Review,* July-August 1980, 67–77.

Hayes, Robert H., and Steven C. Wheelwright. "Link Manufacturing Process and Product Life Cycles." *Harvard Business Review,* January-February 1979, 133–40.

Hirschman, Albert. *The Strategy of Economic Development*. Ch. 8. New Haven, Conn.: Yale University Press, 1958.

Ichniowski, Bernard E. *How do Labor Relations Matter? A Study of Productivity in Eleven Manufacturing Plants*. Doctoral dissertation, M.I.T., 1983.

Katz, H., T. Kochan, and K. Gobeille. "Industrial Relations Performance, Economic Performance and QWL Programs: An Interplant Analysis." *Industrial and Labor Relations Review,* October 1983, 3–17.

Kendrick, John W., and Beatrice N. Vaccara, eds. *New Developments in Productivity Measurement and Analysis.* Chicago: University of Chicago Press, 1975.

Nelson, Richard R. "Research on Productivity Growth and Productivity Differences: Dead Ends and New Departures." *Journal of Economic Literature* 29 (September 1981): 1029–64.

Skinner, Wickham. "The Focused Factory." *Harvard Business Review.* May-June 1974, 113–21.

Commentary
The Micro Approach to Productivity Analysis

Robert B. McKersie

Introduction

The chapter by Hayes and Clark and their associates represents a pioneering venture into the uncharted territory of understanding the dynamics of productivity at the factory level. Now that they have collected mounds of data from twelve plants (of three companies), they liken their analysis to that of an archaeologist who has cut the initial trench through the material—and even this preliminary pass has produced "pay dirt." There is certainly considerable sifting and sorting of the material still to take place. But this project is on to something.

Contribution of This Study

The strength of the project is that they have assembled an extremely rich data set of all the activities, on a month-to-month basis, that might explain variations in productivity at the plant level. No other studies come close (even the work by Casey Ichniowski of MIT does not track information for as wide an array of variables as the present effort). It is clear that managers find this data descriptively accurate and in many ways a better measure of what is going on than normal accounting and control systems.

Ultimately, as the research team analyzes this information more fully, it should be possible to develop guidelines, trade-off numbers— or what more sophisticated analysts would call algorithms—about the various decisions that have to be taken on a regular basis at the factory level. For example, this research work is beginning to shed light on the impact of change in the production process via the institution of en-

I have benefited from discussing this paper with two colleagues: Casey Ichniowski and Harry Katz.

gineering change orders (ECO). With more knowledge about their impact, it ought to be possible for the well-informed manager to know how frequently to institute such changes and also what magnitude of disruption to impose upon the system. The point is that change has to take place, but that a high degree of "choice" is available in how to plan and stage change.

One way to view the role of factory management is as the juggler of a series of inputs or what could be called the elements of the production function. A more thorough analysis of their interactions and their response to key events should enable the process to move more in the direction of a science than an art.

It is not possible here to summarize all of the "yield" that this project has already produced. But some of the particularly interesting findings are the following:

- Managers have not paid sufficient attention to the careful utilization of materials. Given the fact that reduction in the use of materials represents a "win-win" for the organization (since improvement in productivity due to this factor does not reduce the demand for employees), I think this point has considerable appeal and power.
- The manner in which plants within the same company performing similar operations learn from one another is extremely significant: They appear to stand on the performance (or shoulders) of the predecessor in setting up the plant, but once they are launched, competition (to the extent of not sharing process knowledge) seems to take over.
- The concept of confusion and variability caused by different products and engineering change orders is a very fruitful direction for research and represents a major new way of thinking about productivity. We have had helpful concepts in the past, such as the learning curve and capital-labor ratio; we need some way to organize our thinking with respect to continuity and change, so as to understand what is probably the biggest current challenge to productivity improvement.
- The finding that a greater incidence of grievances is associated with lower productivity is significant and parallels the work of some of the researchers in the Industrial Relations Section at MIT.
- The finding about overtime is intuitively plausible: A little is positively related to productivity, but a larger amount leads to a lower level of productivity.

Limitations of the Study

Since the emphasis is on the analysis of month-by-month data for plants already under way, we have much information about *tactics* but not very much about how different *strategic* alternatives have a differential impact on productivity. It appears to be the case that events such as training, maintenance, and the introduction of modifications in equipment all have a negative impact on productivity. But this does not necessarily reconcile with the other point that when a new plant is being established it learns from the experiences and mistakes of existing plants and starts up with substantially more training and better equipment—and as a result enters the learning curve at a higher starting point. Some of the big productivity payoffs probably can be realized from major changes in factory system design, but it is not possible to observe those possibilities on a month-by-month basis within the confines of a plant.

Suggestions for Further Analysis

If a way can be found to standardize the data so that it is comparable across companies, then there might be some analysis to be performed by running regressions for all of the plants in question. I would suggest the use of a productivity *change* variable on the left side of the equation. This would represent a type of index number where for each plant for each month there would be a determination of whether the productivity went up or down, and by what relative amount. The inputs would also have to be normalized, and I am not sure about all of the adjustments that would be involved in this undertaking. But in any event, if that could be done, then the questions about training, maintenance, overtime, grievances—and all of the "windows" that the researchers use for understanding the productivity process—could be examined with a much more comprehensive data set.

A very specific suggestion entails the use of *anticipation* variables as well as lag variables. For example, the relationship between change and work force may be felt a month or two before the actual layoff occurs because of the deadening effect that comes after an announcement about a possible layoff (or at least when workers expect cutbacks); and also because in the month or two before the actual layoff there may be more people than are needed for the production that is required that month.

It would also be helpful to explore the relationship of organizational and industrial relations variables to productivity more thoroughly. In some analysis of plant level data in the auto industry, Katz, Kochan, and Goheille have found that such indicators as absenteeism, grievances, contract demands, and attitudes explain about 30 percent of the variation in productivity.[1]

Additional Conceptualization

As mentioned earlier, some new conceptual categories would help the analysis of this tremendous body of data. The research team makes considerable use of the concept of the learning curve and this is especially useful for understanding the unfolding of productivity in the high tech company. But more can be learned about the interactions of the learning curve with other variables, such as training. Is the learning curve just some inexorable trend line, or is it something that happens only because management finds a way to stimulate, induce, or coerce the organization through the various barriers and problems that are involved in bringing an operation up to normal operating levels? In such a situation, training and development of on-the-job know-how must be intimately involved, and there ought to be a way to better understand this process.

Also, the learning curve way of thinking would be helpful in understanding the impact of such "step-down" events as the institution of an engineering change order, minor maintenance, and the arrival of a new piece of equipment. It is puzzling that in the data set thus far collected the recovery is not as evident as the decline in productivity. But over some period of time there must be a gaining back or movement up the minilearning curve.

Another important conceptual area is that of work-in-process as captured by the much discussed innovation of *kanban,* or in American terms "just in time." The paper does not present any elaboration as to why a reduction in work-in-process inventory should have an improvement on the productivity of the operation. More work needs to take place in this direction.

Also, the authors have not handled this point as carefully as possible. They have not built into productivity for a given month the output that is partially produced in the form of work-in-process. The connection between reducing work-in-process in a particular month and showing a better productivity result is what might almost be called a matter of simple arithmetic, because the "pipeline" was emptied to some extent giving a bigger credit on the output side of the process.

The importance of conceptualizing the authors' interest in confusion should again be emphasized. Increasing attention is being paid these days to flexible manufacturing, and to making it possible for a given lineup of plant and equipment to handle a variety of products and product modifications. These new approaches can be viewed as efforts to deal with the need for variety, while at the same time achieving smooth running operations and continuity.

Implications for Management

Management in two of the companies, the process and fab/assembly operations, is similar to what we used to call "management by exception." The way to think of productivity in these two situations is that of a ship that has been set on its course and the orders are "steady as she goes." Productivity declines, however, seem to arise from unexpected problems that require quick training or quick maintenance. Whether these negative events could be anticipated or even prevented by a different form of work organization (for example, through teams and much more participation by all members of the organization), is something worth thinking about; it also relates to some of the other subjects discussed in this book.

The management process involved in the high tech firm is a different type of activity, and I am not sure we have a good way to accurately depict this process.

When one turns to the challenging question of getting plants that both compete and collaborate with one another (because they produce similar products, yet compete for limited resources) to develop what Eric Trist would call a "learning system," then we are touching some interesting questions that face corporate management. The answer does not necessarily rest in the form of financial incentives wherein one plant literally licenses its ideas to another. Here again the answer is in social innovations that create the openness and participation across levels of middle and upper management of the sort that we now see with increasing frequency on the factory floor.

Additional Work

I am reluctant to suggest any additional information that might be collected, but the analysis could be turned around to examine some of the events that represent the "exceptions" such as absenteeism and the need for training. Using these as the dependent variable would help understand how these events can be predicted, anticipated, and solved from the viewpoint of the factory as an operating system.

Returning to the Macro

The authors start the chapter with the analysis that appears at the beginning of most papers these days on productivity—specifically, we have had a long-term secular decline in the rate of productivity improvement in this country. It is still not clear what the relationship is between productivity at the factory level and what has been going on in the aggregate statistics. I would like to end with this statement, and the belief that the approach these authors have chosen is as likely as any to illuminate this connection.

Note

[1]Harry C. Katz, Thomas A. Kochan and Kenneth R. Goheille, "Industrial Relations Performance, Economic Performance, and QWL Programs: An Interplant Analysis," *Industrial and Labor Relations Review* 37, no. 1 (October 1983): 3–17.

5

Accounting Lag: The Obsolescence of Cost Accounting Systems

Robert S. Kaplan

Historical Perspective

The revolution now under way in the operations of industrial enterprises is of potentially comparable scope and impact to the radical changes that occurred on the U.S. industrial scene in the first decade of this century, and that have affected the practice of management and management accounting ever since.

The period between 1900 and 1910 marked the consolidation of the great industrial enterprises that had emerged in the period after the Civil War.[1] Perhaps the best example of this movement was the 1901 formation, from the nation's three largest steel corporations, of U.S. Steel, the world's first billion-dollar corporation. The largest of the three merging companies was the extraordinarily successful firm owned and managed by Andrew Carnegie whose management philosophy of efficiency and innovation admirably foreshadows the "productivity and technology" title of this book. Carnegie was renowned for his overriding concern to reduce operating costs, which was achieved by, among other means, investing in the latest technology even if this required him to scrap plants less than ten years old. Like similarly inclined managers in Japan almost a century later, Carnegie understood the powerful competitive advantage that accrues to the most efficient producer. Unfortunately, the aggressive entrepreneurial spirit of Andrew Carnegie did not persist among subsequent leaders of the giant steel enterprises so that U.S. technological and productivity leadership was eventually lost to foreign and small domestic competitors.

The first decade of this century also marked the birth of the U.S. automobile industry. In 1908, a high-water mark of about 250 U.S. companies were producing automobiles; even at that time, however, 50 percent of production was concentrated in just three corporations: Ford, General Motors, and the ancestor of the Studebaker Corporation. Ford, in that same year of 1908, introduced the low-priced Model T and, five years later, transformed the industry with the first moving assembly line. The assembly line made possible a great expansion in the number of cars that could be produced, large reductions in the price of cars to expand enormously the market for this product, and a significant increase in the wages that could be paid to attract skilled workers to the assembly-line production process.

The emergence in the early 1900s of the giant steel and automobile companies, plus the growth of corporations in complementary industries to supply these enterprises, provided the motivation and proving grounds for the scientific management movement. The twentieth century marked the development of mass-production enterprises where great efficiencies were achieved through vertical integration and highly specialized machines, processes, and labor. The scientific management movement brought engineers in close contact with the operations of these mass-production enterprises to study how all aspects of the manufacturing process could be made more efficient. Particular attention was devoted to improving the efficiency and productivity of labor in these processes. The writings of Frederick Taylor, Harrington Emerson, A. Hamilton Church, Henry Towne, Henry Gantt, and many others of the scientific management school were appearing at the time of the founding of the Harvard Business School in 1908, and their influence remains strong today. For example, the standard cost model was developed as a natural outgrowth of setting standards for labor and materials utilization by scientific studies of time and output. The standard cost model remains a primary influence on the cost accounting systems of most of today's corporations. As we examine contemporary cost accounting practices in subsequent sections of this chapter, it will be important to recall the origin of these practices in the drive for direct labor and material efficiencies in the mass-production enterprises that were emerging seventy-five years ago.

The final strand in this historical tale can be traced to the organizational innovations of the Du Pont Powder Company, formed in 1903 by consolidating family-owned and other small, family-run firms. The transformation from small, single-activity firms into a large, vertically integrated, multiactivity corporation required new organizational forms and new measures to motivate and evaluate the performance of decentralized operating units. The Du Pont innovations have been chronicled extensively elsewhere.[2] For the purposes of this chapter, the principal legacy was the development of the return on investment measure to serve both as an indicator of the efficiency of diverse operating departments and as a measure of the financial performance of the entire company. While ROI is now ingrained (too firmly, perhaps) as the premier divisional performance criteria, the measures used prior to Du Pont's ROI innovation were profits as a percentage of sales or over costs. One additional financial innovation at Du Pont that has been adopted by virtually all modern corporations was a formal periodic process for operating and capital budgets.[3]

In summary, a keen and far-sighted observer in 1908 would have seen the harbingers and rudiments of virtually all the accounting and financial control practices used by today's industrial corporations. The practices of seventy-five years past have obviously served well the great organizations in existence at the start of this century that prospered and grew for many subsequent decades. Our challenge in the mid-1980s is to take a fresh look at the industrial landscape to see how the changing circumstances compel us to consider modifications and innovations in the accounting and control practices so rooted in the mass-production enterprises of the early twentieth century.

The Modern Industrial Scene and Its Accounting Environment

The vigorous global industrial competition of the 1980s has brought the importance of effective and efficient manufacturing operations to the attention of senior executives. Unlike the environment of the past seventy-five years, however, the factors critical to the success of manufacturing today have little to do with improving the efficiency of direct labor through highly specialized job assignments, working in conjunction with product-specific machinery. Rather, the factors critical to success today center around knowledge; knowing how to produce high-quality products efficiently for rapidly changing consumer demands. The specific requirements to be a world-class manufacturer in the 1980s include:

1. High-quality output: Design quality into products rather than reworking failed items after inspection or repairing defects at the customer's site. Zero-defect goals are established for suppliers and for internal production. Preventive maintenance of equipment is emphasized rather than equipment repair during unscheduled downtimes. Equipment is operated well within design specifications. Design and manufacturability of new products are developed simultaneously to avoid products that cannot be reliably produced.

2. Minimum inventory: Reduce setup times to avoid large batch sizes, implement just-in-time production and just-in-time delivery systems, reduce travel distance and transit time of products in the factory, eliminate safety stocks caused by uncertain quality and delivery from previous stages. Once a product is started into production, keep it moving continually through the factory until completed.

3. Manufacturing technology: Expand the use of computer-integrated manufacturing equipment including robotics, CAD/CAM, and flexible manufacturing systems. Use this technology to enhance flexibility, increase quality, and reduce inventory. The goal is to make small-batch manufacturing as efficient as mass production.

4. Work force management policies: Transform adversarial labor relationships into cooperative, company goal-oriented activities through quality circles, job security, reduced labor classifications, elimination of restrictive work rules, more flexible and comprehensive job assignments, and bonuses and incentives for enhanced productivity.

5. New product development: Reduce time to launch new product from conception in R&D laboratory to commercial introduction. Be able to deliver a product, on schedule, that will work as specified in customer's location and to modify product design after early trials.

6. Worldwide sourcing: Exploit capabilities for mass production of standardized parts in low-cost facilities. Understand marginal cost of production at each site and cost center to facilitate correct make versus buy decisions.

The personnel who make success possible along these dimensions are information workers not traditional blue-collar workers. Firms will need to effectively and efficiently mobilize their technical and managerial personnel—those involved in research, development, testing, product design, industrial and manufacturing engineering; systems programming, computer operations, equipment maintenance, and manufacturing supervision and management. The value added by "blue-collar workers" who actually perform the work may be greater from suggestions for process improvements on the factory floor than from the actual performance of assigned tasks.

Many corporations are making such major changes in their manufacturing operations. Without doubt, much of the impetus for this renewed interest in manufacturing strategy arose from observing the successful innovations of leading Japanese corporations. But the U.S. companies are not simply copying examples established by Japanese manufacturers; they are attempting to implement new practices that will work in the U.S. environment.

But implementing major changes in manufacturing operations in U.S. companies occurs in an environment of extensive financial controls. The cost accounting legacies of the scientific management movement and the management control procedures introduced by 1925 in the Du Pont and General Motors corporations have become the primary information source for budgeting, planning, and evaluating the operations of decentralized operating units. In addition, the cost accounting and management control practices of contemporary U.S. corporations are increasingly being determined by procedures adopted or mandated for external reporting purposes. Thus, decisions on recognition of R&D expenses, lease capitalization, pension cost accruals, interest on capital, and depreciation methods are made to satisfy external constituencies rather than to produce information that will be relevant for management decisions and managerial control.

Against this background, we have now arrived at the central issue of this chapter. Given the rapid changes occurring in the organization and technology of manufacturing operations, what related changes are occurring or need to occur in the firm's cost accounting and management control systems? Are the procedures developed for enterprises seventy-five years ago, as modified to reflect the increased regulation of external financial disclosure, going to be adequate in the new manufacturing environment?

In a recent series of papers (Kaplan 1983, 1984a, 1984b), I have argued that existing cost accounting and management control practices are unlikely to provide useful indicators for managing the firm's manufacturing operations. In particular, traditional cost measurement systems will imperfectly reflect, and with considerable lags at best, the dramatic increase in manufacturing efficiency and effectiveness that occurs when firms achieve total quality control, zero work-in-process (WIP) inventory systems, and enhanced work force capabilities. No system of which I am aware captures the benefits from short product launch times or from the flexibility afforded from computer-controlled production systems. Further, short-term profitability indicators do not signal the decrease in the value of the firm when firms reduce their discretionary expenditures for developing new products, for improving production processes, for maintaining the skill, loyalty, and morale of the work force, for expanding distribution networks and customer awareness, for developing improved software for production and information systems, and for maintaining and improving their physical capital resources. Quite the contrary, the existing financial accounting systems signal short-term increases in accounting profits when firms decrease their economic wealth by foregoing investments in their long-term information and productive capital.

Goals of the Research Study

In an attempt to learn how firms are modifying their accounting and control systems to help them manage in the new manufacturing environment, I visited a select set of innovative firms. These firms were not chosen at random. They were selected to be representative of those U.S. industrial corporations that seemed determined to survive and prosper in the new industrial competition. Thus, they were either leaders in high technology growth industries or firms in mature industries that were actively promoting productivity and new manufacturing technologies in order to be globally competitive. The goal of the study was to learn from innovative firms what changes were being made in their accounting, measurement, and control systems to support the current emphasis on new product and manufacturing technologies.

The study was not approached with a formal research design nor with a set of specific hypotheses to be tested. Our current paucity of knowledge of the accounting and control systems used by innovative firms precludes such a well-structured mode of inquiry. The broad agenda for this initial investigation, encompassing modifications in traditional cost accounting systems, nonfinancial measures of manufacturing performance, and an expanded set of short-term performance indicators for decentralized cost and profit centers, suggested a wide-ranging look at contemporary practices.

To anticipate the findings and conclusions of this preliminary investigation, I found there were many unexploited opportunities to improve the links between firms' measurement systems and their innovations in product technology and manufacturing processes. While it was obvious that each of the firms visited was making significant changes in its manufacturing strategy, it seemed equally clear that comparable changes were not being made in its accounting and control systems. Some may argue that the accounting and control procedures developed seventy-five years ago are robust enough to still be useful in today's radically changed manufacturing environment. Therefore, a discovery of little innovation in contemporary accounting and control systems would be consistent with firms' having made appropriate choices for their information systems. Based on my observations and discussions with senior financial and operating executives, I do not share such a complacent or sanguine view of the current state of managerial accounting systems in U.S. industrial firms. I will attempt to convey to the reader the basis for my conclusions by describing the situations in the firms I visited. To offer candid observations and appraisals of the accounting systems of organizations that I (and many other observers) consider to be among the best managed and most successful U.S. corporations, anonymity has been preserved by referring to companies by coded initials.

Company Experiences: Company V

Company V is a broadly based manufacturer of electrical products and equipment. The corporatewide commitment to improve productivity and product quality was underscored in the 1982 annual report by the Chairman's Stockholder Letter and ten subsequent pages of pictures and text. I examined a division that had recently (in autumn 1982) implemented a major change in its organization of manufacturing operations. The division builds electrical propulsion units for mass transit vehicles. A given propulsion unit could contain between 5,000 and 10,000 different parts. The division has a high percentage of white-collar employees, especially engineers who custom design the units and who are responsible for installation and service of finished units. The production process is predominantly assembly operations and increasingly is using automated equipment.

Under the old production procedures, raw material and work-in-process inventories were stacked on the floor near each work station. Workers were kept busy on a production run until they ran out of operative parts or subassemblies. Partially assembled units, whose production was interrupted because of a faulty or missing part, were stored around the work station until a new part could be delivered and the worker able to start working again on that unit. A local operating rule was to attempt to keep all workers busy at their work stations even if this led to subassemblies being produced well before they could be processed or assembled at the subsequent stages.

Costs were accumulated on a total project basis, where a typical project produced between thirty and fifty identical units. Factory costs were allocated based on net allowed hours, a projection of the total direct labor hours to be worked in the factory during the year. In 1982 this produced a shop labor rate of about $36 per hour of which only 25 percent represented actual direct labor costs. In 1983 the shop labor rate had escalated to more than $50 per direct labor hour; less than 20 percent of this amount represented direct labor costs. The increase in the shop labor rate was caused by a significant reduction in estimated net allowed hours because of increased efficiencies from the new organization of manufacturing (to be described shortly), increased usage of automated equipment, and the higher overhead costs to accumulate and distribute information that enhanced manufacturing efficiencies. Engineering charges were accumulated and allocated to contracts separately. These charges were actually billed at lower rates than the current shop labor rate because of the cost allocation procedure that levied all factory overhead costs onto direct labor.

The division moved to a new organization of manufacturing because it had been steadily losing money for the prior decade. When bidding on jobs, all labor and overhead costs were forecast for the proposed job, and reduced to a cost per estimated labor hour figure. The full cost per-hour figure was then multiplied by the total labor hours for the project, escalated for anticipated inflation and marked up for a planned profit percentage. This procedure of marking up and escalating estimated full costs per hour, at a time when business was contracting, led to high, noncompetitive bids that won few orders. Eventually, the division had slashed cost markups to win new business so that it could maintain an experienced, skilled work force. The division hoped to cut costs below its estimates while working on contracts.

The new concept of manufacturing was explicitly designed to make this division more competitive. A commitment of several million dollars for computer-controlled equipment was made (without formal benefit-cost analysis such as discounted cash flow). An additional major investment was to reeducate and retrain workers, supervisors, managers, and engineers in a new way of conducting business.

The goal of the new system was to have work flow through the assembly process in a smooth, predictable fashion. The new flow process started with 100 percent inspection of purchased items with batches returned to the vendor if any defects were found. The formerly omnipresent (mostly underfoot) raw materials and work-in-process inventories were replaced by limited access, computer-controlled inventory storage locations. Subassemblies were scheduled for production only when they would be needed by a subsequent stage of assembly. Also, work on a subassembly or assembly was not initiated until availability of 100 percent good material was assured. Thus, items were built only as needed, not to keep production workers busy. Inventory was kept in the lowest value state as long as possible. Temporarily idle workers were assigned to other tasks.

A further innovation was a commitment to a model shop where three to five complete prototype units were to be built, tested, and approved before drawings would be released for shop floor production. In this way, design and manufacturing problems would surface early, and efficient manufacturing procedures would be implemented even for the early production runs. Previously, problems and procedures were worked out on the shop floor based on experience in actual assembly and test of finished items. While this trial-and-error approach produced a lovely learning curve over the life of a contract, it led to highly inefficient production for the first batches of units. By developing efficient manufacturing procedures in a model shop and videotaping actual assembly techniques to train factory workers, the efficiencies previously learned toward the end of a production run could now be realized much earlier.

This situation seemed to provide an ideal setting to study the benefits from changing the organization of manufacturing operations. The division had recently won a follow-up order from a customer so that it would be producing a batch of propulsion units in the "new" factory that was identical to a batch produced under the old, traditional manufacturing procedures. A certain degree of care would need to be exercised to control for experience curve effects during production of the first batch of units, differences in quantity discounts from suppliers between the two orders, and changes in price levels since the first batch of units were built. But in principle, these complications could be overcome, and it was hoped that increases in productivity, reductions in WIP, production defects, rework, and scrap, and shortened throughput times would occur and could be documented. Such evidence would provide quantitative measures of the benefits from the new organization of manufacturing, and the returns from the company's investment in the new technology and in training and reeducation costs.

Unfortunately, it proved impossible to perform such a study. The accounting system had been designed to accumulate total project costs, not to measure production efficiencies. The system accumulated detailed product costs, using many subclassifications, on a monthly and contract-to-date basis. But with the exception of direct labor hours, no physical amounts were recorded. Thus, there was no record of the quantity of materials consumed during each month nor the amount of indirect and supervisory labor, and most devastating of all (for the proposed study), no figures on the amount of actual production during the month. Thus, there was no obvious way to relate inventory levels or quantities of labor and materials consumed to quantities of items produced each period. Discussions were held with program managers and production control supervisors to see whether production quantities could be obtained from a production information system, but they did not have this information either.

During the course of these discussions, it became clear to me that not only would it be impossible to reconstruct the unit cost of items produced in the past, but also there would be no way to compute productivity measures or unit costs for items currently being produced using the new manufacturing philosophy. The computer-based cost accounting system was well designed to capture all costs on a total project basis but was too inflexible to be modified to produce unit cost and productivity measurements in the new manufacturing environment.[4]

The senior managers of the division were convinced that significant benefits would be produced from the new organization of manufacturing. Some of these were obvious by inspection. For example, floor space savings up to 50 percent were achieved by eliminating the storage of raw material and work-in-process on the factory floor and at each work station. The division was planning to move the production facilities of a nearby factory into the large space freed up in the redesigned factory. This space became available even after reserving room for the new model shop. But until the division installed a new cost accumulation system, it would not be possible to quantify the benefits from lower defect production, reductions in inventory, and a more orderly flow of production through the assembly process. We see here a theme that will unfortunately be repeated in most of our sites. Firms are implementing imaginative and innovative changes in their manufacturing operations, but continuing to measure and evaluate the performance of these operations using accounting systems from earlier eras.

Company Experiences: Company N

Company N is a leading producer of specialized products for the lumber industry and a manufacturer of diverse products for outdoorspeople and "do-it-yourself" enthusiasts. The company's products are mature and competition takes place along quality, performance, and price dimensions. The company has a long history of emphasizing productivity and performance but a real impetus for change occurred when a senior operating officer made a trip to Japan several years ago. The executive, who had extensive experience in manufacturing operations, reported:

> In October of 1981, I joined twelve other American executives on a trip to Japan. Our mission was to study the reasons for Japan's remarkable achievements. We visited twelve large Japanese manufacturing plants

and spent a full day in each. We discussed management philosophy with the Japanese managers and toured the plants to see their methods of operation. As a result of what I saw on that trip, I very quickly lowered my assessment of our own company's performance in the area of human resource management. I quite suddenly lost my complacency about our invincibility as a manufacturer. Quite frankly, I received a shock when I saw how advanced the Japanese were at managing their people and in their manufacturing methods.

Company N promptly organized a team to study in-depth what would be required to implement Japanese manufacturing concepts in a U.S. environment. By summer 1982, senior executives had articulated a new statement of philosophy for the company that built upon the strong value system already in existence, expanded the company's commitment to people involvement and quality, and articulated a major new thrust to achieve a Just-in-Time Inventory System (JIT). A companywide education and planning program to implement JIT occurred in autumn 1982, and by May 1983, a week-long conference involving worldwide production personnel, and divisional and corporate management, was held to evaluate progress.

Obviously, with less than half a year of effort the progress reported at the conference represented only a fraction of what ultimately will be realized, but the results were still strikingly impressive. The vice president and controller, who organized the conference reported:

> In our _____ Project, inventory is down 92 percent, scrap and rework down 20 percent. In the manufacture of _____ kits, lead times were cut from two weeks to one day. In changing the presses for manufacturing _____, die change time was cut from two and one-half hours to two and one-half minutes. In the manufacture of _____ products, lot sizes were cut from 500 to 30, inventory was reduced by 50 percent and lead times were shortened from six weeks to two days, making possible a make-to-order business.
>
> The award-winning plant had a small but beautiful project. By value analysis, they cut the number of models of handles from 11 to 2. Lead time was cut from 30 days to a few minutes and they now make to order. Work-in-process was reduced from a 40-piece average to one. An amazing feature was that travel distance was cut from 2,000 feet to 18 inches.

Summary data from the conference showed that in five months, inventory was reduced 31 percent, from 194 to 134 days of sales. (Four months later, on 30 September 1983, inventory had been reduced further to 116 days of sales.) Lead times had been reduced from about five weeks to less than five days. *Table 5-1* shows the reduction in set-up time to exchange dies for various products or locations.

The goal was to achieve Single-Minute Exchange of Dies (that is, less than ten minutes) throughout the organization, a goal that had been realized already by many of the locations noted in *Table 5-1*.

Table 5-1
Reduction in Die Exchange Time

Location/Product Type	Exchange Time (12/31/82)	Exchange Time (5/31/83)
1	83 minutes	53 minutes
2	378	162
3	20	.02
4	150	2.5
5	165	.5
6	360	1.7
7	43	17
8	8	2
9	240	10
10	60	20

A tour of a metal fabrication and machining division provided a graphic picture of the improvements that were accomplished within one year of adopting the JIT manufacturing goals. In one welding operation, the substitution of microprocessor-controlled, general-purpose welding machine for a manually operated one had reduced set-up times from three hours to several minutes. This permitted a reduction in lot size from 10,000 to 250 units. With smaller batch sizes throughout the plant, items were moving continually from one stage to the next rather than lying around for a week or more waiting for a large block of time to be freed up on the next machine.

The continual flow of small batches through the factory not only greatly reduced inventory and space requirements but also permitted a large increase in quality. Previously, if a machine or the material being fed to the machine was not in conformance with specifications, an entire batch of 10,000 items could be defective. These defects would be detected at subsequent stages of processing, frequently a week or more later. Engineers would then have to be assigned to salvage the large batch of defective items, either devising some new product that could use these items or conceiving of a rework program to bring the defective items back into specifications. When production shifted to continuous processing of small batches, nonconforming items were detected much sooner and the problem was remedied immediately. Engineers, no longer having to devise schemes to salvage tens of thousands of defective items, could devote all their time to process improvements, thereby producing even greater savings in the near future.

Space savings were enormous. By rearranging machines, moving to Just-in-Time production within the factory, and working with suppliers to deliver in smaller lots, more frequently, and directly to the factory floor, savings in floor space up to 50 percent had been achieved. Formerly, this division anticipated building a new plant in the near future. With the space savings already achieved and anticipated for the future, the division management was confident that a new plant would not be needed before 1988. Travel distance of an item going in and out of inventory, and from one process to the next, had been reduced from three miles to about 100 yards.

The labor savings from these production improvements had also been significant. The company was operating with a no-layoff policy to encourage an active flow of suggestions from the factory workers. In the short run, labor savings were captured by eliminating all temporary jobs, plus the normal attrition of 1.5 percent per month. With the extra space, machine time, and permanent labor time now available from the early success of the JIT program, pressures were building on the R&D program to develop new products that could be produced with the new capacity the division had created through its manufacturing efficiencies.

One more sign of the benefits from the JIT program was the reduction in order lead times from six weeks to less than one week even during a period of increasing sales. Throughput time for some products, measured from the time a batch of units was started into production until the units were ready for shipment had been reduced from four weeks to one shift (eight hours). This increase in order responsiveness was viewed by management as developing a significant marketing advantage for the division.

Accounting System for Company N

The response of the firm's accounting and measurement system had yet to be modified to reflect the new organization and technology of manufacturing. At the large division whose production operations I just described, a traditional standard process costing system was still being used. Production variances were computed at an aggregate plant level so that the significant cost savings achieved by particular products in the plant could not be highlighted. The system itself seemed inconsistent with the major changes occurring in the factory.

For one process I examined (chosen at random), detailed standards were being maintained for each of a sequence of labor procedures. None of these separate procedures existed any longer. They had been combined into a single process that was now being performed by a machine. Thus, in many ways, the highly detailed and complex standard cost system was no longer representative of the simplified production process one could easily observe by walking through the factory.

As another indication of the lack of reality of the standard cost system, standard labor times for each process step were calculated to five significant digits even though factories would be considered operating well within control if labor times were within 1 percent of standard. The ability of industrial engineers to estimate labor standards accurately to within .001 of 1 percent is probably one of the arcane secrets of the profession. Finally, no measures of quality improvements had been developed for reporting systematically to higher levels of management.

To be fair, however, a general awareness existed of the value of supplementing the firm's accounting and control system. Efforts were under way to compute partial productivity indicators such as units produced and value added per labor hour, days' sales in inventory, and throughput time per product. To motivate the efficient use of physical resources, cost centers were allowed to "sell" space and equipment that was no longer needed back to the corporation. These departments were credited for such savings even if they had not yet been realized by the corporation. Manufacturing managers were developing new evaluation criteria based on the percentage of on-time deliveries each month and reductions in lead time rather than the traditional measures of production rates and machine utilization. Cost analysts were attempting to measure actual product costs and provide this information frequently to manufacturing managers so that the benefits from improved production processes could be seen rapidly. This effort, which was still at an experimental stage, revealed that the production cost of one standard metal part (including materials) had been reduced by 40 percent in one year.

The firm's financial executives knew that the JIT production system should eventually permit an enormous simplification and reduction in the cost of operating the firm's accounting system. At present, much of the effort in maintaining an "accurate" cost system is devoted to the detailed record keeping and reporting of in-plant inventories. As the company succeeds in reducing all inventories at the plant level to bare minimum levels (including immediate shipment or assignment of finished goods inventory to marketing departments) and reducing product throughput times from several weeks to several hours, the inventory accounting system can be scrapped. For periodic income measurement, it becomes much simpler and cheaper to do a physical count of the few items around the factory at the end of each period. It seems simpler, however, to eliminate inventory from actual production operations than to modify the record keeping for inventory in the firm's accounting system.

Company Experiences: Company H

Company H is a broad-based manufacturer of computer systems. Division S of Company H designs and produces various models of a major peripheral storage device for the company's computer systems using highly automated and capital intensive production processes. The division has large numbers of "knowledge workers": engineers for product and process design, industrial and manufacturing engineers for process development and improvements, cost accountants and cost engineers, quality engineering and assurance personnel, information systems specialists, test engineers, and materials planners, schedulers, purchasers, and distributors. Given the capital and knowledge-intensive production process, direct labor represents less than 10 percent of total costs.

Company H had recently adopted goals of total quality control and just-in-time production in order to become among the most efficient global producers of computer systems and equipment. Division S had already realized a 50 percent increase in its inventory turnover ratio and anticipated another 50 percent increase during the next three to five years.

As with the other innovative companies we examined, however, the pace of change in Division S's accounting system was much more leisurely than the changes in the organization and technology of the division's production processes. The cost accounting system was traditional, accumulating all overhead expenses into large cost pools. The overhead and indirect expenses included manufacturing engineering and information systems, test engineering, quality engineering, capitalized engineering expenses, depreciation on machinery and facilities, general employee benefits, manufacturing support services, site services, and financial services. These overhead expenses were added together into large aggregate cost pools and allocated to production departments on some objective but arbitrary basis, and subsequently to products on a direct labor hour basis. With direct labor representing a small fraction of total costs, this procedure produced a total burden rate of $90/DLH in 1983 and was forecasted to rise to more than $140/DLH by 1986.

A graphic illustration of the impact of the division's cost accounting procedures is shown in *Table 5-2* that traces the productivity gains and total manufacturing costs for one of the division's fastest growing products. (Numbers have been disguised to maintain confidentiality, but rates of change over time have been preserved.)

We see from *Table 5-2* that the division achieved substantial efficiencies in its manufacturing process. From 1981, the second year of

Table 5-2
Yields, Hours, and Production Costs per Unit

	1980	*1981*	*1982*	*1983*
Quantity produced (1983 = 100)	3	11	58	100
Labor hours/unit	4.	2.4	1.6	1.2
Yield (%)	32	38	67	75
Total manufacturing cost/unit (1983) = 100	152	102	95	100

production, to 1983, the yield of good items doubled and direct labor hours per unit were cut in half. Despite these dramatic improvements in direct labor and material efficiency, total manufacturing costs remained about constant over this three-year period. Since the product was experiencing large increases in sales, one would have expected the per-unit allocation of fixed expenses to have decreased. Therefore, the total manufacturing costs should also have decreased, given the increased productivity of labor and materials, and the expansion in production volumes. But manufacturing costs remained constant clearly showing that the indirect and overhead expenses allocated to the product were increasing at least as fast as the increases in production volumes. How much of this indirect and overhead cost increase represented actual increases in the division's expenses in these categories and how much represented reallocation of already existing costs away from other products could not be determined from the available product cost data. It is obvious, however, that despite the direct labor focus of the cost accounting system, the cost components that needed to be managed and controlled were in the overhead and knowledge worker categories.

Applying overhead and indirect costs on direct labor hours caused managers to focus a large share of their attention on controlling and improving direct labor utilization, even though direct labor was a small percentage (less than 10 percent) of total manufacturing costs. The following behavioral responses to the cost allocation system were described to us:

1. Product managers in several cost centers were recommending a shift from internal production to external vendor supply. Internal production of technically unsophisticated parts at labor rates approaching $90/DLH was hardly competitive with external suppliers. Purchasing externally saves direct labor but increases the personnel required in departments for materials specification and

purchasing, materials planning and scheduling, materials production and control, and materials distribution (these were actual
departments in Division S). The costs of these personnel, however, are aggregated into a common overhead pool and allocated
out on an average basis to the remaining direct labor hours.
Therefore, the buy rather than make decision will lower the costs
assigned to the cost center even though total costs to the division
may have increased.

2. Enormous attention was directed at the measurement of direct
labor hours. Cost center managers were held responsible mainly
for on-time delivery and direct labor hours used. Many hours at
meetings were spent discussing increases or decreases of .01
hours (or smaller) of direct labor per unit. Thousands of dollars of
industrial and manufacturing engineering time were spent for
process improvements to reduce direct labor content by 0.1 hours.
Also, managers attempted to have manufacturing engineers
reclassified from a direct, traceable category into the common
pool where their costs would be shared by other products.

3. Labor-intensive processes seemed much more expensive than capital-intensive ones. Traceable equipment costs were not allocated
to processes that used the equipment. Rather, the equipment
costs were aggregated into a large overhead pool and allocated
back to processes and products on a direct labor hour basis. This
encouraged further capital-labor substitution and buy versus
make decisions for assembly and other labor-intensive processes.

4. There was no incentive for product managers to influence or control the rapid growth of support personnel. First, they never saw
the actual costs of the personnel, since such costs were aggregated
into large overhead pools. Second, they would receive only a fraction of the benefits from reducing or containing the numbers of
these personnel, since the savings would be averaged across all
product groups in the division.

5. Expensive clean room space was used inefficiently. Clean room
space cost twice as much as nonclean room space because of more
costly utilities (to operate air-cleaning equipment), raised floor
construction, and higher capital, installation, and maintenance
expenses. But all space expenses, clean and nonclean rooms, were
added together and allocated to products on a dollar-per-occupied-
square-foot basis. Thus, charges for clean room space were the
same as for nonclean rooms. Predictably, clean rooms ended up
being used (and built) to perform routine operations and to store
items that did not really need a clean room environment.

6. Direct labor time was measured in exquisite detail since the fully allocated labor rate was charged only for hours actually worked. Worker time during idle periods, changeovers, and breakdowns and repairs was charged to overhead categories. One senior financial analyst at the division estimated that 65–70 percent of the computer code for the general ledger was devoted to keeping track of direct labor costs that were less than 10 percent of total manufacturing costs. Also, while (or because) direct labor occupied so much attention in the accounting system, physical measures of materials consumed or capital employed in the production process were not available so that productivity measures could not be easily computed.

Fortunately, there is also a "good news" counterpart to the above litany. In early 1983, the product manager for one of the four major components in the storage device established a task force to study and make recommendations to improve production costing and organizational procedures. The task force's recommendation, to create "a focused factory" within the larger plant organization, was adopted and implemented as of January 1984. The focused factory was somewhat fictitious but it implied specific identification of all overhead, support, and indirect personnel and costs necessary to produce the component. (Perhaps coincidentally, another division of Company H at a completely different site had implemented the identical concept, calling it the "plant within the plant.") With this scheme, the product manager is charged directly for almost all the overhead personnel and costs being allocated to the component, and he contracts with the various support functions for an appropriate level of service.

Many expenditures that previously were lumped together and allocated on a common basis would now be collected and allocated on a disaggregate basis. For example, separate occupancy rates would be developed for clean and nonclean room space. The single gas or electric meter for the entire site would be replaced by local meters for energy consumption at each cost center. The single rate previously used to allocate all manufacturing engineering costs would be replaced by five separate rates that would reflect better the different tasks performed by various categories of support engineers. Only a few service functions, considered inherently nontraceable, such as payroll, accounting, and personnel, would remain in a common overhead pool to be allocated on a basis such as head count.

All these overhead costs for the component would be allocated to finished products based on expected production volumes; that is, overhead costs would be reduced to a cost per unit produced, rather than a cost per direct labor hour. The allocation on a unit basis is possible because there was little product variety in the cost center; whatever variety did exist could be handled by developing relative complexity factors for the different products and using these to compute a weighted average of equivalent production volume each period.

In summary, the focused factory proposal at Division S will make overhead costs visible to the product manager at a much more disaggregate and controllable level of detail. The manager can then negotiate to reduce support services that he feels are redundant or too expensive. The proposal is being implemented for the simplest component in the storage device produced by the division. Costs for the other components would continue to be collected and allocated on the old basis during the experimental period. While it is too early to determine the impact of the focused factory accounting approach, some reductions in the controller's and industrial engineering staff were already appearing. Significant personnel reductions in other engineering and overhead functions are expected to occur during the initial year as the product manager attempts to eliminate superfluous tasks and makes the continual tradeoffs between costs and work performed that are necessary for efficient operations.

Company Experiences: Company M

Company M is a worldwide semiconductor manufacturer. The company's senior management consists of the engineers and scientists who founded the company. The influence of these technically sophisticated leaders pervades the operations and reporting systems of the organization. To a degree not closely approached by any other organization I visited, the executives of Company M rely on raw operating statistics, rather than financial data, to understand and manage their business.

This operating philosophy probably has several origins. First, with their technical backgrounds, the top managers have more faith in measures of physical quantities than in summary financial measures. As one senior executive said, "I have a need to see 'inside' the process, to be assured everything is running smoothly and operating properly." Second, there exists one physical variable that has more to do with the success of the company than any set of financial variables. Production costs arise from fabrication of silicon wafers into usable chips. If the yield of chips increases by 50 percent, then production costs per chip can drop by one-third. Therefore, the single most important factor affecting unit production costs is the percentage yield of good chips.

Third, the company has been in existence for only slightly more than a decade. It does not have professional managers who would run the company via financial numbers because they do not understand or are not interested in learning about the manufacturing technology. Thus, the use of summary financial statistics to shield the senior managers from the details of week-to-week operations has not occurred and will not occur in the foreseeable future given the strong technology culture in the corporation.

Charts are used everywhere in the organization. As one walks in the corridors surrounding every production facility, one sees charts of yields, quality, activity levels, and deliveries. Production supervisors are provided with more than one hundred indicators on a frequent and regular basis. Senior managers, up through the vice presidents and the president of the company, receive about 100 charts of key indicators every week. *Table 5-3* summarizes the nature of the charts seen by these executives.

The items in *Table 5-3* illustrate the diversity of indicators seen by Company M's management. They include measures of output, productivity, resource utilization, and unit costs. While costs are certainly among the set of data monitored by managers, costs are never among the first measures (or even in the top half of measures) to be reported. The managers seem satisfied with the indicator system. The only complaint that emerged during my discussions was not on the quantity of measures produced, but that the indicators have not changed as rapidly as the business; that the system was getting too ponderous and was not responsive to changing conditions. I will return to the issue after a brief description of the cost accounting system used by Company M.

The company uses a relatively simple process cost system. Actual costs are accumulated into ten major cost pools: Raw Materials, Masking Plates, Direct Labor, Indirect Material, Equipment Maintenance, Depreciation, Facilities, Process Overhead, Plant Overhead, and General Overhead. Each cost pool is allocated to processing activities based on the relative difficulty or complexity of that activity. Thus, detailed costs are not collected for each activity. But rather than allocating costs to activities on a simplistic basis (such as direct labor hours), costs are allocated after a study of the degree of difficulty of each process. Also, as in any process cost system, the accumulated cost of scrapped wafers is spread over the remaining good wafers. Yields, therefore, have a dramatic impact on the unit cost of completed wafers.

It was interesting to learn that until three years ago, costs were allocated on a direct labor hour basis. It was even more interesting to

Table 5-3
Charts of Manufacturing Performance

Fabrication	Assembly	Test
1. Yield	Number units shipped to	Number units shipped
Wafers out/wafers in	test	Number units processed
Rework percentage	Number units assembled	Average test time
2. Production	(by package type)	Throughput time
Activities performed	Number leads/package	Test yields
Wafers produced	Yields by package type	Test per operator hour
Chips produced	Leads completed per	% Lots rejected
Equivalent chips pro-	operator hour	Equipment uptime
duced	Shipment per indirect	Personnel turnover
% Delivery commit-	labor head count	Test of ongoing quality
ments met	Cost per unit shipped	Costs per unit
Throughput time	% Units shipped on	% Units tested on sched-
3. Productivity	schedule	ule
Activities/operator		
hours		
Activities/payroll $		
Chips/payroll $		
4. Equipment maintenance		
Equipment utilization		
% Hours with no un-		
scheduled downtime		
5. Engineering		
Equivalent chips pro-		
duced/good wafers		
6. Financial		
Total expenses		
Average cost/chip		
Revenue/chip		
Margin/chip		
7. Summary measures		
WIP measures		
WIP turnover		
Personnel turnover		
Absenteeism		

have a vice president state that only in the last three years have cost numbers begun to be developed seriously. My interpretation of these seemingly contradictory statements is that managers did not use product cost numbers derived by allocating overhead costs based on direct labor hours. In summary, the cost system struck me as reasonable and functional. It did not seem expensive to operate and probably did a sensible job in tracing and allocating costs to products. As mentioned already, the main influences on unit costs are wafer and chip yields.

Beyond this, and once the obviously traceable costs are allocated to specific products, it would not matter greatly how costs are allocated among the different types of wafers produced.

Even the extensive set of indicators used by Company M, though, was not adequate to reflect changes in the product and process technologies and in the market conditions for the firm's products. We can see in *Table 5-3* that many of the indicators are either simple counts of output (number of wafers produced, number of chips produced, number units shipped, number units assembled and tested) or ratios involving simple counts of output (wafers out/wafers in, rework percentage, chips produced/good wafers, number leads/package, tests per operator hour). These measures were developed when the company had only a few principal products, all using a similar production technology. Over time, the product line has diversified into many component types so that current production includes static Random Access Memories (RAMs), dynamic RAMs, microprocessors, and microcontrollers, among others. In addition, much higher densities of patterns can now be engraved on the silicon wafer by exploiting new technology developments. The company is simultaneously producing chips using three fundamentally different technologies, each having differing processing characteristics and yields. Thus, summary measures of numbers of wafers and chips produced or units assembled and tested no longer reflect the varying diversity and complexity of the output. This tends to distort output and productivity measures.

This output measurement problem has been recognized by management, but a solution is still in the experimental stage. A complex normalized measure of output, called an equivalent functional chip, has been developed that controls both for the shrinking size of each chip (when using the more advanced technology) and for the density of the patterns given the chip size (to control for the alternative functions a chip could perform). Manufacturing managers consider this normalized measure more representative of actual output, but other managers are reluctant to reduce their reliance on the simpler and more familiar measures that sum up the actual wafers, chips, and finished units produced, regardless of the technology or function of the units. The episode is an example in which a company has made great advances in its product and manufacturing technology but has been slower to update its measurement and control system to be consistent with the new product and process environment.

The use of a simple sum of diverse and noncomparable items had also created a problem in measuring production activity. Initially, wafer output was used as an indicator of production activity. As the diversity and complexity of wafers increased, simple counts of wafer capacity or wafers produced were no longer meaningful. Some wafers can be produced rapidly and in great quantities, while the more complex and dense wafers require both many more processing stages and increased time at each stage. Therefore, six years ago, the company changed its production measure from counting wafers to counting the number of activities required to produce each type of wafer. The basic unit of production was defined to be one wafer processed through one machine stage. Complex wafers have many machine processing stages; simple wafers have only a few. Thus processing complex wafers to completion requires more "activities" than completing simple wafers. Manufacturing output each month is measured by the number of activities accomplished (total number of wafers processed through each major machine process).

The problem with this measure is that there is enormous variation in the complexity of activities. An easy step in wafer production has a throughput of 300 wafers in an hour (an output rate of 300 activities/hour) whereas a complex printing process requires eight hours to finish one wafer (a rate of only .125 activities/hour). When the time to accomplish a unit of activity varies by more than three orders of magnitude, it is unlikely that summing up all activities will be a useful measure of the production quantities of different facilities.

Again, some normalized measure of production activity, to reflect the great variation in time and complexity of different stages in the wafer production process, would seem to provide a better summary both of production capacity in a facility and of the actual production accomplished in a period. As an extreme case, perhaps only one or two stages, in a fabrication process requiring up to forty stages, may be limiting the output of finished wafers; that is, these one or two stages represent bottleneck resources. At a time when potential sales are considerably in excess of production capacity (the situation from mid-1983 through March 1984), these bottleneck resources should become the focus of all managers' attention. Unlike the previous situation, however, in which a new summary product measure was being developed, the managers of Company M were still using the old summary measure of total activities accomplished each period to monitor and evaluate production performance. It is another example in which a measurement system developed for one environment was not modified when production technology and market conditions changed.

A third measurement issue also became obvious for the first time during 1983 when sales began to exceed production capacity. Product yield had historically been used as the key measure of manufacturing effectiveness and becomes even more critical when demand exceeds current capacity. But other factors that increase production rates should also be highlighted for managerial attention. Improved use of bottleneck resources is one such factor, as discussed in the preceding paragraphs. Another factor is to obtain maximum use of equipment by avoiding unscheduled downtime. Indicators of unscheduled downtime and percentage of working hours without unscheduled equipment downtime had only been recently formulated and had not yet become a permanent part of the reporting system. Thus the measurement system was slow to provide information on machine availability, a key target now for management attention and control.

These examples illustrate an underlying theme that has emerged throughout the chapter. Managerial accounting systems cannot be developed and maintained in isolation from the organization and technology of a firm's manufacturing processes. Changes in these processes will likely make the accounting system less useful to motivate and control manufacturing performance even for accounting systems that go beyond traditional financial summaries to use a broad variety of direct physical measurements.

Discussion

Let us summarize the incidents we found in the four companies. The electrical propulsion division of Company V had completely reorganized its manufacturing operations. The benefits from this reorganization were impossible to quantify, however, since the accounting system accumulated only total project costs. Thus, per unit reductions in labor hours and average inventory levels could not be determined. Nor could we learn whether the introduction of a model shop, to build a few prototypes and debug product designs and manufacturing techniques, succeeded in flattening out the learning curve.

Company N had made great progress within a short time period to achieve its goal of a Just-in-Time Production System. Set-up times, batch sizes, material travel distances, WIP and raw material inventory, product throughput times, and space requirements had been greatly reduced, some by remarkable percentages. Yet the company was still using a standard cost system based on highly detailed and frequently obsolete labor assignments. Actual product costs had to be calculated by a separate process that was still under development. No reporting system had yet been established to monitor progress on reducing inventory levels or in the cost reductions that were the consequence of inventory reduction activities.

The cost accounting system in Division S (of Company H) allocated all costs to departments and products through a burden rate on direct labor hours, even though direct labor represented less than 10 percent of total manufacturing costs. The focus on direct labor hours was accompanied by excessive growth and inefficient use of nondirect personnel. Some evidence of distortions in make versus buy decisions, in the use of scarce capital, such as clean room space, and in the resources used to record and process direct labor time also were associated with the cost allocation procedure.

Company M relied much less on financial measures to monitor its manufacturing performance. But even with its extensive use of direct physical measurements, the periodic management reporting system was not revised responsively when major changes in product characteristics, process technology, and the market environment made the critical measures in the system unrepresentative of current conditions.

These examples were not isolated instances designed to provide support for a prior hypothesis of an accounting lag phenomenon. These companies and divisions were chosen because we knew they were innovative manufacturers and therefore offered the best hope for finding either new management accounting procedures or new procedures to integrate management accounting personnel closer to the production environment. In fact, three of the companies were in the process of making experimental changes in their accounting and control systems, but these changes were lagging behind their innovations in the organization and technology of manufacturing operations.

I have also talked with senior partners active in the manufacturing consulting practice of four of the "Big 8" public accounting firms. They confirmed the view that corporations have been slow to modernize their cost accounting systems. Other companies that I am talking to or working with also fail to provide instances of innovative or responsive management accounting systems. A division controller in one company indicated that not only were the cost accounting systems of the thirteen plants in his division incompatible with each other but that he would classify nine of them as below a minimal level of adequacy.[5] In another company I visited, a company with a deserved reputation for product excellence and customer service, the major financial controversy was on the allocation of company profits to manufacturing plants, even though the plants were totally managed as cost centers. An effort was just under way to develop improved measures of manufacturing performance, such as timeliness, quality, and inventory management, but this effort had been sidetracked until the role of manufacturing plant "profitability" could be settled.

Therefore, a primary goal of this exploratory investigation was not realized. I had hoped to be able to document the incidence and value of innovative accounting and control systems for the new industrial competition and to learn how firms making major changes in their manufacturing operations were developing and using measures of quality, inventory reductions, manufacturing flexibility, employee morale and abilities, productivity, and new product effectiveness. Instead I found that changes in accounting procedures lag far behind changes in the real production phenomena they are supposed to represent.

The demand for changes in management accounting systems can only accelerate in the years ahead. Seventy-five years ago, the emphasis was on using direct labor and materials efficiently. The cost accounting systems developed at that time, and which have persisted until today, reflected this goal by keeping detailed records of direct labor and inventory. With the new organization and technology of manufacturing operations, variable direct labor and inventory are vanishing from the factory. Cost accounting systems should reflect this phenomenon and start to provide meaningful, detailed costs on the capital and knowledge worker inputs that are much more critical to manufacturing success than being able to keep track of and allocate all costs to direct labor.

Existing cost accounting systems will become even more obsolete as companies invest further in computer-integrated manufacturing processes. With this technology, almost all relevant manufacturing costs become fixed costs; in fact, they are not only fixed, they are largely sunk costs because the expenditures on the equipment and on the extensive software required to operate this equipment must be incurred before production can ever begin. Attempting to manage virtually unmanned production processes with a cost accounting system designed to control direct labor costs will certainly provide an interesting new challenge to U.S. executives. Surely, however, there will be enough new challenges in the coming decades that we do not have to create unnecessary ones.

Conclusions and Recommendations

Companies are making fundamental changes in the organization and technology of their manufacturing processes. The four companies described in this paper provide good examples of the new procedures and equipment for contemporary manufacturing operations. Set-up and lead times have been reduced by one and two orders of magnitude; microprocessor and other computer-controlled equipment acquired, installed, and made operational; personnel retrained to produce with greatly reduced defects and buffer inventory levels; much WIP inventory removed entirely; suppliers trained to deliver items 100 percent in conformance with specifications and just when needed; and large machinery modified and moved around to facilitate the smooth flow of products through the factory. Amidst all these changes, the one constant is the firm's management accounting system.

Relative to the real changes occurring in the firm's manufacturing operations, it would seem simple for accountants to change the way they move numbers around on their ledgers or in their computers. Transforming symbols should be easier than transforming real objects or motivating, educating, and training real people. Yet when manufacturing operations change, the last and most difficult component to change is the accounting system. Ironically, if the accounting system is not representative of actual operations, and not useful in understanding or controlling these operations, it has little other justification for existence. Why then do accounting systems lag so far behind the pace of change in the phenomena they purport to represent?

One reason for accounting lag may be the lack of adequate role models. Much of the impetus for the dramatic changes in the organization and technology of manufacturing operations came from observation of Japanese manufacturers. The experience of the CEO of Company N (the second firm described in the chapter) was typical of the reaction of many U.S. executives when they learned what leading Japanese firms could accomplish with a commitment to total quality control and zero inventory production systems. As this realization sank in, either by direct observation of Japanese production techniques or from the competition of high-quality, low-priced Japanese products, alert U.S. manufacturers started to adapt innovative quality and inventory-reducing practices to their own operations. It seems, however, much more difficult to observe the details of Japanese accounting and control systems. Therefore, comparable examples of innovative accounting systems are not available to U.S. firms.

Other sources of innovation for U.S. manufacturers are the suppliers of computer-integrated manufacturing equipment such as robots, CAD/CAM, flexible manufacturing systems, and cellular technologies. The analogous suppliers of accounting systems, such as the major public accounting firms, have not been quite as imaginative in devising new accounting systems for the contemporary manufacturing environment. Also, textbooks and articles on managerial accounting mostly employ the simple, static, single-product, single-stage, high direct labor model of manufacturing processes as articulated seventy-five years ago by the scientific management engineers. Therefore, even firms that recognize inadequacies in their existing management accounting systems do not have alternatives readily available to use in their place. Each firm has to innovate on its own rather than being able to share in the experience of successfully innovating firms.

A second possible explanation for accounting lag is the prevalence of computer-based accounting systems. In theory, having an accounting system stored in a programmable computer should permit considerable flexibility for implementing changes. In practice, however, it seems difficult to modify accounting programs without risking damage to the entire transactions-based accounting system that provides the entries for the firm's financial and tax statements. Thus, complex and not easily modified computerized accounting systems provide a barrier to innovative and adaptive changes in the firm's managerial accounting system. Computerized systems supply efficient processing of transactions data but the potential flexibility for modifying instructions in stored programs is rarely achieved in practice.

Fortunately, some relief from the inflexibility of large, centralized accounting systems is now possible. The growing availability of inexpensive yet powerful personal computers (PCs) will permit much latitude for local initiatives to develop more relevant and responsive managerial accounting systems. Plant controllers can customize their internal reporting systems to aid the accounting, planning, and control requirements of manufacturing and plant managers. Ideally, much of the transactions data for the local accounting system can be obtained from the same system used to collect and report information for the companywide accounting system. Even if local PCs cannot access the centralized data base, however, the relevant data may still be entered manually and the processing and graphics capabilities of the PC used to prepare regular reports for shift supervisors and manufacturing and plant-level managers. One can be quite optimistic that the increased supply of inexpensive personal computers, excellent financial software packages, and computer-literate accounting personnel will permit much more innovation in local managerial accounting practices than was previously possible.

The role for divisional management will be to encourage such innovation and to not put imaginative accounting personnel in a straitjacket by insisting that all internal financial reports be prepared in accordance with centralized accounting practices. It should be obvious that the traditional ways of measuring and motivating manufacturing performance are not adequate for the contemporary organization and technology of manufacturing operations. The alternatives to the traditional and accounting system, however, are not so obvious. A period of experimentation is needed to adapt managerial accounting practices to each company's and each factory's particular needs. It is fortunate that low-cost, high-capacity local computing capacity is now available to permit such experimentation without compromising or jeopardizing the integrity of the transaction-based centralized system.

A third explanation for the lack of responsiveness of current accounting systems arises from the emphasis on financial accounting even among managerial accountants. Recall that most of today's cost accounting practices can be traced to the scientific management movement. The innovators of the scientific management movement were engineers, intimately involved in their company's manufacturing operations. In the past seventy years, however, the operation of the firm's accounting system has been delegated to professional accountants frequently separated from plant operations. During this time there has been a great growth in the importance of the financial reporting system for external constituencies (stockholders, investors, lenders, public regulatory and tax authorities). The firm's accountants became more concerned with recording transactions and allocating costs in a consistent and objective manner for these external constituencies. They became removed from concerns as to whether the numbers they were objectively and consistently recording held any relevance for describing, motivating, and controlling the firm's manufacturing performance.

The emphasis on external reporting and the deemphasis on internal relevance was also reflected in the academic training of accounting professionals. Educational programs, strongly influenced by the training demands of the public accounting profession, concentrate on financial accounting courses (introductory, intermediate, and advanced financial accounting, auditing, tax, and financial accounting theory). These financial accounting, auditing, and tax courses have undergone major changes over the years in response to changes in the regulatory and legal environment. In contrast, cost accounting courses remain focused on the simple production model of the turn-of-the-century firm. Embellishments have been added to emphasize the importance of distinguishing fixed from variable costs, and the decision relevance of incremental and opportunity costs. But the greater complexity of manufacturing processes in the past seventy years has not changed the production model used to illustrate cost accounting practices. Certainly, the major innovations now under way in the organization and technology of manufacturing operations are hardly anywhere reflected in contemporary cost accounting courses and materials. Also, it would be unusual for an accounting major to take a course in production, manufacturing processes, or technology.

Thus, accounting students receive extensive training in external reporting requirements and innovations but virtually no training in contemporary manufacturing operations. Industrial companies aggravate this imbalance by frequently hiring their key financial people from public accounting firms. An alternative, but rarely followed, practice would have firms promoting their manufacturing engineers and production supervisors into managerial accounting positions. Personnel with good technical backgrounds should not find it difficult to master the relevant features of the standard cost model, overhead allocations, variance analysis, and cost-volume-profit analysis. Promoting manufacturing engineers into responsible financial positions would generate a supply of personnel for operating the firm's internal measurement and control system who would be more comfortable with the underlying manufacturing operations. We could even hope that such personnel, knowledgeable about the technology and organization of manufacturing, could devise appropriate performance measures and, in effect, recreate the innovative environment that occurred earlier in this century when engineers were intimately involved both in redesigning the factory and in developing representative measurement systems.

One company we spoke with has instituted an imaginative program with a nearby university to train a new generation of management accountants. It has encouraged, and helped to finance, a joint undergraduate degree program between the industrial engineering and accounting departments. Students in this program will receive training both in contemporary manufacturing processes and in accounting, particularly management accounting. It is interesting to note that the large state university near the company, with one of the largest and finest accounting departments in the nation but with close ties to its public accounting firm constituency, was not receptive to instituting such a joint program on its campus.

The fourth and most important explanation for accounting lag, however, is that senior company management has not emphasized the need to improve the relevance and responsiveness of its management accounting systems. Top executives must recognize that they have complete control over choosing their measurement and control systems. The internal accounting procedures can and should be different from those used to prepare financial and tax statements. Also, the accounting system should be continually scrutinized so that it remains consistent with and relevant to current manufacturing technology and operations.

A strong recommendation from the case studies described in this chapter is that accounting personnel should be working much more closely with manufacturing managers and product and process engineers. When significant changes are made in manufacturing operations, the former accounting system will become obsolete. Rather than wait for confusing and misleading information to be produced from the old accounting system, it would be preferable for a new set of measures, aggregations, and allocations to be available simultaneously with the introduction of the new production procedures. This will require accounting and control personnel to be part of any task forces responsible for developing and implementing manufacturing process changes so that measurement systems can be developed that will be functional for the new manufacturing environment. In this way, firms will avoid the current practice in which accounting measures and reports continue to be produced long after major changes have occurred in the environment for which they had been designed.

Accounting systems must serve the objectives of the firm. We do not have a universal accounting model that works well in all circumstances. While the choice of appropriate measures, aggregations, and allocations is an art, it is an art that must be practiced in conjunction with the strategic goals of the firm and in close communication with the rapid changes occurring in firms' manufacturing processes. This requires that the choice of an internal accounting system be made explicitly and simultaneously with the choice of a firm's corporate and manufacturing strategy.

Notes

1. The historical material was extracted from chapters 2 and 3 of Lawrence and Dyer (1983) and from Chandler (1977).
2. See, for example, Chandler (1977) and Johnson (1975).
3. About the only features of modern financial control systems that were developed after 1908 were the innovations introduced to manage the multidivisional firm by General Motors in the 1920s. GM's system featured "centralized control with decentralized responsibilities" (see Sloan [1964] and Brown [1927]) and is the model used by most firms today with market-oriented decentralized profit centers.
4. In principle, one could compare the total costs of two orders for the same propulsion units performed before and after the reorganization of the factory. In practice, one would be unable to disentangle the experience curve effects during each order, different material price discounts, and changes in the price level for material and labor. Also, working with only a single estimate of unit

costs (computed as total project costs divided by number of units produced) gives the analyst no degrees of freedom to compensate for random, noncontrollable influences on costs. Also, lacking data on monthly production, one cannot determine the division's success in reducing average inventory levels.

5. The incompatibility of cost accounting and management control systems of similar plants in the same division points out a hidden cost of growth through acquisition. As we understand better the rigidity of existing accounting systems, we can expect that growing by acquisition will likely lead to multiple, noncomparable measurement systems in various plants of a company. In contrast, internally generated growth gives companies the opportunity to install their preferred measurement system in newly established plants.

References

Brown, Donaldson. "Centralized Control with Decentralized Responsibility." American Management Association Annual Convention Series, no. 57, 1927. Reprinted in H. T. Johnson, ed., *Systems and Profits: Early Management Accounting at DuPont and General Motors*, New York: Arno Press, 1980.

Chandler, Alfred D. *The Visible Hand: The Managerial Revolution in American Business.* Cambridge: Harvard University Press, 1977.

Kaplan, Robert S. "Measuring Manufacturing Performance: A New Challenge for Management Accounting Research." *The Accounting Review*, October 1983, 686–705.

———. "The Evolution of Management Accounting." *The Accounting Review*, July 1984a, 390–418.

———. "Yesterday's Accounting Undermines Production." *Harvard Business Review*, July-August 1984b, 95–101.

Lawrence, Paul R., and Davis Dyer. *Renewing American Industry.* New York: The Free Press, 1983.

Sloan, Alfred P. *My Years with General Motors.* New York: Doubleday, 1964.

Commentary
The Growth of "Worrying" about Management Accounting

Anthony G. Hopwood

Until recently it has been rare for accounting to be interrogated in the name of either its organizational functioning or its precise organizational effects. Accounting discourse has remained a purely technical one. Little effort has been invested in exploring the ways in which it intersects with other organizational processes, the actual consequences which it has, and the implications of these for organizational performance. The justifications given for accounting practice, both contemporary and prospective, not only have continued to reside in the technical domain but also have been content to draw on presumptions of its organizational desirability rather than a more pragmatic concern with its actual effects. The result is that accounting, although undoubtedly an influential part of organizational practice, nevertheless has remained an isolated craft, with its normative presuppositions only rarely tested against the very practical contexts that its practitioners somewhat paradoxically continue to emphasize.

Now, however, there are some encouraging signs that these manifestations of the accounting past are slowly starting to change in both the worlds of academic inquiry and practice.

Professor Kaplan's chapter is both symptomatic of, and a significant contribution to, the changes that are taking place in management accounting research. Rather than being content with designing, at a distance, ever more sophisticated technical procedures that seemingly have the potential to improve organizational decision making and control, researchers increasingly have become more interested in understanding management accounting as it is, the factors that influence the forms it takes and the organizational consequences it actually has. Albeit slowly, management accounting research is starting to confront management accounting practice.

Of course, this development is manifested in many and various

227

ways. Accounting practice is being interrogated from a number of very different perspectives. There are those who seek to understand its economic rationality in organizational terms. Others place the emphasis directly on the organizational or social or even political nature of accounting practice. More significantly, perhaps, even the newer variety of management accounting researchers seemingly are content to remain theorists of the accounting craft. Despite the growing concern with confronting practice that is implicit in a number of the new approaches, very few have sought to directly observe management accounting in practice. Kaplan is one of these few and, because of this, his contribution is even more significant.

Kaplan's arguments also are interesting because they are reflective of a growing realization that management accounting not only is not what it should be but also might even be having effects that it shouldn't have. Of course the later realization that practice is subject to unanticipated dysfunctional consequences certainly is not a new one, not least in the research community. Until recently, however, it is fair to say that it has been possible to presume that, although present, the undesirable "side effects" did not prevent the achievement of the main management accounting task. The icing, in other words, was perhaps starting to deteriorate but the cake itself was still regarded as wholesome. Such a presumption, however, is now being questioned. A more radical view that something "might," but only might, be more fundamentally astray with the management accounting craft interestingly started to emerge in the corporation rather than in the academy and Kaplan has provided the first research statement of this growing focus of "corporate worrying."

The history of the development of worrying about management accounting has not been documented as yet. Indeed I sense that much of it has been masked as corporations have simply introduced other management strategies and techniques that complement the increasingly limited and rigid practices of accounting. Other control techniques have been made to operate alongside management accounting, as Kaplan notes. Lateral overlays of information have been introduced to provide the integration that has become more important in organizations segmented by the vertically oriented influence of accounting practice. Other management disciplines even have started to confront the problems involved in the control of cost structures very different from those that both accompanied management accounting's birth and underlie many of the pronouncements made in the textbooks and manuals of the craft. However, despite these important complementary developments, there nevertheless is now a more direct history of practical worrying about management accounting.

The organizational rigidities that were furthered by many management accounting practices were of concern to those who sought to implement more flexible forms of work organization in the late 1960s and early 1970s. The limited notions of costliness incorporated into traditional systems were clearly identified at the same time. At a more general level, a number of major manufacturing organizations started to realize how their existing management information and control systems, including the management accounting systems, might be implicated in the narrowing of management attention onto the purely economic; in the construction of far too short conceptions in time; in a rigidity of organizational structures that was clearly dysfunctional in an era of uncertainty and change; and in a costly regime of suboptimal decision making.

In the early 1970s Philips was one of the earliest corporations to specifically identify this disease. In subsequent years other major corporations came to a similar realization, particularly as a result of an intensification in their competitive environment which highlighted the organizational costliness of their cost accounting systems. The rise of strategic notions of corporate management only served to further the perception of a problem as management strategists grappled with the difficulty of relating traditional short-term, accounting-based oriented management information systems to the needs of a more aggressive formulation and monitoring of corporate strategy.

The net result of these developments was a slowly growing corporate awareness of the types of problems discussed in Kaplan's chapter. Some organizations established working parties and study groups in the area. One even restricted any changes in its financial control systems until it had a better idea of where it was going. The Ford "After Japan" ("AJ") program was seen to have implications for their massive existing commitment to financial control systems. In numerous other organizations the traditional accounting information flows are being supplemented, particularly in the name of the vocabulary of "strategy."

Still, however, traditional notions of the management accounting craft are firmly entrenched, as Kaplan's chapter makes clear. As someone from the United Kingdom, surely one of the most accounting-intensive countries in the Western world, I have to agree with his view that accounting is still about accounting. In most of its manifestations it appears to remain an organizational practice rather loosely connected with changes occurring in other organizational arenas. Its emphasis is still on the narrowly financial, the short term, and the organizationally constraining. Although there are some signs of change, these are slow to emerge, contained within relatively few organizations and very poorly known and understood.

Kaplan seeks to account for the seeming permanence of the old in terms of organizational lag and traditionalism. Again, coming from the United Kingdom, I cannot disagree with many of the points he makes in this respect. Management accounting as we now know it did arise amidst the very specific cost structures and control problems that characterized manufacturing organizations of the past. Accounting system reform does appear to be an unknown art. Financial accounting has had a dominant influence, and one that might still be increasing. Textbooks, in particular, and the accounting education process, more generally, are still firmly grounded in the traditions of the past. Until recently, information processing technologies have provided a very constraining influence. And few, if any, alternative conceptions of accounting have been, or even are now being articulated. Accounting still is accounting.

However, although I share Kaplan's view that these factors are implicated to a significant extent in the conservatism that pervades accounting practice, I am far less convinced that together they give an adequate account of accounting as it is. I admit the problems of articulating alternative explanations: Accounting practice is an inadequately researched domain. It is even difficult to isolate the full variety of forms that it takes, let alone outline the factors that lie behind its development and the linkages that it has with other organizational practices. Be that as it may, other considerations are involved in accounting as it is. Some of them, at least, might help us to understand why senior corporate management has not sought to grapple with the problems of accounting practice in the ways that Kaplan might have expected.

The first such factor relates to some of the diverse and conflicting influences that have an impact on accounting practice. Kaplan emphasizes the needs of new manufacturing processes, their attendant cost structures and control needs, and a more competitive environment. But the very same competitive environment that has highlighted the importance of flexibility, noneconomic competitive advantages, and the significance of a more strategic, longer term perspective, also have reinforced the relevance of the immediate and the traditionally economic. Budgets have not only been tightened but revised much more frequently. Standards have been cut. Cash controls have been introduced to complement cost controls. A renewed emphasis has been placed on financial responsibility, accountability, and control. In many organizations these complementary factors have resulted in a vast increase in the regime of economic calculation that pervades organizational life.

So, not only is accounting alive and well, but so is a concern with many of its traditional emphases. The short term has been of significance alongside the longer term. The economic has been emphasized alongside the noneconomic. The very real requirements for flexibility have had to compete with a renewed interest in the constraining and the specific. In other words, all the accoutrements of what has been provocatively called "newly poor behavior" (Olofsson and Svalander 1975), in which accounting traditionally has been implicated, have been very actively competing for organizational space, visibility, and significance with what might be seen as the very different management practices associated with the rise of the strategic and its less direct concerns with the economic. And no doubt a lot of the balancing of these competing pressures has been done by practitioners firmly grounded in the concerns of the past.

It would have been illuminating if Kaplan had specifically sought to identify the positive interests that there might have been in the accountings of the past rather than just confronting the difficulties faced by the emergence of the new. Further research most definitely needs to confront the variety of current organizational forces influencing accounting. Accounting needs to be seen as emerging and functioning in a conflicting domain with divergent interests, needs, and perspectives seeking to attach themselves to its technical procedures.

A second factor lying behind accounting practice as it is might reside in the diversity of roles that accounting serves in organizations. In part, Kaplan points to this when he contrasts the needs of the new with management accounting's present domination by the dictates of an increasingly regulated corporate financial accounting. Of course the two need not be so tightly coupled. They were not in the past and they are not in some other national contexts. However, one would like to know more about what is at stake in the intertwining that we see today. Rather than too readily labeling it as a manifestation of lag or ignorance or both, one might probe more into the roles that perhaps are being asked of accounting practice in organizations.

In saying this I draw on a view of the roles that accounting serves that go beyond the directly decision-facilitating ones that are implicit not only in Kaplan's paper but in much of the contemporary accounting literature (Burchell et al. 1980). Although the reformist rationales that underlie that decision-facilitating role are valuable, they should be complemented with a much more explicit appreciation of how accounting has been involved in the construction and furtherance of organizational power structures, in the creation and propagation of the goals of organized endeavors, and in the establishment of a dominant pattern of economic visibility that pervades the organization.

When seen in such terms, accounting is involved with much more than directly facilitating managerial action. It is concerned with making visible and thereby governable the detailed work processes of an organization. It provides for both aggregating and disaggregating organizational actions and outcomes—a powerful tool in the hands of organizational managers. It is involved with the establishment of a language of organizational motive, with rendering into the domain of the economic important aspects of the physical and task reality of the organization. And it is quite centrally involved in the construction of operational concepts of accountability, responsibility, and even performance which play a significant role in the creation of a manageable organizational regime.

Such wider organizational roles provide an important basis for understanding not only the development and present functioning of accounting but also the paradoxes and seeming inadequacies of its practice which Kaplan so acutely observes. Although accounting's involvement with facilitating operational decision making is important, not least in the management of change and improvement, that alone cannot provide anywhere near a complete basis for appreciating accounting as it is, the conflicting nature of the organizational pressures on it, and the effects that it actually has. The language of motives, power, and control must be utilized alongside that of decision making. Accounting has to be seen as an influential organizational ritual and an instrument of control and governance as well as a decision aid. The metaphors of acccounting as an "ammunication" and "rationalization machine" need to complement those of the "answer" and "learning machines" that characterize so much of official accounting discourse (Burchell et al. 1980).

A third factor lying behind the present practice of accounting is the professional competition that pervades the management arena. Organizations may need to be managed and controlled, but that can be done in a multiplicity of different ways. Different organizations have invested in different regimes of control. Control practices and emphases have changed over time. And of particular importance in the present context, different occupational and professional groups have competed for the right to control the corporate arena (Armstrong, 1985).

When seen in such terms, a reliance on accounting controls cannot be dissociated from the rise to power of the corporate accountant and financial manager as compared with, for instance, the engineer or the personnel manager. This is not the place to discuss what might have been at stake in the growing significance of industrial accountants and the techniques and procedures that they brought into the organizational arena. Suffice it to say that the conflict for control of the management of the corporation has been resolved in different ways in different contexts. The accountant as a corporate manager is very much a phenomenon of the Atlantic fringe countries of the United States, the United Kingdom and, possibly, the Netherlands—all countries that are playing a leading role in the worrying that is taking place over the adequacy of management accounting practice. As Horovitz (1980) makes clear in his comparative study of management control practices in European countries, not only are financial management practices less well developed in continental European countries but also a much greater investment has been made in the creation of alternative visibilities in the organization. There appears to be a more active competition for management attention between the visibilities of the technical, the human, the financial, and the marketplace.

Comparative and historical studies may play an important role in helping us understand the factors implicated in the accounting practices of today. Equally, but somewhat more provocatively, they might well show how the imperatives and justifications that are so often associated with different management practices emerge from, as well as result in, the practices that we observe today.

One final factor is of importance in understanding management accounting as it is. Most justifications and indeed studies of accounting practice emphasize its internal organizational roles. Kaplan's chapter has adopted this viewpoint, as has this commentary so far. However, further insights into both the practice and functioning of accounting, not least in manufacturing organizations, can be gained from an appreciation of how it came to be involved in the social as well as the organizational management of the corporation.

The discussion so far has been suggestive of this point. This commentary has emphasized the potential of accounting for furthering particular conceptions of organizational power. Attention has been given to the regime of economic visibility created by accounting practices. Accounting's involvement in the construction of governable organizations has been highlighted. And accounting's dependency on a significant professionalized body of practitioners has at least been considered. All of these points provide a basis for understanding the significant linkages between the organizational and the social practice of accounting.

Accounting, when seen in such terms, is more than a mere technical organizational practice oriented to the furtherance of pregiven conceptions of organizational efficiency and achievement. It is a practice that has come to play a significant role in the very articulation and furtherance of the concepts on which it is grounded. Operating, as it does, in organizations where the elucidation of both the ends and the means of organized endeavor resides in a contested domain rather than in one that is subject to the dictates of a pregiven rationale, accounting can be seen as having the characteristics of an interested practice that is concerned with creating and quite actively mobilizing, rather than merely facilitating, the context that it is used to regulate.

Such a perspective is particularly useful when comparative understandings are needed of accounting practice—not an insignificant stimulus for the present questioning. In some contexts the corporation may have been a less significant site for social control. Organizational participants may have already been inculcated into the norms appropriate for the operation of a manageable organizational regime. Accounting then may well have been able to concentrate on its organizational roles. Elsewhere, however, any such presumption may not have been in order. With the corporation itself being a very active site for social action, investments were made in organizational practices that sought to create a more disciplined and controllable work force, an economic vocabulary of organizational motive, and a legitimacy for organizational authority and influence as well as an effective management process. In many Western countries accounting was created and often still functions at just such an intersection of the organizational and the social. It is doubtful whether its development, present functioning, effects, and the contradictions to which it is subjected can be understood outside of this context.

On this basis I therefore conclude these comments by emphasizing that a recognition of accounting as being such a multifaceted practice is important for understanding many of the problems with today's practices. Residing in the realms of both the organizational and the social, they are subjected to both the demands of control and decision making. While undoubtedly influenced by the dictates of traditionalism, accounting also has been shaped by occupational competition, very diverse organizational demands, and even conflicting contemporary pressures. So although often treated as an isolated and purely technical organizational phenomenon, the history of the emergence of accounting as we now know it, its present organizational functioning, and its specific consequences and effects, cannot be understood in such isolated terms. Any accounting of accounting, be it to use the accounting language, historical or current, must be based on a wider appreciation of the contexts in which it emerged and the very diverse expectations that are held of it.

Such a perspective is helpful for understanding the dilemmas, undesirable effects, and even lags identified by Kaplan. It can provide a way of understanding the contradictions currently faced by accounting practice. It can illuminate the factors that both mobilize and constrain accounting developments. And it can provide a basis for appreciating the changing pressures that are impinging on accounting as we know it. For the corporate arena is not a stable one. The salience of past needs can change. The expectations that are held of particular management practices can be volatile, and different occupational groups can seek to renegotiate the interests and influence they have in corporate control.

When seen in such terms, Kaplan has provided us with some significant insights. His chapter provides us with a rich, provocative, and illuminating start on a wider exploration of the accounting craft. His contribution has served to problematize the accounting craft. That has not been done so succinctly and pertinently before. Not only has Kaplan usefully questioned the effects that accounting has, but he has also highlighted the very real need for research to confront the specifics of accounting as it is. I share Bob Kaplan's view of a new, more organizationally grounded appreciation of accounting. Equally, however, I share his view of the sheer magnitude of the steps that are needed to create a different accounting future. A considerable organizational and intellectual distance still needs to be traversed.

References

Armstrong, Peter. "Changing Management Control Strategies: The Role of Competition Between Accountancy and Other Organizational Professions." *Accounting, Organizations and Society*, 1985.

Burchell, Stuart, Colin Clubb, Anthony Hopwood, John Hughes, and Janine Naphapiet. "The Roles of Accounting in Organizations and Society." *Accounting, Organizations and Society*, 1980, 5–27.

Horovitz, Jacques H. *Top Management Control in Europe*. London: Macmillan, 1980.

Olofsson, C., and P. A. Svalander. "The Medical Services Change Over to a Poor Environment." University of Linkoping Working Paper, 1975.

6

From Control to Commitment: Transforming Work Force Management in the United States

Richard E. Walton

The healthy restructuring of American industry depends upon our ability to diagnose its deficiencies, to develop new approaches to replace deficient ones, and to adopt and adapt the more productive approaches.[1] This paper examines U.S. industry's ability to progress in one area, the organization and management of work.

There is good reason to reexamine American management strategies in various policy areas, including product development, inventory systems, and vendor relationships. Attitudinal changes also are important: American management must cultivate higher standards of excellence, especially with respect to quality, and longer time perspectives, especially in judging financial performance. Except for standards of excellence, these areas of change are not the subject of this paper, but all may be interdependent with changes in the work force management strategy.[2]

A broad consensus has emerged that U.S. managers generally have come to rely upon poor models for managing their work forces, to expect and accept much less from workers than is potentially available. Management has failed to motivate the work forces and to use and develop their latent capacities. In the case of organized labor, U.S. trade unions must share with management the responsibility for failing to achieve a partnership that will serve the interest of all stakeholders in the enterprise.

American managers have been in the forefront of the criticism, recognizing that their old work force management solutions were not working and that they needed to go back to the drawing board. American managers have also been in the lead in developing alternatives. Journalists have helped raise our consciousness of the deficiencies, and academics have helped shape these new approaches. But the search for a new work force management model has been carried on in large part by managers themselves, sometimes joined by trade union officials.

The major features of the commitment model (or models) have emerged. The task now is to continue defining the new model while promoting its diffusion. The work of definition involves finding optimal policies, deciding how much emphasis to give to various features of the model, and resolving some of its problematic aspects. In promoting diffusion, a critical question is how rapidly American management can replace its less productive approaches. In the case of the work force management, the transformation involves changes in attitudes, skills, structures, and systems. Above all, it involves a change in management philosophy and trade union policies.[3]

The Emerging Model and the One It Replaces

Recognizing that the new model is still evolving, we can nevertheless sketch its broad outlines. We will describe illustrative applications and contrast the attributes of the emerging model with those of the prevailing one. Finally, we will identify a transitional model.

Illustrative Developments

The most dramatic evidence of U.S. management's interest in developing new models of work force management appeared in the new plants built during the 1970s.[4] The more visible pioneers included General Foods at Topeka, Kansas; General Motors at Brookhaven, Mississippi; Cummins Engine at Jamestown, New York; and Procter & Gamble at Lima, Ohio. The following description of one of these plants is illustrative of the innovative greenfield plants started up during the 1970s and early 1980s:

> The work force of the new plant is organized into teams responsible for segments of the work flow. They are delegated many self-supervisory responsibilities. They make internal work assignments, make production trade-off decisions, diagnose and solve production problems, and select personnel replacements to their team. Support functions such as quality control and maintenance are integrated into team responsibilities. Team members are paid for acquisition of additional skills, not for doing a particular job. Common parking lots, cafeterias, and other symbols de-emphasize status. Employees do not punch the time clock. Supervisors are expected to be facilitative, exercising progressively less direction and control as team capacities develop. Employees exercise voice over a wide range of conditions that affect them. Finally, and critically important, the organization is characterized by very high expectations about task performance and about people treatment.

During the early 1970s new plants with this kind of design were all nonunion. By the end of the decade, similar designs were developed jointly by General Motors and the United Auto Workers. A leading example is the Cadillac plant in Lavonia, Michigan.

Sometimes inspired by the achievement of these new plants and sometimes driven by a breakdown in functioning in their own plants, managers of existing facilities also began to revise their approach to managing. The dramatic turnaround of General Motors' assembly plant in Tarrytown, New York, stimulated other union-management efforts in this spirit.[5] The typical pattern of these efforts is as follows:

> Local management and local union officials enter into a dialogue about the nature of their common interests and the barriers to communication and problem solving. When the parties have passed a threshold of mutual trust, they agree to jointly sponsor quality of work life (QWL) or employee involvement (EI) activities. They establish a joint structure to guide these activities, which typically involves workers in joint problem solving of production and people difficulties that arise in their work areas. Training in participative problem solving for workers, supervisors, and union officials supports the change. Often the training is conducted by trainers drawn from both union and management ranks. Worker participation is voluntary. Assurances are given that production improvement will not result in layoffs. Often individuals or labor-management centers serve as joint consultants to the companies and unions in facilitating this process.

These joint ventures typically have been initiated and sustained by efforts of local managers and union officials. One major exception is the joint effort between the Communication Workers of America (CWA) and American Telephone and Telegraph Company (AT&T) to promote QWL throughout the Bell System, which has been led by CWA President Glenn Watts and AT&T Vice President Rex Reed. Another exception is the UAW-Ford Employee Involvement program which was launched and energized centrally by Don Ephlin of the UAW and Pete Pestillo of Ford. The earlier UAW-GM effort also had national champions in Irv Bluestone and Steve Fuller, but the change strategy relied primarily on stimulation and education of local leaders, rather than on central direction. While a growing number of officials at the national levels of unions, such as the steelworkers, are now supporting union involvement in QWL activities, they remained a minority in 1983.[6]

In some instances the combination of the QWL spirit and threatening competition have prompted the parties to break new ground in union-management relations. Ford-UAW offers the most striking example:

> In 1982, the Ford Motor Company won wage concessions from the UAW and in return agreed to profit sharing, limitations on plant closing and outsourcing, and experimental approaches to job security. The parties

agreed to a joint venture in retraining and agreed to meet in Mutual Growth Forums. UAW's Don Ephlin was given an opportunity to meet periodically with the board of directors of the Ford Motor Company. As important as the specific outcomes of this 1982 negotiation was the spirit in which the parties chose to cast them. The parties signaled that they were entering into a new partnership based on joint initiative and a strong sense of the mutuality of their interests. The statements of the parties clearly indicated that they were less concerned with preserving prerogatives than with finding solutions to joint problems.

Most concession bargains between companies and unions, including the GM-UAW negotiations that followed, have not sent out such strong signals about the dawning of a new era of mutuality in labor relations. However, these negotiations have often moved the parties along the path of emphasizing their common fate and relinquishing some prerogatives or principles previously held sacred. In the nonunion sphere, the spirit of the Ford-UAW agreement was matched by the workers of Delta Airlines, who showed their loyalty to the company and their support for management by collecting monies to help fund the acquisition of a new plane.

A more recent development that appears to be gaining momentum since the late 1970s is "management restructuring." Changes at the plant floor have redefined the management task, and the minimal management structures incorporated in many new plant designs have proven effective. Consider the following illustrative example of management restructuring:

> After evidence of increased self-management and problem-solving capabilities of the work force, and with the stimulus of the division manager, a plant task force developed a phased plan to be implemented over three years. The plan was to remove two levels of the plant hierarchy, increase substantially supervisory spans of control, integrate the quality, development, and production activities at a lower level of the organization, structurally combine the production and maintenance organizations (except for some specialized maintenance functions), and open up new career path possibilities for managers and professionals. The plan was implemented on schedule. These changes achieved increased responsiveness, improved effectiveness, and better management development. Although decreased salaried personnel costs were not the primary motivation, they were a welcome benefit.

This pattern of restructuring to increase responsiveness is not confined to manufacturing organizations. Sales organizations and staff departments such as purchasing, materials management, and engineering have also eliminated managerial layers that were passing along information without adding value.

Finally, the movement that began in the plant is now finding expression at the corporate level. In many companies that have had some local successes of the types just described, top managements have begun to chart the organizational renewal of the entire company.[7] Cummins Engine Company, for example, has drawn up a statement of its ambitious intentions in this respect. Cummins' new management principles are intended to "achieve the most productive organization possible." These include an unprecedented effort to inform employees about the business; leadership that encourages participation by *everyone*; and jobs that involve greater responsibility and more flexibility. Cummins' statement spells out the implications of these and other principles for the role of the supervisor (less control, more facilitation); for union-management relations (more joint sponsorship); and for staff organization (smaller size as others grow in capacities to do multiple tasks).

Similarly, the founders of certain new companies, working with a clean slate, have chosen to adopt a bold, ambitious, and comprehensive work force management model. When Don Burr left Texas International Airlines to found Peoples Express with a group of his colleagues, he was committed to creating an organization that would be extraordinarily effective in developing and utilizing its people. The following is a description of their initial human resource policies:

> People Express featured a minimal hierarchy of three levels and positions with exceptionally broad scope. Every full-time employee was a "manager." Flight managers were pilots who also performed other tasks such as dispatching and safety checks. Maintenance managers were technicians who oversaw maintenance of P.E.'s airplanes, which was subcontracted to the maintenance departments of other airlines; they also performed various other staff jobs. Customer service managers performed all passenger-related tasks, such as security clearance, boarding, flight attending, ticketing, and food service.
>
> Everyone, including the officers, was expected to be "cross-utilized" and to rotate among functions, in order to increase their understanding of the business and to promote their own personal development. The work force was organized into three- or four-person work groups as an alternative to larger groups with supervisors. Teams and the individuals within them were expected to be self-supervising and to collaborate with others. Performance reviews were based on peer feedback gathered by the person under review.
>
> Salaries at the first level were very competitive. Those at the two higher levels were more modest. However, base salary for all employees was supplemented by a very ambitious set of policies for tying employees' financial stake to the company's: two forms of profit sharing and stock ownership. All employees, as a condition of employment, were required to buy, at a greatly discounted price, shares of P.E. stock. In addition P.E. awarded stock option bonuses.
>
> There was a plan providing for broad-based participation in the governance of the corporation.
>
> Finally, the recruitment, selection, and training were all designed to produce a work force that would work effectively under the above management strategy.

It is too early to judge the effectiveness of the People Express policies and practices, indeed even their workability. A case study reporting on the first year of operation described some striking achievements that could be attributed to certain organizational policies.[8] But in some other areas, such as the governance structure and the cross-movement policy, implementation had not yet occurred because of the demands of growth and the strain from heavy workloads. The experience of People Express is cited here as illustrative of the visions of a growing fraction of those who are fortunate enough to have a chance to found a new company today.

The Control Model for Work Force Management

The traditional model for managing the work force was refined and institutionalized over the first half of this century. In this model, *job design* is based on subdividing work into small tasks, clearly fixing job responsibilities, and holding individuals accountable for specific job requirements. Planning work is separated from implementation activities. *Performance expectations* are expressed as "standards" that define minimum acceptable performance. Both standards and job definitions are based on the least common denominator concept, in terms of the worker skills and motivations they assume. In the *management organization*, managerial roles and departmentalization also follow the same spirit of specialization and top-down control and coordination. Management prerogatives and positional authority are emphasized, and status symbols are allocated in ways that reinforce the hierarchy. Inevitably, layering develops and is justified by control considerations.

Worker compensation in the traditional model is based on a fair day's pay for a fair day's work. Because job requirements are carefully prescribed, they can be systematically evaluated and priced. Fairness in compensation is assured by comparing jobs. When jobs are deskilled, this leads, justifiably, to a lowering of the fair day's pay. Where feasible, pay is varied to provide individual incentives for meeting performance expectations.

In practice, the degree of *employment security* offered by companies has varied widely, even when other elements of the work-force management model are similar. Strong employment assurances are sometimes given, reflecting the values of the founders or a belief by management that this policy was of strategic importance in avoiding unionization. However, the basic logic of the traditional work force management model is that labor is and should be managed as a variable cost.

In the traditional model, there is generally little policy definition with regard to *employee voice,* unless the work force is unionized, in which case damage control strategies predominate. If the work force is not unionized, management relies on an open-door policy and devices such as attitude surveys to learn about employees' concerns. If the work force is unionized, then management is forced to bargain terms of employment and to establish an appeal mechanism for resolving disputes under the contract. Labor relations specialists are expected to handle these activities as separately as possible from line management's task of managing work.

Labor relations strategy follows naturally from the other policies, which emphasize interest conflict between employees and employers, and between managers and the managed. Adversarial relations are often an accepted corollary of the traditional work force management model.

Finally, the *management philosophy* associated with the traditional model emphasizes property as a source of management prerogatives and management's exclusive obligations to the shareowners. Employee claims, when enforced by bargaining power, are treated as constraints.

The common theme of the many elements of the traditional model is to establish order, exercise control, and achieve efficiency in the application of the work force. The model's antecedents include the bureaucratic organizations of the military and church. But it is Frederick W. Taylor who deserves credit for developing and promoting the industrial model. Because it was consistent with the prevailing ideologies of U.S. management and because it worked satisfactorily for many decades, the model was internalized by successive waves of managers. It has been reinforced by the policies of the U.S. labor movement.[9]

Two developments have prompted the current movement away from the control model. First, as workers' expectations changed over time, the control and efficiency measures often led to employee alienation, which in turn undermined both control and efficiency. The old model began to break down because it too severely violated current expectations. This development had been forecast by organizational psychologists a decade or two earlier,[10] but it did not manifest itself in a way that compelled management rethinking until the late 1960s and early 1970s.

Intensified competition was a second force hastening the obsolescence of the traditional work-force management model. The control model can operate satisfactorily with moderate to moderately low employee commitment. The system of policies and practices is designed to produce reliable if not outstanding performance. Beginning in the mid-1970s, it became increasingly apparent to many managers that this "satisficing" solution was not sufficient. The emergence of foreign competition in several industries set significantly higher standards of excellence. The heightening of domestic competition also placed "satisficing" organizations at risk. High-performance organizations require high-commitment work systems. More highly committed work forces required a radically different management model.

The Commitment Model

Over the past fifteen years a new model of work force management has emerged.[11] This commitment model, as portrayed in *Table 6-1,* can be found in the design of new plants and of newly founded companies such as People Express and Transtech, a subsidiary of AT&T. Hewlett-Packard, Digital Equipment Corporation, and many other high technology companies also represent variations of the high-commitment model. We can review the features of this model, acknowledging that some elements are still in the early stages of definition.

In the new model, *jobs are designed* to be broader and to combine planning and implementation activities.[12] Individual responsibilities often are contingent upon changing conditions and extend in any event to upgrading the system. Teams, rather than individuals, often are the unit accountable for performance. *Performance expectations* are set relatively high; they are "stretch objectives," rather than definitions of minimum performance. These expectations are dynamic, emphasizing continuous improvement, and often are oriented to the marketplace. (The control model's static standards, in contrast, are based on measurement of the work itself.) The *management system* tends to be flat, rely upon shared goals for control and lateral coordination, base influence on expertise and information rather than position, and minimize status differences.

Compensation policies place more emphasis on reinforcing group achievements. Acknowledging the broader and more contingent nature of job definitions, and therefore the expanded scope for individual contributions, pay is geared less to the logic of job evaluation and more to skill or other proxies for contribution. In some cases, gain sharing, stock ownership, or profit sharing is a cornerstone of the commitment model. In others, there is nothing of this sort. In fact, in some organizations there is a counter trend to emphasize individual merit pay. This is true for schools, government agencies, and some industrial organizations where merit pay has not been practiced. No clear pattern of policies has yet emerged.

Employment assurances are recognized as an important element of the new model; often companies go to great lengths to avoid unemployment or to assist in reemployment. Existing employees may be given high priority in training and retraining as old jobs are eliminated and new ones created. However, here again, no dominant pattern of policies has emerged.

Employee voice is a central feature of the new management model. If the work force is not unionized, management provides a variety of mechanisms for giving more employees more voice on more issues. This includes more assurances of due process. In unionized settings, both the representative systems and the mechanisms for direct participation are elaborated to provide greater employee consultation. At the same time, a more systematic effort is made to inform the work force about the business conditions affecting the workplace.

Union-management relations is by definition not an issue for many of the organizations that have pioneered the high-commitment model because their work forces have never been unionized. It is, however, an important question for corporations with unionized work forces that are committed to evolving toward a new model, such as Dana, Ford, Goodyear, and AT&T, to mention a few. The new model requires that union-management relations become less adversarial. Just how far the unions and companies are prepared to go toward broadening the agenda for joint problem solving and planning remains a major question and one of the problematic aspects of the new model, as we will discuss below.

The management philosophy that supports the new commitment model typically is inspiring or compelling in its content and is usually embodied in a published statement. The legitimate claims of *multiple* stakeholders—employees, customers, and the public, as well as owners—are usually acknowledged. The fulfillment of many employee needs is taken as a goal rather than merely a means to other ends.

The common thread of the policy elements of the new model is first to elicit employee commitment and then to expect effectiveness and efficiency to follow as second-order consequences. The theory is that these policies can both generate high commitment and provide ways to translate that commitment into enhanced performance. In the absence of the requisite high commitment, the work-force management systems based on these policies are distinctly more vulnerable than control models.[13] If broader and more contingent jobs, more general supervision, and more dynamic performance expectations are to be effective, there must be trust between levels of organization. Without trust, management is forced to reinstitute controls to ensure acceptable performance.

Transitional Model

While some new organizational units have adopted a comprehensive version of the commitment model, the transformation from control to commitment that occurs in established organizations usually involves a more limited set of changes. Usually only certain elements of the work-force management model are affected. We refer to this typical cluster of changes as a "transitional model." It appears to represent a sufficient degree of change to modify expectations, to make credible the leaders' stated intentions to move toward a more comprehensive commitment model, and to support and reinforce the initial changes in behavior. We believe that the transitional model can achieve a temporary equilibrium, but only if there is evidence of movement toward the more comprehensive commitment strategy.

The cornerstone of the transitional model is the widespread involvement of employees in problem-solving groups. Such groups are sometimes called quality circles, but they can have many other names as well. These groups expand the individual's responsibilities from performing the immediate job to upgrading the larger performance system. In unionized organizations, the precondition for this type of employee involvement is union-management dialogue leading to a jointly sponsored program. In any event, this type of employee involvement must be supported by additional training, a shift in management style, and additional communication. Participation is voluntary. Often managers develop ad hoc mechanisms for consulting employees about changes that affect them. Assurances are given that productivity improvements will not result directly in layoffs, and extra effort is made to avoid, defer, or minimize layoffs that result from technological change or decreased volumes. When layoffs or compensation concessions are necessary, they conform to the principle of "equality of sacrifice," and involve all employee groups, not just the hourly work force. Some visible changes are also made to deemphasize status differences.

Several elements of the work-force management model typically are not affected in the first major movement that creates the transitional model. The basic design of jobs, the compensation system, and the management structure and systems ordinarily remain unchanged. Over time, these elements are examined and modified in ways that will support the commitment strategy.

Potential Benefits from the Commitment Strategy

Those who advocate the commitment model believe it is superior in several respects. Properly implemented, it is more competitive—in terms of quality, cost effectiveness, and adaptiveness to change, including technological change. It provides more satisfying work and a more humane work environment. It accords more legitimacy to the management of the enterprise. In short, it does well in balancing and integrating the contemporary interests of the many stakeholders of the enterprise.

Is the superior potential from commitment universally available? Or do different task technologies offer different potential advantages from the commitment strategy? Theory indicates the latter.[14] Practice requires a more complicated assessment.

Both theory and practice confirm that some work technologies are more suited to an *ambitious* version of the commitment model, for example, those technologies that inherently require intricate team work, problem solving, learning, and self-monitoring. These conditions characterized many of the organizations that pioneered the high-commitment strategy—a fertilizer plant in Norway, a refinery in the United Kingdom, a paper mill in Pennsylvania, a food processing plant in Kansas. All were continuous process technologies. Capital intensive and raw material intensive, all provided high economic leverage to any improvements in human skills and attitudes. All were capable of providing a high level of intrinsic job challenge.

Is the converse true? Is an extreme version of the control model appropriate when the work can be completely prescribed, where it will remain static over time, and where the tasks are inherently individualized? These conditions may be met literally in the case of prisoners breaking rocks with sledgehammers in a prison yard. Mass production, epitomized by the assembly line, also was thought to illustrate these conditions, but this view is changing. In fact, U.S. management's interest in moving from control to commitment has been as strong in assembly-line units as in other task technologies.

Although the assembly-line task has seemed to emphasize reliable productivity, some managements have reconceived the work force's tasks in larger system terms and in more dynamic terms. Many elements of the assembly task do not change, but a role in process problem solving and methods improvement is added.

While the commitment model may yield greater absolute economic benefits and more impressive job satisfaction and human development in certain continuous process technologies, the incremental economic benefits and human gains in assembly lines may be equally important to the survival and prosperity of companies applying the commitment strategy to their operations of this type.

What are the costs and benefits of the commitment approach? When it has been implemented effectively and succeeds in eliciting high commitment, management reports the following types of benefits: higher in-plant quality, lower warranty costs, lower waste, higher machine utilization, increased total capacity with the same plant and equipment, fewer operating and support personnel, lower turnover and absenteeism, and faster start-up of new equipment. To achieve these gains, managers have had to invest extra effort, develop new skills and relationships, cope with higher levels of ambiguity and uncertainty, and experience the pain and discomfort associated with changing habits and attitudes. Some managerial skills have become obsolete, and some managerial careers have been casualties of change.

When union officials have entered into joint sponsorship of QWL and similar programs, they report improved product quality; reduced absenteeism and turnover; reduction in discharges, disciplinary layoffs, and grievance load; reelection of union officials who are proponents of QWL; increased dignity; and enhanced financial rewards.[15] Their basic motivations for entering into joint sponsorship include increased job security for the work force and the advantages to the union that come from influencing this transformation rather than standing apart from it. Like their counterparts in management, union officials have had to make the investments and to experience the difficulties associated with changing attitudes and skills.

For the worker, the quid pro quo includes greater autonomy and more influence in return for accepting more responsibility; potentially more social support in return for operating in more interdependent modes; and more opportunity for development and self-esteem in return for accepting greater uncertainty, including the possibility of failure.

Research generally supports the hypothesis of a net advantage to moving toward the commitment strategy.[16] That is, the *average* effectiveness of these units appears to be higher than the average of the more conventionally organized but otherwise comparable units. Poorly conceived or badly implemented commitment-oriented systems are undoubtedly less effective than the better managed conventional ones.

Problems and Progress in the Transformation Process

What type of errors have companies made as they search for conceptually sound and implementable versions of the commitment model? What are the most problematic aspects of the new model? And what factors and forces are determining the rate of transformation in U.S. industry?

Errors en Route to a New Model

Overreaching. In most management policy areas, the appropriate direction of change is clear, but the amount of change must be determined through a process of initial judgment, experience, and subsequent adjustment. For example, we envision jobs that are broader in scope, that incorporate planning as well as doing. But how broad? We are seeking optimal, not maximum breadth.

The optimum in terms of job scope, delegated self-supervision, voice, and other elements depends in part upon the degree of choice provided participants. In the initial redesign or in new organizational start-ups, individual participants may have had a personal influence on the design of the more ambitious version of the commitment model. Such involvement typically helps create a higher resolve to make the new model work. Those who join the organization later may not feel the same high resolve, nor may employees in organizations where the commitment model is initially implemented without the involvement of the work force.

In most cases of ambitious designs of a new organization, whether a single plant or a new enterprise, the planners initially overreach with respect to one or more elements of the model. In one plant, planners assigned an unduly large role to peer influence on decisions about pay adjustments. In another plant, they underplayed the role of first-line supervisors as a link in the chain of responsibility. In still another plant, they overemphasized learning of multiple skills and flexibility at the expense of depth of mastery in critical operations. In a new financial services company, the initial structural design called for unmanageably large spans of control. In the People Express case, the planners overestimated by a wide margin the amount of personnel flexibility and therefore individual job movement that would be feasible. These design errors, by themselves, are not fatal to the develop-

ment of a high-commitment work system. Some balance between prag-
matism and conceptual purity is necessary, however, and the
organization must be especially competent in monitoring and adjusting elements of its work-force management strategy.

Tokenism. A common error in the transformation from a control-
based to a commitment-based strategy is to make only token changes.
To be effective, modifications to the existing model must reach critical
mass. The coordinated set of changes that we have identified as the
"transitional model" in *Table 6-1* suggests the rough magnitude of
change required.

Over several decades U.S. management has made a series of attempts to modify the control model, but only on the margin. Management experimented with a succession of technique-oriented changes:
job enrichment, sensitivity training, management-by-objectives, group
brainstorming, and so on. In the past decade, quality circle programs

Table 6-1
Work Force Management Models

	Traditional Control Model	*Transitional Model*	*New Commitment Model*
1. Job Design Principles	Individual attention limited to performing individual job.	Scope of individual responsibility extended to upgrading system performance, via participative problem-solving groups in QWL, EI, and quality circle programs.	Individual responsibility extended to upgrading system performance.
	Job design deskills and fragments work and separates doing and thinking.	No change in traditional job design or accountability.	Job design enhances content of work, emphasizes whole task, and combines doing and thinking.
	Accountability focused on individual.		Frequent use of teams as basic accountable unit.
	Fixed job definition.		Flexible definition of duties, contingent on changing conditions.
2. Performance Expectations	Measured standards define minimum performance.		Emphasis placed on higher, "stretch objectives," which tend to be dynamic and oriented to the marketplace.
	Stability seen as desirable.		
3. Management Organization: Structure, Systems and Style	Structure tends to be layered, with top-down controls.	(No basic changes in approaches to structure, control, or authority.)	Flat organization structure with mutual influence systems.
	Coordination and control rely on rules and procedures.		Coordination and control based more on shared goals, values, and traditions.

Table 6-1 (*continued*)

	Traditional Control Model	Transitional Model	New Commitment Model
	More emphasis on prerogatives and positional authority.		Management emphasis on problem solving and relevant information and expertise.
	Status symbols distributed to reinforce hierarchy.	A few visible symbols change.	Minimum status differentials to deemphasize inherent hierarchy.
4. Compensation Policies	Variable pay where feasible to provide individual "incentive."	Typically no basic changes in compensation concepts.	Variable rewards to create equity and to reinforce group achievements: gain sharing, profit sharing.
	Individual pay geared to job evaluation.		Individual pay linked to skills, mastery.
	In downturn, cuts concentrated on hourly payroll.	"Equality of sacrifice" among employee groups.	Equality of sacrifice.
5. Employment Assurances	Employees regarded as variable costs.	Assurances that participation will not result in job loss.	Assurances that participation will not result in job loss.
		Extra effort to avoid layoffs.	High commitment to avoid or assist in reemployment.
			Priority for training and retaining existing work force.
6. Employee Voice Policies	Employee input allowed on relatively narrow agenda. Attendant risks emphasized. Methods include open-door policy, attitude surveys, grievance procedures, and collective bargaining in some organizations.	Addition of limited, ad hoc consultation mechanisms. No change in corporate governance.	Employee participation encouraged on wide range of issues. Attendant benefits emphasized. New concepts of corporate governance.
	Business information distributed on strictly defined "need to know" basis.	Additional sharing of information.	Business data shared widely.
7. Labor-Management Relations	Adversarial labor relations; emphasis on interest conflict.	Thawing of adversarial attitudes; joint sponsorship of QWL or EI; emphasis on common fate.	Mutuality in labor relations; joint planning and problem solving on expanded agenda.
			Unions, managements, and workers redefine their respective roles.
8. Management Philosophy	Management's philosophy emphasizes management prerogatives and obligations to shareowners.	Ad hoc shifts in stated priorities.	Management's philosophy acknowledges multiple stakeholders—owners, employees, customers, and public.

often have been implemented in this same spirit. If quality circles or any other technique is implemented without corresponding changes in other areas of the work force management model, and/or without a genuine change in management philosophy, positive effects will be limited and will decay rapidly.

Implementation deficiencies. Implementation failures are perhaps the most common form of error in moving toward a commitment model. In participative systems, for example, it is very important to define the boundaries of participation skillfully, so that one fully taps the creative energy of subordinates but does not generate unrealistic expectations. This is easier said than done. Similarly, effective groups must develop peer influence mechanisms but must also internalize restraints and standards of due process to temper the power of the group vis-à-vis the individual. Considerable conceptual clarity and skill are needed in shaping the norms of the organization.

Problematic Aspects of the Commitment Model

Continued development and definition are required in all elements of the model. In several areas, the search is for an optimum that will remain a moving target. This applies to broadening job design, to streamlining management structure and systems, and to the narrowing of status differences. In five areas of the work force management mode, more basic difficulties are apparent.

Employment assurances. It is difficult to create high commitment on the part of employees unless there is some reciprocal employment commitment to them. Why should employees strive to produce changes that may cost them or their fellow employees their jobs? Many U.S. observers see the lifetime employment guarantees extended to some segments of a corporation's work force as a cornerstone of the successful Japanese management system. Many U.S. managers in heavy manufacturing have become more interested in employment assurances because they would fit the new work-force management model. At the same time, however, current economic realities make employment assurances a less available policy alternative. Similarly, many high technology companies that pioneered high-commitment work systems and have emphasized employment security are now forced to rethink this aspect of the model.

What will emerge from this dilemma? Will the model provide lifetime assurances for the few, the employees who are able to reach ten, fifteen, or twenty years' seniority, as is illustrated by one type of experiment in the auto industry? Or will the model incorporate a policy that requires the company to make special efforts to avoid layoffs, thus clarifying that while the employment commitment for employees is not absolute, it is high priority—significantly higher priority than under the control models. Still another policy alternative is for the company to accept greater responsibility for outplacement of redundant employees.

I personally expect that the model will combine the second and third policy options. In any event, the commitment model is likely to incorporate a new level of effort to retrain existing employees to move from eliminated jobs to newly created jobs.

Compensation. If the work force management model is based on higher performance expectations and succeeds in both utilizing and developing employee capacities, it would be appropriate and just for employees to receive more generous financial rewards. Never has it been more appropriate in this sense to increase real wages and never has it been less feasible. This condition exists today because in the United States not only has the work force been underutilized, but also the wage rates have risen to levels that render many industries noncompetitive internationally. In certain industries, for example, trucking and airlines, new sources of domestic competition have placed companies that maintain the prevailing wage rates at a significant disadvantage.

Wage freezes, pay cuts, and concession bargaining create handicaps to commitment that must be overcome by other aspects of the workforce management model. Moreover, it is difficult to develop new compensation concepts at a time when the overall level of compensation cannot be raised and it may even be necessary to reduce pay to survive and to save jobs.

Even if overall levels of compensation were not a problem, it would not be obvious what type of compensation policies would best reinforce the commitment model.

New organizations search for alternatives to pay structures based on traditional job evaluation, the mainstay of the control model. Traditional wage structures involve dozens of job classification levels, with each job closely analyzed and differentially priced. For trade unions, rigid job demarcations have been a basis for limiting supervisors' latitude in directing the work force; they also help to protect jobs. For the individual worker, these carefully drawn and enforced demarcations give a sense of job ownership and accommodate his or her territorial instincts. Thus within the spirit of the control model, job evaluation has served the interests of all stakeholders.

However, the job evaluation structures tend to become counterproductive in the context of the commitment model, which emphasizes broader individual responsibilities, an orientation to end results rather than to minutely prescribed job input, and flexible, multiskilled workers.

New organizations pursuing the commitment model frequently base their pay structure on the employees' skill levels. The principles of skill-based pay structures have long been practiced in the engineering profession and skilled crafts, but have not been applied to many other employee groups. The extreme version of this system is to pay all job entrants at the same rate initially, and to move individuals to a progression of higher rates as they master additional skills and become more knowledgeable about the total work process and better able to take on assignments throughout the system. The motivational rationale for this system is that individuals will be reinforced for developing their capacities, for attending to the needs of the larger work process, and for accepting the uncertainty associated with changing assignments in response to business requirements. In designing the system, an economic analysis must ensure that the advantages resulting from the redundancies in skills generated, the positive motivational effects, and the work-force flexibility will more than offset the higher average wage that results when the system matures and a larger percentage of the work force becomes highly skilled.

This economic advantage is more readily assured in capital-intensive or raw material–intensive businesses in which the total payroll is a relatively small percentage of the costs of goods. But even when there is a good conceptual fit between skill-based pay and the rest of the work force management model, and the design of the structure is economically justified, many implementation difficulties remain to be solved: how to measure skill mastery and adhere to common standards in pay progression decisions, how to allocate opportunities for employees to learn new skills, how to ensure an optimal amount of breadth and flexibility versus depth and stability, how to handle the potential demotivating effects of topping out in a system in which the individual previously has been repeatedly reinforced for growth.

In existing plants, a traditional wage classification structure cannot be converted overnight to a skill-based structure because of the vested interests of those who occupy the more highly rated classifications. However, it is sometimes possible to progressively reduce the number of job classifications, to build more contingent duties and requirements for flexibility into certain key jobs, and to adjust the pay for those jobs accordingly. This is a common approach to moving beyond the transitional model.

Many organizations reaching for the commitment model adopt some form of gain sharing. Conceptually, profit sharing and group productivity bonuses both fit with a work system that emphasizes collaboration, coordination based on shared goals and values, and ambitious standards of performance. Profit sharing is an available option in many situations and contributes to a general sense of equity, but its positive effect on commitment often is relatively modest. The most widely recognized form of gain sharing is the Scanlon Plan, which shares with workers any gains in productivity, measured by improvements in the ratio of payroll to the sales value of production. Such group bonus schemes may have potential merit in a wide range of situations, but what is conceptually appropriate cannot always be implemented. For example, at the plant level, often one simply cannot devise a formula for sharing productivity gains that is readily understood, adequately responsive to employees' efforts, and appropriately independent of factors beyond their control. Smaller organizational units that are stand-alone businesses, employ mature technologies, and participate in relatively stable markets, are more likely to be able to devise a satisfactory gain-sharing scheme.

Work technology policy. The application of computer-based technology has profound implications for the evolution of work force management.[17] This technology can be either designed and implemented in a way that reinforces the control model or shaped so as to facilitate movement to the commitment model. To date, the directional effects have been variable and mostly unplanned. The following illustrates the variability:

- Applications of this type of technology sometimes narrow the scope of jobs and sometimes broaden them.
- They may emphasize the individual nature of task performance or promote the interdependent nature of the work of groups of employees.
- They may change the focus of decision making toward centralization or decentralization, with further implications for the steepness of the hierarchy.
- They create performance measurement systems that emphasize learning and self-control or surveillance and hierarchical control.
- They may transfer certain work functions from the unionized work force to supervisory or professional groups, or they may provide developmental opportunities for the workers.
- They can increase the flexibility of work schedules to accommodate human preferences or they can decrease flexibility and introduce shift work.

- They often contribute to social isolation, but sometimes they have the opposite effect.

Research indicates that when a technological application had effects that promoted commitment, these consequences were as likely to be accidental and unanticipated as were effects that reinforced the control model. The directional effects often were not inherent in the technology; that is, the control effects could have been minimized or revised had they been attended to early in the design and implementation process.

Both management and union have reason to give priority attention to the work force implications of new computer-based work technology. Without attention to both human concerns and business requirements, neither will be best served by the technology that results. Effective utilization of technology depends upon serving the needs of both.

As a rule, however, neither management nor union officials presently recognize the extent to which new work technology can be better managed in the interests of both parties. They share with many others in contemporary society an assumption about "technological determinism"—the idea that the side effects of technological progress are given and that individuals, organizations, and society must learn how to cope with them. Even in organizations otherwise pursuing the commitment strategy, there has been relatively little appreciation of technology policy as a manageable element of the model. In fact, it can be argued that computer-based technology is the least deterministic, the most flexible technology to affect the workplace since the beginning of the industrial revolution. Because these technologies are less hardware dependent and more software intensive and because of the rapidly declining cost of computer power, the basic technology permits an increased number of technical options. Thus, one can solve the business requirements with a greater variety of technical configurations, *each with a different set of human implications.* Progress in making better use of new technology and in using it to promote the commitment model requires a recognition of this potential by managers and by labor leaders.

Progress also depends on another type of knowledge—*how* to influence the technology development process at the design and early implementation stages. Line managers and senior union officials, who are one more step removed from the process, often are awed by the technology development process and do not know how or when they could intervene to ensure that social criteria are considered in addition to economic and technical criteria. Thus, a second need is to develop methods that influence but do not encumber the technology development process. These methods will need to include involvement by workers who will operate the new work technologies.

Progress in aligning the design of work technology with the commitment approach also depends on another factor—changes in the nature of the union-management relationship. Some work force issues, especially job skill, job pressure, and job satisfaction, are very difficult to address in a conflict-bargaining mode; integrative solutions to these issues are possible but can only be found through joint planning and problem solving. Limited experience with joint problem-solving processes and perceived risks associated with joint planning processes are factors that must be addressed.

Role of the supervisor. The commitment model implies a new set of role requirements for first-line supervisors: they should facilitate rather than direct the work force, impart rather than merely practice their technical and administrative expertise, and promote the development of self-managing capabilities of individual workers or work terms. In short, supervisors should delegate themselves out of their traditional functions—if not completely, then almost.

This role prescription is regarded as essential to support other commitment elements, especially meaningful jobs, lean and flexible management, and effective employee voice. However, supervision has proven to be one of the more problematic aspects of the commitment model.[18] Difficulties are encountered both in implementation and in basic conception.

Some of the implementation shortfalls of early projects are gradually being remedied: failure to train, support, and reinforce first-line supervisors for their team development task; and failure to recognize the supervisors' own needs for voice, dignity, and fulfillment while directing them to attend to the same needs in the work force.

Conceptual dilemmas are signaled by the titles often used in newly founded organizations, for example, *team advisers* or *team consultants* rather than *supervisor* or *team manager.* Taken literally, these titles signal that, unlike their supervisors, advisers and consultants are not in the chain of responsibility. In practice, however, team advisers are expected to be directive if necessary and to reassume functions delegated to the work force if they are not being performed. It is not surprising that the team advisers find this role exceedingly difficult. In many cases management has confused the *style* that supervisors are expected to use with the basic *responsibilities* they are expected to assume. The ideal style is advisory, but the responsibilities are to achieve certain human and economic outcomes. Interestingly, this ambiguity in titles has not extended to other management roles, such as plant manager, which are nevertheless expected, in the commitment model, to be performed in a participative and advisory style. I expect that with experience management will gradually regard the issue of delegation between the first-line supervisor and workers as similar to the delegation between other levels of the organization, that is, one delegates what subordinates are ready and able to perform. Then titles will not attempt to signal otherwise.

Other difficulties with the supervisory roles are even less tractable. The role in a commitment strategy requires relatively sophisticated interpersonal skills and some conceptual abilities often not present or potential in the existing supervisory work force. Many supervisors are not able to adapt to the new role.

Some companies have tried to provide the quality of talent required by the newly defined role by using it as an entry point to management for college graduates. This may work where the work force already has acquired the necessary technical expertise. However, it blocks a route of advancement for the blue-collar work force and sharpens the dividing line between management and the work force, thus weakening the thrust of other commitment practices. Moreover, unless the company is growing rapidly enough to open up higher-level positions for those college-educated supervisors, it is likely to find them increasingly impatient with shift work and other conditions of the first-line supervisor.

Where the new supervisory roles are filled from the ranks, even supervisors who become effective face dilemmas. If they successfully develop the teams they supervise and delegate their functions, what new responsibilities are delegated to them so that their own capabilities are fully utilized? Do their capabilities match the other managerial work that could be transferred? If fewer and fewer supervisors are required as they broaden their span of control from one to two to three teams, then what promotional opportunities exist for those who are no longer required?

The search continues for a viable and satisfying role for the first-line supervisor in the commitment model.

Union-management relations. Many companies that have pursued the commitment strategy, some for several decades, are not unionized and are not likely to become organized. Many companies that are trying to move away from the control approach do deal with unions. Often these companies have unions in most of their plants (the older ones), while a few newer plants are not unionized.

Some managements aspire to decertify their existing unions or render them ineffective. They expect other policy elements of the commitment strategy to strengthen employees' tie to the company and weaken those to the union. They hope that employees no longer will see the need for a third-party organization to represent them. With this set of hopes and expectations, they attempt to change the other policy elements with as little involvement by the union as possible. The obvious risk is that the union will perceive the threat and find ways to block both the policy changes and the attitudinal changes in the work force that management seeks. I do not expect this particular management strategy to be successful.

Other managements have decided to actively promote more cooperative relations with their existing unions. They have concluded that they could not successfully transform their work force management strategy without the active support of their unions. General Motors, Ford Motor Company, and AT&T offer well-publicized examples of this management approach. The unions in these instances and many others often have responded cautiously but also positively, for their own reasons. As indicated earlier, they may value the prospect of increasing the involvement of the work force; they may see this involvement as instrumental to improving competitiveness and preserving jobs. In addition, they may see in it the opportunity to expand the union-management agenda and therefore their own influence.

Management's interest in cooperative relations intensified in the late 1970s when it became evident that improved work force effectiveness would not close the competitive gap in many industries and that wage concessions and unprecedented wage constraints would be necessary for survival. On the basis of their own analysis of competitive conditions, unions agreed to wage concessions but often secured in return more influence over matters previously strictly within management control.

These developments have presented both unions and management with new challenges and dilemmas.

1. When companies pursue the so-called double-breasted strategy—trying to promote collaborative union relations in their unionized plants, but to keep the union out of any plants not yet organized—should the union attempt to force the company to choose? After General Motors had seen the potential from its joint QWL program with the UAW, the company conceded a neutrality clause (in 1976) and then adopted an automatic recognition policy in new plant start-ups (in 1979). The UAW has been insistent on these issues. If forced to choose, what should other managements do?[19]

2. Where union and management have collaborated in promoting QWL throughout the work force, how can the union prevent management from using the program to appeal directly to the workers about issues, such as wage concessions, that are subject to collective bargaining? This became an urgent concern of the UAW as it approached the 1982 negotiations with General Motors.

3. If, in the spirit of mutuality, the parties agree to expand their joint agenda, do they both recognize the demands for symmetry? Effective mutuality will require that the union approach some traditional adversarial bargaining items (for example, job classification and job security) in a problem-solving mode, and that the management bring into the agenda some items it has traditionally handled unilaterally (for example, technology plans, major investments, and outsourcing policies). As the parties expand the mutual agenda, what new risks will they face? Will management unduly complicate its strategic decision making? Will the union become too closely associated with actions that, however necessary, will be unpopular with its membership?

4. Do union officials have the expertise to deal effectively with the new agenda items, whether they be investment, pricing, or technology? They already have had to expand their skills and direct their resources to support QWL activities. The paradox is that shrinking employment has reduced the unions' membership and thus their financial resources at the very time they need to beef up their expertise by getting more training for current officials and bringing additional analytical specialties onto their central staffs.

5. Even if all the dilemmas described above can be handled satisfactorily, the union faces a major challenge in redefining its role and ideology to be sometimes an adversary and sometimes a partner of management.

It will take the better part of a decade for these dilemmas to be worked out in a large enough segment of industry to establish the prevailing pattern.

Rate of Transformation

How rapidly is the transformation described here occurring? To my knowledge, no studies have yet attempted to quantify the rate of change. It is not clear what operational indices one would use to chart this cultural change, inasmuch as the early stages of a shift in approach can be reflected by changes in any of several policy areas—job design, management restructuring, or participation. Moreover, the same phenomenon—for example, the establishment of quality circles—may reflect a basic shift toward commitment in one organization but be merely a gimmick within the control model in another organization. The headquarters executives of large companies often are not aware of what is happening in their own plants and offices or do not know how to interpret what they hear. Admittedly, those in companies actively promoting their transformation usually can offer an educated guess about the extent of change. For example, in 1981, a vice president of General Motors estimated that roughly equal proportions of GM plants had significant QWL activities, some activities, and none. In 1982, a few years after launching their joint QWL effort in 1980, executives of AT&T and CWA estimated that 5 percent of the vast Bell System's vast work force was involved in participative problem-solving groups. Unfortunately, few company-level estimates of this type are available.

Since we lack more systematic data, let me note some trends that I find indicative of the pace of change.

In 1970, only a few plants in the United States were systematically revising their approach to work force management. It was possible for those of us interested in this phenomenon to learn about most of these cases. By 1975, hundreds of plants were involved. I have learned in subsequent years of major projects that were under way in 1975, of which I was not then aware. I estimate that by 1980 thousands of plants were undertaking the comprehensive type of change that was limited to a few in 1970.

Within each of several companies I have observed over the past decade, the numbers of active plants grew from a few in the early 1970s to a dozen or dozens in the early 1980s. These companies include Owens-Illinois, Procter & Gamble, TRW, Goodyear, Butler Manufacturing, and Cummins Engine.

The source of initiatives within companies has shifted upward, and the change process is no longer experimental but rather a matter of policy. In the early 1970s experimental projects were generally initiated and sponsored by plant managers. Later the projects tended to receive more support from division-level management. In the early 1980s, company presidents and CEOs were increasingly structuring policy to promote companywide change.

Many of the managers who were associated with this type of innovative change at the plant level in the early or mid-1970s are in senior management positions today. Transformation of work force management remains one of their principal means for achieving enterprise effectiveness.

Certain structural factors are contributing to the shift in the model approach. First, a growing fraction of the U.S. industrial plants have been built in new locations since management began to take advantage of these greenfield opportunities to pioneer the new commitment model. Second, some industries, characterized by a commitment approach, such as computers, are expanding, whereas many industries (for example, auto, steel, and electrical equipment) that find it more difficult to replace the control model are declining.

The transformation is gaining momentum in part because of growing pressures for change. In addition, we are learning from experience. In 1974 I published an article that analyzed why a very small fraction of the innovations in the early pilot studies had spread within their own firm.[20] Within several years I could publish a report on the successful or promising diffusion strategies of three leading companies.[21] Today, most companies have experienced some diffusion of their successful innovations in the commitment approach.

We have been referring primarily to the blue-collar work forces. Where clerical operations resemble factory operations, the shift from control to commitment is conceptually analogous to the blue-collar transformation. However, the rate of change in these clerical operations has been slower, in part because the control model has not produced such overt employee disaffection; in part because management has been slower to recognize the importance of quality and productivity improvement in offices. Today, these conditions are changing, increasing management's interest in investing in the commitment model.

There has been more change in the model for managing the blue-collar work force than in the model for managing professional employees, in part because it is more readily apparent how to reform blue-collar (and clerical) operations. In a sense, the blue-collar reforms are a move in the direction of the model already idealized in managing professional forces. Apart from improvements in implementation and some marginal changes, for example, in consultation, no major options are being considered for the management of professionals.

The control model evolved over a long period, and it would not be surprising if several decades were required for the evolution and establishment of the commitment model. A more rapid transformation is to be encouraged, however. Here we analyze some of the factors pacing the diffusion of the new model.

We have already identified several factors: employee disaffection in the early 1970s, increased competitive pressure in the later 1970s, and concession bargaining in the early 1980s. The sequence and pacing of these developments was especially favorable to the emergence, diffusion, and testing of the commitment model. The earlier symptoms of disaffection provided the critical diagnostic insight that the work force management model was severely flawed. The increase in competition gave the diagnosis more urgency and expanded the constituencies concerned. Finally, concession bargaining came at a time when it risked cancelling some of the progress made under QWL activities, but it also confirmed the wisdom of undertaking those activities.

Our progress to date must be credited to certain industry and union leaders. For example, General Motors' effort, while overtaken recently by Ford's and AT&T's centrally directed change programs, was the most credible industrial pioneer during most of the 1970s. The UAW's Irv Bluestone and Don Ephlin inspired their colleagues to see the positive possibilities in QWL and were the most credible pioneers in the trade union movement during this same period.

The Japanese contributed to the transformation not only by the competitive pressure they generated but also by providing a striking illustration of the power of high-commitment work systems.

I do not expect a period of economic prosperity in the United States to retard the rate of transformation in companies and unions already committed to change, but it may slow down the rate at which new parties become part of the transformation process.

The amount of change achieved does not seem to be closely tied to the strength of the threats to an industry's or company's survival. The type of threat that the automobile industry experienced in the last half decade came earlier to the steel industry, but steel lagged behind autos in developing and diffusing a new work-force management model. General Motors was more secure than either Chrysler or Ford but took the lead in pioneering the search for a new model. AT&T and the CWA were dealing from strength when they undertook their joint sponsorship of QWL in 1980. Similarly, Goodyear enjoys a leadership position among tire makers, but it has been the most aggressive and systematic in drastically revising its work force management model. While competitive threats increase the general sense that change is required, those who lead in the change process will not necessarily be those who feel the threats most sharply.

What does differentiate the early changers from the followers? Executive leadership? Yes. A prior management philosophy that emphasizes people and therefore makes high commitment a more credible policy objective? Absolutely. General managerial competence in implementation? Certainly. Visionary and secure union leadership? Indeed. Later changers appear to be influenced by the apparent successes of the leaders. These views are based on a decade of personal observation and my reading of the literature on the subject; they are offered here as working hypotheses.

Notes

1. William J. Abernathy, Kim B. Clark, and Alan M. Kantrow, *Industrial Renaissance* (New York: Basic Books, Inc., 1983); Paul R. Lawrence and Davis Dyer, *Renewing American Industry* (New York: Free Press, 1983); Rosabeth Moss Kanter, *The Change Masters* (New York: Simon and Schuster, 1983); Michael Maccoby, *The Leader* (New York: Simon and Schuster, 1981); William G. Ouchi, *Theory Z* (Reading, Mass.: Addison-Wesley, 1981).

2. Abernathy et al., *Industrial Renaissance*, 91.

3. George C. Lodge, *The New American Ideology* (New York: Alfred Knopf, Inc., 1975).

4. Edward E. Lawler III, "The New Plant Revolution," *Organization Dynamics,* Winter 1978, 2–12.

5. Robert Guest, "Quality of Work Life—Learning from Tarrytown," *Harvard Business Review,* July-August 1979, 76–87.

6. Thomas A. Kochan, Harry C. Katz, and Nancy R. Mower, "Worker Participation and American Unions: Threat or Opportunity," Sloan School of Management Working Paper, Massachusetts Institute of Technology, May 1983.

7. Eric Trist has distinguished four strategic options for management regarding QWL: rejection, laissez-faire, selective development, and corporatewide commitment. The more advanced companies in the United States are pursuing a combination of the last two options. See Eric Trist, "QWL and the 1980s," chapter 3 in *The Quality of Working Life and the 1980s,* edited by Harvey Kolodny and Hans van Beinum (New York: Praeger, 1983), 48.

8. Debra Whitestone and Leonard A. Schlesinger, "People Express (A)," Harvard Business School Case No. 483-103, 1982.

9. Michael J. Piori, "Why Unions Don't Work Anymore," *INC Magazine,* March 1982, 16–17.

10. Chris Argyris, *Personality and Organization* (New York: Harper and Bros., 1957).

11. Others have drawn attention to the emergence of a new dominant pattern in work organizations. For example, Trist has articulated contrasting "organizational paradigms" that are in much the same spirit as the more detailed distinctions I made here between the control and commitment workforce management models. He refers to them as the "Old Paradigm" and the "New Paradigm." See Trist, "QWL and the 1980s," 47.

12. J. Richard Hackman and G. R. Olsen, *Work Redesign* (Reading, Mass.: Addison-Wesley, 1980).

13. Richard E. Walton, "Establishing and Maintaining High Commitment Work Systems," in John R. Kimberly, Robert H. Miles, and Associates, *Organization Life Cycles* (San Francisco: Jossey-Bass, Inc., 1980).

14. Tom Burns and G. Stalker, *The Management of Innovation* (London: Torestock Publications, 1961); Walton, "High Commitment Work Systems."

15. Irving Bluestone, "Labor's Stake in Improving the Quality of Working

Life," in *The Quality of Working Life and the 1980s*, edited by Harvey Kolodny and Hans van Beinum (New York: Praeger, 1983), 33–41.

16. Raymond A. Katzell and Daniel Yankelovich, *Work, Productivity and Job Satisfaction: An Evaluation of Policy-Related Research* (New York: Harcourt Brace Jovanovich, Inc., 1975); Hackman and Olsen, *Work Redesign;* Robert Zager and Michael R. Rosow, eds., *The Innovative Organization: Productivity Programs in Action* (New York: Pergamon Press, 1982).

17. Richard E. Walton and Wendy Vittori, "New Information Technology: Organizational Problem or Opportunity?" *Office: Technology and People* 1 (1983): 249–73; Richard E. Walton, "New Work Technology and Its Workforce Implications: Union and Management Approaches," Harvard Business School Working Paper, April 1983; Joel A. Faden, "Automation and Work Design in the United States," Center for Quality of Working Life, Institute of Industrial Relations, University of California, Los Angeles, 1982.

18. Richard E. Walton and Leonard A. Schlesinger, "Do Supervisors Thrive in Participative Work Systems?" *Organizational Dynamics,* Winter 1979. Leonard A. Schlesinger and Janice A. Klein, "The First Line Supervisor: Past, Present, and Future," in *Handbook of Organizational Behavior,* ed. J. Lorsch (Englewood Cliffs, N.J.: Prentice-Hall, 1985).

19. Thomas A. Kochen, Robert B. McKensie, and Peter Cappelli, "Strategic Choice and Industrial Relations Theory and Practice," Sloan School of Management Working Paper, Massachusetts Institute of Technology, October 1983.

20. Richard E. Walton, "The Diffusion of New Work Structures: Explaining Why Success Didn't Take," *Organizational Dynamics,* Winter 1975.

21. Richard E. Walton, "Successful Strategies for Diffusing Work Innovations," *Journal of Contemporary Business,* Spring 1977.

Commentary
The Commitment Model: From "Whether" to "How"

J. Richard Hackman

Introduction

A couple of years ago a senior manager at Cummins Engine visited my class on organizational design for self-management to talk with students about the company's innovative plant at Jamestown, New York. One of the class members asked, quite reasonably, for the visitor's views about the circumstances under which a high-commitment organizational design, such as the one at Jamestown, would be preferred over a traditional organizational model. "That's last year's question," he responded. "The question for today's managers is not *whether* to design organizations for high involvement and self-management, but *how* to do it, and how to do it well."

Walton appears to share the assumption of the Cummins executive as do I. If they are structured and managed competently, organizations based on what Walton calls the "commitment" model generally outperform those based on the "control" model. Yet the "if" must be taken seriously: There are many high-commitment organizations that perform far below their potential, and less well than competently managed traditional firms. The Cummins executive and Walton agree that we have a great deal still to learn about high-commitment work organizations.

Walton examines two sets of problems that are impeding progress in the transformation of the workplace: The first set deals with errors in implementing the commitment model, and the second addresses problematic aspects of the model itself. Since I find little to quarrel with either in Walton's descriptions of the commitment and control models or in his list of errors and problems, this commentary will add to and elaborate on certain items in his list. In doing that, two messages are intended. One, it is *difficult* to manage in accord with the commitment model—more difficult than many managers who wish to reap the benefits of high-commitment and better human resource utilization in their organizations realize. And two, the considerable effort required to develop new organizational forms, and to learn new ways of behaving within those forms, is a far more engaging and ultimately productive enterprise than continuing the time-worn debates about when "participation" is and is not a good idea.

Errors en Route

Walton lists three problems that are encountered in attempting to move from a control to a commitment model: overreaching, tokenism, and deficiencies in implementation. To these, the following additional difficulties can be added, each of which I have encountered in my own research on organizations that aspire to the commitment model.

1. *Managerial reluctance to exercise legitimate authority in setting direction.* People are often ambivalent about exercising authority, and people who happen to be managers are no exception. Confronting issues about which we are ambivalent is invariably anxiety-arousing, and it is tempting to keep those anxieties under control by wholly embracing one or the other side of such an issue. So, in a control-oriented organization, we sometimes observe managers making decisions and giving orders in ways that make it clear to all just who is in charge—even if the ideas and involvement of others are closed off in the process. In commitment-oriented organizations, on the other hand, we sometimes see managers declining to take a personal position about *anything*, even if that sometimes blurs the direction and identity of the enterprise. Both patterns of behavior make life at work a little easier for a manager who is conflicted about his or her own authority, but neither may be in the best interest of the organization.

Now, it is clear that the "I am the boss, and what I say goes" syndrome is wholly inappropriate for managing a high-commitment organization. It is perhaps less clear, but also true, that a managerial style in which consensus is relentlessly pursued is also inappropriate in such organizations. In fact, some things are *not* open for discussion and negotiation even in high-commitment organizations. Those who own an enterprise, for example, or who act on their behalf, have the right to specify the directions and aspirations of the organization—to say, in effect, "This is the mountain we will climb. Not that one, this one. And while many aspects of our collective endeavor are open for discussion, choice of mountains is not among them."

Will such an assertion depower and alienate organization members?

No. On the contrary, having a clear statement of the direction of an enterprise tends to be *em*powering—something that helps energize people and direct them toward common goals, even when those goals may not be ranked highest on the individuals' personal lists of aspirations.

What is depowering is to exercise authority about details of the behavior that individuals exhibit in pursuing collective aspirations. So, while an effective manager in a high-commitment organization may be clear and insistent about the choice of mountain to be climbed, he or she will suppress any inclination to dictate how each stream should be crossed on the way up the mountain, or to ask individuals to await his or her instructions at each fork in the trail.

Managers in a high-commitment organization must be clear and articulate about organizational directions without falling into a syndrome of close, hands-on supervision. Making this distinction, and behaving in accord with it, turns out to be a considerable personal challenge for many managers. And, overall, I find that I spend far more time encouraging managers in high-commitment organizations to exercise their authority about directions than I do discouraging them from being excessively directive.

2. *Setting "stretch" objectives without providing the support needed to achieve them or holding people accountable for them.* Walton points out that high-commitment organizations tend to have expectations about performance that stretch and challenge people, implying that such organizations may give relatively less attention to the definition and enforcement of minimum standards of acceptable performance. I agree that stretch objectives are characteristic of high-commitment organizations and believe them to be a positive influence on organizational effectiveness. For this reason, helping members develop engaging and challenging performance objectives is an important part of the manager's role in such organizations. Yet I have repeatedly observed managers in these organizations being satisfied with the articulation of challenging objectives—overlooking the conditions that must be put in place to support work toward their accomplishment, and failing to hold people accountable for whether or not they are attained. From the behavior of these individuals, one might infer that they believe that high aspirations are not only necessary for organizational excellence, but that they also are about all that is needed to achieve it.

In one organization, for example, senior managers spent a great deal of time and effort developing and communicating the overall aspirations of the organization and were both clear and articulate about the meaning of—and the need for—superb performance by all members.

They were successful in engaging the motivation of the great majority of the people, and in directing them toward worthy goals. But, with that accomplished, their attention turned to other matters. No one worried much about whether or not the people had the material resources and organizational supports they needed to achieve the stretch objectives, nor were individuals or teams held directly accountable for accomplishing them. Member effort and commitment, initially quite high throughout the firm, gradually slipped as people experienced frustration and occasional disillusionment with how the organization was functioning. Top management responded by reinforcing educational programs intended to teach members about the directions and objectives of the organization, and by exhorting people to view the performance difficulties as an olympic challenge to be surmounted. Yet the continued insufficiency of resources and organizational support for the work gave many people an easy explanation for their own less-than-olympic performance and, worse, a good reason to forgive poor performance by others. The functioning of the organization deteriorated markedly before top management recognized the importance of attending to resources, support, and accountability in addition to the "stretch" objectives they had spent so much time formulating and communicating.

If anything, seemingly mundane matters such as resources, support systems, and accountability are even more important in high-commitment organizations than they are in more traditional enterprises. To ask someone to reach for the moon is to incur an obligation to be especially attentive to what he or she needs to get there. Many managers in high-commitment organizations seem not to understand this or fail to recognize its importance. And consultants to such organizations seem invariably to find such matters less worthy of their time than conceptual work on the design and direction of the enterprise as a whole. If the commitment model is to prosper, I suspect there may have to be a reemphasis, by managers and consultants alike, on developing and implementing the organizational supports that people need in their day-to-day work. For only if that work gets done well can the achievement of "stretch" objectives become a realistic possibility.

3. *Assuming that "the group will work things out."* As Walton notes, groups and teams of various kinds pervade almost every high-commitment work organization. Groups provide a setting in which people can learn how to work together on shared objectives, they promote norms of collaboration, and they provide a close-to-home site where the inevitable tensions between individual and collective aspirations can be addressed and negotiated among peers. Altogether,

groups are natural and appropriate features of high-commitment organizations.

Yet members of such organizations often act as if they believe some sort of magic takes place in groups. Teams are formed casually, tossed important but ill-defined tasks, and sent away to let group process do its magical work. Far too often the outcome is a late product of dubious quality and deteriorated relationships among team members—resulting in frustration and disappointment that is shared by the task-giver and the team members.

Does it need to be said again that it makes a difference how a group is composed—how large it is, the mix of members, the clarity of group boundaries? Or that some team tasks engage and motivate members, while others serve mainly to frustrate and alienate them? Or that the reward and information systems of an organization can profoundly affect how members behave in a team and how well they perform? Or that the kind of support and assistance provided to the group sometimes spells the difference between a group that gets over the hurdles it inevitably encounters and one that finds its progress blocked by them? No, such things need not be said. We already know they are true.

Then why do we see groups created and managed so casually in organizations, particularly in high-commitment organizations where they are such a key design feature? There are several possible responses to this question. One is that groups are sometimes used inappropriately. A team may be given a task that can be done more efficiently and creatively by an individual working intensively on his or her own. Or a team may be used as a place to "dump" a problem that no one knows quite what to do with. Since the right way to proceed is unclear, the thinking goes, let's form a task force to take a look at it. Team members are then selected (perhaps based on who has some time available, or on political considerations), the group has a meeting with a senior manager who gives them a general sense of the problem to be addressed, and the manager is then able to put the troublesome matter out of mind—at least for a time.

Another possible response is that we do not know nearly as much as we think we do about the conditions that actually must be in place to foster effective team performance. As a result, we unintentionally design groups in ways that impede rather than foster their effectiveness. Then, when team performance turns out to be substandard, we have trouble figuring out what the problem was. Still another response is while we do know generally what needs to be in place to help a group do well, we do not have the skills to execute our good intentions—or, perhaps, we do not think it is worth the time and trouble to do so.

Whatever the reason, I have found in my research far too many groups given important work to do in high-commitment organizations that do not have a realistic chance to succeed. The way they are formed, and how their tasks are designed, stack the cards against them before members have their first meeting. And that disability is reinforced thereafter by the absence of the organizational and managerial supports the team needs to perform its work well.

Creating effective teams in organizations is not a simple or straightforward task; neither is being an effective member of an organizational team or task force. Both managers and group members need to know some things about the determinants of group effectiveness, and to develop some skills in using *what* they know, if the considerable potential that work teams have in high-commitment organizations is to be realized. I wish the need for this kind of learning were more widely recognized than I think it is—and I wish I knew more managers who were actively working to hone their skills as designers and managers of organizational groups.

The concerns about learning expressed above apply not only to the design and management of groups but also to the other issues on Walton's list of problems. Because they are new, the management behaviors required to create and maintain high-commitment work organizations will seem unfamiliar and awkward to many managers, and hard for them to perform well. But that is true for any new endeavor. Trying to make sense of a balance sheet, for example, or designing a new production technology, can also feel awkward and unfamiliar, and be just as hard for an unpracticed manager to do well. Yet for some reason we are far more willing to acknowledge the need for training and experience in those areas than we are in aspects of work having to do with the effective use of human resources.

Managing a high-commitment work organization is every bit as tough as figuring out what to do about the numbers on a balance sheet and requires just as much education, practice, and coaching. The sooner we recognize this, the sooner we can be on our way to developing a cadre of managers who are able to harvest the considerable contributions that high-commitment work organizations have to make to the people who own them, the people who work in them, and the people who are served by them.

Problems with the Commitment Model Itself

What if we did learn how to overcome the problems en route and found ourselves with a good number of organizations operating in accord with the tenets of a commitment model? Is the model sturdy enough to withstand success? Walton's paper suggests that the answer is not yet clear and identifies five aspects of the commitment model that remain problematic (employment assurances, compensation, work technology policy, role of the supervisor, and union-management relations). Unless the issues Walton raises can be resolved, the model is likely to be self-limiting. That is, after one makes some amount of progress in realizing the aspirations of the commitment model, further progress will be frustrated by properties of the model itself.

But what if we surmount those difficulties as well? What are the longer-term implications of the model? Does it provide a relatively stable and potentially enduring alternative form of work organization, or is it more likely to prompt a new set of problems and instabilities in the workplace and in society? This commentary concludes with some speculations about these questions, specifically as they apply to the first two of Walton's five problematic issues.

Employee assurances. As organizations become successful in using the commitment model, they may find that they are able to get more work done better, with fewer employees. What is to be done with the surplus staff? Are jobs to be secure only for certain groups of employees, perhaps those who have seniority in the firm? Will organizations be expected to carry on the employment rolls people who are not really needed? Are elaborate outplacement programs the answer? Walton raises all these options for consideration, and they all deserve discussion. But none of them seems up to the challenge that would be posed by widespread and enduring adoption of the commitment model. One cannot simply write off younger people in the work force. Nor is it consistent with the tenets of the commitment model to have people employed who have little productive work to do. Nor is the outplacement option viable if other organizations also have a surplus rather than a scarcity of qualified staff.

The problem would be less severe if we could count on sustained economic growth, because that would provide a continuous influx of new opportunities for productive work by people not needed in existing organizational units. But imagine for a moment that the rate of growth of the economy as a whole slows significantly (as population growth approaches zero), at the same time that existing organizations become leaner and more effective. What would be available to people who are "free" for meaningful employment under such circumstances? To expand welfare services and compensate such individuals for *not* working seems inconsistent with the core premises of the commitment model. Can we, then, imagine groups of public philosophers, artists, and poets compensated by society for enriching the intellectual and aesthetic environment? An interesting possibility, surely, but one that would require radical rethinking of the goals of society and the way shared resources are allocated toward achieving those goals.

Because there appear to be no easy answers to the employment assurance problem in the long term, the issue deserves hard and systematic thought by those who have interest in the evolution of the commitment model. And when strategies for dealing with the problems *are* developed, I suspect they will raise fundamental questions about social values and have major implications for social and macroeconomic policy.

Compensation. In the early days of job enrichment, a number of managers and scholars assumed that having interesting work would be sufficient reward to compensate people for working harder and producing more than they did when their jobs were routine, simplified, and segmented. We now have ample evidence that this assumption was badly flawed: When people do more for an economic organization, they expect (and often demand) more in return—specifically, more dollars. How, then, should people be compensated in a high-commitment organization, where everyone is expected to work hard and collaboratively in pursuing organizational goals?

Walton notes that the dominant compensation model in start-up organizations that aspire to the commitment model is one that bases compensation on employees' skill levels. As people learn how to do more jobs in the organization, they are paid at higher rates, thereby providing a powerful incentive for continued learning. My sense of the evidence is that the model works as intended: People work hard to learn more in start-up situations, partly because the learning is intrinsically rewarding but also because learning contributes to their personal economic well-being.

I have two concerns about the long-term viability of the skill-based compensation model. The first (and less serious) is whether most organizations actually need everyone to know how to do everything. While some firms do have this need, other organizations may wind up with groups of people who have skills they do not use and that the organization does not need, at least not in such quantity. Like having a larger staff than is needed to get the work done, this would be inconsistent with the tenets of the commitment model. My second concern is with what happens when most people in an organizational unit have reached the ceiling—that is, they know how to do all the available jobs, and they perceive little opportunity for future increases in compensation. This plateau has been reached in a number of new plants organized in accord with the commitment model, and it appears to have deleterious implications for the future development of the organization and the people.

A common response to this state of affairs, as Walton observes, is some kind of gain-sharing or profit-sharing plan. Such plans have much to recommend them in high-commitment organizations. For one thing, they foster and reinforce collaborative thought and effort to improve the effectiveness of the enterprise as a whole. For another, they reward actual organizational *performance* (or improvements in performance) rather than simple increases in individuals' repertoires of skills (something far more appropriate during start-up than when the collective challenge is to sustain growth and profitability). Moreover, these plans encounter a ceiling only when (if ever) there are no further improvements to be made in productivity and profitability—surely providing people with greater opportunity for continued growth in compensation than is the case for most skill-based plans.

Yet, taking the longer perspective, I suspect that gain sharing and profit sharing may also turn out to be transitional programs. Without straining one's historical eyes too seriously, one can discern a trend in compensation arrangements from hourly wages, to flat salaries, to skill-based programs, and now to gain- and profit-sharing programs. Accompanying this trend, for many organization members, has been an increase in the desire to have a "say" in how the firm operates (and a greater feeling of legitimacy in asking for it), and a stronger insistence on sharing in any increases in the overall financial worth of the entity as a whole. That these matters are the traditional prerogatives of owners is precisely the point. As members of the work force are increasingly asked to *behave* like owners (for example, by taking responsibility and accepting accountability for significant pieces of work, and collaborating with others to improve the functioning of organizational units beyond one's own job or section), they also increasingly expect to be *treated* like owners, enjoying the prerogatives and exercising the rights that owners traditionally have in a capitalist economy.[1]

This trend—if indeed it is a trend, and if it continues—may have consequences that extend far beyond what happens in single high-commitment firms. Over the long term, for example, there would be substantial changes in the structure and distribution of ownership of economic organizations, changes that would alter how decision-making power and political influence are distributed in society at large. Indeed, the meaning of "capitalism" in our society, and the way it operates, would gradually but inevitably change. Such changes, in my view, have much to recommend them. But, like the longer-term implications of employee *assurance* programs under the high-commitment model, they have a vaguely revolutionary flavor. That flavor, as delectable as it may be to some, surely will offend the palates of those who presently have the larger share of power and wealth in our society. Should the commitment model indeed prosper and diffuse throughout the economy, we may have some interesting political times ahead of us.

Conclusion

The management literature is filled with various theories and techniques intended to contribute to organizational effectiveness through better utilization of human resources. These devices typically have a fairly short and predictable life cycle: they prompt much excitement when introduced, yield well-publicized early successes, are found to be more difficult to implement and diffuse than originally thought, and eventually give way to yet another exciting new idea. Is the commitment model just one more entry in this continuing parade of management fashion?

I think not. To be sure, various writers have, at various times in recent years, identified programs such as quality circles, job enrichment, autonomous teams, gain sharing, and labor-management committees as the key to improving productivity and human resource utilization in work organizations. Devices such as these are common in high-commitment organizations, and some of them, indeed, have followed the life cycle sketched above. But the commitment model itself is considerably more than the aggregation of specific programs and techniques. It is, instead, an approach to the design and management of organized endeavor that challenges many well-accepted ideas about how to structure work and authority, about ways to develop and effectively employ human resources, and about the proper distribution of voice and economic benefit among an organization's many constituencies. The commitment model is not merely the latest management fad.

I am, nonetheless, unsure whether the model will continue to prosper and diffuse throughout society. Even if the executive quoted at the beginning of this commentary is right that we have broken through the *whether* barrier to more productive questions about *how* to structure and manage high-commitment organizations, the road ahead will not be smooth. The conceptual, practical, political, and ideological questions that remain to be addressed are difficult, controversial—and may even be unanswerable. Walton's chapter is a great help in sorting out those questions, and in providing conceptual directions and practical insights for dealing with them.

Note

1. Advocates of worker cooperatives have been espousing the virtues of ownership and collaborative effort for years—but, perhaps because cooperatives often are small, capital poor, and shy on business expertise, there are only a few worker cooperatives that can be held up as models to illustrate the benefits of ownership. It would be ironic if established businesses, often used as a point of contrast for worker-owned enterprises, should turn out to provide a better means of realizing the values of ownership than cooperatives that have been founded specifically to pursue those values.

Part Two
Discussion Summary

Introduction

The identification by the Hayes-Clark chapter of disruptive "confusion" as a key factor in U.S. plants was regarded by the colloquium participants as an important addition to the general debate about productivity and innovation. It formed one of five key themes that were explored during the discussion of this group of papers. The others were:

- The need for more effective management of organizational learning, and ways to encourage it;
- The tendency of American firms to direct their capital investment mainly toward reducing direct labor, and the fact that such investments appeared to have a diminishing impact on productivity;
- The need for firms to replace their outdated measurement and accounting systems with ones that better reflect the needs and capabilities of new manufacturing approaches and technology;
- Whether the new "commitment" model of employee relations is applicable generally, or only useful in certain situations.

The "Confusion" Syndrome

The Hayes-Clark chapter's discovery of the extraordinary impact of factory "confusion" prompted an intense debate about its causes and consequences, and about ways in which it might be reduced.

Changes, either in engineering requirements or in schedules, had been "the biggest single cause of low productivity in our plant" until corrective action was taken, conceded the senior divisional manager in a "smokestack" industry, Carl Schlemmer (vice president and general manager, GE Transportation Systems).

Nor was the problem confined to the maturer industries. High technology process industries were forced continually to introduce a lot of frontier-pushing processes that were not fully understood, pointed out Bob Slade (advisor, manufacturing technology, IBM). The result was *"a constant flow of changes," and repeated transitions to the start of a new learning curve.*

Jeffrey Miller (professor, Boston University) estimated, on the basis of a comparative study, that the frequency of engineering changes for the typical U.S. firm was as much as twice that of a Japanese company. The same ratio of discrepancy applied to the practice of changing schedules in midstream, he reported. Engineering change orders became increasingly disruptive with higher volume, emphasized Ray Abu-Zayyad (vice president, IBM).

The prevalence of work-in-process (WIP) in U.S. firms was closely associated with the instability of U.S. production environments, suggested Miller. "WIP is there for a purpose. It's there because you've got lots of engineering changes, or because you're rushing something up ahead of something else"—or, indeed, because the whole system was geared to anticipating such changes. In the words of Dale Hartman (director of manufacturing technology, Hughes Aircraft), "WIP reflects the American approach of 'just in case,' in contrast with the Japanese 'just in time.' "

Criticism of American laxity in measuring the use of materials came from Gerhard Veller, whose company, Van Leer B.V., has purchased several subsidiaries in the United States in recent years. In his industry, raw materials accounted for between one-half and two-thirds of total selling prices, yet he saw U.S. companies as still relatively unaware of their materials usage. "To us it is inconceivable not to know, almost from day to day, the raw materials usage and all the other factors that have an influence on manufacturing cost."

Trying to "tame" the incessant change and confusion in many U.S. plants would have considerable implications not only for the relationships between manufacturing and development, but also for the R&D process itself, warned Miller (for a further discussion of this issue, see Part Three).

Describing how his firm had set about resolving the problem—and implicitly challenging the thesis that investment in innovative production technology necessarily creates a damaging form of confusion in the manufacturing process—Schlemmer said GE had done it primarily through technology: It now had "the ability to generate the information necessary to reprogram the machine tools on an instantaneous basis, using a computer." Yet Abu-Zayyad warned that more controls and more equipment did not necessarily bring a better manufacturing process; complexity created confusion in manufacturing and is "an indication of an ill-defined manufacturing process."

The Learning Conundrum

Confusion was also the result of companies learning "on-line," rather than "off-line," suggested Geoffrey Place (vice president, research and development, Procter & Gamble). In a process industry, such as aerospace, a considerable investment had to be made in the learning process at the start, so that the aircraft flew "from the word go." At the other extreme was the typical assembly operation, where one sometimes could get away with very little learning; one "dumped" work on the plant and hoped that over the following two or three years it could sort itself out and get up to a reasonable level of efficiency. "But," said Place, "if you look at the total costs in that situation, then not doing the learning ahead of time can in fact be a very high cost strategy."

This was very much a political issue within companies, noted Place. Many up-front costs, called "R&D budget items," "engineering appropriations," or whatever, were "highly visible, big chunks of money." But when included in the much larger manufacturing budget, such items tended to be, if not invisible, regarded as almost inevitable.

For this reason, and many others, "the way we manage learning," from development through to production, was of fundamental importance, stressed Slade. "Sharing and interaction are critical," added Ikujiro Nonaka (professor, Hitotsubashi University). John Doyle (vice president of research and development, Hewlett-Packard) pointed out the difficulties involved in transferring learning between plants. Hewlett-Packard had considerable experience in this, having established an average of two new plants each year since 1957. In the early life of a plant, he said, there tended to be considerable willingness to learn from others, but this rapidly attenuated. He had therefore come to appreciate the importance, as in Japan, of lifelong learning "as a value in and of itself."

The Bias to Labor Saving

A major reason for the lack of impact of capital investment in American industry, according to Slade, was that "we...often apply capital in the wrong places." Applying it to labor, for example, attacked only "a tiny part of the productivity problem," since labor was less than 20 percent of the costs in many industries, and probably under 10 percent in most of them. Together with slowness in learning, this explained why "sometimes we don't achieve the degree of productivity we'd like."

A vivid example of the problem was provided by Hartman. His company had recently completed a study of a major manufacturing operation, employing about 4,000 people, where direct labor currently accounted for 12 percent of costs. Indirect labor and support activities represented 38 percent, and the remaining 50 percent was attributable to materials and subcontractors. Over the next five years the plant was expected to shift to 5 percent or less in direct labor, with a commensurate increase in the indirect and support areas.

Linking this issue directly to Kaplan's chapter on the outdated nature of most companies' cost accounting systems (see discussion below), Robert Hayes (professor, Harvard Business School) argued that "one of the reasons companies pay so much attention to direct labor, and to reducing it, is because that's what their accounting systems are set up to measure." Harold Edmondson (vice president of manufacturing, Hewlett-Packard) emphasized that other types of productivity were of equal importance, such as getting new products into manufacture quickly, adapting the production process to be more flexible to consumer needs, and so forth.

The Cost of Blinkered Accounting

"How did we get into this mess?" (the overwhelming predominance of narrow, often inappropriate, short-term financial measures of manufacturing performance that are described in Kaplan's chapter). Edmondson answered his own question by explaining that "it's the lowest common denominator syndrome. You try to measure two divisions within a company, or two companies within an industry. . .and you keep looking for measurements and rejecting them because they aren't quite the same. Finally you work your way down to a few things (usually aggregates) that are comparable."

In addition to the usual financial yardsticks, Edmondson said Hewlett-Packard had recently recognized that "there are some other things that we want to measure. A number of our divisions are in different businesses, and we are expecting different things of their manufacturing organizations." The old rule had been to demand, for example, that "three months' inventory is what you've got to have. Anybody with more than three months, that's bad; anybody with less than three months, that's good."

The company, Edmondson said, had "finally recognized that there are some other things that affect those numbers, such as the business you're in, but more specifically what's being asked of the manufacturing organization." Hewlett-Packard was "taking a step back, and try-

ing to make sure we know what we want from each of the fifty individual organizations. We're going to try to develop some measures based on specific strategies. We may come up with a system that says the accounting numbers don't have to be only dollars, but could be other things, such as months between a pilot run and the first shipment of a new product, or other measures that are not currently considered to be very important because they don't come out of the accounting department." Not only had his company recognized the inadequacy of its accounting system, said Edmondson, but fundamentally "we've . . . recognized the inadequacy of our whole measurement system."

Reaffirming that "accounting is merely a communication device, which is always late," Stephen Willey (senior vice president, Kimberly-Clark) said his company's U.S. consumer businesses had converted their system from being based on external requirements to what was needed internally: such data could then be converted easily for external use.

Debating whether or not Japanese companies make heavy use of financial measures, Owen Robbins (vice president for finance, Teradyne) said, "They are not nearly as concerned with accounting numbers as we are." But Kim Clark (professor, Harvard Business School) maintained that "the Japanese crunch numbers a lot more than we do. The difference is that they're very focused, often using physical quantities rather than financial data." He agreed, however, that the Japanese manufacturing plant was not "run by the numbers"; instead, "number-crunching" was a central staff function.

Several participants suggested that changing the "informal" measurement systems that underlay the formal structure was the most promising approach. But Clark pointed out that this would not necessarily resolve the problem, since informal measures were always influenced by the formal system. "Plant managers get obsessed by the financial accounts they receive" (from corporate)—so much so that they sometimes neglect to make the most basic and necessary physical measurements. The management of one factory had had to be informed by one of Clark's research assistants that its physical output had halved over a period of several years, even though its dollar output was almost the same as before. "You've got to change the formal system if you want to alter the informal," Clark concluded.

"Dollars and cents aren't gospel, customer satisfaction is," agreed James Bakken (vice president, Ford Motor). But "many operating managers still look at the accounting system within their company as sacrosanct and not to be challenged." So change would not be easy to achieve.

Several participants were more optimistic, looking to the arrival of personal computers to enable companies to start making use of a wide range of more appropriate measures, whether financial or physical. "Selective and judgmental use is the answer," said Doyle. Otherwise, the accounting profession, which (like the law) was "fundamentally attached to past practice," would continue to be "an antidote to boldness"—when boldness was precisely what companies frequently needed. "There's a tyranny in any single set of figures," agreed Miller.

The most far-reaching view of all came from Place. The use of numerical systems of any sort actually hindered comprehension, he argued. So "shouldn't we be moving back from quantitative management to qualitative?" After all, that was how companies basically managed R&D and personnel.

"Control" versus "Commitment" Models of Management

The financial function has tended to be the center of corporate control, declared Bakken, in challenging Walton's view that the "control" and "commitment" models were cleanly separable. Robert Hayes also questioned Walton's assertion that a number of U.S. organizations were in a transition stage between the two extremes, and claimed that "we are misinterpreting the lessons of the Japanese model." In contrast to the picture painted by much of the recent literature on Japanese management, Hayes said, "there's no ambivalence about the role and authority of managers there"—Japanese workers "are very tightly controlled." Rather than the final stage of a transition process, the emerging U.S. commitment model may eventually be seen as itself a transition toward more effective use of the control model, Hayes suggested.

William Van Sant (president, Cessna Aircraft), argued that the pyramid model was still correct. "There always has to be a leader with vision." The key question should be "what kind of chemistry is necessary to instill that vision throughout the organization?"

Although other participants questioned the general applicability of the commitment model and its resilience in certain circumstances, several related more positive first-hand experiences.

Jon Kropper (executive vice president, Wang Laboratories) conceded that the model could work well in rapidly growing companies, but asked if it could take root and survive in slower growth businesses, which were under a different kind of pressure. Charles Eberle (vice president of manufacturing, Procter & Gamble) replied that it was even more compelling in such businesses, though he admitted there *could well be thorny questions about "employment assurance" (a company's ability to promise long-term employment).*

A high commitment system, agreed Robert McKersie (professor, MIT), made it difficult for management "to make some of the tough decisions further down the road." To which Richard Hackman (professor, Yale University)—who, like Walton, studies commitment-based organizations—conceded "that's why its long-term effect may be revolutionary." In an organization where all employees were owners, one set of owners (management) would find it difficult to press another (the work force) to make sacrifices.

To Doyle, a key difficulty was how to prompt management to work with ambiguity and uncertainty without themselves being either dictatorial or ambivalent. As he put it, "How do you teach people to live in that kind of world and still be effective leaders?"

This was not just a matter of relations between senior management and the hourly paid, stressed Bakken. The impact on—and role of—middle management was generally not discussed in the literature, he complained. Yet "this is the biggest single stumbling block. The question they have is 'what on earth happens to us?' " Securing agreement from the various levels of management, and getting them to behave in a fashion conducive to commitment, was not easy, emphasized Abu-Zayyad. The executives leading the change needed to be selected very carefully.

To some of these doubts and questions, reassurance was offered by Frank Pipp (corporate group vice president, Xerox), Gordon Forward (president and CEO, Chaparral Steel), as well as by Richard Walton (professor, Harvard Business School) himself.

In the case of one unionized plant, reported Pipp, his company had shifted to the commitment model at a time of zero growth and was able to reduce the work force by half and management by 60 percent. The basis of this successful transition had been twofold: "competitive benchmarking" (competitive comparisons that, because they were objective and well done, were accepted down through the organization), and effective and consistent communication.

Conceding that a growth environment facilitated such improvements, Forward said that such growth might include dimensions other than sales or profits—it could equally well concern quality or the reliability of delivery.

In the early 1970s, Walton admitted, he had been concerned that a sizable fraction of employees in organizations that were shifting toward a commitment approach would not want to invest more responsibility in their jobs. But he had since come to the view that 85 percent of the existing hourly paid work force could be expected to participate in the model. Responding to some of the other doubts and questions expressed by the participants, he stressed that he was "not talking about a system which isn't under control"; and that if companies took the trouble to communicate effectively about the new model and the changes needed to make it operative, "then people would get the message and respond."

To Hayes's question, "What evidence do we have that the commitment model is enduring?" Walton pointed to the record of adoption, and especially to the way that some firms that experimented with it in the 1970s are now moving to companywide implementation. Managers do believe it works, emphasized Walton—even to the extent that some of them comment: "I've never had so much power since I started giving it away."

Part Three

Technology: Harnessing "Creative Destruction"

Overview

Introduction

Few aspects of management are more characterized by tension and ambiguity than is technological innovation. The tentacles of the pervasive productivity-technology dilemma—the subject of this volume—embrace a series of "microdilemmas" within the innovation process itself: whether to invest in research or in development; to give priority to product or process development; to conduct the various phases of development sequentially or in parallel; to stimulate individual creativity or group dynamics and control; to encourage organizational centralization or decentralization; and whether governments should adopt a laissez-faire approach or provide incentives for specific kinds of R&D activity. In each case managers must wrestle with trade-offs between efficiency and creativity, and seek ways to foster both simultaneously.

The first three chapters in this section provide a broad overview of some of the key issues in the management of innovation: the generation and development of radical ("extraordinary") product and process innovations, as distinct from those of a step-by-step ("incremental") type (chapter by Professor Richard Rosenbloom, Harvard Business School, and commentary by Dr. Roland Schmitt, senior vice president, corporate research and development at General Electric); the management of accelerated product development programs in Japan, which increasingly underpins that country's industrial success (chapter by Professors Imai, Nonaka, and Takeuchi of Hitotsubashi University, and commentary by John Doyle, vice president for research and development at Hewlett-Packard); and the effectiveness of government subsidies of R&D (chapter by Professor Edwin Mansfield, University of Pennsylvania, and commentary by Dr. Lewis Branscomb, vice president and chief scientist at IBM). The final chapter, by Professors Kim Clark and Robert Hayes of Harvard Business School, provides a statistical analysis of the relationships linking different management policies and industry characteristics to both new product innovation and productivity growth. Unusually broad ranging in its coverage, it *readdresses several of the issues raised in previous sections and ties them in with those focused on in this final one. It therefore serves both as a reprise and an appropriate conclusion to this volume.*

Underlying all the chapters, commentaries, and discussion, as in Part Two, is the complex role played in the innovation process by human software—or, in more conventional terms, the generation and application of knowledge. The nature of the discovery, knowledge-creation, learning, and synthesis processes that are appropriate in the early phases of the development of a new technology differs markedly from that appropriate to incremental product or process improvements, where one is building on a known technological foundation. Hence the considerable differences in emphasis and approach between the Rosenbloom chapter and that of Imai, Nonaka, and Takeuchi. It also underlies the repeated emphasis in the commentaries and discussion that there is no one best way to manage innovation.

Yet certain conclusions of general validity do emerge from the chapters, commentaries, and discussion. They include:

- *The interaction of process innovation and product innovation is more complex than is generally understood;*
- *The technology development process may be more effectively and speedily managed in overlapping phases, delaying final specifications as long as possible, rather than through the sequential pattern widely practiced in Western companies;*
- *This has dramatic implications for organizational cultures, structures, and control systems—especially in their tolerance of extensive and prolonged ambiguity;*
- *The various phases of the overall process need to be better understood: just as R&D are not one process, despite their usual juxtaposition, so development consists of a number of different steps stretching forward into manufacture and commercialization;*
- *The much-vaunted Japanese supplier network provides manufacturers with substantial advantages in product and process development, as well as in production itself;*
- *The conflict between efficiency/productivity growth and innovation is affected by, among other things, the nature of a firm's production technology and the maturity of its products;*
- *The age of a firm's production equipment seems to bear little relationship to its innovativeness or productivity growth—this suggests that it is difficult to overcome problems in either areas through capital investment alone;*
- *The importance to the innovation process of organizational learn-*

ing and unlearning *has been underrated, and the development process itself can be a valuable tool for improving the learning process throughout the firm.*

Managing Technology for the Longer Term

Rosenbloom's chapter begins by drawing attention to the risks of pursuing extraordinary innovations. They are surrounded by such uncertainty that even if most of the key technological variables are known, critical uncertainty may still exist about such factors as the innovation's timing, its target market, and its financial viability once it has been introduced.

Drawing on the work of Abernathy and Clark, he distinguishes between the "entrenching" effects of "regular" innovations, and the "transilience" of extraordinary ones (that is, "the capacity to transform established systems of technology and markets"). He argues that a managerial perspective on extraordinary innovations is greatly needed because "academic literature provides little guidance to managers concerned with extraordinary opportunities for change." Not only do most studies deal exclusively with incremental innovation, but the results of many of them recently have been opened to question.

Reviewing the economic literature on innovation, Rosenbloom points out that rival firms "often follow markedly different courses even though they are influenced by similar economic forces." Why, for instance, in what was eventually to become the home video player industry, did the (then) largest manufacturers of consumer electronics—RCA, Matsushita, and Philips—make such different choices?

Taking home video as his main source of examples, Rosenbloom concentrates on providing a simple framework for thinking about generic elements of the process by which innovations are conceived, developed, and implemented, and about characteristic decisions taken by managers in the course of these activities. Rosenbloom divides the innovation process into three phases:

- *Formulation (of a core concept)*
- *Gestation*
- *Exploitation*

He emphasizes, however, that the phases need not be sequential—they can be carried out at least partly in parallel.

Among his observations are the following:

- *The same perceived opportunities can drive prospective innovators along very different formulation and development paths;*

- *"Invention" may occur well into the innovation process, rather than at its start, as most conventional models of innovation assume;*
- *The importance of nontechnical decisions to the success of an innovation (for example, Xerox's decision to invent a new distribution system to launch its copying business, or Matsushita's selection of VCR playing time as a key marketing factor);*
- *The sharp difference between the types of managerial activity that are required in the gestation phase, on the one hand, and during exploitation on the other;*
- *Radical technical change "casts a long shadow before it," so that an extraordinary innovation seldom should take management by surprise.*

Rosenbloom goes on to explore the difficult balance between exploratory and targeted development work. In common with the subsequent chapter by Imai et al., he also examines the question of how far to prolong the exploratory phase (what the Japanese chapter calls "the postponement of variety reduction").

The chapter concludes with an agenda for systematic research into these factors. Among many other questions raised in discussion, Rosenbloom doubted whether an organization structured for incremental innovation could successfully accomplish extraordinary innovation.

Managing the New Product Development Process in Japan

The chapter by Imai, Nonaka, and Takeuchi concentrates specifically on Japanese manufacturers that have excelled in making incremental innovations—they have not only developed new products rapidly, they have also been highly responsive to changing technological and market environments. The competitive advantages attainable through this proficiency are now beginning to be recognized by their Western competitors.

The authors studied the new product development process at five companies: Fuji-Xerox, Honda, Canon, NEC, and Epson. Although the products developed were all based on highly imaginative concepts, in technological terms they were considered to be incremental improvements. Moreover, all were seen as "hero projects" within the companies concerned, because of their importance to the firms' success in key markets.

Seven key determinants of success were found by the researchers:

1. Top management as catalyst. *Top management rarely handed down a clearcut goal or well-defined product concept. Rather, it*

established highly challenging parameters, created a certain level of tension within the organization, and set in motion a crisis-solving project team.

2. Self-organizing project teams. *A multifunctional team (in some cases composed of engineers with little prior experience in the technology to be developed) was empowered with considerable autonomy and allowed to operate entrepreneurially.*

3. Overlapping development phases. *Several phases of the development process often overlapped, or two phases were combined into one. (This approach contrasts with the type of sequential approach advocated by the National Aeronautics and Space Administration. Known as phased program planning, this relies on a formal division of labor and a careful evaluation at the end of each phase.)*

4. Multilearning. *This loose coupling of phases fostered learning at different levels—individual, group, and organizational. It also encouraged learning across functional areas, as project members were stimulated to become generalists. This learning was fed back to the organization and served to upgrade continuously the quality of the work force.*

5. Subtle controls. *Top management avoided chaos by implanting what the authors term "subtle" controls and checkpoints within the development process: selecting the right people for the team, creating an open working environment, encouraging visits to customers, and setting up an evaluation system based on group performance. (John Doyle remarks in his commentary, however, that these controls seem far from "subtle.")*

6. Organizational transfer of learning. *Although the knowledge so accumulated was transferred to subsequent projects and eventually became institutionalized, the emergence of another crisis might force the organization to "unlearn" the lessons of the past (a process that Schumpeter referred to as "creative destruction").*

Doyle's commentary discusses the considerable extent to which many of these factors are also common to leading U.S. firms. But, because of its almost complete absence fron the U.S. industrial scene, he places particular emphasis on the final factor:

7. Interorganizational network building. *The speed and/or flexibility of the product development process was also supported by the existence of a close network of outside suppliers (for example, affiliated companies, subcontractors, and vendors) who often participated in all stages of development.*

The paper concludes by suggesting three key differences between how Japanese and U.S. companies approach the product development process:

- *Japanese "trial and error," versus American formal systems;*
- *Japanese companywide learning, versus American emphasis on the role of a technical elite;*
- *The central role of product development in Japanese strategy formulation.*

Despite their praise of the Japanese approach, the authors admit it has some drawbacks: Among others, it may not apply to technological "breakthroughs," and it requires a quite extraordinary effort on the part of those involved (to the extent, suggests Doyle, that it might not be acceptable in an American context).

Public Policy toward Innovation

Tax incentives are only one way to offset the underinvestment in R&D which is thought to occur—for a variety of reasons—in market economies. Another approach is for the government to subsidize civilian R&D projects. Of course, many countries use both approaches, although the mix varies considerably over time and from country to country.

General R&D tax incentives involve less direct government control than do other techniques for promoting research, such as federal contracts and grants. Moreover, they tend to be relatively easy to administer. Among the disadvantages of R&D tax incentives, however, are that they may reward firms for doing R&D that they would have done anyway, and they may not help unprofitable (non-tax-paying) firms. They may also encourage dysfunctional behavior, such as efforts to redefine non-R&D activities so that they qualify for incentives.

These are some of the central issues addressed by Mansfield, and by Branscomb in his commentary. As will be evident from Mansfield's point-by-point riposte to Branscomb, their papers were marked by strong, contrasting opinions.

Mansfield's chapter concludes that in the United States, Canada, and Sweden, R&D tax credits and allowances appear to have had only a modest effect on R&D expenditures, on the order of 1 to 2 percent. In each case, the increase in R&D seems to be substantially less than the tax revenue lost. In each case, too, there is substantial evidence that the incentives resulted in a considerable redefinition of other activities as R&D, particularly in the first few years after their introduction.

While emphasizing that the results of his surveys must be viewed with considerable caution, Mansfield considers them to be consistent and accurate. His chapter therefore concludes that such R&D incentives, in their present form, are unlikely to have a major impact on a nation's rate of innovation: "As long as [they] result in only a modest reduction in the price of R&D, as long as they do not apply at all to a substantial proportion of firms, and as long as the price elasticity of demand for R&D is rather low."

Branscomb counters with the argument that the U.S. tax credit has had a substantial effect on R&D spending by IBM, and by the electronics industry in general. He argues that Mansfield's conclusions about the U.S. tax credit are premature and believes it should be extended. Beyond this disagreement, he presents the case against alternative, more interventionist, measures, for promoting innovation. In this he and Mansfield are in agreement.

Government actions can have both positive or negative effects on industrial innovation. On the one hand, "rifle shot" policies, of the sort favored by some advocates of "industrial policy," are extremely difficult to devise and to apply without having unintended consequences. On the other hand, more general measures aimed at improving the overall environment for innovation run the risk of being wasted on low-value projects.

Above all, Branscomb believes, public policy should promote stability. Given the long time scales of innovation, political fine tuning can only be disruptive. This is one of the few areas where Schumpeter's "winds of creative destruction" can do more harm than good.

Trade-offs between Innovation and Productivity Growth

Much of the advice that business managers receive today is based on casual empiricism (informal studies of a few companies and particularly powerful anecdotes) and even more casual intuition. In some cases it has grown out of a comparative analysis of a few U.S. and Japanese or European companies, or out of studies of the characteristics of specific successful U.S. firms.

Although this work has provided new perspectives and hypotheses about the influence of managerial practices, its reliance on relatively small samples in a few, nonrandomly selected industries leaves the generality of its findings open to question. Moreover, the recommendations it makes about managerial policy rest on a set of largely implicit assumptions about the nature of competition, and about the role that technology and productivity play in industrial success. Making these assumptions and related hypotheses explicit, and studying them in the context of data obtained from over 900 manufacturing businesses, is the purpose of the final paper. A particularly valuable dimension of its analysis is its distinction between two groups of businesses according to the basic nature of the production process involved: "process" or "fabrication/assembly."

Within this framework, it sheds new light on the managerial actions that appear to stimulate productivity and/or product innovation. The nature of competition, the speed of diffusion of new technology, and the impact of vertical integration are quite different in these two groups. On the other hand, the authors find in both industries that technological instability appears to have a significant influence on product development, but little impact on the growth of Total Factor Productivity (TFP). Moreover, certain management policies appear to affect productivity growth in different ways at different stages of industry development.

Their analysis of the impact that, for example, vertical integration and proprietary technology development have on TFP growth and product innovation provides support for the notion that a firm in a given business cannot be all things to all customers. A choice of competitive strategy that emphasizes flexibility (to change products and processes) appears to require managerial policies that limit the firm's effectiveness in improving productivity, at least in the short run.

The chapter concludes that managerial behavior must be tailored to the firm's specific competitive and technological environment. Moreover, basing one's analysis and prescription only on studies of fabrication/assembly production processes—which is the tendency of much of the management literature—can be dangerously misleading.

7
Managing Technology for the Longer Term: A Managerial Perspective

Richard S. Rosenbloom

Introduction: The Nature of Extraordinary Innovation

Technological innovation is a pervasive element of modern business activity. Most innovations represent small increments of change in an established order. On occasion, however, an innovation sets in motion a sequence of events that can transform organizations, industries, or whole economies. Such innovations are distinguished from the "ordinary" pattern of technical change both by the way thay relate to customary patterns of technical and commercial practice and by the way they affect firms and markets. These "extraordinary innovations" exemplify Schumpeter's notion of "creative destruction." Although limited in incidence, they are substantial in their consequences for industrial societies.

Examples abound of companies making major commitments in prospect of exploiting an extraordinary innovation. CBS, IBM, and Sears formed a venture to develop videotex services for information and transactions[1]; Cross and Trecker explained its acquisition of the troubled Bendix machine tool businesses as a step toward strengthening its capacity to participate in the market for "flexible manufacturing systems"; investors everywhere bid up the price of stocks of small firms venturing to exploit the new technologies of recombinant DNA.[2]

The active pursuit of extraordinary opportunity in this manner entails extraordinary risks. In industry, as in affairs of state, a position on the front lines of a revolution is necessarily hazardous. Because extraordinary innovations require extended periods of time for conception, development, and exploitation, they make unique demands on established operating organizations. A high degree of novelty and distant time horizons combine to create substantial uncertainty about payoffs. A demanding task performed against great uncertainty will

297

often result in failure. Industrial history is strewn with carefully conducted, ambitious, and costly attempts that came to naught—as, for example, Kettering's famous "copper-cooled engine," or the recent experience of RCA with the videodisc.[3]

It is the cumulation of several inherent elements of uncertainty that makes these risks so great. First, not all envisioned opportunities are realized. Like the economist whom critics accused of forecasting eleven of the last five recessions, aspiring innovators, gullible journalists, and many other observers speculate freely about revolutions that never occur.[4] More than a few expire without serious attempts at commercialization, and others are attempted without success, or, at best, remain eternal "good prospects."

Even if they were armed somehow with foreknowledge that a certain idea would lead to a "successful" innovation, executives would still face substantial uncertainty about its relevance to particular firms. For example, suppose that one were certain that videotex services would be common in U.S. households by the end of the century. To make a business decision one would have to make judgments about its timing—will diffusion to mass use result from the services now in commercial use, or will those prove to be false starts with mass adoption coming from other initiatives a decade later? Equally important would be an assessment of its character—will videotex emerge primarily as an information-oriented service (for example, weather, stock market data, shopping information) or as a transaction-oriented service (for example, home banking, shopping, travel and entertainment bookings, stock market trades), or both? If these issues are so uncertain in 1984, when commercial-scale services are already in use, imagine the risks of evaluating videotex as an opportunity when development began in the 1970s.

Adding to the uncertainties is the awareness that participating in a successful revolution in technology, by itself, offers no assurance that a given firm will reap economic rewards. Dozens of firms conceived and developed home videoplayer products in the early 1970s; only a few found the right combination of technology and user needs. Even a firm that gets that combination right may be defeated in the marketplace. A dramatic example was the collapse of the EMI CT Medical Scanner business within a few years of the introduction of a revolutionary product for which EMI was the pioneer.[5]

While the objective risks inherent in a prospective innovation are great enough, the perceived risks may be even greater. The core idea of an extraordinary innovation necessarily will challenge prevailing traditions of practice, strengthening skeptical arguments. Often it will have arisen outside the community of organizations likely to be most affected. The exotic is easier to dismiss as misconceived, sometimes thus paving the way for the familiar case of innovation by invasion.

In the face of great uncertainty, managers in most established and successful firms will find the weight of rational argument on the side of deferring or, at least, limiting the commitment of resources to an extraordinary innovation. With time, perhaps as a result of efforts by less cautious organizations, or as a consequence of developments in ancillary fields, the technical and commercial uncertainties will be reduced.

Yet there is growing recognition in management that this posture also carries substantial risks to the future of a firm. To everything there is a season; no formula for success endures forever. On occasion an industrial organization must be prepared to commit itself, at risk, to an extraordinary innovation.

Defining Characteristics

What makes an innovation "extraordinary"? Clearly, what's "extraordinary" is relative, contrasted to what is "ordinary" in a particular setting at a point in time. The setting comprises firms and associated markets; an extraordinary innovation makes special demands on the capacities of the firms and has consequences that alter the character of both firms and markets. Historians can write confidently about the sources and consequences of "the turbojet revolution" (aircraft propulsion) or a "revolution in miniature" (semiconductors).[6] Managers, experiencing these forces in real time, sometimes struggle to perceive the "revolutionary" implications of an innovation in the making.

Abernathy and Clark present a framework for classifying innovations according to the degree and character of their effects. As they point out:

> . . . some innovations disrupt, destroy, and make obsolete established competence; others refine and improve. Further, the effects of innovation on production systems may be quite different from their effects on linkages to customers and markets.[7]

With a simple distinction between "entrenching" and "disruptive" consequences in two domains—the technological and market systems—Abernathy and Clark define four "modes" of innovation. Innovations that serve to entrench established skills, systems, practices, and relationships in both domains are said to constitute the "regular" mode of technological change. Other innovations are said to exhibit a property they call "transilience," a term indicating a "capacity to transform established systems of technology and markets."[8] An innovation having a high degree of transilience falls outside the "regular" mode; it is, in other words, an "extraordinary" innovation.

A complementary definition emerges from the framework suggested by Edward Constant in his fascinating history of the development of turbojet propulsion for aircraft. As he notes, within any established community of technical practitioners, one finds "an accepted mode of technical operation, the conventional system for accomplshing a specified technical task." Constant defines "normal" technical progress as that which fits established traditions of practice:

> Normal technology—what technological communities usually do—comprises the improvement of the accepted tradition or its application under "new or more stringent conditions." It is technological development. It is, like Thomas Kuhn's normal science, "puzzle solving." That is not to say that the problems of normal technology are easy or obvious of solution, just that their solution is sought within the limits of the received tradition and that their solution is presumed to exist within those limits.[9]

A "received tradition" shapes behavior in the commercial domain as well as in technology. For some innovations, the technology is "normal" (in Constant's sense) but the commercial approach is extraordinary. An oft-cited example is the introduction of the Timex pin-lever mechanical watches, which challenged the received tradition that watches were sold primarily as adornments through outlets able to provide service and repair. A simple timekeeper, inexpensive enough to be replaced when broken, cut across the normal mode of commercial practice and revolutionized an industry.[10]

The Need for a Managerial Perspective

The academic literature on innovation provides little guidance to managers concerned with extraordinary opportunities for change. Early empirical studies viewed an innovation as the outcome of a simple process and sought statistical relationships between characteristics of the process and its outcomes.[11] Most studies encompassed incremental, that is, "ordinary," innovation. Even within that domain, recent critiques have questioned the validity of some of the main findings of these studies and their salience for decision makers.[12]

Recent scholarship has emphasized the evolutionary character of most technological change, its complexity, and the pervasive role of uncertainty.[13] This work has generated new theoretical perspectives on the economics of innovation and useful insights on public policy issues. Historical studies of technological "revolutions" help to clarify how the process unfolds, though they seldom provide much insight into the managerial forces at work.[14] Taken together, these studies from the varying perspectives of history, economics, and public policy provide a coherent view of the main features of the process of innovation.

As Nelson and Winter emphasize, the core of the problem of conceptualizing innovative processes is finding a way to treat them as "purposive, but inherently stochastic." For example, the extension of integrated circuit techniques into the domain of Very Large Scale Integration (VLSI) creates new possibilities on which it is possible to build a myriad of applications. As Rosenberg and Steinmueller point out, each particular application "entails a subtle combination of technical sophistication with the identification of specific but unsatisfied human needs." The combinations, of course, are primarily put together by firms, either as producers of components or equipment, or as users of them. Nelson and Winter suggest the concept of a "selection environment" as a way of understanding some of the forces governing the way that technologies like this ultimately will be used. Competitive markets provide one kind of selection environment; variations in market structure between sectors presumably affect the ways that technology develops in those sectors. Rosenberg and Steinmuller,[15] in their analysis of VLSI, also focus on economic factors.

But economic factors alone are unlikely to explain more than a small part of the variation in the innovative behavior of firms. In pursuit of opportunities for extraordinary innovations, rival firms often follow markedly different courses even though they are influenced by substantially similar economic forces.

For example, *Table A7-1* (see *Appendix* at the end of this chapter) identifies a dozen companies that led in the development of home video players in the early 1970s.[16] The products they demonstrated between 1969 and 1972 were based on nine different technical approaches to magnetic, film, or disc technologies. These were no casual engagements—three-quarters of the developments were carried through to commercial introduction, representing aggregate investments of many hundreds of millions of dollars. In the end, of course, only one of these approaches, the helical-scan magnetic videocassette recorder, has prospered in the mass market.

How are we to understand why these companies acted so differently in pursuit of the same prospective market opportunity? Why, in particular, did the (then) largest producers of electronic consumer products—RCA Corporation, Matsushita Electrical Industries, and N.V. Philips—make such different choices? Each of those three had the technical capability to address any one of the possible approaches to this innovation; all three had substantial financial resources, were of comparable scale, and operated in similar market environments.

In analyzing these sorts of differences in the innovative behavior of companies, one should look beyond economic descriptors to examine the inner workings of the firm. To do that in systematic research, one could take as the basic unit of analysis the activities of a given firm with respect to a given innovative opportunity. By identifying generic choices taken (at least implicitly) by managers in such circumstances, the differences between firms could be examined on a common basis. Explanatory propositions could then be framed in terms of the kinds of choices taken and the economic, organizational, and other differences between the companies.

As a step toward making such research possible, the following sections of this chapter suggest a simple framework for thinking about generic elements of the process by which innovations are conceived, developed, and implemented, and about characteristic decisions taken by managers in the course of those activities.

Generic Elements of the Process of Innovation

Firms capture the benefits of an innovation by selling or using the novel products or processes that embody the innovative idea. Creating suitable embodiments—through design, development, and commercialization—requires a certain period of "gestation" before benefits accrue. But understanding what is worth embodying is itself a significant task.

It follows from this that a firm's first engagement with a particular opportunity for innovation can come in any of three major elements of the evolution of that innovation. If the combination of technology and application is only partially or diffusely identified (for example, "to exploit applications of genetic engineering in agriculture"), the first tasks are aimed at *formulation* of a core concept worth developing further. The *gestation* of a suitable core idea comprises tasks aimed at design, development, and preparation for commercialization. In some cases, the firm's first involvement will come after others have carried the idea through to commercial use, when the remaining task is only *exploitation*.

Formulation

On occasion it may appear that an important innovative idea has sprung, full-blown, into the mind of its creator. Alistair Pilkington, for example, is said to have conceived the idea of the float glass process one day while washing the dishes. But this sort of story is more often the stuff of legend than the experience of innovators. More commonly the formulation of a successful innovative idea is the result of a subtle and lengthy process to which many persons contribute.

The shaping of the idea of a home videoplayer illustrates the point. It began in 1951, twenty years before the first successful product was developed, when David Sarnoff called on RCA Laboratories to create a method of recording television programs that would be as cheap and simple as available methods for sound. One application of this, he speculated, would be the emergence of a "theater in the home" in which viewers could have their choice of programs. The concept gained adherents, stimulated by the success of Ampex Corporation with the invention of videotape recording. Subsequent innovations leading to simple, low-cost machines, the pioneering of Peter Goldmark with "electronic video recording," and the work of RCA Laboratories on several other technologies in the late 1960s, lent greater credibility to the idea that a practical means of creating a home videoplayer was within reach.

As noted earlier, technical possibilities proliferated, and with them emerged different conceptions of how such a player would be used. Some innovators believed that consumers would want to own a "library" of programs; others that users would rent programs, perhaps "refilling" specially designed cartridges.

In retrospect we can see that the successful products were conceived with the benefit of ideas put forth and lessons learned by a number of rivals. Especially instructive were the highly visible failures of the first generations of products: Sony and Ampex home recorders in the mid-1960s and the more costly adventures in the early 1970s of the EVR Partnership and of Cartrivision.

This example illustrates one of the ways in which a sense of "opportunity" drives prospective innovators to chance the risks and pursue the formulation of novel ideas. The character of the opportunity varies from case to case. The first stimulus may be provided by a novel technological capability, such as is provided by new methods of genetic engineering. Alternatively, it may come from the perception of an unfilled need, as in home video. The technology in question may be novel or it may be familiar; the need may be manifest and widely recognized or it may be latent and perceived by few.

Sometimes the "opportunity" may appear to be a "cure" for which there is, so far, no known "disease," or vice versa. An opportunity becomes the core idea for an innovation when the complementary element has been added by the identification of a specific application for the technology of a specific means of serving the need. Fully formed, the core idea for an innovation thus embraces elements from two domains: technology, which determines how things can be done; and use, which determines why things are worth doing. An idea that is vague about the suitable technical approach or about economically valuable applications is incomplete.

Sometimes all that is required to complete the concept is a single creative insight. But in most instances today, formulation is a task, not an event. Synthesizing the appropriate technical elements and applications ideas provides a goal for which resources are mobilized and toward which the coordinated activities of a firm (or, perhaps, an alliance of firms) are directed. In some cases, formulation can be a lengthy activity, as when it turns out to be impossible to fill in the missing elements until exogenous changes—introduction of related technologies, or shifts in the marketplace—have occurred.

New ideas, of course, are created by people, not by organizations. As one experienced industrial research manager observes, "Solutions to problems occur when the knowledge of a need and the technical or scientific knowledge to cope with that need finally come together in one head."[17] But in a world of complex technologies and markets, organizations have an essential role in elaborating and refining an idea, testing its feasibility and utility, and identifying the technical and commercial issues that would have to be resolved to succeed with an innovation.

Managing a task like the formulation of an innovative idea is sure to be different from other responsibilities of the managers of an established industrial firm. To begin with, the work of formulating an extraordinary innovation centers on abstractions—technical concepts and envisioned applications—and on tangible steps (tests, and so forth) designed mainly to indicate, at least in principle, that the concepts can be made real. The process is necessarily iterative—ideas put forth, examined, revised, tested again, and so forth.

In the early 1960s, for example, engineers at Ampex, Sony, Matsushita, and elsewhere, experimented with various helical scanner configurations for VTRs and speculated about potential applications in which this technology might meet a real need. Unlike the original Ampex innovation in transverse recording, which was targeted on the demanding performance requirements of a specific (broadcasting) application, the formulators of helical product concepts had to speculate not only about technical possibilities, but also about users and their requirements. Early efforts concentrated on achieving the maximum degree of cost reduction and simplification consistent with "acceptable" image quality. Prototypes were made "for practice," and the first products were marketed by Sony and Ampex in part to learn what sorts of customers might be interested.

This kind of activity makes special demands on managers. The prevailing mode of behavior is best characterized as "speculative." It exhibits qualities associated with three common connotations of that word, being (1) "contemplative," reflecting on or considering a subject; (2) "conjectural," employing an orderly process of reasoning based on inconclusive evidence; and (3) marked by "risky commitments." No lengthy exposition is required to establish that this is very different from the normal mode of management in established firms.

The story of the phonograph, invented by Thomas Edison, illustrates the vagaries of the process by which economically valuable applications of an imporant new technology are discovered. In current usage, a "phonograph" is a machine that reproduces music recorded on plastic discs. To Edison, it meant a "sound-writing" (phono-graph) machine, which used cylinders as the recording medium. More than a dozen years passed before the phonograph technology was used commercially to play music.

The fundamental invention was made by Edison in the fall of 1877. Public response was rapid and gratifying. Appreciative crowds gathered wherever it was demonstrated. While it seemed to suggest many and wondrous possibilities, none held the promise of economic returns. Edison's own speculations were recorded thus in his journal:

> I propose to apply the phonograph principle to make Dolls speak sing cry and make various sounds also apply it to all kinds of Toys such as Dogs animals fowls reptiles human figures to cause them to make various sounds to Steam Toy Engines exhausts and whistles—to reproduce from sheets music both orchestral and instrumental and vocal the idea being to use a plate machine with perfect registration and stamp the music out in a press from a die or punch previously prepared by cutting in steel or from an Electrotype or cast from the original of tin foil—a family may have one machine and 1000 sheets of the music thus giving endless amusement I also propose to make toy music boxes and talking toy boxes playing several tunes also to clocks and watches for calling out the time of day or waking a person for advertisements rotated continuously by clockwork. . . .[18]

None of those applications made economic sense in 1877; Edison put the phonograph aside to work on the more attractive possibilities of electric power. A decade later, experimental demonstrations by others excited the interest of court reporters in Washington, D.C., persuading the developers that a "dictating machine" might be a profitable product. Both Edison and his rivals developed and commercialized a design for that application, which proved somewhat less than a bonanza outside the Capitol. A California distributor, in financial trouble because of disappointing demand, was creative enough to set one up with a coin-slot control to play "music for a nickel" in a San Francisco bar. Despite Edison's strong objection to an application that seemed to trivialize his noble invention, the demand evoked responses from others and Edison was forced to join in. A rival technical concept, the flat-disc gramophone, emerged to challenge Edison's cylinders. Thus were born—some fifteen years after Edison's invention—the innovations that gave rise to the "record business" and the first segment of the home entertainment equipment industry.

The story of television includes similar elements. Primitive television systems were demonstrated in the nineteenth century and the conceptual outlines of an "all electronic" system were sketched in by 1912. Yet speculation about applications was sterile until the emergence of radiobroadcasting created the model. David Sarnoff was able to introduce the new technology in 1939 as a means of "adding sight to sound" in what was by then a major industry providing entertainment and information for mass audiences.[19]

In both of these stories, the initial stimulus came from a novel technological capability, the utility of which remained to be discovered. There are complementary examples in which the leading element defining the opportunity was the perception of potential applications for which there was no evident practical technology, or, much the same, many candidate technologies with no clear front-runner. The 1970s' boom in "alternative energy technologies" provides an apt example. The opportunity was clearly perceived: Fossil fuels were finite in supply and apparently sure to increase in cost. The answer would logically lie in developing renewable energy sources, but none was then, or is now, competitive with fossil fuels for any but a few specialized applications.

Gestation

To create or transform a business, ideas are not enough. Two principal milestones mark the sometimes lengthy path from recognition of a core concept to its realization in routine use. The first, completion of the technical design, provides a detailed specification of the materials, components, and procedures necessary to realize the envisioned product, process, or system on a commercial scale. The second is reached when the design has been embodied in an operating system capable of delivering the new good or service to users as a routine commercial activity. One can think of these steps as constituting a period of "gestation," which begins with conception of the core idea and ends with the birth (or rebirth) of a business segment built upon it.

Once the basic technical approach and the primary intended applications have been formulated, the next task is to create detailed and documented designs, prototypes, and so forth, on the basis of which a commercially useful embodiment could be created. One part of this work is engineering design—selecting constituent elements or configuring systems to satisfy stated requirements. Another facet is invention—creating new capabilities by enhancement of known technologies or the creation of novel ones.[20] An assortment of technical elements—some novel, some familiar—will be joined in the synthesis of a completed design. The technologies of those elements may need refinement, enhancement, or fundamental improvement, and their interrelations need to be understood.

For example, the work of the Ampex team that invented the VTR began with commitments to a specific technical approach—using rotating heads—and to a specific application—"time-shift" for broadcasting. Several fundamental inventions and the enhancement of numerous available technologies were necessary to create the prototypes demonstrated in 1956. But these achievements, impressive as they were, represented only a portion of the innovator's task.

Commercial introduction, which marks the end of the "gestation" phase, requires that a firm have an operating system capable of manufacture and distribution of the new product, process, or system. Facilities and procedures for manufacture and distribution have to be planned and created, operating personnel recruited and perhaps trained, and so forth. In the Ampex case, this required another eighteen months, a substantially greater investment of funds, and the efforts of a much larger and more diverse team of engineers and operating executives.

The character of the resultant innovation is shaped, step by step, by problem-solving activities in design and commercialization. The possible outcomes are constrained by the perceived requirements of the application (which define the context) and the perceived limits of technologies and operating systems (which define the capabilities of the innovative system). The degree of difficulty in development depends as much upon the definition of the intended context as on the state of the art in the technology.

In the Ampex example, two characteristics of the broadcasting environment were highly influential. First, established technical standards set a high requirement for the quality of recorded images. Counterbalancing this was the high cost (to the stations) of alternative time-shift methods. The interplay of these factors led to development of a complex and expensive machine that was highly successful in a particular niche but unsuited for a wider range of applications in other environments.

The logical structure of these sorts of design decisions is explored in a recent paper by Kim Clark. He argues that both the logic of problem solving in design and the formation of concepts that underly choice in the marketplace impose a hierarchical structure on the evolution of technology. At the apex is a "core concept," which is particularly trenchant in its impact on other aspects. The choices shaping this are "core" in the sense that they dominate the others. The characer of the core concept, according to Clark, "establishes the agenda for a product's technical development within a particular functional domain."[21]

Clark's aim was to explain the evolutionary advance of technology stemming from the extension and refinement of existing ideas. He shows how the process of "regular" innovation (in Abernathy's sense) can be viewed as "moving down the hierarchy," to refine or elaborate the implications of established higher-order concepts of technology or demand. Our interest, of course, is in changes that embody significant departures from established concepts to create new agendas, moving "up the hierarchy." But Clark's ideas can be extended to conceptualize choices made in the gestation of an extraordinary innovation.

Technical development implies the discovery and resolution of discrepancies between the intended context of use and the projected innovative system. The problems thus identified are related hierarchically; some components of design are more trenchant in their implications than others. The "agenda" for development comprises a hierarchical array of problems to be resolved in design and commercialization. This agenda has two interrelated segments: one that is primarily "technical" in character, another that is "commercial." Both segments are dynamic, their composition changing, sometimes dramatically, as a result of experience in the laboratory, in the marketplace, or in use.

The technical agenda is defined by the logic of design, the characteristics of the technologies, and the implications of the intended context of use. That agenda influences and, in turn, is influenced by, the commercial agenda. The latter is defined by factors that are, in part, firm-specific, such as the capabilities of available systems for production and distribution or the business objectives of the innovator.

For example, in the development of the first magnetic videotape recorder the alternative technical approaches to scanner design (fixed versus rotating heads) necessarily gave rise to different hierarchies of problems to be solved to achieve commercial utility. But the inherent character of the technologies employed and the applications envisioned are insufficient to explain all the formative choices made in development and commercialization of that product. Ampex was a very small firm seeking to preempt a market pursued by larger and stronger rivals. The firm's capabilities and the strategy it chose to follow created a "commercial agenda" for the innovation to which the technical agenda had to conform.

Exploitation

Although studies of innovation often focus on what we have called "gestation," behavior during exploitation can also be decisive in shaping outcomes. Successful commercialization of an innovation creates a substantial pool of benefits to be shared by producers and users. The size of the pool and the way it is divided depend not only on inherent characteristics of the innovation, but also on choices made by the firms promoting it.

For example, once the engineers of the Haloid (now Xerox) Corporation had completed the design of what became the 914 office copier product, the exploitation of that innovation was blocked by a poor fit between characteristics of the product (high initial cost of the machine) and circumstances of the context in which it would be used (the office copier equipment market). By inventing a different distribution system in which machines were leased at prices determined by volume of usage, the company eliminated that mismatch and made successful innovation possible. The insight that one could sell copies rather than machines made the difference. Most observers would agree that this key decision about exploitation of the product influenced the outcomes at least as much as any technical choice during development.

Another classic example is provided by the case of the home videocassette recorder innovation. Sony created the first successful formulation of this innovation—marrying the technology of helical recording to the market appeal of a "time-shift" machine for television viewers. Embodying that in the Betamax, Sony managed design and commercialization very expeditiously and reached the market first with a successful product. Matsushita, resisting pressures to adopt Sony's standard, differentiated its product by the VHS format, aggressively made its product available under other brands, and correctly identified the duration of playing time per cassette as an important factor to users. Thus, despite Sony's lead, Matsushita ended up with the dominant position in a large new industry.

The most significant fact for managers is that a wholly different mode of activity is required during exploitation of an innovation to capture the fullest measure of the benefits. The capabilities required to bring an extraordinary innovation into being are different from those suited to the more mundane tasks of operating and adapting a business organization—making, selling, planning, organizing, and so forth. Rivals are sure to emerge, and the skills needed to gain competitive advantage are not those that will have produced the innovation in the first place. Yet innovative activities endure as well, aimed at improvements or the next transformation.

Summary of the Process of Innovation

The view of the process we have been describing can be summarized as shown in *Table 7-1*.

Three phases of firm involvement have been identified. Associated with each phase is a distinctive mode of activity. The formulation of a suitable core concept is fundamentally a creative activity in a "speculative" mode. The decision to pursue a specific embodiment entails a shift to a more systematic, problem-solving mode—developmental in character. Commercialization introduces additional activities aimed at timely and cost-effective implementation of a delivery system, while developmental work continues. Once they are complete, successful exploitation calls upon a different mix of skills, largely in a competitive or commercial mode.

While the inherent logic can be presented in these simple terms, the reality of an evolving innovation, of course, is seldom so simple. The various tasks are interrelated and mutually influential. For example, because design choices constrain options for exploitation, those choices

Table 7-1
The Process of Extraordinary Innovation

Phase	*Modality*	*Tasks*	*Products*
Formulation	Speculative	Experimentation Evaluation	Core concept of an innovation
Gestation	Developmental	Design Test Evaluation Implementation	Technical design Operating systems
Exploitation	Competitive	Marketing Manufacturing	Economic returns

made sensibly will anticipate such consequences. A firm possessing (or lacking) a certain kind of manufacturing or distribution network will want to ensure that designs reflect those circumstances. Problems in manufacture may lead to revision of the design; experience in the marketplace may lead to reformulation of the basic concept.

Nor should this framework be interpreted as a simple "linear" model of innovation. In "real time," an organization's activities directed at a prospective innovation may exhibit characteristics of several elements at once. Experience in development may lead to reformulation of the core concept. Progress from one to the next is seldom smooth. Exploitation may begin while development is still incomplete; failure at any point may inspire conclusions leading to reformulation of the concept, or to development along different lines.

Managerial Choices

Radical technical change casts a long shadow before it. Except in rare cases, the realization of an extraordinary innovation represents the flowering of ideas that have been around for a long time. To senior executives of firms affected by such an innovation, the possibility of its occurrence should represent no surprise. To be sure, uncertainties also abound. One may be surprised by the timing of commercialization, the efficacy of a new technology in use, the rate at which users adopt it, and other significant characteristics. But the concept of the innovation should rarely astonish.

Even if forewarned, a firm can be forearmed only if its leaders act affirmatively. Management's role begins with these choices: whether to commit resources to a prospective innovation and, if so, how? and when?

We can think of the first important choice as defining the organization's posture (at a point in time) with respect to the opportunity perceived. The first branch of the decision tree, at least implicitly, presents the choice between an active and a passive posture. As the chief executive of a large diversified firm once remarked to this author, "Choices are unavoidable; you can't march in every parade." The first reaction of most firms to most opportunities probably is to elect to watch the formation of the "parade" for a while, rather than to join it.

Even a very innovative firm may choose to "watch the parade" on some occasions. For example, while all three of its largest rivals—Matsushita, Philips, and RCA—sought to pioneer in the establishment of different videodisc technologies for mass consumer use, Sony's management remained skeptical of the prospects and the company took no active role in that field. As it turned out, Sony's was the wisest course in that situation.

In a firm that chooses an active posture, managers must make several basic choices to define objectives and set the direction of activity. As Michael Porter suggests,[22] there is a choice between pursuing a leadership position and aiming to be an active follower. While deliberately eschewing leadership may be repugnant to some executives, the alternative posture should not be rejected without analysis. As the success of Matsushita in home videocassette recorders illustrates, long-run market leadership may sometimes be gained by intelligently following the leading innovators.

In pursuit of either leadership or "followership," management shapes the innovation by the way it defines the direction of the firm's work. One dimension of choice is the extent to which work is "targeted" on a particular outcome, as opposed to being "exploratory." For example, in the early development of consumer videorecorders, several technical approaches and several possible applications were candidates for development. Within the family of helical scanners, high-level alternatives on the hierarchy of technical choices included the number of heads on a scanner (one, two, three, or four?) and the method of encoding color signals. On the applications side, no one understood whether users would want the machines to make the equivalent of "home movies," to play prerecorded programs, or to record broadcasts. Some firms targeted their work to create a specific embodiment for a particular use; others explored several technical approaches and kept options open for various applications.

Conceptually, one can think of four generic strategies defined by the extent to which choices have been made among competing technical approaches and applications possibilities (see *Figure 7-1*).

Figure 7-1
Development Strategies

		Domain of Technology (technical approaches)	
		One	Many
Domain of Use (applications)	One	Product targeted	Application targeted
	Many	Technically targeted	Exploratory

Before the innovation can be exploited, a firm's efforts must come to focus on a specific technical approach and on a chosen application. But an active posture can be implemented without so specific a commitment to its outcomes being present at the start. Instead, initial activities may contemplate diverse applications, diverse technical approaches, or both.

This is not just a matter of sorting out rival notions of the most suitable core concept. Lower-level choices can also matter significantly. For example, a century ago, there were two rival approaches to embodying Edison's phonograph invention: Edison's "phonograph," using a cylinder, and the "playback-only" gramophone, using a disc. For each approach, a hierarchy of lower-level technical choices enabled the development of a family of related but varied embodiments. Early phonographs used treadles, springs, batteries, and household current for motive power; Edison even produced one model driven by water (from a tap). Work that was focused on only one approach necessarily constrained the application possibilities. The gramophone, for example, could not be used for dictation. Even lower-level choices were significant—a battery powered version of the phonograph was the only practical choice (in 1891) for the first nickel-in-the-slot applications.

Although senior managers cannot concern themselves in detail with the problem-solving agendas of development or commercialization, they ought to be concerned about shaping the overall direction of work. My observation of some cases suggests that managers can accomplish that by the way they define a "keynote" for each of those agendas. For example, the keynote of a technical agenda would specify the core concept (or concepts) worth working on and the system of priorities by which choices should be made at lower levels of the hierarchy. The corresponding commercial keynote would specify the customer or market segments targeted and the significance of the innovation to the firm.

The managerial determination of "direction" operates not only in the substantive dimension defined conceptually by technical and applications approaches, but also in terms of time and resources. Managers can choose when to initiate organized activity and when to make the important transition to commercialization.

For example, in an interesting article with the provocative title "Where is Tom Edison Now That We Need Him?" Roland Schmitt argues that the best way to deal with some uncertainties of innovation "isn't by doing forecasts or market studies—it's by Edison's method . . . . introduce the innovations, and let the public tell in the marketplace what it thinks of them."[23]

Alternatively, a management may prefer to remain longer in an exploratory mode of development, deferring the more substantial costs of commercialization until prospects seem surer.

Resource utilization, of course, will be driven by (or drive) these choices of direction. Hence, at least implicitly, a management must formulate a definition of direction that is consistent in all three dimensions: substance, timing, and resources. Moreover, it must review those choices periodically; a decision on posture or direction, once taken, cannot be immutable. Circumstances change, and the courses of action pursued by prospective innovators must adapt to them.

Issues for Research

The history of industrial innovation makes clear that pioneering in the development of an extraordinary innovation sometimes brings extraordinary returns, and sometimes not. We have outlined a way of thinking about the possibility of a salient extraordinary innovation. Other conceptualizations are possible, and each must be tested by looking at what managers actually do.

Research so far provides little understanding of why firms in apparently similar business situations often adopt radically different postures and work in different directions when facing the same opportunity for innovation. Neither does any academic theory or managerial doctrine provide reliable guidance as to the circumstances that should be considered when a firm adopts a posture toward and sets the direction of efforts for an extraordinary innovation. Better understanding is a prerequisite for prescription.

Inquiry should begin with comparative descriptive studies. Among the questions that should be addressed are: What circumstances govern when a firm will adopt an active posture? Once it has done so, what determines how and when it decides whether to try to lead or to follow? What does the choice between leading and following imply about behavior toward the formulation, gestation, or exploitation of the innovation?

To explore these questions, one must consider three aspects of the situation: the inherent nature of the innovation; the elements of innovation involved (formulation and so forth); and the context in which the work is carried out. By context we mean both the "internal" characteristics of the firm and the character of its external environment (for example, industry structure). We suggest that all three sets of influences interact to influence the "agendas" of work to be done and that they, in turn, shape performance.

The links between direction-setting choices and outcomes of the innovative process also should be explored. Retrospective studies suggest that certain choices in the formulation, gestation, or exploitation of an innovation prove to be disproportionately important in determining outcomes. My impressionistic interpretation of several histories of extraordinary innovation is that these highly consequential choices may occur in any phase of the process and that their significance is not often appreciated at the time that they are made.

A final area in need of attention concerns the question of organization. While most modern firms are well adapted to promote and assimilate "normal change," managers in many firms have come to believe that novel mechanisms may be necessary to manage extraordinary innovations. It seems likely that they entail a process of change that is inherently different from the normal experience of an established industrial or commercial organization. For these reasons, some firms assign responsibilities for extraordinary innovation to units not involved in current operations. In some cases it becomes part of the mission of a corporate research laboratory; others experiment with novel organizational forms—a "skunk works," perhaps, or task forces or venture teams. Whatever the form, the task of managing the development of technologies that "don't fit," of exploring the potential of opportunities that are still on the horizon, conflicts with the premises of established and otherwise successful management concepts and systems.

In summary, these words are intended to encourage systematic inquiry into management's choice of the strategy ("posture" and "direction") and structure of activities aimed at extraordinary innovation. A historical sense of the trajectories along which technologies evolve, or the microeconomists' rigorous analyses of industries in which firms are mainly anonymous, will help, but they aren't enough. These familiar academic perspectives help us to understand the issues. But, as we have argued, the managerial role needs to be brought into the foreground of our research frameworks if findings are to contribute to improvement of practice.

Notes

1. Videotex is a generic term for an interactive communication service that provides text and graphic displays on a television receiver or similar terminal. The joint venture is described in the *Wall Street Journal*, 15 February 1984, 3.

2. For the Cross and Trecker acquisition, see *Wall Street Journal*, 13 April 1984, 16. Biotechnology investments are described in "Biotech Comes of Age," *Business Week*, 23 January 1984, 84–94.

3. Alfred P. Sloan, Jr., *My Years with General Motors* (Garden City: Doubleday & Company, Inc., 1964), chapter 5: "The 'Copper-Cooled' Engine," 71–94; a good, brief review of the RCA videodisc innovation appears in *Electronic News,* 16 April 1984.

4. For an interesting review of unfulfilled prophecies of this sort, see "If This is the Future . . .", *Science 84,* January-February 1984, 34–43.

5. See "Sober Diagnosis," *Wall Street Journal,* 6 May 1980, 48.

6. Edward W. Constant II, *The Origins of the Turbojet Revolution* (Baltimore: Johns Hopkins University Press, 1980); Ernest Braun and Stuart MacDonald, *Revolution in Miniature* (Cambridge: Cambridge University Press, 1978).

7. William J. Abernathy and Kim B. Clark, "Innovation: Mapping the Winds of Creative Destruction," Harvard Business School Working Paper 84-32 (25 July 1983), 3.

8. Abernathy and Clark, "Innovation," 13.

9. Constant, *Turbojet Revolution,* 10.

10. David S. Landes, *Revolution in Time* (Cambridge: Harvard University Press, 1983), 339–40.

11. For a useful review, see James Utterback, "Innovation in Industry and the Diffusion of Technology," *Science* 183 (1974): 620–26.

12. David C. Mowery and Nathan Rosenberg, "The Influence of Market Demand Upon Innovation: A Critical Review of Some Recent Empirical Studies," in *Inside the Black Box: Technology and Economics,* by Nathan Rosenberg (Cambridge: Cambridge University Press, 1972), 193–241; and Richard S. Rosenbloom, "Technological Innovation in Firms and Industries: An Assessment of the State of the Art," in *Technological Innovation: A Critical Review of Current Knowledge,* ed. P. Kelly and M. Kranzberg (San Francisco: San Francisco Press, Inc., 1978), 215–30.

13. See, for example, Rosenberg, *Inside the Black Box;* Richard R. Nelson and Sidney G. Winter, "In Search of Useful Theory of Innovation," *Research Policy* 6 (1977): 36–76; and William J. Abernathy, Kim B. Clark, and Alan M. Kantrow, *Industrial Renaissance* (New York: Basic Books, 1983).

14. See, for example, Constant, *Turbojet Revolution;* and Braun and MacDonald, *Revolution in Miniature.* A useful exception is William J. Abernathy, *The Productivity Dilemma: Roadblock to Innovation in the Auto Industry* (Baltimore: Johns Hopkins University Press, 1978).

15. Nathan Rosenberg and W. Edward Steinmueller, "The Economic Implications of the VLSI Revolution," in Rosenberg, *Inside the Black Box,* 178–92.

16. Frequent use will be made throughout this paper of examples from the history of the development of magnetic videorecording technology and associated home videoplayer innovations. A summary of that history is given in the *Appendix.*

17. Ralph E. Gomory, "Technology Development," *Science* 220 (1983): 576–80, quotation from p. 579.

18. Quoted in *A Streak of Luck,* by Robert Conot (New York: Seaview Books, 1979), 106 (from Edison manuscript dated 23 November 1877).

19. Baird's abortive first effort in 1928, interestingly, was based on an analog to the gramophone; he sold primitive videodiscs in Selfridge's, London, but was about fifty years ahead of the technology.

20. Unexpected invention may result from problem-solving efforts well after the design process has begun. For an example, see the discussion of GE's invention of a superior technique for CT scanning mentioned in Roland Schmitt's commentary on this chapter.

21. Kim B. Clark, "How Industries Evolve: The Interaction of Design

Hierarchies and Market Concepts," Harvard Business School Working Paper, HBS 84-20, Ocotber 1983, quotation from p. 15.

22. Michael E. Porter, "The Technological Dimension of Competitive Strategy," in *Research on Technological Innovation, Management and Policy*, vol. 1, ed. Richard S. Rosenbloom (Greenwich, Connecticut: JAI Press, 1983), 1–33.

23. *Research Management*, September-October 1983, 7–9.

Appendix

Origins of Magnetic Video Recording

Magnetic recording of information, an exotic and rarely used technology of the 1940s, is a ubiquitous part of life in the industrial world of the 1980s. Its applications are now many and varied: the magnetic stripe on plastic cards used for financial transactions; the floppy and rigid discs and the reels of tape used as computer memories; the sound cassette in a Sony Walkman; the videocassette for education or home entertainment; the devices that make instant replay possible. All these utilize the same phenomenon of physics: Certain ferromagnetic materials, used as coating on suitable nonmagnetic substrates, will retain the "imprint" left by a magnetic "head" that scans the coated surface. The recorded imprint is a magnetic analog of a varying electrical current, the "signal," which in turn has been created by an associated device to represent, perhaps, your bank balance, or the voice of a tenor, or the image of a sporting event.

Magnetic recording was invented at the turn of the century by Valdemar Poulsen, a Danish telephone engineer and a pioneer in wireless (radio) technology. Early machines used wire as the recording medium; recordings were noisy and distorted, limiting the commercial utility of the technology. In the 1930s, the first good quality sound recordings were being made in Germany, using machines of advanced design produced by AEG-Telefunken and greatly improved tapes, made by what is now BASF.

American companies "reverse engineered" new products from captured German Magnetophones after World War II. The first substantial commercial market for this equipment was provided by commercial radio networks and affiliated stations. By 1950, a small California company, Ampex Corporation, had become the dominant supplier of high-quality audio tape recorders for broadcast and professional use.

Ampex had been founded in 1944 in San Carlos, California, by 52-year-old Alexander M. Poniatoff (his initials, plus "ex" for "excellence" provided the name and set the tone for the new company). The first products were high-precision motors for wartime radar equipment.

When he first encountered the Magnetophone, in late 1946, Poniatoff was looking for a commercial product to sustain his young firm.

The origins of Sony Corporation present a striking parallel. One of Sony's founders, Masaro Ibuka, had operated a small wartime factory making precision equipment for the Japanese navy. Struggling to keep his small firm alive in the postwar devastation of Japan, he was joined by Akio Morita. Searching for a product that could be sold in volume, he was shown an early-model tape recorder by a member of the American Occupation forces. Ibuka recalls that he was "immediately convinced that this was the product they had been looking for." And so it was.[1]

Video Recording

While the business of making magnetic sound recording equipment was being born, two other new technologies, digital computing and television broadcasting, were beginning the transition from laboratory marvels to significant commercial enterprises. In the ensuing decades, both of these developments would create enormous demands for magnetic recording equipment.

By 1951, the year in which IBM committed itself to its first mainframe computer, the 701, and to magnetic tape as a principal memory medium for it, television had already become a major industry in the United States. More than 11 million U.S. households owned television receivers; a half-million more were being added every month; standards for color broadcasting were being debated hotly; and coast-to-coast transmission of network programs was on the horizon.[2]

Because the United States spans three time zones, West Coast broadcasters need a way to delay their transmission of programs originating in the East. When the first coast-to-coast telecasts began, the only available means was "hot" kinescope, a photographic technique of adequate quality (at least for monochrome images) but excessive complexity and cost. The need for an alternative was evident; the analogy to audio recording made magnetics a prime prospect.

But much more than mere enhancement of audio techniques would be needed to make video recording a reality. Video signals used a much broader segment of the frequency spectrum than did audio. Both the high frequencies (3,500,000 Hz. versus audio's roughly 15,000 Hz.) and the wide range of frequencies posed extremely tough challenges. To record the high frequencies, the magnetic head must scan the tape at very high speeds (100 times faster than the best audio recorders). Recording the broad frequency band of the video signal was also difficult, because of inherent biases in the translation of the electronic signal into its magnetic counterpart.

Early Approaches to Video Recording

The magnetic elements—the recording medium (coated tape, disk, or card) and the head—are at the heart of any magnetic recording system. Unless they perform well, the system will not. Also important are the scanner and associated transport mechanism, through which the head scans the medium to "read" or "write," and the electronic circuitry, which both processes the signals to and from the head and controls the mechanical actions of scanner and transport.

The critical design choice in developing a videorecorder pertained to the type of scanner; there are three basic "families" of approaches, as follows (see *Figure A7-1*):

1. *Longitudinal scanners* in which the medium is scanned along its length by moving the tape past a fixed head at a velocity equal to the desired "writing speed";
2. *Transverse scanners* in which the medium is scanned across its width by heads rotating (at the writing speed) in a plane perpendicular to the (much slower) motion of the tape;
3. *Helical scanners* in which the tape is scanned in a pattern slanted across its width by heads rotating in a plane set at an acute angle to the motion of the tape.

Whichever technical approach they adopted, aspiring inventors had to produce a design capable of meeting demanding requirements in three principal respects: (1) frequency response—to attain a high enough "writing speed" to record the high frequency video signal with then available heads and tapes; (2) time-base stability—to attain a very high degree of stability in the scanning motion (a timing variation of one part in a million would disrupt the video image); and (3) standardization—to maintain the geometry of the scan over time and across machines so that a recorded signal could reliably be recovered at a later date or by a different piece of equipment. Details of the mechanical design of the scanner and the design of its associated electronic circuitry determined how well a videorecorder would meet these requirements. The design problems to be resolved in each case differed greatly according to which basic design "family" was being developed. At the same time, there were certain other problems—particularly in the design of recording heads and in obtaining tape of adequate quality—that arose in common for all three approaches.

Figure A7-1
Scanner Formats

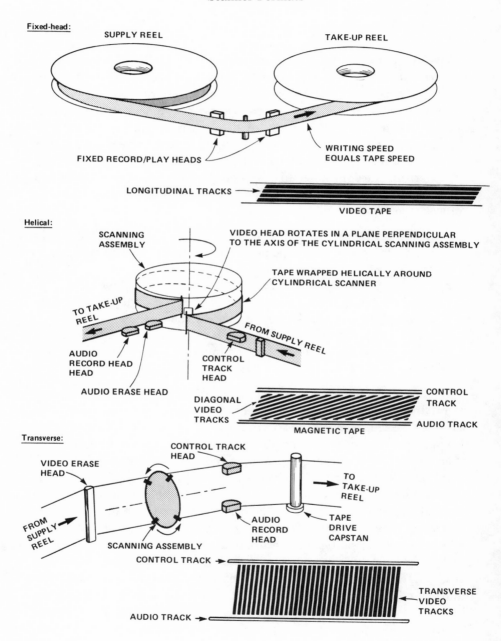

Fixed-head:

SUPPLY REEL

TAKE-UP REEL

FIXED RECORD/PLAY HEADS

WRITING SPEED
EQUALS TAPE SPEED

LONGITUDINAL TRACKS

VIDEO TAPE

Helical:

SCANNING
ASSEMBLY

VIDEO HEAD ROTATES IN A PLANE PERPENDICULAR
TO THE AXIS OF THE CYLINDRICAL SCANNING ASSEMBLY

TAPE WRAPPED HELICALLY AROUND
CYLINDRICAL SCANNER

TO TAKE-UP
REEL

FROM SUPPLY REEL

AUDIO
RECORD HEAD
HEAD

CONTROL
TRACK
HEAD

AUDIO ERASE HEAD

DIAGONAL
VIDEO
TRACKS

CONTROL
TRACK

AUDIO TRACK

MAGNETIC TAPE

Transverse:

CONTROL TRACK
HEAD

VIDEO ERASE
HEAD

TO
TAKE-UP
REEL

FROM
SUPPLY
REEL

AUDIO
RECORD
HEAD

TAPE
DRIVE
CAPSTAN

SCANNING ASSEMBLY

CONTROL TRACK

TRANSVERSE
VIDEO
TRACKS

AUDIO TRACK

The first commercially practical videotape recorder, invented at the Ampex Corporation and first demonstrated in March 1956, used a transverse scanner. While the Ampex team was developing its design, engineers in other organizations in North America, Europe, and Japan were experimenting with other approaches to videorecording, using both fixed-head and helical scanners. Of those efforts, the best-funded and most publicized was the project at the RCA Laboratories in Princeton, New Jersey.

In a widely quoted speech, delivered at Princeton in September 1951, David Sarnoff, RCA's chief executive, challenged his company's technical community to invent a practical videorecorder, which he suggested would become the visual equivalent of the popular phonograph. In December 1953, RCA demonstrated a system using a fixed-head scanner that could record and play back good quality video in monochrome or color. The engineer in charge kept the RCA project focused on the fixed-head scanner in the belief that the apparently more complex mechanical demands of rotating heads would make them impractical, especially for RCA, which viewed itself as an "electronics" company. The fixed-head scanner required much more sophisticated electronic circuits but mechanically was similar to existing audio recorders.

Other development teams pursued similar goals at the same time in projects sponsored by Bing Crosby Enterprises in the United States (the singer had been the first to use audiotape in radio broadcasting) and the BBC in England. All these designs, while capable of good recordings, had a fundamental handicap: The tape had to run at exceptionally high speeds. In the RCA design, for example, the tape moved at 30 feet per second (versus 1.25 ft./sec. for audio); huge reels holding 7,000 feet of tape had to spin at as much as 600 rpm and still would provide only four minutes of playing time. The announced goal of the RCA team was a fifteen-minute play from a nineteen-inch reel of tape.

The alternative design concepts, using rotating heads, posed different but equally daunting technical obstacles and were more difficult to bring to a state where a picture could be demonstrated. The logic of the technology led a number of prospective inventors independently to pursue similar approaches. An Italian, Luigi Marzocchi, was granted European patents in the 1930s for a variety of design ideas for moving scanners for magnetic recording of high frequencies. Similar ideas were investigated by Marvin Camras at the Illinois Institute of Technology in the 1940s. Earl Masterson, an engineer at RCA, filed a patent for a helical scanner in 1950. Experimentation with helical scanners at Telefunken in Germany and Toshiba in Japan produced patents filed also in the early 1950s.

The impetus for the project that first succeeded in inventing a practical videorecorder came from a 1951 demonstration of Camras's concepts for rotating head scanners, witnessed by an Ampex engineer. Poniatoff and his associates saw this as a promising approach to video. They hired a young broadcast engineer, Charles Ginsberg, and assigned him to develop a videorecorder. At first alone, and then with a student assistant (Ray Dolby, later to become famous as an audio inventor), Ginsburg developed equipment capable of recording and playback of crude video images. The project was officially shelved in mid-1953 but gained new life the next year as Ginsburg, working "unofficially" with another engineer, developed new ideas that led to formal reinstatement in mid-1954 and expansion of the team to five persons.

By early 1955 the Ampex team could demonstrate all of the basic technological capabilities needed to design a magnetic videorecorder suitable for use in broadcasting. The most novel elements were the scanner design and the electronic circuits used to process the video signal for recording and recovering it on playback. While the Ampex scanner was true to the original concept of multiple rotating heads, it had been fundamentally changed by the addition of a fourth head and by adoption of an axis of rotation parallel to the motion of the tape. The breakthrough in circuitry came with the decision to encode the video signal by modulating the frequency of a "carrier" signal.

On 2 March 1955 the team demonstrated its accomplishments to the Ampex board of directors, which authorized them to proceed with the design of a commercial product, to be demonstrated, they hoped, within a year. Ampex aspired to preempt the dominant position as supplier of videorecorders to television networks and stations. The problems to be solved were entirely technical, not commercial. The customers' need for a videorecorder was manifest; the missing ingredient was a workable product. By inducing broadcasters to adopt its recording format as the standard for the industry, Ampex would gain a decisive competitive advantage. To do that, Ampex would have to be first to the market with machines designed so that each one could play back tapes recorded on any other machine of the same "format."

The Ampex team had invented the technical basis for just such a product; the task of the development project was to refine certain critical elements and to embody the whole design in a way that would meet conventional requirements of manufacturability and usability. The urgent tone of the development project derived directly from the commercial imperatives—the product had to be ready for shipment (not just demonstration) early enough to preempt the market and create a de facto standard. With the same goal being pursued as high priority by RCA Labs with its awesome resources and reputation, Ginsburg and associates believed that they were in a tough race.

Optimization of design was not a goal. The design had to be workable, and it had to be ready soon; refinements could come later. One consequence of this was the adoption of a format that used a great deal of tape per unit of time (750 square feet for an hour, about $200 worth). But measures that would increase recording density might negatively affect signal quality, and the team chose to build in a margin for error.

A prototype was demonstrated to thirty Ampex employees in February 1956. Its performance astounded the audience and management committed the company to introduce the product commercially with a demonstration in April at the annual Convention of the National Association of Radio and Television Broadcasters. That first public demonstration electrified the broadcasters, who signed orders for 100 machines during the four days of the convention.

To ensure adoption of its format, Ampex offered to ship a few custom-made prototypes in 1956, at a premium price of $75,000. CBS used the first of these on the air in November. The first production models, offering the important feature of interchangeability of tapes between machines, were delivered in late 1957. A "regular" process of innovation ensued in the broadcast recorder business. Color circuitry was developed; all the circuits were embodied in solid-state designs; suppliers developed improved materials for the recording heads and better tapes; adaptations to specialized niches appeared in the form of portable equipment and a cassette-playing machine for commercials. But despite these developments, the original recording format remained unchanged for decades, and, while it did, Ampex remained the dominant supplier of videorecorders to broadcasters.

While the transverse-scanner design met an important need in broadcasting, its complexity made it inherently expensive and difficult to maintain and operate. The dramatic success of videorecording sparked speculation about applications in a wide assortment of other settings, which in turn stimulated exploration of scanner designs offering greater simplicity.

Characteristic of the speculation at the time was this excerpt from an investment banker's sober appraisal of Ampex in 1958:

> It is impossible to estimate the potential market over the long run for videotape recording equipment, so many are its applications. Video tape recorders may some day be found in offices, plants, and homes; eventually,

small hand cameras using magnetic tape rather than film might be used by home and professional movie makers; video tape recorders might play these films back through conventional TV sets.[3]

In pursuit of this potential market, firms in Europe, North America, and Japan undertook development of VTRs based on helical scanners and, in some cases, on more radical fixed-head designs. The first helical-scan recorders were introduced as commercial products in 1962 by Sony and Ampex itself. While these machines could not compete with the transverse-scan design in the demanding technical environment of broadcasting, their low cost and relative simplicity found buyers for other applications.

In contrast to the enduring standardization of the recording format used for the transverse-scan broadcast machines, each new generation of helical scanners brought the introduction of new formats, with rival producers seldom collaborating to standardize. One positive consequence of this was that there was a continuing increase in recording density, leading to reduced consumption of the still-expensive recording tape, and to more compact equipment designs. *Figure A7-2* tracks the improvements in unit prices and in tape utilization for innovative designs introduced through four generations of helical recording tech-

Figure A7-2
VTR Technological Trends: Cost and Performance 1955–1980

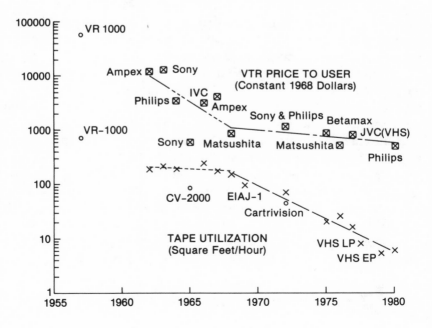

nology, showing the same data for the Ampex VR-1000 (transverse scan format) for comparison.

As the figure illustrates, firms in Europe, North America, and Japan participated in the evolution of the helical technology. By 1975 that sequence of developments had led to "fourth generation" designs (Beta and VHS formats) with equipment costs (in constant dollars) reduced and tape utilization (recording density) improved by nearly two orders of magnitude each.

The constituent improvements came from many sources and were quickly adopted by the producers of recorders. Significant inventions in scanner design were made at Ampex in the late 1950s and early 1960s. Ampex, Matsushita, and others pioneered in cartridge-loading designs that simplified use. Sony and Philips introduced cassette-loading methods that soon became standard. Better ferrite materials and experience in volume manufacture of heads facilitated formats that made more efficient use of the recording medium. New media, like Du Pont's chromium dioxide and the Japanese cobalt-doped coatings, enabled good quality color recording and higher densities in recording. Increased densities made cassettes practical; combined with increasing use of integrated circuits, high-density recording facilitated compact and easy-to-use equipment.

While the technology was advancing, the industry was searching to find applications for which helical machines could be sold. Working on the assumption that American consumers would buy a VTR for home use if it cost less than $1,000, Ampex and Sony (followed by others) launched the design and commercialization of such products in the mid-1960s, selling recorders and cameras for "home movie" applications. The premise was wrong, but the producers quickly discovered applications in replacement of 16mm movies for education, training, and so forth, opening up a "professional" market for helical VTRs.

By the time the first cassette- and cartridge-loaded VTR designs began to surface in the early 1970s, substantial interest in home video had been built up within the worldwide consumer electronics industry. Many factors contributed to widespread industry acceptance of the proposition that a billion-dollar market was latent, waiting for the right technology to tap it. The product concept with the greatest currency envisioned the development of a simple, low-cost "box" (the player) with which consumers could reproduce prerecorded entertainment from some sort of "cartridge" for viewing through the household's television receiver.

The proponents of magnetic recording asserted that VTRs would prove effective for that consumer application, while offering the added

Table A7-1
"Home" Videoplayers under Development—Early 1970s

Technology	Company	First Demonstration	Commercial Introduction
Magnetic Tape			
Helical cassette	Sony	1969	1972[a]
	Matsushita	1969	1972[a]
	Philips	1969	1972[a]
	RCA	1972	X
Helical cartridge	CTI/Avco	1970	1971
	Ampex	1970	X
Longitudinal	Arvin	?	X
Plastic Film			
EVR	CBS and Partners	1968	1970[a]
Holotape	RCA	1969	X
Super-8	NordMende	1969	X
Disc			
Pressure	Teldec	1970	1975
Optical	Philips	1972	1978
	Thomson	1972	X
	MCA	1972	1978
Capacitance	RCA	1972	1981

[a] Not to consumer market.

benefit of recording capability. Others remained skeptical that the complex and (for mass market purposes) relatively expensive magnetic machines could be improved sufficiently to be successful for this purpose. Other technologies offered appealing advantages, though all were limited to use only for playback of recordings made by producers.

During the early 1970s, demonstration models of home videoplayers based on nine different technologies were shown publicly by firms striving to take the lead in developing the new home video market. Dozens of firms on three continents made substantial commitments— spending hundreds of millions of dollars in aggregate—to develop products from these technologies. *Table A7-1* lists the more prominent of these developments and the firms associated with them.

None of the designs listed in the table proved successful in the consumer marketplace. But the progress of magnetic recording technology continued and the fourth-generation designs, led by Sony's Beta and JVC's VHS formats, finally tapped the mass market in the late 1970s.

Ampex and Sony had drawn important lessons from their first experiences with the consumer market in the 1960s. Interviews and the evidence of products later commercialized suggest that commercial "agendas" were reformulated to emphasize performance improvements, and particularly greater recording density. The first generation of cassette-loading, color recorders (1972) stimulated growth in professional applications, but one more generation was needed to open the consumer market. When that happened, it was not for machines that played prerecorded programs, despite an avalanche of speculation in the period from 1968 to 1972. The failure of such products (the Cartrivision magnetic recorder, and CBS's film-based EVR) persuaded Sony to look elsewhere. The result was the "time-shift" campaign for Betamax, and the birth of a major industry.

Appendix Notes

1. For more of the story of the origins and early growth of Sony, see Nick Lyons, *Sony Vision* (New York: Crown Publishers, 1976).
2. For a discussion of these developments in the context of the industry as a whole, see Richard S. Rosenbloom and William J. Abernathy, "The Climate for Innovation of Industry," *Research Policy* 11 (1982):209–25.
3. Carl M. Loeb Rhoades & Co., "Ampex Corporation: A Study of the Leading Manufacturer of Professional Tape Recording Machinery," July 1958, 8.

Commentary
Extraordinary Innovation: Experiment, Organization, and Teamwork

Roland W. Schmitt

Professor Rosenbloom's chapter raises many interesting issues. This commentary focuses on three of them. First, it discusses the general framework he proposes as a setting for managerial decisions. Second, it comments on the relationship between organization and innovation. Finally, it considers whether extraordinary innovation can be fostered by institutions designed to achieve ordinary innovation.

First the framework. Professor Rosenbloom observes that "the academic literature on innovation provides little guidance to managers concerned with extraordinary opportunities for change." I agree. But the principal outcome of academic studies in this field will be understanding, not guidance—at least for the present. The two are not synonymous. Ex post facto studies of extraordinary innovations, cast in the framework provided by Professor Rosenbloom, could provide a deep, sound basis for understanding differences between innovations that succeeded and those that failed. This would be helpful background knowledge for managers faced with ongoing decisions in real-life cases of extraordinary innovation.

But it would provide only one element of the guidance such a manager needs. Because often it is not a failure of "knowing what to do" that frustrates success, but a failure to "make it happen." And making it happen depends heavily on exogenous factors that could only be captured in psychological and sociological studies that were as deep and thorough as those encompassed by Professor Rosenbloom's framework.

For example, one cannot imagine going into a meeting with the chief executive officer or with an operating group executive of General Electric armed with the argument that the developments at issue should be "application targeted because there are several technologies applicable to the domain of use" and that our posture "should be an active follower rather than a passive or an active leader."

Even if these arguments were to be cast into the specifics of the particular case and then related to the prevailing competitive and market environment, they would still miss what are often the most important factors such as the degree of candor permitted in such discussions, the element of trust between an operating manager and an R&D manager, the climate for risk, the consequences of failure, and many more. In short, an understanding of extraordinary innovations that is sufficient for guidance cannot be achieved within the framework of Professor Rosenbloom's chapter.

The value and originality of the chapter consists in his focus on the nature of managerial decisions in each phase of innovation—formulation, gestation, and exploitation. Even the formulation phase is a sequence of decisions. Formulating a new concept is, in Professor Rosenbloom's happy phrase, "a task, not an event." The gestation phase, again viewed as decision making, is also an extended process. Initial technical choices create an agenda for decision. Finally, in the exploitation phase, the agenda of technical decisions is overlaid with an agenda of commercial ones.

Raising questions about management decisions is the great merit of Professor Rosenbloom's chapter. One is somewhat uneasy, however, with some features of his model. Despite his disclaimer that he is not presenting a "fixed linear sequence," what he presents sounds very much like one. One's own preference, as he notes in his paper, is to view innovation as an experimental process. This experimental process is a balance of vision and reality, of theory and testing, of adaptation and persistence. These are elements of successful innovation, just as they are elements of successful research. This view is not totally at variance with Professor Rosenbloom's framework. In fact, there are complementary features. But these comments will emphasize the differences.

According to a linear scheme, phase one must be finished before another phase begins. That is not necessarily true, however, for making innovations.

Frequently the new ideas that occur during the development of a technology are so fundamental that they ought to be regarded as a new conception. Perhaps the wheel should not be reinvented. But other important technologies are reinvented, over and over again, in fundamentally different, new ways.

A case that Professor Rosenbloom alludes to, but does not develop, illustrates this reinvention process. The CAT scanner was indeed invented by Geoffrey Hounsfield of EMI. That company had carried it all the way into the exploitation phase before General Electric got involved. EMI was selling scanners like hotcakes, if you can imagine a $500,000 hotcake. Too slavish a devotion to a linear model of innovation might have persuaded General Electric that it was too late to reformulate the invention, and that it should worry only about the exploitation phase—that is, we should either license and stick to EMI's technology package, or we should stay out and leave the field to them.

However, we did not take this view. Instead, we went back to an earlier phase—whether it was formulation or gestation is a matter of terminology. We started out experimentally, working on a scanner for the detection of breast cancers. In the process, we found that a technically original route—the fan-beam approach—looked superior to the EMI pencil beam method. In midexperiment, as market conditions and technical options continued to change, we shifted our goal from the breast scanner to a whole-body scanner based on the fan beam. We gestated that idea as fast as possible—in fact, it took about nine months. We gave birth not to a me-too product, but to a technically distinct one. It became the market winner.

As important as the technical and management decisions that contributed to this success was the fact that there were two entrepreneurially oriented business managers in tandem in operations. Both knew what to demand and to expect of a forefront corporate R&D organization. So when decisions were made in favor of innovative but risky new technical approaches, they were psychologically in tune with such a course and prepared to share its risks.

We now view this effort as one of our most successful. It illustrates a process of repeated invention, not a linear sequence of conception, gestation, and exploitation.

Much the same thing can be said of many of the other extraordinary innovations that have originated in the General Electric R&D Center. The Lucalox lamp, a major advance in high-efficiency lighting, came about as a result of research in ceramics that was only later redirected into a lighting application. The discovery of polymerization by oxidative coupling at the laboratory opened up a fundamentally new way of making polymers, as well as the conception of a specific new polymer. But it took a second conception, a polymer blend conceived after that first polymer had been introduced, to bring about the commercially successful product, Noryl resins.

We now move to a second issue. Why do different firms take such different organizational approaches to innovation? The answer here is looking at innovation in a way that transcends typologies of linear schemes. A firm's attitude toward innovation arises out of its attitude toward its market and its mission.

Looking at the sort of innovation I know best—innovations coming out of a corporate research laboratory—consider the comparison between two exemplars of corporate-level research, Bell Laboratories and the General Electric Research and Development Center. Both are successful. But they have achieved their successes with very different philosophies of operation.

Those philosophies are a consequence of the nature of the companies they serve. AT&T—the old AT&T—was a regulated company with a regulated market and a regulated mission. So its technical efforts were focused on that mission of communications and its scientific foundations, rather than on the development of new products that it would not have been allowed to sell, or the opening up of new markets that it would not have been allowed to enter.

AT&T's principal technical organization, which was, like the company, highly centralized, put heavy emphasis on generic research. That research was often only loosely coordinated with markets, but more tightly coordinated with the performance and cost of the telephone system. Bell Laboratories became, and remains, most renowned for the depth of its scientific efforts, and the excellence of its fundamental research.

General Electric, on the other hand, early in its corporate career renounced any ambitions of being the AT&T of electric power. GE decided not to own the electric power system, but to sell products to it—and in the process, to branch out into products that owed their technical origins to electricity, but were not necessarily electrical themselves. Thus the blue glow inside Edison's light bulbs became industrial electronics; the resins stuck to the outside of copper wires to keep in the electrons became engineering plastics; and the rotating machinery of a turbine became the jet engine.

But though these lines of technical descent were clear, nothing could have been more disastrous than to run electronics as a part of the light bulb business, polymers as part of the wire and cable business, and jet engines as part of the steam turbine business. Each of those products needed to be developed and marketed by organizations that understood the businesses. Those organizations needed their own R&D resources, and they put them in place.

So, today, about 95 percent of the 17,000 people with technical degrees who do research and development for GE do it in the company's decentralized operations. Corporate R&D exists to do the technical work above and beyond what the operations do for themselves. But

GE's long and continous history of establishing new businesses, setting up new ventures, and exploring new markets has resulted in a "hands-on" entrepreneurial climate that pervades all its technical organizations. As a result, the corporate laboratory works closely with the business operations. Targeted programs, and awareness to market needs are the strengths of General Electric's corporate R&D organization. It has become most renowned for its ability to generate a wide range of successful new products and services for the company it serves—everything from new classes of electronic devices to a radically new form of projection television, from new wire enamels to new types of high efficiency lamps.

The two companies discussed here adopted different philosophies of innovation management because they had different markets, missions, and corporate climates. So we should not be surprised that scientists at Bell Laboratories invented the transistor—a sold-state electronic switch essential to the future communcations mission of the company. And we should also not be surprised that scientists at the General Electric Research and Development Center invented the first reproducible process for making diamond—an extraordinary invention in Professor Rosenbloom's sense, yet for GE a logical extension of its existing market for tungsten carbide cutting tools, which in turn was an extension of its role as a maker of tungsten filaments for incandescent lamps.

This subject of corporate-level research and development provides a large part of the answer to that final question: Are institutions adapted to ordinary development also the right places to carry out extraordinary development? As Professor Rosenbloom puts it, "Some firms assign responsibilities for extraordinary innovation to units not involved in current operations. In some cases it becomes part of the mission of a corporate research laboratory."

Extraordinary innovation is indeed the mission of the corporate laboratory, at GE, Bell and many other places. But there is more to it. The corporate laboratory must have a partner in company operations. That partner must be strong in both marketing and technology, and coupling between that partner and the laboratory must also be strong.

The popular ways of categorizing innovation—as either technology push or market pull—oversimplify the situation and distract attention from that need for a strong technology-business partnership. Both the push and the pull can be present, but nothing will happen until the partnership gets established.

Consider, for example, General Electric's work in the field of power electronics for motor control. This field is in a state of fairly rapid technical evolution. But its commercial impact is revolutionary. A great majority of the hundreds of millions of electric motors out there in our factories and our homes are targets for replacement by electronically controlled motors.

The GE R&D Center had developed one of the world's leading technical efforts in this area by the late 1970s, and the markets were beginning to emerge. But nothing much happened until one of General Electric's entrepreneurial managers arrived at the laboratory and essentially told us, "Look, the time has come to make the variable speed alternating current drive into a product. Here are the specifications that must be met. Now you guys go out and make the inventions."

It must be admitted that when he presented those specifications for the first time, some of our people were skeptical about meeting them at all, much less within his ambitious timetable. But in fact, once that crucial teamwork was set up between the laboratory and operations, the team did come up with the inventions and put them into the product in even less time than that demanding schedule had called for. In the process, they made a couple of major developments—a new type of power switch and a high-voltage integrated circuit—that will be important products in their own right.

So to take advantage of either the push or the pull you need strong teamwork between the laboratory and the people who are going to use the technology. If managers try teaming up with a corporate laboratory a few times, they can learn to make a habit of it.

Jack Welch, General Electric's current chief executive officer, rose through the company by—among other things— knowing how to use corporate R&D. The businesses he ran are exemplars of successful exploitation of a corporate laboratory. GE's Plastics Business Group has repeatedly worked with the R&D Center on the development of highly successful new engineering plastics—first Lexan polycarbonate resin, later Noryl resin, and most recently the high-performance thermoplastic ULTEM resin.

And the partnership of the R&D Center and GE's Medical Systems business that led to fan-beam computed tomography is now doing it again with magnetic resonance diagnostics—a new method of taking cross-sectional images of the body, or of doing medical diagnosis, that uses the combination of a strong magnetic field and radio waves in place of x-rays.

These examples are cited to underline the need to not give the generator of technology—or even the director of the corporate laboratory— too much of the credit for innovation. It's just as important, and perhaps more difficult, to be a good receiver—to know how to put new technology to work in new products.

These examples only hint, however, at the variety of forms the innovation partnership can take. Each one is a different experiment. Which brings us back to the main point of this commentary. Innovation is an experimental process rather than a sequence of invariable stages. Different techniques work at different times. Different firms will organize differently for innovation because they have different markets, different missions, and different corporate climates. And, for all its effectiveness, corporate-level R&D is not the whole story of innovation. We must not forget the important role of the receiver, and of the partnership between the people who know technology and the people who know markets. That's what makes innovation happen.

8

Managing the New Product Development Process: How Japanese Companies Learn and Unlearn

Ken-ichi Imai

Ikujiro Nonaka

Hirotaka Takeuchi

Introduction

In our travels through corporate America several years ago, we found America in search of itself. "What went wrong?" many would ask. The talk would be about Rip van Winkle and about the past.

In our most recent travels through corporate America, we found it ready for action. "Can we do it?" many would ask. The talk would be about the future, about renaissance, renewal, and turnaround.

We heard a number of suggestions concerning how to bring about a more competitive future for corporate America. Not surprisingly, many emphasized innovation as the key missing link. For example:

- Abernathy, Clark, and Kantrow note that a change in the nature of innovation is both a sign of dematurity in process and, in competitive terms, its most far-reaching effect.[1]
- Lawrence and Dyer believe that a readaptive process—"the process by which organizations repeatedly reconcile efficiency and innovation"—is essential to renewing American industry.[2]
- Kanter argues: "As America's economy slips further into the doldrums, innovation is beginning to be recognized as a national priority. But there is a clear and pressing need for more innovations, for we face social and economic changes of unprecedented magnitude and variety, which past practices cannot accommodate and which instead require innovative responses."[3]

We were asked, by practitioners and researchers alike, to offer them clues on how the Japanese do it. How can Japanese companies be productive and innovative at the same time? How can they support such a rapid new product development program? How can they be so flexible in seeking out new technology and, at the same time, adaptive to changing market requirements?

It is with this kind of an orientation that we embarked on our investigation of the innovative behavior of Japanese companies with respect to new product development. Two dimensions of new product development were highlighted: (1) the speed with which new product development takes place, and (2) the flexibility with which companies adapt their development process to changes in the external environment. The basic rationale for treating speed and flexibility as the central issues of our research rests on our belief that they collectively lead to competitive advantages in the forms of increased productivity, reduced costs, improved quality, and higher market share, among others.

Methodology

To understand the dynamic process that enables certain Japanese companies to develop new products rapidly and with maximum flexibility, we selected five innovative models as our primary units of analysis. They include: (1) the FX-3500 copier made by Fuji-Xerox; (2) the City box-car made by Honda; (3) the Auto Boy lens shutter camera made by Canon (known as Sure Shot in the United States); (4) NEC's PC 8000 personal computer; and (5) Epson's MP-80 dot-matrix printer. These five models were selected with the following criteria in mind: market success, innovativeness of product features, strength of impact and visibility within the company as being a "breakthrough" development process, variety of product and process technology utilized, and spread of product categories along the product life cycle curve. See *Table 8-1* for a more detailed description of our units of analysis.

In-depth field research was conducted with the five manufacturers mentioned above, as well as with their affiliated companies and subcontractors. The latter group was included since product development in Japan cannot be viewed solely as an intrafirm activity. As is discussed below, an interorganizational network formed between the manufacturer and its outside suppliers plays an important role toward making speed and flexibility possible. As shown in *Table 8-2*, interviews were conducted with more than forty people from thirteen companies over a six-month period.

Table 8-1

Description of the Units of Analysis Used in the Study

Brand (company)	Product Description	Innovative Features	Life Cycle of Product Category	When Introduced	Approximate Peak Production Units per Year (peak year)	Share of Relevant Domestic Market
1. FX-3500 (Fuji-Xerox)	Medium-sized plain paper copier	• One-half the cost of a high-speed copier • Speed of 40 copies/min. • Compact size	Growth	1978	30,000 (1978)	60%
2. City (Honda)	1200cc box-car	• "Tall and short" car concept • Large interior • Fuel efficient	Mature	1981	125,000 (1982)	12%
3. Auto Boy (Canon)	Lens shutter camera	• Fully automatic camera with automatic winding and rewinding	Mature	1979	1,400,000 (1982)	20%
4. PC 8000 (NEC)	8-bit personal computer	• First fully packaged personal computer introduced in Japan	Introduction/ growth	1979	105,000 (1981)	45%
5. MP-80 (Epson)	Dot-matrix printer for personal computers	• Separate unit from computer • Compact	Introduction/ growth	1980	700,000 (1981)	60%

Table 8-2

Interview List

Brand	Company	No. of Interviewees	Total Interview Hours
FX-3500	Fuji-Xerox[a]	7	16
	Dengen-Automation[b]	2	2
	Sanyo Seisakusho[b]	1	1
	Toritsu-Kogyo[b]	4	2
	Tesco Industrial Co.[c]	1	1
	Mitsuba Electronics[c]	1	1
City	Honda	8	12
	Masuda Manufacturing[b]	1	1
Auto Boy	Canon	6	5
PC 8000	NEC	5	7
MP-80	Epson[d]	4	7
	Shiojiri Kogyo[b]	1	1
	Standard Press[b]	1	1
		42	57

a. Joint venture between Xerox Corporation and Fuji Film.
b. Primary subcontractor.
c. Secondary subcontractor.
d. Independent subsidiary of Seiko Group.

Descriptive Model

The key to identifying the various factors that make speed and flexibility possible is to view product development as a dynamic and continuous process of adaptation to changes in the environment. Within this framework, which is presented in *Figure 8-1,* companies adapt to changes or uncertainties in the market environment through an iterative process of variety reduction[4] and "learning-by-doing." Even a seemingly minor change in competitive behavior or consumer preference forces a manufacturer to make choices and to engage in learning, as Abernathy et al. point out:

> For whatever reasons—a sudden shift, say, in the prices of substitute products—a demand may arise among buyers for new dimensions of product performance or for a different set of trade-offs among product attributes. If this demand is sufficiently unlike the one it supersedes, producers may need to seek out new technology, to revise design concepts, to reintroduce innovation as an important element in competition, and to undertake a new round of iterative learning.[5]

A large proportion of the differences in the product development process between Japanese and U.S. manufacturers can be explained by examining how variety amplification, variety reduction, and learning actually take place.

Intrafirm Process

This chapter consists partly of a seven-piece jigsaw puzzle. In this section, six of the pieces are identified and put into place; they all are factors supporting a speedy and flexible new product development process from the inside. The final and missing piece, which identifies the contribution of outside suppliers, is examined in the next section. Needless to say, only after all the pieces are put in place can the entire picture be appreciated.

The process of developing new products within Fuji-Xerox, Honda, Canon, NEC, and Epson itself resembles the way in which a jigsaw puzzle is put together. It requires an incremental and iterative process of what Abernathy calls "learning-by-doing" as opposed to "analytic-strategy-synthesis."[6] The "doing" sometimes comes before the "thinking" part. Or in the words of Weick, "How can I know what I think until I see what I say?"[7]

The two processes are also similar in other respects. Variety reduc-

Figure 8-1
Descriptive Model for New Product Development

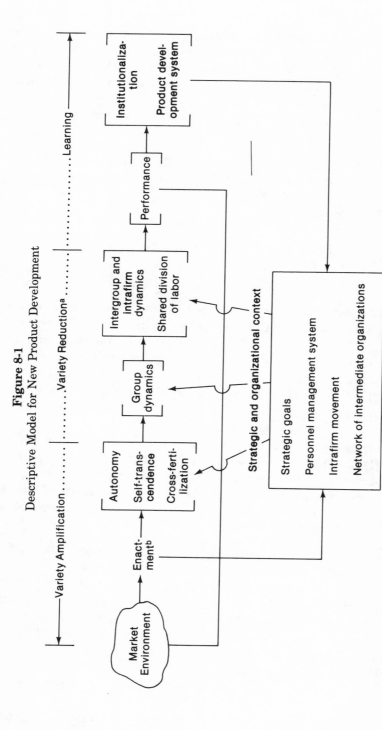

a. Dotted lines indicate considerable degree of overlap among variety amplification, variety reduction, and learning.
b. Enactment is defined as subjective perception of the external environment.

tion occurs in jigsaw puzzles by "building up" the pieces from scratch. It is often easier to finish a puzzle if others chip in, especially if they see things differently. Learning takes place as well, as one moves on from a seven-piece set to a more challenging one, with more pieces, almost as a natural course of events.

The six intrafirm factors that contribute to a speedy and flexible development process are as follows:

1. Top management as catalyst
2. Self-organizing project teams
3. Overlapping development phases
4. Multilearning
5. Subtle control
6. Organizational transfer of learning

Top Management as Catalyst

Top management plays a key strategic role in new product development. It provides the initial kickoff to the development process by signaling a broad strategic direction or goal for the company. Top management rarely hands down a clearcut new product concept or a specific work plan. Rather, it intentionally leaves considerable room for discretion and local autonomy to those in charge of the development project. A certain degree of built-in ambiguity is considered healthy, especially in the early stages of development.

Top management decides on a broad strategic direction or goal by constantly monitoring the external environment—that is, competitive threats and market opportunities—and evaluating company strengths and weaknesses. Competitive threats from rival companies, for example, forced Fuji-Xerox and Canon to seek a *reactive* strategic direction:

- Prior to 1970, Fuji-Xerox was the only plain paper copier (PPC) manufacturer in Japan. But starting with the entry of Canon in the fall of 1970, Japanese manufacturers (such as Konishiroku, Ricoh, Minolta, Copia, and Toshiba) began to make inroads into the PPC market, especially at the low end. By 1977 Ricoh, which introduced a liquid dry PPC model called "DT 1200" in 1975, had overtaken Fuji-Xerox as the market leader in terms of units installed. Fuji-Xerox therefore launched the development of FX-3500 with a sense of urgency and a determination to regain market leadership.
- Canon was the undisputed leader in the medium-priced 35mm lens

shutter camera market in the 1960s, as a result of the 1961 introduction of Canonet, a lens shutter camera with an electric exposure capability. It also became the leader in the higher-priced 35mm single-lens reflex (SLR) market with the successful 1976 introduction of the AE-1, which was the first automatic exposure SLR camera with a built-in microprocessor. But while Canon was concentrating its effort on the SLR market in the mid-1970s, Konishiroku overtook it in lens shutter cameras, increasing its share of the Japanese market to over 40 percent by introducing two new Konica models, one with a built-in flash and the second with an automatic focus. It was this serious competitive threat from Konica that prompted Canon to redirect its development efforts behind Auto Boy.

An assessment of market opportunities and company strengths and weaknesses led Honda, NEC, and Epson to pursue more of a *proactive* strategic direction:

- Honda's top management felt a sense of crisis as its best-selling lines—Civic and Accord—were beginning to lose their appeal to the youth market. The City development project was initiated in 1978, just as the postwar generation (under thirty-three years at the time) began to outnumber the prewar generation. The City was targeted toward the youth segment and developed by a young project team, whose average age was only twenty-seven. As is described in greater detail below, this team was given full autonomy to develop "the kind of car that we, the young, would like to drive."
- NEC's strength in microprocessors led to the eventual development of its personal computer PC 8000. NEC began to mass produce microprocessors to reduce costs and, at the same time, broaden their application base. Mr. Watanabe, head of the PC 8000 development team, was originally asked by top management to create a market for microprocessors and to sell them by the bundle. He visited Silicon Valley and saw the successful launching of personal computer prototypes in the United States, which confirmed the large market potential of microprocessor applications within personal computers. As a result, TK 80, a training kit for hobbyists and the predecessor to PC 8000, was introduced in 1976.
- Ever since its establishment in 1961, Epson's history has been marked by what appears to be almost an obsession with creating a market for "products of the future." Epson, which was originally a parts manufacturing plant for Seiko, was the first company in Japan to enter the miniprinter market with its EP-101 just as elec-

tronic calculators were taking off in the late 1960s. Epson also developed an electronic printer (MP-80) just when the personal computer market was beginning to boom. And it introduced a letter-sized computer (HC-20) in 1982, opening up a market for handheld computers. Top management constantly keeps its watchful eye on tomorrow's growth opportunities and directs its development people to think the unthinkable.

Regardless of whether the strategic direction or goal is determined reactively or proactively, it is stated in rather nonspecific terms. For example, Canon's top management directed the Auto Boy team "to think of something new that will surpass all preceding competitive brands." Honda's top management told the City team "to create a radically different concept of what a car should be like." Top management at Fuji-Xerox instructed the FX-3500 team "to come up with a product head and shoulders above others." These directions or goals are intentionally left vague, to give the development team maximum latitude toward creative problem solving.

But, at the same time, top management is not at all hesitant about setting very challenging parameters. Canon's Auto Boy team, for example, was given a free hand to develop an auto-focus camera as long as it was done "on its own." Unlike all other front-runners, who licensed the auto-focusing technology from Honeywell, the challenge was to develop the new product using Canon's original core technology. Similarly, Honda's top management asked for a radically different concept within the constraints that City be a "resource-saving, energy-efficient, mass-oriented automobile." Fuji-Xerox's FX-3500 team was given two years to come up with a new product that could be produced at half the cost of the high-end line and still be equipped with similar performance standards. As a point of reference, it took five years for Fuji-Xerox to develop an earlier domestic model (FX-2200) and over four years for Xerox Corporation in the United States to develop a model comparable to the FX-3500 at that time.

Top management implants a certain degree of tension within the project team by giving it a wide degree of freedom in carrying out a project of great strategic importance to the company and by setting very challenging parameters. This creation of tension, if managed properly, helps to cultivate a "must-do" attitude and a sense of cohesion among members of the crisis-solving project team. Examples of how tension is created are described by top management in the following manner:

- Mr. Kawamoto, vice president of Honda in charge of development, remarked: "At times, management needs to do something drastic like setting the objective, giving the team full responsibility, and keeping its mouth shut. It's like putting the team members on the second floor, removing the ladder, and telling them to jump, or else. I believe creativity is born by pushing people against the wall and pressuring them almost to the extreme."
- Mr. Kobayashi, president of Fuji-Xerox, noted: "I kept on rejecting the proposals repeatedly for about half a year. In retrospect, I'm amazed how persistent I was about sending them back. Engineers can think up all kinds of reasons why something is impossible to do. But I was able to resist giving in because everyone in the company shared an acute sense of crisis."

Self-organizing Project Teams

A new product development team, consisting of members with diverse backgrounds and temperaments, is hand picked by top management and is given a free hand to create something new. Given unconditional backing from the top, this team begins to operate like a corporate entrepreneur and engage in strategic initiatives that go beyond the current corporate domain. Members of this team often risk their reputation and sometimes their career to carry out their role as change agents for the organization at large.

Within the context of evolutionary theory, such a group is said to possess a self-reproductive capability. Several evolutionary theorists use the word "self-organization" to refer to a group capable of creating its own dynamic orderliness.[8] A recent study by Burgelman found that a new venture group within a diversified firm in the United States takes on a self-organizing character.[9] Another study by Nonaka has shown that Japanese companies with a self-organizing characteristic tend to have higher performance records than others.[10]

The creation and, more importantly, the propagation of this kind of self-organizing product development team within Japanese companies represents a rare opportunity for the organization at large to break away from the built-in rigidity and hierarchy of day-to-day operations. It is quite difficult for a highly structured and seniority-based organization to mobilize itself for change, especially under noncrisis conditions. The effort collapses somewhere in the hierarchy. A new product development team is better suited to serve as a motor for corporate change because of its visibility ("we've been hand picked"), its legitimate power ("we have the unconditional support from the top to create something new"), and its sense of mission ("we're working to solve a crisis situation").

To become self-organizing, a group needs three qualifications. First of all, it has to be completely autonomous. Our case studies support this condition. For example:

- A Honda City design engineer recalled: "It is incredible how the company called in young engineers like ourselves to design a new car and gave us the freedom to do it our way." Mr. Kawashima, then the president of Honda, promised at the outset that he would not intervene with the City project. "Yes, we've given them freedom," commented Mr. Kawamoto, vice president in charge of development, "but we've also transferred a strong sense of responsibility to them."
- Mr. Watanabe, who headed the PC 8000 project for NEC, recalled: "We were given the go-ahead from top management to proceed with the project provided that we would work all by ourselves in developing the product and be responsible to manufacture, sell, and service the product on our own as well."

Second, given this autonomy, a group comes up with extremely challenging goals on its own and tries to keep elevating these goals. It does not seem to be content with incremental improvements alone and is in constant pursuit of a quantum leap. We observed this tendency toward "self-transcendence," or the creative overcoming of the status quo, in all of the development projects we analyzed. For example:

- Epson typifies a company with a never-ending quest for approaching the limit. Its corporate target is to have the next-generation model developed by the time the first-generation model is introduced on the market. There is an unwritten rule that the next-generation model be at least 40 percent better than the existing model.
- The self-motivating factor behind Canon's Auto Boy development team was to improve on the company's achievement with its AE-1 in the single-lens reflex camera market. "You weren't even considered human at that time if you weren't somehow associated with the AE-1," said one of the Auto Boy team members, half jokingly. "We wanted to challenge that legacy." The end result was a fully automatic lens shutter camera with an improved auto-focusing technology that became the top-selling brand immediately after introduction, despite a two-year lag in market entry.

- Both Fuji-Xerox and Honda challenged the status quo. Fuji-Xerox overcame the preconceived notion within the company that a new product normally be developed through conversion engineering (of a U.S. model) and undertook a self-development program. Similarly, Honda overcame what appeared to be an unshakable market preference for a "long and low" car and developed a "short and tall" City.

Third, a self-organizing group is usually composed of members of diverse functional specializations, thought processes, or behavior patterns. The total becomes much more than the sum of its parts when these members assemble and begin to interact with each other. Variety is amplified and new ideas are generated as a result. We found this phenomenon, which can be termed cross-fertilization, to be widespread among the companies interviewed. Cross-fertilization can be seen in the following examples:

- Honda's City development team members included representatives from product development (D), production engineering (E), and sales (S), as shown in *Figure 8-2*. Interactions across these functional boundaries were substantial. Throughout the City development project, which took three years, more than 2,000 visits from E to D and back were recorded by team members and other employees involved in the project. The two physical locations (Suzuka for E and Wako for D) were 300 miles apart, or five hours by train.
- Fuji-Xerox's FX-3500 was also developed by a multifunctional team, consisting of managers from planning, design, production, sales, distribution, and evaluation. Unlike City, these managers were physically located in one large room where open communication and sharing of information took place continuously.

Figure 8-3 is a listing of the functional backgrounds of the key team members for the five development projects we analyzed.

Overlapping Development Phases

The group dynamics of the self-organizing team strongly influence the manner in which the development project proceeds. The autonomous, self-transcendent, cross-fertilizing nature of the group produces a unique set of dynamics. For example:

- Cohesion is promoted as team members face some challenging goals. The broad nature of the goals also helps to alleviate detailed differences.

Figure 8-2
Development System at Honda

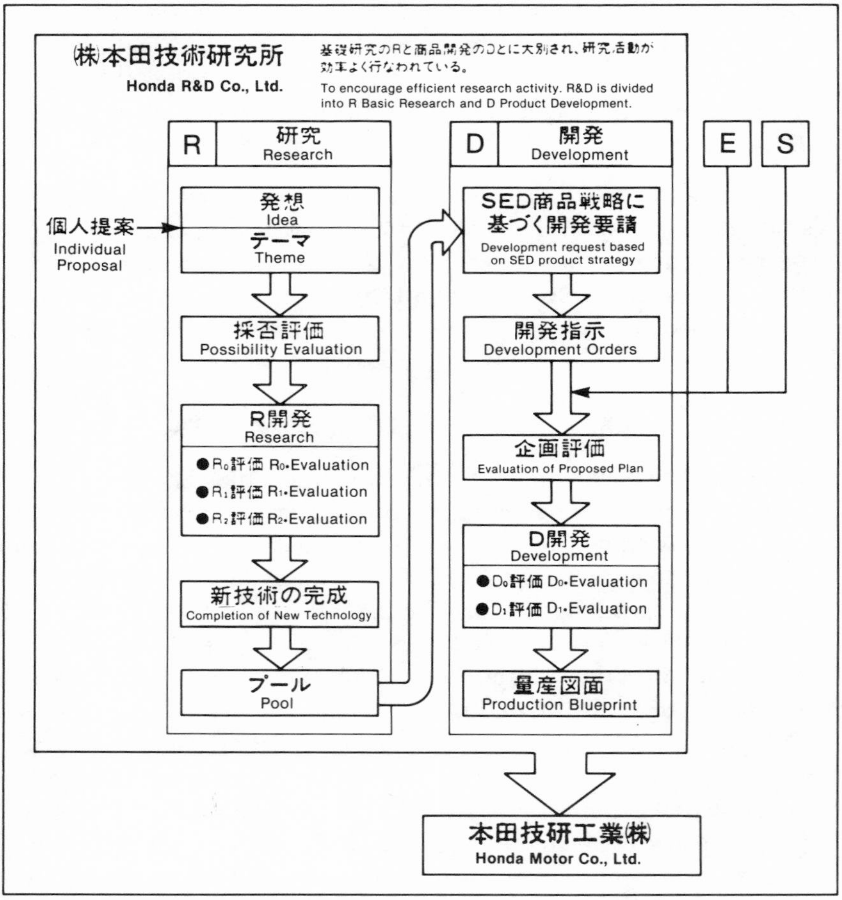

- Ambiguity is tolerated, given the diverse backgrounds of the group.
- Overspecification is avoided, since it may impair creativity.
- Sharing of information is encouraged so as to become better acquainted with the realities of the market.
- Decision making is intentionally delayed to extract as much up-to-date information as possible from the marketplace and technical communities.
- Sharing of responsibility is accepted as the group embarks on a risk-taking mission.

Figure 8-3
Functional Background of the Key
New Product Development Team Members[a]

Company \ Functional Background[b]	R&D	Production	Sales	Planning	Service	Quality control	Others	Total
Fuji-Xerox	5	4	1	4	1	1	1	17
Honda	18	6	4	-	1	1		30
Canon	12	10	-	-	-	2	4	28
NEC	5	-	2	2	2		-	11
Epson	10	10	8	-	-		-	28

a. Numbers indicate number of key team members.
b. Designates the assignment prior to joining the new product development team.

These dynamics help to explain why phase management in the Japanese companies we investigated tends to be holistic and overlapping rather than analytical and sequential. Variety reduction is delayed as long as possible in these companies as the self-organizing team engages itself in the search for information—from both the marketplace and the technical communities—and in an iterative process of experimenting even at the very late phases of the development process. As mentioned earlier, variety reduction under the analytical/sequential approach is conducted more systematically, and as early as possible.

A simplified illustration of the overlapping nature of phase management is depicted in *Figure 8-4*. The sequential approach, labeled Type A, is typified by the NASA-type phased program planning (PPP) system adopted by a number of U.S. companies. Under this system, a new product development project moves through different phases—for example, concept, feasibility, definition, design, and production—in a logical, step-by-step fashion. The project proceeds to the next phase only after all the requirements are satisfied, thereby minimizing risk.

Figure 8-4
Sequential (A) versus Overlapping (B and C) Phases of Development

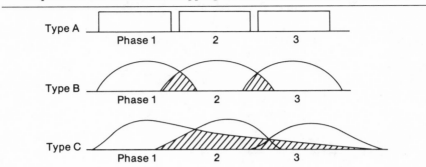

But, at the same time, a bottleneck in one phase can slow down the timetable of the entire development process. The overlapping approach is represented by Type B, in which the overlapping occurs only at the interface of adjacent phases, and Type C, in which the overlapping extends across several phases. The product development process at Fuji-Xerox and Honda is closer to Type C than to Type B.

The overlapping approach has its merits and demerits as well. The more obvious merits include: faster speed of development, increased flexibility, and sharing of information. It also leads to a more subtle, but equally important, set of merits dealing with human resources management. Among others, it helps to do the following:

- Foster the more strategic point of view of a generalist
- Enhance shared responsibility and cooperation
- Stimulate involvement and commitment
- Sharpen a problem-solving orientation
- Encourage initiative taking
- Develop diversified skills
- Create grounds for peer recognition
- Increase sensitivity of everyone involved to changes in market conditions

On the other hand, the burden of managing the process increases exponentially. By necessity, the overlapping approach amplifies ambiguity, tension, and conflict within the group. The burden of coordinating the intake and dissemination of information rises as well, as does the responsibility for management to carry out on-the-job training on an ad hoc and intensive basis.

The loose coupling of phases also makes division of labor, in the strict sense of the word, ineffective. Division of labor works well in a Type A system where the tasks to be accomplished in each phase are clearly delineated and defined. Each project member knows his or her responsibility, seeks depth of knowledge in a specialized area, and is evaluated on an individual basis. But such segmentalism, to use Kanter's terminology,[11] works against the grain of a loosely coupled system (that is, Type B and Type C) where the norm is to reach out across functional boundaries as well as across different phases. Project members are expected to interact with each other extensively, to share everything from risk, responsibility, information, to decision making, and to acquire breadth of knowledge and skills. Under a loosely coupled system, then, the tasks can only be accomplished through what we call "shared division of labor." This shared division of labor takes place not only within the company but also with outside suppliers. We witnessed varying degrees of coupling or overlapping among the Japanese companies:

- Fuji-Xerox revised the PPP system, which it inherited from the parent company, in two respects. First, it reduced the number of phases required to develop FX-3500 from six to four by redefining some of the phases and aggregating them differently. Second, a linear, sequential system was changed into what Mr. Kobayashi referred to as a "sashimi" system. Sashimi—or sliced raw fish—is served in Japan by tilting the slices and placing them on a plate with one piece overlapping another. (See *Figure 8-5* for a detailed graphic representation.) Such a system requires extensive social interactions on the part of all those involved in the project, as well as the existence of a cooperative network with suppliers. On this latter point, a project member in charge of design commented as follows: "We ask our suppliers to come to our factory and start working together with us as early in the development process as possible. The suppliers also don't mind our visiting their plants. This kind of mutual exchange and openness about information works to enhance flexibility. Early participation on the part of the supplier enables them to understand where they are positioned within the entire process. Furthermore, by working with us on a regular basis, they learn how to bring in precisely what we are looking for, even if we only show them a rough sketch. When we reach this point, our designers can simply concentrate on work requiring creative thinking." As a result of these efforts, Fuji-Xerox was able to shorten the development time from thirty-eight months on a similar prior model to twenty-nine months for FX-3500.

Figure 8-5
Overlapping Nature of the Development Schedule at Fuji-Xerox

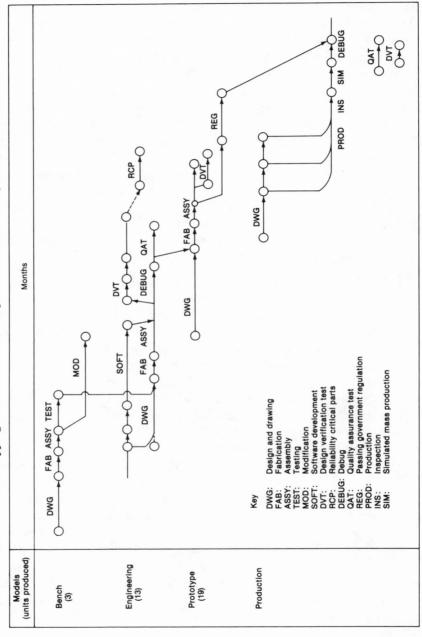

- Canon experienced several conflict situations as the Auto Boy development proceeded with an extensive degree of overlapping. One project member recalled: "Someone from development thinks that if one out of 100 is good, that's a clear sign for going ahead. Someone from production thinks that if one out of 100 is not good, we've got to start all over. That gap has to be narrowed. But both sides have absolutely no question in their minds that the conflict can be resolved." Conflict induces high levels of social interaction, which in turn gives rise to creative solutions, according to the same project member: "The design people keep a watchful eye on the entire project to make sure that their original design becomes converted into a truly good product at the very end. The production people, on the other hand, try to come to grips with what the designer had in mind by asking themselves, 'Why did he do it this way?' Creative solutions are born by each side intruding on the turf of the other." This mutual "reaching out" enabled Canon to remain flexible even under intense conflict situations.

- Honda's City team adopted what we decided to call a "rugby" approach toward product development. Mr. Watanabe explained: "I always tell my team members that our work cannot be done on the basis of a relay. In a relay someone says, 'My job is done, now you take it from here.' But that's not right. Everyone has to run the entire distance. Like in rugby, every member of the team runs together, tosses the ball left and right, and dashes toward the goal." The important point to remember here is that critical problems occur most frequently at relay points within the sequential approach. The "rugby" approach smoothes out the process by involving everyone in the development project. Individual initiative is also a prerequisite, argued Mr. Kawamoto: "If each and every one of us does his or her job well, then we basically won't need a structure." In fact, we found that Honda's project members deviated freely from the step-by-step structure for product development, shown in *Figure 8-2.*

Multilearning

The five Japanese companies in our study have another commonality that became increasingly clearer as our study progressed. They possess an almost fanatical devotion to learning—both within organizational membership and with outside members of the interorganizational network. To them, learning is something that takes place continuously in a highly adaptive and interactive manner. This discovery is neither new nor original. Lawrence and Dyer, for example, point this out as follows: "Japanese management does not now need to be convinced, if it ever did, that their organizations are learning and social systems as well as production systems."[12]

What is somewhat new and original is the discovery that learning plays a key role in enabling companies to achieve speed and flexibility within the new product development process. Continuous interactions with outside information sources, for instance, allow them to respond rapidly to changing market preferences. The iterative process of trial-and-error or learning-by-doing gives considerable degrees of freedom in responding to outside challenges or to challenging goals emanating from within. The constant encouragement to acquire diversified knowledge and skills also helps to create a versatile team capable of solving a wide array of problems in a relatively short period of time.

Broadly speaking, learning manifests itself within the organization along two dimensions: across multiple levels, and across multiple functions. We decided to refer collectively to these two types of intrafirm learning—that is, multilevel and multifunctional—as "multilearning."

We witnessed Japanese companies promoting learning at three levels—individual, group, and companywide. Examples of each are described below:

- Epson encouraged learning at the individual level to develop as many generalists within the company as possible. Mr. Aizawa, executive vice president in charge of R&D, stressed this point when he said: "I have been telling my development staff members that they need to be both an engineer and a marketer in order to be promoted within our firm. Even in an engineering company like ours you can't get on top without the ability to foresee future developments in the market."

- Honda fostered learning within the production group by establishing a special corner within the factory where the rank-and-file workers could experiment with work simplification ideas during normal working hours, using tools and materials provided by the company. Referred to as the "handmade automation" program, it has been instrumental in elevating the skill levels of workers in the manufacturing group and in positioning automation within the minds of the workers as a positive force that could make their work simpler and safer.

- Fuji-Xerox utilized the TQC (Total Quality Control) movement on a companywide basis as a means of learning how to bring about a more creative and speedy new product development process. The switch from the PPP system to the "sashimi" system came about as a result of the TQC movement.

We also witnessed Japanese companies treating "learning in breadth," or learning across functional lines, as the cornerstone of their human resources management program. Several examples of this very pervasive practice include the following:

- All of the project members who developed Epson's first miniprinter (EP-101) were mechanical engineers. They knew very little about electronics at the start of the project. In fact, Mr. Aizawa, also a mechanical engineer by training, returned to his university and studied electrical engineering for two years as a special researcher while trying to serve as the project leader of the EP-101 team. All project members were well versed in electronics by the time EP-101 was completed.
- A small group of sales engineers from the Electronic Devices Division, who originally sold microprocessors, were responsible for developing NEC's PC 8000. They acquired much of the necessary know-how by (1) putting TK 80, a computer kit, on the market two years prior to the PC 8000 introduction; (2) setting up an NEC service center called BIT-IN in the middle of Akihabara, a consumer electronics center in Tokyo, soon after introducing TK 80; (3) stationing themselves for about a year, even on weekends, at BIT-IN; and (4) interacting with hobbyists who frequented BIT-IN, which almost became a "club," and extracting as much useful information from them as possible.
- Mr. Nakamura, who had recently become a department manager of the assembly line operation at Honda's motorcycle plant in Suzuka, said that the recent lateral move took him by surprise. He admitted: "After all, I was in the painting operation for twenty-two years. I guess management wanted some change. But for me, it meant learning everything all over again from scratch."

Honda also has a so-called "practical training" program in which all department managers, like Mr. Nakamura, are asked to select a functional area in which they have never worked before and to spend one week every two years "getting their hands dirty." NEC enhances mobility across functional lines by transferring technical people from its R&D center to its divisions. As Mr. Miya, director of R&D, noted: "When a researcher starts producing results, the division comes to us and says, 'Give us that person.' Our current president started out in

Figure 8-6
Job Rotation Plan of R&D Researchers at NEC[a]

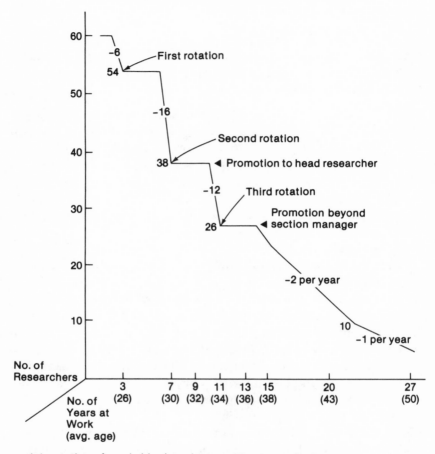

a. Job rotation of newly hired graduates with a master's degree.

R&D and was transferred to the division." NEC's rotation plan, shown in *Figure 8-6*, calls for a transfer of more than half of the newly recruited researchers (holding a master's degree) from R&D to the divisions at the end of about ten years and more than 80 percent after twenty years. Canon also utilizes similar programs of employee exchange and job rotation to encourage its employees to become "U-shaped" individuals—that is, individuals with a broad base of skills and knowledge.

Other personnel policies commonly found in Japanese companies—such as long-term employment and group evaluation—also foster multifunctional learning. Long-term employment makes the retention of valuable lessons from the past possible. Since people do not leave the company, members of a project team can easily seek out past "stars" and extract words of wisdom from them. Group evaluation enhances interactions within the group and fosters sharing of skills and know-how among each other.

From management's point of view, a new product development project offers an ideal springboard for creating a group of employees with broad skills and knowledge and an organizational climate conducive to bringing about change. But from the team members' point of view, multilearning requires an extraordinary amount of effort and dedication. Of course, it helps to have the rails already laid out (in the form of personnel policies that facilitate multilearning). It also helps to be working with a self-organizing team, a crisis situation, and an overlapping system of development. But management did not happen to find these supporting factors by chance. Rather, management made them happen.

Subtle Control

Some checks are needed to prevent looseness, ambiguity, tension, or conflict from getting out of control. These are manifested within the five companies we studied in subtle forms of control, rather than in more formal or systematic forms. Consistent with the self-organizing nature of the team, the emphasis is on self-control and on control through peer pressure or "control by love." More specifically, management uses selection of team members, openness in working environment, sharing of information, group-oriented evaluation, and sharing of values as a mechanism for implanting subtle control within the product development process. Each of these mechanisms is discussed below.

First, management implants the seeds of control by selecting the right people onto the project team, constantly monitoring the balance in team membership, and adding or deleting specific members if deemed necessary. For example:

- Honda handpicked team members mostly in their twenties to develop the youth-oriented City. As Mr. Kawamoto noted: "It's our responsibility to assign the right individuals to the appropriate positions. We also need to monitor the project closely and transfuse new blood midstream into the project. An elderly or conservative member may be added to the team when the balance shifts too dangerously toward a radically new approach. Or an engineer with a different technical background may be added when the project appears to have hit a stalemate."[13]

- Mr. Yoshino, who supervised the FX-3500 project, recalled: "When the design manager was assigned, I told him to give me the names of people he'd like to have. It wasn't 100 percent, but we were able to uproot the people we wanted with a probability of about 90 percent. And if we thought that someone was not living up to our expectations, I'd send the word out to have that person replaced midstream in the process."

Second, subtle control is exercised in the form of an open and visible working environment. For example:

- Honda enhances visibility by holding meetings in a large room with glass walls. "We can see what other people are up to," commented a City team member. This philosophy is also reflected at the executive level, where all the top executives have desks in one large room and hold meetings (among themselves and with those reporting to them) around three round tables situated in the center of that large room.
- Fuji-Xerox also espouses this so-called "large-room" system. Mr. Suzuki, a project member for FX-3500, gave the rationale for this system as follows: "When all the team members are located in one large room, someone's information becomes yours even without trying. You then start thinking in terms of what's best or second best for the group at large and not only about where you stand. If everyone understands the other person's position, then each of us is more willing to give in or at least try to talk to each other. Initiatives emerge as a result."

Third, management implants seeds of subtle control by encouraging team members to extract as much information from the field—from customers and competitors—and, more importantly, to bounce them off other members. This sharing of information helps to keep everyone up to date, build cohesion within the group, and act as a source of peer pressure:

- Fuji-Xerox encourages its design people to go out into the field to talk with users and suppliers during slack periods. A member of the design team commented: "We go out into the field to listen to the voice of our customers, study our competitors' models, or search for any useful research findings. As a result, we are in a better position to finalize the product concept as we see fit and to respond to what a planner has to say about quality, cost, or delivery time.

We try to digest what we sensed in the field and have it reflected in the design. This exposure helps in a lot of ways. For example, a designer may be tempted to take the easy way out at times, but he may reflect on what the customer had to say and try to find some way of meeting that requirement. Even if we get into an argument, we can go back to what we saw and heard in the field and build a consensus around our common experience. As you can see, we're constantly trying to find ways of feeding back the demands from the field into the design of the product."

- Sharing information about competition also helps to push the project to a higher level. As the same member of the Fuji-Xerox design team observed: "The development process in Japan is characterized by a daily influx of information about competition. This information exerts pressure which, in turn, acts as a driving force for us to do better. I wonder if this kind of pressure we feel in Japan—i.e., pressure every day by every member of the team—is felt in the U.S. as well."

Fourth, the Japanese evaluation system, which is based on group rather than individual performance, serves as another form of subtle control. Such a system encourages the formation of a self-organizing team and fosters multilearning among the team members. It also helps to build trust and cohesion, on the one hand, and peer pressure, on the other.

Lastly, management exerts subtle control by establishing some overriding values shared by everyone in the organization. These values or basic beliefs give people within the organization a sense of how to behave and what they ought to be doing. The shared value at NEC is "C & C," which stands for "Computer and Communication." NEC, which started out as a communications company, has made major inroads into the computer business under this slogan. The shared value at Canon is to become a "superior company." It is now in the second phase of the "superior company" plan, whose core theme is the strengthening of its R&D capability. The shared value at Epson, which is "thinking the unthinkable," sets a very aggressive pattern for product development, as exemplified by the unwritten "40 percent improvement" rule.

Organizational Transfer of Learning

We noted earlier that all those involved in the development project are engaged in a constant process of learning, across both levels and functions. The know-how accumulated at the individual level is transferred to other divisions or to subsequent projects within the organization and becomes institutionalized over time. Lawrence and Dyer describe this process as follows:

> It is true. . .that members of an organization cannot only learn as individuals but can transmit their learning to others, can codify it and embody it in the standard procedures of the organization. In this limited sense, the organization can be said to learn. When certain organizational arrangements are in place, an organization will foster the learning of its members and take the follow-up steps that convert that learning into standard practice. Then it is functioning as a learning system, generating innovations.[14]

We observed the process of institutionalization most vividly within Fuji-Xerox and Canon:

- The FX-3500 project was instrumental in making self-development the standard practice within Fuji-Xerox. Prior to this project, new product development was synonymous with conversion engineering, in which a basic U.S. model was converted into a Japanese one through minor engineering modifications. As mentioned earlier, self-development was accompanied by major process improvements, including the condensing of phases from six to four.
- Canon established a model for new product development through the AE-1 project and refined it in the Auto Boy project. Prior to these projects, Canon did not have a standardized format for new product development. One former member of the Auto Boy project team recalled: "When we were developing Auto Boy, we used to meet once a month or so to exchange notes on individual subprojects in progress, and once in three months or so to discuss the project from a larger perspective. We didn't know it at the time, but the pattern became institutionalized into monthly and quarterly progress reviews later." The know-how accumulated in these two camera projects was transferred to the Business Machines Group when it developed PC-10, a personal or microcopier introduced in 1982. Project members for the PC-10 sought out previous leaders of the AE-1 and Auto Boy projects to extract as many live lessons as possible.

The importance of having a role model within the organization is emphasized by Mr. Kawamoto of Honda as well: "Leave the organization somewhat untidy and leave sufficient room for self-growth to emerge. Everyone will be able to see that one team is doing something outstanding. There's no need for everyone to be doing it, but one outstanding example will set the standards for others." But since these teams are dissolved after the product is developed, whatever learning takes place is carried over to the next generation through individual team members. Mr. Kawamoto continued: "If the factory is up and running and the early-period claims are resolved, we dismantle the project team, leaving only a few people to follow through. We only have a limited number of very able people, so we turn them loose to another key project immediately."

Besides passing down "words of wisdom" from the past and establishing standard practices within the organization, we also noticed a simultaneous attempt on the part of Japanese companies to "unlearn" the lessons of the past and to engage themselves in a continuous process of what Schumpeter called "creative destruction." This process of unlearning helps to prevent the development process from becoming too rigid. It also acts as the springboard for making further incremental improvements. For example:

- Fuji-Xerox has been reviewing and refining its "sashimi" approach toward product development. Compared with the days of the FX-3500, the manpower required to develop a comparable new product today has been reduced to about one-half and the product development cycle to twenty-four months. Among other things, it allowed suppliers to participate from the early stages of development and eliminated the prototype production phase from the development process.

- Mr. Aizawa of Epson described the continuous nature of the development process as follows: "We have this constant fear that we're going to be left behind. That's why we want to have a product in test production when a new product is being introduced in the market." Epson always approaches a new product idea from two opposing points of view. One idea is pitted squarely against another even when developing the next generation model of a successful product already on the market. This approach opens the door for unlearning to take place and helps to maximize flexibility within the development process.

- Honda had to unlearn the lessons from the past to develop a totally new concept of cars. Mr. Watanabe recalled: "At one point in time, we had a choice between a modified version of Civic or a totally different 'short and tall' car. We opted for the latter, knowing full well the risks involved."

We also observed that much of the unlearning is triggered when a new crisis from the market environment confronts the organization.

What used to work in the past is no longer valid, given the changes in the external environment. To adapt to these changes, the challenge is to retain some of the useful learning accumulated from the past and, at the same time, throw away that portion of learning which is no longer applicable. In this regard, we agree with Levitt, who says that "translation of knowledge into results is almost surely a matter of 'tinkering' and, more importantly, a matter of management."[15]

Interorganizational Network

Six intrafirm factors that lead to speedy and flexible new product development processes in Japan have now been examined. To use a mundane analogy, we have just completed looking at the inside of the house we are interested in buying. To stop here is like deciding to buy a house without even looking at the outside. This section of the paper examines the impact of the outside—that is, outside suppliers and the interorganizational network surrounding our five companies—on new product development. Our study shows that interorganizational factors make just as important a contribution as intrafirm factors in speeding up the new product development process, as well as in making it more flexible.

What do we mean by an interorganizational network? The concept may still be somewhat foreign to many U.S. executives, although Schonberger observes the following: "In the past few years U.S. executives have been exposed to news stories on the Japanese success phenomenon, including stories on the Japanese tendency. . .to rely heavily on extensive networks of suppliers."[16]

Most of the large Japanese companies in the machinery business, including our five sample firms, utilize an interorganizational network similar to the one presented in *Figure 8-7*. The overall framework consists of three separate networks:

(A) Affiliated network: consists of affiliated companies that supply raw materials and parts or serve as sales organizations. Honda, for example purchases parts from outside vendors, such as Nippon Denso, but also buys from its affiliated companies such as Keihin Seiki and Yachiyo Kogyo.

(B) Supplier network: consists of small- and medium-sized companies that manufacture and process parts. These companies are also starting to take the initiative of developing and test-producing their own parts.

(C) R&D network: consists of research institutions (either com-

Figure 8-7
Interorganizational Network

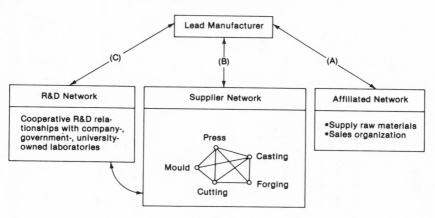

pany-, government-, or university-owned) with a cooperative relationship on R&D.

Of these three, we will focus our attention on the supplier network in this chapter, since it has the most direct impact on the speed and flexibility of new product development.

To cite a specific example on how a supplier can speed up product development, consider the progress made by two vendors of Fuji-Xerox in shortening the delivery time for some parts, as shown in *Table 8-3*. Both vendors have been able to reduce the delivery time at least by one-half between 1978 and 1983.

To illustrate how flexibility can be achieved, consider how the supplier network is structured for Fuji-Xerox (see *Figure 8-8*). Toritsu-Kogyo, one of its primary subcontractors, operates a factory of its own

Table 8-3
Time Required to Deliver Parts to Fuji-Xerox

	Model/Year			
Vendor/Part	*Model 3500* *1976*	*Model 4800* *1978*	*Model 4370* *1981*	*1983*
Dengen Automation, Inc.				
Bench model	10 mos.	6 mos.	—	3–4 mos.
Feasibility model	4 mos.	4 mos.	2 mos.	2 mos.
Sanyo Seisakusho, Inc.				
Specific part (A)		1.5 mos.	1 mo.	3 wks.
General part (B)		4 wks.	3 wks.	2 wks.

Figure 8-8
Interorganizational Network for Fuji-Xerox

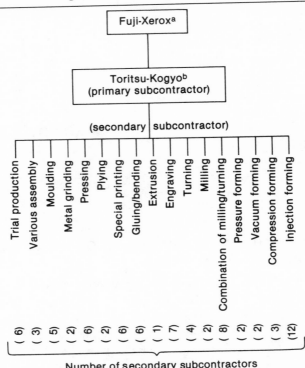

Number of secondary subcontractors

a. Has other primary subcontractors.
b. Serves as subcontractor for other manufacturers.

and utilizes seventy-seven secondary subcontractors. A large number of these subcontractors are located within walking distance from To-ritsu-Kogyo. Toritsu-Kogyo is a fairly large subcontractor, by Japa-nese standards, with sales of about 7 million and fifty employees, while most of the secondary subcontractors have fewer than ten employees. A clear-cut division of labor sets in as each secondary subcontractor tries to differentiate itself from the rest according to two criteria. The first differentiation occurs on the basis of the seventeen skills shown in *Figure 8-8*. The second differentiation takes place on the basis of prod-ucts handled. The six secondary subcontractors in pressing, for ex-ample, may each handle a different-sized product.

Because of this division of labor, each secondary subcontractor ac-quires a high level of technological skill in one specialized area, as well as a high level of competence in problem-solving. Thus, secondary subcontractors can respond very quickly to special requests made by either Toritsu-Kogyo or Fuji-Xerox, and can adapt very effectively to changes in the environment.

Fuji-Xerox can consider these secondary subcontractors as highly specialized and skilled task forces possessing up-to-date information who can be called into the product development process when necessary. All seventy-seven of these task forces can be mobilized very quickly since they are physically located in one general area. They can be mobilized in any combination or in any sequence as Toritsu-Kogyo selects and coordinates the most appropriate secondary subcontractors for the job at hand.

An understanding of how the network is structured is a prerequisite for studying the dynamic process by which speed and flexibility are achieved within the supplier network. The general conceptual framework for analyzing the intrafirm process presented earlier (*Figure 8-1*) applies, to a large extent, to the interorganizational process as well. Suppliers also adapt to changes and uncertainties in the market environment through an iterative process of variety reduction and learning-by-doing. The similarities as well as some differences are discussed below to further understanding of how a supplier network can contribute to new product development.

Self-organizing Network

Various supplier networks emerged in Japan during the postwar economic boom as a natural response to the expansion in the market size for goods and services. One similarity of these interorganizational networks to the intrafirm development teams is the self-organizing manner in which they both emerged. For one thing, supplier networks are made up of autonomous firms that gathered around the lead manufacturer's plants, most of which were located in Tokyo because of its development in the postwar period as the focal market for most goods and services. So it was only natural for the suppliers to locate in Tokyo as well, since that proximity would bring several mutual benefits, such as shorter delivery time, lower inventory carrying costs, lower transportation costs, and improved communication.[17]

The number of these Tokyo-based suppliers grew rapidly, as expert machinists with an entrepreneurial flair left their positions in larger companies to start up their own ventures. Each supplier, equipped with a unique set of skills, would initially enter the market in a small way by finding a particular niche. As these ventures grew, some of the more talented employees would create spin-offs by developing new skills or mastering a new technology. Since these employees were usually treated like members of the extended family, their former bosses viewed these spin-offs as a natural course of events, like a child leaving home to become independent. Some would even go as far as lending financial support.

These spin-offs are also viewed positively by the lead manufacturer. They generally raise the overall level of skills and technology within the network as each start-up company enters the market with some sort of incremental improvement. As the number of narrowly focused firms proliferates, they also give the lead manufacturer a greater degree of freedom in selecting a subcontractor.

In addition to being autonomous, these small firms possess a strong motivation to constantly upgrade their skills or technology, thereby satisfying the second qualification for self-organization (self-transcendence). Most of the suppliers pride themselves on running a flexible operation capable of producing special-order or experimental items at short notice. But each time the lead manufacturer makes very tough demands—shorter delivery time or higher technical content— the suppliers have to overcome the status quo and reach out for something higher.

The third qualification for cross-fertilization is also evident as suppliers with differentiated functional skills, technological backgrounds, and behavior patterns are assembled in one general location to form a loosely coupled network. Although these suppliers are autonomous units, we observed substantial degrees of social interaction, open communication, and information exchange taking place among them.

Shared Division of Labor

Self-organization fosters variety amplification as the number of start-ups and spin-offs proliferates within the process. Variety reduction takes over as these autonomous units form a loosely coupled network and begin to exercise shared division of labor. Recall how members of the development team reached out across functional boundaries, interacted with each other, and shared risk, responsibility, and information among themselves. A similar phenomenon occurs among members of the supplier network as well.

Each supplier knows that it cannot survive on its own. Its survival is very much a function of how well it can coexist with others within the network. To coexist, each supplier has to think of the common good and behave like a team player. But coexistence alone does not ensure growth. Each member has to sharpen its own skills, and at the same time, mutually support the continuity of the network at large. Mutual support is enhanced through tightly knit interactions among the members on a day-to-day basis to exchange relevant business information and ideas. Continuity is maintained by establishing a system of shared division of labor among the network members.

The Fuji-Xerox network, presented in *Figure 8-8,* shows how seventy-seven secondary subcontractors are organized to perform seventeen separate functions for Toritsu-Kogyo. A clear-cut division of labor is in place as each of the seventy-seven specializes either on the basis of function performed or product type handled. The Toritsu-Kogyo example may suggest that the network is composed only of subcontractors with very specialized skills. But a separate group of subcontractors who handle standardized processing is also in existence. Such nonspecialized subcontractors take part in the division of labor by working on evenings or holidays to speed up the overall process.

The shared nature of division of labor can be graphically represented by taking the static organization chart shown in *Figure 8-8* and overlaying horizontal lines interconnecting the seventy-seven subcontractors. In other words, these subcontractors are mutually dependent and are in constant interaction with each other. A considerable amount of reaching out takes place as they try to share risk, responsibility, and information. For the entire network to be effective (or to put it differently, for each subcontractor to survive), the subcontractors need to run together like a rugby team, maintaining cohesiveness and balance.

A company's new product development project benefits from the existence of an interrelated group of specialized suppliers on the outside. It is in a position, for example, to invite specific suppliers to join the project team in the early phases of the program to develop or test produce some parts. In the case of Fuji-Xerox, 90 percent of the parts used during test production are manufactured outside. In the later phases of the project, including mass production, it can rely on the primary subcontractor to select and control the right number of qualified secondary subcontractors. This delegation of authority to someone outside adds another level of flexibility to the new product development process. All of the Japanese companies in our study rely heavily on outside suppliers to produce parts at the mass production stage. The percentage of parts produced outside for our units of analysis (that is, FX-3500, City, and so forth) were roughly 90 percent for Fuji-Xerox, between 70–75 percent for Honda, about 65 percent for Canon, over 70 percent for NEC, and 70 percent for Epson.

Learning

We noted earlier that learning at the intrafirm level played a key role in enabling companies to achieve speed and flexibility within product development. The same conclusion can be drawn about learning at the interorganizational level, although the nature of learning is quite different at the two levels. In the former, learning (or multilearning as we called it) has a strong human resources management orientation, whereas learning at the latter has a straightforward economics orientation.

We know that learning takes place within the production process in the form of lower costs as the production volume increases over a given period of time. This so-called "learning curve effect" takes place, albeit to a lesser extent, among subcontractors as well. We observed a learning curve among them, both for lot production and for line production, indicated by line A in *Figure 8-9*.

Can we expect a similar learning curve effect during trial production? In general, the answer is no, since requests for a bench model or a prototype come a little at a time and trial production volume is low. But subcontractors within the supplier network are an exception. They are able to realize a learning curve effect even for bench models.

This exception is made possible through what we call "learning in arrangement." Although numerous companies order bench models and their specifications call for different shapes and sizes, many of the orders require the same production technology and skill. So the basic difference boils down to the materials used and the arrangement of work flow. Thus, if learning can take place in how to arrange the work flow effectively, some savings in cost and time are possible. Even if

Figure 8-9
Learning Curve Effect among Subcontractors

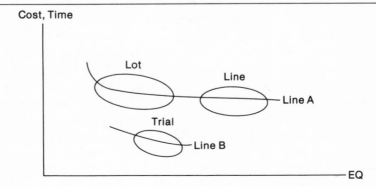

different types of bench models are being produced, the production process can be made to run continuously without having to halt every time a new bench model is introduced.

A supplier network facilitates learning in arrangement for the following reasons. First, several suppliers that specialize in prototype production exist within the network. In the supplier network for Fuji-Xerox, six such subcontractors were present (see *Figure 8-8*). Second, since each of these six specialized further according to the types of products handled, members of the network knew which type of prototype to send to whom. Third, this specialization allows the subcontractors to receive the same kinds of orders from numerous sources, thereby giving them some advantage in volume. Fourth, the geographic concentration of these specialized subcontractors in or near Tokyo prompts referrals from other companies outside the network.

Lower costs and time—achieved through learning at an early phase of product development—have a positive impact on the overall process. The manufacturer is induced to experiment with a wide variety of prototypes, thereby keeping flexibility at the maximum. At the same time, it speeds up the development process.

Information Exchange

As noted earlier, members of the supplier network try to build mutual support by actively interacting with each other and exchanging as much useful information as possible. These exchanges help them to keep abreast of the most recent developments in the marketplace and the technical community. They also expedite the development process, as suppliers can have vital parts ready just in time for the manufacturer.

Information exchange takes place both laterally and vertically. Lateral exchange in the case of Toritsu-Kogyo occurs among its seventy-seven secondary subcontractors. These subcontractors share several commonalities that facilitate the flow of information. First, they all work for the same primary subcontractor. Second, their factories are located within walking distance from each other in downtown Tokyo. Third, most of the owners live there as well, which means that they can be in touch with each other even after working hours. Fourth, almost all of the owners are machinists by training and, therefore, share similar backgrounds. Fifth, they tend to share a trait typical of downtown Tokyo when communicating with each other—to use few words and be as straightforward as possible.

Lateral flow of information is also intensified as a result of the "weak tie" nature of the way in which the secondary subcontractors are organized. Previous research has shown that a weak tie makes a faster and broader exchange of information possible.[18] Those who emit the information feel free to say whatever they please on a wide variety of topics; they feel it is the responsibility of those receiving the information to screen out and digest what they have heard. Contained in this kind of free-wheeling exchange is "leading-edge" information on what is happening in the marketplace and the technical community, as well as hints on how to improve existing products or what new products to develop in the future.

Vertical information exchange occurs within the three levels of hierarchy—the lead manufacturer, primary subcontractor, and secondary subcontractor. The "strong tie" nature of the organization of the vertical network gives rise to a more orderly and planned exchange of information. For example, both top-down flow and bottom-up flow of information are funneled through the primary subcontractor, which plays an important role as the link between the lead manufacturer and the secondary subcontractor.

But the tie is not so strong as to prevent direct exchange of information from taking place. A division or department manager of the lead manufacturer may visit a secondary subcontractor on occasion to learn as much from "the man on the spot" as possible. The reverse also takes place when a secondary subcontractor visits the lead manufacturer to participate in a new product development project or to discuss specific ideas on quality improvement. The most frequent exchange, of course, is undertaken between the engineers from both sides who can talk freely about technical matters without having to go through middle managers or the salespeople. This direct linkage not only saves time but makes the subcontractor far more a part of the new product development team than an outside vendor.

Reciprocity

Information is only part of what members of the network give and take. Many of the business transactions that take place within the network are also based on a give-and-take relationship. Two such transactions are highlighted here.

First, the lead manufacturer may sometimes push its subcontractors very hard to have some part delivered by a certain deadline but compensate them well when the task is accomplished. For example:

- Fuji-Xerox decided to change the basic design of a certain part midway in the development process and made an extremely tough demand of one of its subcontractors about when the delivery should be made. The subcontractor complied with this "utterly insane" request by working at night and completing the assignment on time.

Fuji-Xerox reciprocated later by paying the subcontractor handsomely. Mr. Kawamoto of Honda summed up this reciprocal relationship when he said, "We're buying time with money."

Second, where market conditions are unfavorable, a lead manufacturer may sometimes make a quite unreasonable demand on the subcontractor about the purchase price of a certain part. It tries to make up for whatever opportunity loss the subcontractor may have incurred by giving it very attractive margins when conditions turn favorable at a later date.

There is no guarantee that the lead manufacturer will return the favor in the future. Written contracts are unheard of. But if the lead manufacturer delivers, a trusting relationship begins to develop. In the long run, this kind of relationship leads the subcontractors as a group to accept the lead manufacturer as the legitimate leader and establish a strong cooperative system in support of it. A set of "shared network norms" is established over time, laying out a basic understanding of how business should be conducted within the network. Such a norm may tolerate an unreasonable demand made by the lead manufacturer during times of competitive crisis.

Subcontractors are willing to make sacrifices in the short run because they understand that their own survival is largely dependent on how well the leader performs in the market. They also know that certain new product development projects are a matter of life or death for the leader and, therefore, go out of their way to help. "Unreasonable demands are easier to swallow during wartime than peacetime," commented one subcontractor.

Conclusion

We embarked on this study by observing the dynamic process by which new products are developed within five Japanese companies. We then tried to put some order to what we observed by identifying seven commonalities in the process. This section compares and contrasts what has been learned from these Japanese companies with what is known about the new product development process in the United States.

Our conclusions are speculative at best since we have not conducted a comparable in-depth interview of U.S. companies. But our involvement in a recent comparative study of management practices in the United States and Japan[19] has given us a basic understanding of how U.S. companies approach the development process. Our exposure to corporate America and to leading U.S. researchers in this field has given us further insights. With this limitation in mind, we highlight three major differences between the United States and Japan.

First of all, the process itself is viewed differently. In general, new product development within U.S. companies is viewed more as an analytical and systematic process. Many companies utilize a sequential approach involving some variation of the phased program planning system. Variety reduction within such a system takes place in a top-down manner, with as many uncertainties as possible removed upstream in the process.

In contrast, Japanese companies view new product development as a trial-and-error process (learning-by-doing) and resort to a considerably looser format of phase management. Top management keeps goals purposely broad and tolerates ambiguity to encourage an iterative process of information-seeking and solution-seeking to emerge in a bottom-up manner. Variety reduction is conducted on a more ad hoc basis and is more spread out across the overlapping phases. This allows a more flexible response to last-minute feedback from the marketplace.

Second, a different kind of learning takes place. In the United States, product development is undertaken by a highly competent and innovative group of specialists. Most of the learning is done by an elite group of technical people, largely on an individual basis, within a narrow area of specialization. Thus an accumulation of knowledge based on "learning in depth" takes place.

In contrast, product development in Japan is often undertaken by a team of nonexperts who are encouraged to become generalists by interacting with each other throughout the development process. The development project may be headed by a nontechnical person, as in the case of the FX-3500 made by Fuji-Xerox, or by a sales engineer from a different division, as in the case of NEC's PC 8000. Everyone participating in the development process is engaged in learning, even outside suppliers. Learning also takes place across all phases of management and across functional boundaries. It is this kind of "learning in breadth" that supports the dynamic process of product development among Japanese companies. This learning emanating from the development process, in turn, serves as the trigger to set total organizational learning in motion. In this sense, new product development is the particular device that fosters corporatewide learning.

Third, the organizational impact is different. In the United States, new product development is an important strategic tool that enables companies to adapt to changes in the external environment by taking advantage of market opportunities or responding to competitive threats. As such, it plays a central role in strategy formulation.

In addition to its impact on strategy, product development in Japan takes on another important role. It serves as a change agent for reshaping corporate culture. Product development breaks down the hierarchy or rigidity normally associated with Japanese organizations—such as the seniority system or lifetime employment. Management gives the development team very broad but challenging goals as well as full autonomy to come up with something new. It uproots a competent middle manager from the hierarchical organizational structure and assigns innovative young talents to the team. Management gives unconditional support and legitimizes these unconventional moves by declaring a state of emergency or crisis. As mentioned earlier, organizational members and outside suppliers are willing to "swallow" more during times of war than during peacetime. The multilearning that takes place during wartime often breaks down the traditional ways of doing things. These changes are institutionalized within the entire organization until another crisis situation forces it to unlearn the lessons of the past. In a sense, management entrusts to the new product development team the mission to bring about an iterative process of learning and unlearning within the entire organization.

Caveats

Some final words of caution are in order. First, the Japanese approach toward product development has some built-in limitations, among which are the following:

1. It requires an extraordinary effort on the part of all project members during the entire span of the development process. Monthly overtime of 100 hours during the peak and 60 hours during the rest of the time is not uncommon.
2. It may not apply to breakthrough projects requiring a truly revolutionary innovation, as in the areas of biotechnology or chemistry.
3. It may not apply to mammoth projects, as in the aerospace business, where extensive face-to-face interactions are limited by the sheer scale of the project.
4. It may not apply within organizations where new product development is carried out by a genius at the top who makes the inven-

tion and hands down a well-defined set of specifications for people below to follow.

Second, we can expect our findings to be relevant in the short run; but given the evolutionary nature of the new product development process in Japan, they may soon be outdated. Extensive reliance on CAD/CAM, for example, may have far-reaching implications for how product development is managed within the organization. Externally, recent developments in telecommunications may make an interorganizational network based on geographical proximity obsolete. In fact, a recent study by Imai has already documented the rise of a telecommunications-based network in Japan.[20]

Finally, we must recognize that generalizations are misleading. For lack of better terminology, we labeled what we observed in the five Japanese companies as the "Japanese approach." Such a generalization may not necessarily apply when the sample size is enlarged, although our instincts tell us otherwise. We have also generalized about U.S. companies, describing their approach as analytical and sequential. For some companies, such a description may be very far from reality. For example, we see a flexible approach in place among a few U.S. companies that have established such systems as internal corporate ventures,[21] product champions,[22] skunkworks,[23] and others. The difference between the United States and Japan, therefore, may not be so much a "difference of kind" but more a "difference of degree."

Notes

1. William J. Abernathy, Kim B. Clark, and Alan M. Kantrow, *Industrial Renaissance* (New York: Basic Books, Inc., 1983), 107.

2. Paul R. Lawrence and Davis Dyer, *Renewing American Industry* (New York: The Free Press, 1983), 8.

3. Rosabeth Moss Kanter, *The Change Masters* (New York: Simon and Schuster, 1983), 19.

4. Variety is defined as the number of distinguishable elements, as used in cybernetics. A company reduces the number of options available by making choices on an iterative basis.

5. Abernathy et al., *Industrial Renaissance*, 27.

6. William J. Abernathy, abstract to "The Anatomy of the Product Development Cycle: An Historical Perspective," Colloquium on Productivity and Technology, Harvard Business School, March 1984, 27–29.

7. Karl E. Weick, *The Social Psychology of Organizing* (Reading, Mass.: Addison-Wesley, 1979), 133.

8. See Eric Jantsch, "Unifying Principles of Evolution," in *The Evolutionary Vision,* ed. E. Jantsch (Boulder, Colorado: Westview Press, 1981); Devendra Sahal, "A Unified Theory of Self-Organization," *Journal of Cybernetics* 9 (1979): 127–42.

9. Robert A. Burgelman, "A Model of Internal Corporate Venturing in the Diversified Major Firm," *Administrative Science Quarterly,* June 1983, 223–44.

10. Ikujiro Nonaka, "Evolutionary Strategy and Corporate Culture" (in Japanese), *Soshiki Kagaku* 17, 3 (1983): 47–58.

11. Kanter says segmentalism obstructs innovation and change in the following manner: "Segmentalism sets in when people are never given the chance to think beyond the limits of their job, to see it in a larger context, to contribute what they know from doing it to the search for even better ways. The hardening of organization arteries represented by segmentalism occurs when job definitions become prison walls and when the people in the more constrained jobs become viewed as a different and lesser breed." Kanter, *Change Masters,* 180–81.

12. Lawrence and Dyer, *Industry,* 262.

13. A similar finding is reported by Quinn who responds in the following manner to the question, How do executives cross-sectionally coordinate the various interacting subsystems in the decision dynamic? "In addition to selecting people with the technical skills most likely to be relevant over the time horizon of the strategy, most top executives tried consciously to team different management styles together: a 'tough' manager with a 'people-oriented' manager, a conceptualizer with an implementer, an entrepreneur with a controller, and so on." James Brian Quinn, *Strategies for Change: Logical Incrementalism* (Homewood, Ill.: Richard D. Irwin, 1980), 138–39.

14. Lawrence and Dyer, *Industry,* 263.

15. Theodore Levitt, *The Marketing Imagination* (New York: The Free Press, 1983), 164.

16. Richard J. Schonberger, *Japanese Manufacturing Techniques* (New York: Free Press, 1982), 175.

17. This supplier proximity to lead manufacturer plants also took place in the United States in the heavy-industry region around the Great Lakes and Ohio. According to Schonberger (ibid., 173), "Independent machine shops and foundries abound, locating near to buyer plants that make farm machinery, autos, machine tools, and so forth."

18. Mark S. Granovetter, "The Strength of Weak Ties," *American Journal of Sociology* 78 (1973): 1360–80; Everett M. Rogers, *Diffusion of Innovations,* 3d ed. (New York: The Free Press, 1983), Chapter 8, 293–303.

19. Tadao Kagono, Ikujiro Nonaka, Kiyonori Sakakibara, and Akihiro Okumura, *An Evolutionary View of Organizational Adaptation* (Tokyo: Nippon Keizai Shinbun, 1983). An English translation is forthcoming from North-Holland.

20. Ken-ichi Imai, *Japanese Industrial Society* (Tokyo: Chikuma Shobo, 1983), in Japanese.

21. Burgelman, "Internal Corporate Venturing."

22. Thomas J. Peters and Robert H. Waterman, Jr., *In Search of Excellence* (New York: Harper & Row 1982).

23. Thomas J. Peters, "The Mythology of Innovation, or a Skunkworks Tale Part II," *The Stanford Magazine,* Fall 1983, 11–19.

Commentary
Managing New Product Development: How Japanese Companies Learn and Unlearn

John L. Doyle

Introduction

Different kinds of novelty can be generated by product development. Discovery, invention, and innovation are all possible, but the last has the characteristics of being both demandable and predictable within a finite time, while the first two are not. Innovation is a derivative process while the others are discontinuities.

It is not clear which of these categories we are dealing with in the products cited in the chapter by Professors Imai, Nonaka, and Takeuchi, but from my knowledge of them innovation seems the prevalent theme. When this is so, completion date is a function of the number of essential product development steps and the degree of innovation demanded. A process that innovates must be not only flexible, but responsive to external stimuli.

The authors view product development as "a dynamic and continuous process of adaptation to changes in the environment." I think the U.S. definition of product development normally also includes the notion of endogenous creativity that fills needs customers do not even know they have until the solution is proposed. Examples include Hewlett-Packard's HP 35 calculator, the broad band spectrum analyzer, the pet rock, and the hula hoop.

We may thus be comparing different processes with subtly different objectives, rather than different processes with the same objectives as this paper suggests. There is, however, great value in a business strategy based on rapid evolutionary innovation, and in this light alone the paper has considerable interest.

377

The Seven "Key Factors for Success"

The paper identifies six factors internal to the company, and one external, to explain the speed and flexibility with which the five selected products were developed. My comments follow the same order:

Top management as a catalyst. Top management can have a vital role in the development of a few products in any one firm, but it surely cannot be the normal case. Its involvement usually comes where there is an external threat or crisis (Fuji, Canon, Honda) or where an unusual opportunity exists in diversification or timing (NEC, Epson). Top management in the example cited appears to set quite precise goals, either picks or anoints the team, and then applies pressure. None of these activities seems catalytic in nature, but rather directly operational.

The quotations ascribed to Kawamoto (Honda) and Kobayashi (Fuji-Xerox) reflect a tolerance that may be restricted to Japanese engineers. Most of the American engineers I know, if put under similar pressure continuously, would soon be looking elsewhere for employment.

Self-organizing team. Multifunctional teams handpicked by top management and given simple goals are likely to be very capable and achievement-oriented. The interaction of marketing, manufacturing, sales, and service with product development is almost invariably beneficial and should be much more widely adopted. In *Figure 8-3* it is instructive to note that the number of people with a production background is 60 percent of those with R&D origins. On the complete team, R&D is outnumbered by non-R&D professionals.

Although the degree of self-motivation of such teams may be high, it can also lead to isolation and elitism, as is shown, for example, by the comment "You weren't even considered human at that time if you weren't somehow associated with the AE-1."

Overlapping development phases. It is highly effective to achieve overlap, even parallelism, when possible, particularly when a high degree of innovation is demanded. The points in favor of overlap are well covered by the authors but are not uniquely Japanese. Broad-based collaboration and generalism are also encouraged at many U.S. companies, as both Ouchi[1] and Peters and Waterman[2] have pointed out.

Multilearning. This seems to stem in part from the picking of a multifunctional team and the overlapping phases. Pressure also usually enhances the learning process. TQC (Total Quality Control) is a useful way of setting multilearning expectations and opportunities, as the authors point out; this is a valuable observation that could benefit project teams of all kinds. On the other hand, it is hard for me to accept that a team of mechanical engineers could become "well versed in electronics" by the end of a single project, especially if it required a large amount of overtime.

Subtle control. Selecting the right team, setting clear goals, and establishing an evaluation based on group performance do not seem to be examples of *subtle* control, but encouraging the team to gather copious information from the field is an interesting, subtle, and powerful control mechanism. The reality of the marketplace is a wonderful control from which project teams are too often protected. Too much time spent studying competitive products in detail, rather than customer needs, however, can stunt invention and induce copying. It is important to concentrate on *what* is done for the customer by competitors, not so much on *how* they do it.

An open environment is usually conducive to effective team performance which depends on efficient communication. The chief barriers to efficient communication are walls, doors, and status, and the removal of these barriers can only be beneficial.

Organizational learning. Successful, highly visible projects will always be studied and often copied by others in the company. The danger of top management involvement is that people will always demand it or have an excuse for failure when it is not present. Untidy organizations that have room for experimentation and growth are an important feature of a learning society and one that knows how and when to forget. Learning on its own is an important feature of a climate designed to encourage innovation and invention.

Interorganizational network building. Here is the most startling insight into process differences between Japan and the United States. For Fuji-Xerox to have seventy-seven subcontractors, most of whom have fewer than ten employees, all within walking distance of each others' factories, describes a resource that in my experience is nonexistent in the U.S. electronics industry. Moreover, these subcontractors appear to be almost wholly dependent on Fuji and therefore extremely responsive. It is my understanding that they also have very different wage, benefit, and working conditions from the major corporations they serve. Few Western companies have access to such a compliant network.

It seems that the financial and timing effects of this resource upon the product development process need to be more thoroughly studied before conclusions about the relative effect of the seven factors can be reached. It is also necessary to study the effects of the product development process on these subcontracting entrepreneurs and their employees. The percentage of the final product produced by firms of this type (estimated at the end of the section) shows a very small degree of vertical integration compared with the U.S. companies that I know well. The pressure on these subcontractors is clearly severe, as shown by the comment, "Unreasonable demands are easier to swallow during wartime than peacetime."

Observations on Hewlett-Packard Practice

Direct influence on the part of the management of Hewlett-Packard, although rare, is effective in the case of any particular project. But it tends to have negative side effects on other projects, by upsetting priorities and the evenhanded reward system that normally operates. "Hero" projects, as they are sometimes called, usually result from unsuccessful strategies of product development at other times and cannot be the general practice. At HP, only 1–2 percent of the projects in process at any one time have direct top management interaction. Highly decentralized companies cannot have much top management involvement. Our goals tend to be set at a higher level of abstraction.

We focus on two major thoughts, "doing the right thing" and "doing that thing rightly." In the examples quoted, it appears that the top management of the Japanese companies has already done the first (and most difficult) part. Teams are never handpicked by top management, and strategies are largely devised at the project and division level within a defined business strategy.

A great emphasis on invention rather than innovation necessitates an early phase of doing the difficult parts first, followed by an overlapping in the execution phase. Several limitations on the general applicability of the Japanese method are mentioned in the chapter, including the extraordinary effort required of all project team members, and the fact that it may not apply to breakthrough projects requiring a truly revolutionary invention. These limitations seem applicable in the case of my company. We definitely discourage continuing overtime of the amount reported, especially in view of the point noted by Kawamoto: "We only have a limited number of very able people, so we turn them loose to another key project immediately." My concern is that a company's best people would thereby be forced into a life of unrelieved drudgery.

The smallness of our divisions encourages cross-functional understanding. It also leads to considerable interdivisional dependence, which may have all the disadvantages of subcontracting with few of the potential advantages, such as lower investment and personnel costs.

Our Japanese joint venture talks about the "2 Cs and 2 Qs" of successful projects: Cost, Combination, Quality, and Quick. This seems to imply that some aspects of the authors' model are more general than can be indicated by the five examples.

Conclusion

While the paper raises interesting ideas and some lessons for U.S. managers, I am uneasy about basing recommendations for change on the findings derived from so small a sample, particularly since there was little attempt to measure or compare the "success" of the projects investigated in a rigorous way. Nor does the chapter distinguish between invention and innovation, and it is hard to tell which was occurring in the cases discussed.

The emphasis placed on learning by the project team, both from the marketplace and from competitors, however, is extremely important and rather often neglected.

The value placed on learning itself as a goal also is admirable and useful and helps prevent self-satisfied complacency.

Finally, the reliance on subcontracting is extremely interesting and merits a thorough study in its own right.

The authors have presented an interesting and successful process for achieving R&D effectiveness but it is not at all clear that this is *the* method. Despite the quotations from U.S. authors at the beginning, the study does not establish that the products described are better or better developed than similar projects at U.S. manufacturers.

It is worth noting, however, that the Fuji-Xerox team, with just five R&D professionals and seventeen in total, regained a major market share in one year with a product developed in two years. Behind these facts lies a product development challenge that the United States cannot ignore.

Notes

1. William Ouchi, *Theory Z* (Reading, Mass.: Addison-Wesley, 1981).
2. Thomas J. Peters and Robert H. Waterman, Jr., *In Search of Excellence* (New York: Harper & Row, 1982).

9

Public Policy toward Industrial Innovation: An International Study of Direct Tax Incentives for Research and Development

Edwin Mansfield

During the past twenty years, in an attempt to encourage industrial research and development, tax credits and allowances for R&D have been introduced in at least ten nations, including the United States, Sweden, Canada, Japan, and the Federal Republic of Germany.[1]

Unfortunately, there is a remarkable dearth of systematic empirical evidence on the extent to which these tax incentives really have increased company-financed R&D expenditures. Despite their widespread adoption throughout the industrialized world, and the fact that some countries have used them for many years, surprisingly little quantitative evidence has been collected about their effects.[2] In considerable part, this is due to the many formidable problems and difficulties that studies of this sort encounter.

The purpose of this chapter is to provide very detailed evidence of this sort for the United States and Sweden and to summarize briefly such data for Canada. Although this evidence is subject to many limitations, it seems to be the most detailed and comprehensive available

The research on which this chapter is based was supported by a grant from the Division of Policy Research and Analysis of the National Science Foundation, which of course is not responsible for the views expressed here. I am particularly indebted to the more than 200 firms that provided me with data. In Sweden, I received important help from Ove Granstrand of Chalmers University of Technology, Tage Berglund of the Swedish National Central Bureau of Statistics, Thomas Sidenbladh of the Ministry of Industry, and Gunnar Blockmar of the Swedish Royal Academy of Engineering Sciences. In Canada, I benefited from discussions with D. McFetridge of Carleton University, R. Gillis, R. Swann, and D. Thom of the Ministry of State for Science and Technology, T. Roseman of the Department of Finance, and H. Stead of Statistics Canada. In the United States, I received very helpful comments from Eileen Collins, Margaret Grucza, and Rolf Piekarz of the National Science Foundation.

to date.[3] Particularly since many countries are evaluating and reevaluating their tax policies in this regard at present, the results should be of interest to managers, government officials, and policy analysts.

The R&D Tax Credit in the United States

Although the pros and cons of adopting an R&D tax credit have been discussed in the United States for decades, it was not until 1981 that adoption occurred. In August of that year, the Congress passed the Economic Recovery Tax Act, which provided for a 25 percent tax credit for R&D expenditures in excess of the average of R&D expenditures in a base period (generally the previous three taxable years). Expenditures qualifying for this incremental tax credit are "in-house" expenditures for R&D wages, supplies, and the use of equipment; 65 percent of the amount paid for contract research; and 65 percent of corporate grants to universities and certain scientific research organizations for basic research. The credit was applicable to expenditures made after 30 June 1981 and before 1986. Unused R&D tax credits can be carried forward up to fifteen years. According to the Treasury, the revenue loss due to the tax credit will be about $1 billion per year. (During 1981, it was estimated to be about $0.6 billion.)[4]

In 1981 about half of the credits went to sixty-five large firms, although almost 12,000 corporations reported qualified incremental R&D expenditures. Only about 59 percent of the credits could be claimed currently, the rest being carried forward. On the average, the largest firms were able to use a larger percentage of their credits currently than could the smallest firms. Reported company-financed R&D expenditures increased as a percentage of sales in practically all U.S. industries during 1981 and 1982, the years when the tax credit went into effect (*Table 9-1*). Some observers have speculated that this increase has been due in part to the tax credit, while others have pointed out that the surge in company-financed R&D spending began before the enactment of the tax credit, and that the percentage increases in company-financed R&D expenditures in 1981–83 were less than those in the immediate prior years. Very little systematic study has been carried out on this score.

In 1983 Treasury officials expressed support before Congress for a three-year extension of the credit so that firms would be able to plan R&D activities "with certainty that the credit would be available." At the same time the Treasury recommended that a number of changes be made. (1) The R&D activities that qualify for the credit should be

Table 9-1

Company-financed R&D Expenditures as a Percent of Sales, United States, 1975, 1980, 1981, and 1982

Industry	1975	1980	1981	1982
Aerospace	3.2%	4.5%	4.8%	5.1%
Appliances	1.2	1.8	2.0	2.0
Automotive	2.7	3.7	3.5	3.8
Building materials	1.2	1.1	1.2	1.3
Chemicals	2.6	2.4	2.5	2.9
Conglomerates	1.5	1.8	2.0	2.8
Drugs	4.7	4.9	5.3	6.0
Electrical and electronics	3.0	3.2	3.4	3.5
Food and beverages	0.5	0.6	0.7	0.7
Machinery	2.1	2.1	2.4	3.0
Instruments[a]	5.4	4.2	4.6	5.2
Leisure time[a]	1.7	2.7	4.4	4.8
Metals	1.2	0.9	1.1	1.2
Miscellaneous manufacturing	1.8	2.1	2.0	2.4
Fuel	0.42	0.40	0.46	0.55
Office equipment and computers	5.6	6.0	6.1	6.5
Oil service	1.2	1.6	1.8	2.1
Paper	0.8	0.8	0.9	1.0
Personal care	1.6	1.8	2.0	2.3
Steel	0.6	0.6	0.6	0.7
Textiles and apparel	0.5	0.4	0.5	0.6
Tires and rubber	1.9	1.8	2.0	2.3
Tobacco	0.5	0.3	0.5	0.5
Telecommunication	1.9	1.0	1.2	1.3
Total	1.8	2.0	2.0	2.4

a. There are marked changes in the composition of the industry between 1975 and 1981–82.
Source: *Business Week.*

defined more precisely. (2) The base level of expenditures used to compute the amount of the credit should be indexed so that credits are not awarded merely for keeping up with inflation. (3) The credits should be altered to benefit start-up companies which frequently do not have any income tax liability against which to apply the credit.[5]

Effects of U.S. R&D Tax Credit: Survey Results

As pointed out above, a basic objective of the R&D tax credit was to increase the amount of company-financed R&D. To estimate the extent to which the tax credit has achieved this objective, we surveyed a carefully designed sample of all manufacturing firms spending over $1 million (or 1 percent of sales, if sales were at least $35 million) on R&D in 1981. This universe of firms accounted for $32.1 billion of company-financed R&D, or over 90 percent of the total. Considerable care was taken in the design of the sample. This universe of firms was divided into two strata, one stratum consisting of the 301 firms that spent $10 million or more on R&D in 1981, the other consisting of the 475 firms that spent between $1 million (or 1 percent of sales, if sales were at least $35 million) and $10 million. A random sample was chosen from each stratum. Optimum allocation rules were used to determine how many firms to pick from each stratum. The total sample size was set at 110 firms, since this seemed large enough to obtain the desired precision. It turned out that the sample included about 30 percent of all company-financed R&D in the United States.[6]

Surveys have been used frequently by economists to obtain information concerning the effects of particular economic variables or policies. For example, surveys have been conducted to investigate the effects of a variety of factors on business investment.[7] An unusual feature of the present survey is that it is in fact a random sample from a well-defined universe or frame. The great advantage of this procedure is that it enables us to calculate confidence intervals based on accepted statistical principles. In contrast, there is no way of estimating the sampling errors (or biases) in judgment samples, which are generally used. The disadvantage of our procedure is that it is relatively expensive both in time and money.

Before contacting the firms in the sample, we tested and sharpened the questions to be put to them. About twenty-five other firms (not in the sample) were visited and written to, and a number of variants of the questions were tested. Finally, after having revised the wording of the questions, we contacted one or more of the principal officials of each of the firms in the sample, and asked them to estimate the effects of the R&D tax credit on their firm's R&D expenditures in 1981, 1982, and 1983. In some cases, we visited the firm and interviewed each official in person for about an hour; in other cases, we carried out some or all of the interviews on the telephone; in still other cases, we used correspondence and mail questionnaires. The choice of these communication media was randomized, but the probability of a personal visit was lower for some areas than others to reduce travel costs. Further, an attempt was made to contact a mixture of R&D executives, financial and tax executives, and chief executive officers, since their perception of the effects of R&D tax credits may be somewhat different.

Fortunately, there was very little problem of nonresponse. (Of

Table 9-2

Estimated Percentage Reduction in Company-financed R&D Expenditures
without Tax Credit, Eleven Industries, 1981–83

Industry	Percent Reduction[a]		
	1983	*1982*	*1981*
Chemicals and drugs	1.7	1.5	0.7
Electrical and electronics	0.4	0.3	0.0
Machinery (including computers)	1.0	0.7	0.0
Instruments	5.9	3.7	0.4
Metals and steel	4.9	2.4	4.2
Oil and oil supply	0.3	0.6	0.1
Aerospace	0.0	0.0	0.0
Telecommunications	1.4	1.4	1.5
Rubber	2.2	0.6	0.6
Paper	0.7	0.4	0.0
Other	0.3	0.2	0.2
Total	1.2	1.0	0.4

a. The summary figures in the last row are the unbiased estimates described in note 8
divided by the total company-financed R&D expenditures in the population. The industry figures show the percentage reduction in the total company-financed R&D expenditures of the firms in the sample. Figures have been rounded to the nearest tenth of a
percentage point. Thus, 0.0 does not mean that the effect is zero.
Source: See the section entitled "Effects of U.S. R&D Tax Credit: Survey Results."

course, each respondent was assured that his or her response would be
confidential.) Although it frequently took some time before an appoint-
ment could be made with the relevant official or before a response was
forthcoming, in only a few cases did a firm refuse to participate in the
study. (Generally, the reason given for nonresponse was lack of time on
the part of the relevant executives.) In these few cases, we substituted
a randomly chosen firm of approximately the same size from the same
industry for the firm that did not respond. Equally important, the
executives seemed to feel reasonably confident that they could provide
useful responses. Although it is obvious that any estimate of this sort
is approximate, there was no indication that they felt that their responses were subject to very large errors.

The results, summarized in *Table 9-2*, indicate that the R&D tax
credit has had only a modest effect on firms' R&D spending. Without
the tax credit, the R&D expenditures of the 110 firms in the sample
(which, to repeat, accounted for about 30 percent of all company-
financed R&D in the United States) would have been about 0.4 percent
lower in 1981, about 1.0 percent lower in 1982, and about 1.2 percent

lower in 1983 than in fact was the case, according to the firms themselves. (Based on the sample, it appears that the credit had more effect in instruments and metals than in other industries.) The estimates in *Table 9-2* contain sampling errors. But, as pointed out above, a major advantage of our sample design is that, based on the firms' estimates, we can compute a probable range (or "confidence interval") for the extent of the total increase in R&D expenditures (by the population of 776 firms) due to the tax credit. Using the customary statistical procedures, we find that a 95 percent confidence interval for the total tax-credit-induced increase in R&D expenditures in 1983 is $277–638 million, or 0.6–1.8 percent. For 1982, it is $151–538 million, or 0.4–1.5 percent. For 1981, it is $38–208 million, or 0.1–0.6 percent.[8]

Thus the relatively small effects shown in *Table 9-2* cannot be attributed to sampling errors, since, if we take proper account of these errors, it is very unlikely that the true effect exceeded 1.8 percent in 1983. Moreover, based on the firms' estimates, it is a very safe bet that the extra R&D stimulated by the tax credit has been considerably less than the revenue loss to the Treasury. For 1981, whereas the above confidence interval indicates that it is very unlikely that the tax-credit-induced R&D exceeded $208 million, the revenue loss was $600 million (according to the Treasury). For 1983, whereas the above confidence interval indicates that it is very unlikely that the tax-credit-induced R&D exceeded $638 million, the revenue loss was estimated to be about $1 billion.

Evaluation of the Survey Results

While these survey results are of interest, it is obvious that they should be treated with caution. For one thing, even though there was no evidence (that we could detect) that firms responded in a self-serving way, such a bias may exist. Since firms generally have favored the introduction of such tax credits and have been inclined to argue that they will promote additional R&D, one might think that they would tend, if anything, to overestimate the effectiveness of the credit in stimulating additional R&D. If so, the results of the previous section may overstate the tax credit's effect.

Whether or not the effects of the tax credit are overstated, it seems fair to characterize them as modest, based on *Table 9-2*. Is this result reasonable? Is it in accord with other relevant evidence? The answer seems to be yes. One reason why the effects are modest is that many firms are unaffected by the tax credit. Some firms, for a variety of reasons, want to cut back on their R&D expenditures. For example, 20 percent of the firms spending over $10 million on R&D in 1981 reduced their R&D spending from 1981 to 1982.[9] For firms that do not increase their R&D expenditures over the base amount, the credit is essentially irrelevant. In addition, some firms do not have any income tax liability against which to apply the credit. Although such firms can carry the credit forward to be claimed against future tax liabilities, this reduces its value to the firm and cuts its effectiveness. According to the Treasury, firms in 1981 could use only about 59 percent of the R&D tax credits, the rest being carried forward.[10]

For firms that do intend to increase their R&D expenditures over the base amount and that have an income tax liability against which to apply the credit, the after-tax price of an extra dollar's worth of R&D is reduced by the credit. However, for firms that intend to increase their R&D expenditures for each year in the foreseeable future (and this includes most firms, if for no other reason than that inflation pushes up nominal expenditures), the tax credit does not reduce the after-tax price of an extra dollar's worth of R&D by 25 cents. Because an extra dollar of R&D this year increases the base amount during the next three years, it reduces the credits available then. Assuming that the credit remains in effect for the following three years, and that the interest rate is 15 percent, the reduction really equals only about 6 cents.[11]

For firms that do not intend to raise this year's R&D expenditures above the base level or that do not have an income tax liability against which to apply the credit, the price reduction is far less than 6 cents. According to Eisner, Albert, and Sullivan (1983), "the effective rate of credit for firms with tax liabilities and increasing R and D is in the order of only a few percent."[12] If so, this certainly would suggest that the average price reduction may be less than 6 percent.[13]

Although relatively little is known about the price elasticity of demand for R&D, the few available estimates suggest that it is rather low. Mohnen, Nadiri, and Prucha (1983) find that the price elasticity of demand for R&D in U.S. manufacturing is about 0.3 in both the intermediate and long run.[14] Using data for the Bell System, Nadiri and Schankerman (1981) estimate that the long-run price elasticity is about 0.3. In our interviews, many R&D executives said that it was lower than 0.3 because R&D is viewed as one component (and often a small one) in a package of inputs that must be combined in relatively fixed proportions to launch an innovation. For the sake of argument, suppose that the price elasticity is about 0.3. If the tax-credit-induced price reduction is 6 percent or less, one would expect the tax credit to increase R&D by 1.8 percent or less. This compares with the 1983 confidence interval from the survey of 0.6–1.8 percent. Thus, based on these crude estimates, the survey results seem reasonable.[15]

The Redefinition of Activities as Research and Development

It is important to recognize that the firms in the survey were asked to estimate the effect of the R&D tax credit on their R&D expenditures, holding constant the definition of R&D. As implied earlier, the credit may have induced firms to redefine some activities as R&D. Many activities that could legitimately be called R&D (or at least are in a gray area) have not been broken out and identified as such in the past, because there was little or no incentive to do so. When the tax credit was introduced, an incentive was provided, and it was only natural that such redefinitions would occur.

An important question is: To what extent has reported R&D expenditure increased merely because of the tax-credit-induced redefinition of activities as R&D? To obtain information on this score, we posed this question to a randomly selected subset of the firms in our sample. The results indicate that, taken as a whole, the reported R&D expenditures of these firms increased by about 4 percent per year during 1982–83 for this reason alone. Obviously, this estimate is very rough.[16] (For one thing, firms may be inclined to underestimate the extent of the redefinition since it may seem to smack of deception.) Nonetheless, it is interesting to note that American experience in this regard, as measured by this estimate, is strikingly similar to the reported behavior of Canadian and Swedish firms described below.[17] If our experience parallels theirs, this redefinition of activities as R&D will tend to peter out in the mid-1980s after reported R&D expenditures have risen in total by about 13–14 percent for this reason alone.

In a preliminary and crude attempt to see how consistent the above result is with the observed behavior of reported R&D expenditures during 1981–82, we used a naive forecasting model to predict (on the basis of pre-1981 data) the 1981 and 1982 R&D expenditures of forty-two firms. These were the firms (in the six major R&D-intensive industries in *Table 9-3*) that reported spending more than $100 million in 1982. Two forecasts were made for each firm. Both forecasts were based on firm-specific multiple regressions (using pre-1981 data) in which the firm's R&D expenditure is a function (linear for the first forecast, nonlinear for the second forecast) of its sales and time. The results, shown in *Table 9-3*, indicate that the firms' reported spending on R&D was, on the average, considerably higher in 1982 and somewhat higher in 1981 than would have been expected on the basis of these naive

Table 9-3
Average Percentage Increase in Reported 1981 and 1982 R&D
Expenditures[a]

Industry	Linear Equation[b]		Nonlinear Equation[c]	
	1981	1982	1981	1982
	(Avg. percentage increase)			
Aerospace	11%	23%	9%	17%
Chemicals	12	22	6	4
Drugs	10	24	8	20
Electrical and electronic	8	29	−4	−17
Oil	19	35	15	22
Computers	0	8	−1	7
Average	10	23	5	9

a. This increase is over what would have been expected on the basis of naive forecasts, forty-two firms with over $100 million in R&D, six industries.
b. Each firm's R&D expenditure is assumed to be a linear function of its sales and time.
c. The logarithm of each firm's R&D expenditure is assumed to be a linear function of time and of the logarithm of its sales.
Source: See the section entitled "The Redefinition of Activities as Research and Development."

forecasts. While the results in *Table 9-3* cannot indicate the extent to which reported R&D expenditures were pushed upward in 1982, and to a lesser extent in 1981, by the redefinition of activities as R&D (as well as by the real effects of the tax credit), the survey findings indicate that these factors played a noteworthy role.[18]

The R&D Tax Allowance in Sweden

An important way to enrich and extend our knowledge of the effects of any policy mechanism is to compare and contrast its effects in various countries. This is particularly true in the case of tax incentives for R&D, because U.S. experience is severely limited by the fact that they were introduced here only about two and a half years ago. Another industrialized country that has a longer experience with them is Sweden. What has been the effect of the R&D tax allowance in Sweden? Has it been similar to our results for the United States? Although there are many important institutional and other differences between Sweden and the United States (including the obvious fact that the Swedish and American tax laws differ), it is instructive to see the extent to which Swedish experience seems to conform to the pattern described in previous sections.

In Sweden, current R&D expenditures are deductible in the year in which they are incurred, and capital assets used for R&D must be depreciated over their normal economic life. In addition, a special R&D tax allowance was instituted in 1973; this allowance equaled 10 percent of the firm's R&D expenditures plus 20 percent of the increase of this year's R&D expenditures over the previous year's. For example, in 1974, when the allowance really began, it equaled 10 percent of the firm's R&D expenditures plus 20 percent of the difference between 1974 and 1973 R&D expenditures. For this purpose, R&D expenditures were defined as 1⅔ times R&D salary costs plus whatever amount the firm pays others for R&D minus the amount the company receives in government subsidies for R&D. In contrast to the American tax credit, the Swedish tax allowance is a deduction from taxable income, not a reduction in tax liabilities.[19]

In 1981 the form of the tax allowance was changed, more emphasis being placed on the increment in R&D and less on the level of the firm's R&D. Specifically, the new allowance equaled 5 percent of the firm's R&D expenditure plus 30 percent of the increase over the previous year. Also, whereas the salaries of employees formerly were regarded as R&D if more than half of their time was devoted to R&D, now the salaries of employees devoting more than 25 percent of their time to R&D could be included. In addition, R&D salary costs were multiplied by 5/2, rather than 5/3. The revenue loss to the Swedish government due to the R&D tax allowance is shown in *Table 9-4*. In the early 1980s, the value to firms of this tax allowance was over 200 million Swedish kronor, in contrast to about 100 million Swedish kronor in 1974.

Effects of the Swedish R&D Tax Allowance: Survey Results

As in the case of the U.S. tax credit, we carried out a survey of firms to shed light on the extent to which the Swedish tax allowance resulted

Table 9-4
Cost to the Government of Swedish R&D Tax Allowance, 1974–82

Year	Cost (millions of kronor)
1974	100
1977	130
1979	160
1980	158
1981	176
1982	230 (est.)

Source: Swedish Ministry of Industry (correspondence with Thomas Sidenbladh).

in an increase in company-financed R&D expenditures. The universe of firms from which the sample was drawn consisted of all Swedish manufacturing firms in *Moody's International* and *Dun and Bradstreet International*, together with a group of other Swedish manufacturing and mining firms known to carry out R&D. The (over 200) firms in the frame account for more than 90 percent of all company-financed R&D of Swedish manufacturing (and mining) firms. The universe of firms was divided into two strata, one stratum being composed of the top fourteen R&D spenders in Sweden (see Granstrand 1983), the other being composed of all other firms in the frame. A random sample was chosen from each stratum. The total sample equaled forty firms, since this seemed large enough to provide the required accuracy. Indeed, this sample includes over 80 percent of all company-financed R&D in Sweden. Rules of optimum allocation were used to determine how many firms were chosen at random from each stratum.[20]

After the sample was chosen, we spent a considerable period of time testing the questions and obtaining background information from government agencies and firms, some of which were in the sample, some of which were not. (Professor Ove Granstrand of Chalmers University of Technology set up many of the interviews and provided very valuable advice.) Finally, we contacted the major officials of each firm in the sample, and asked them to estimate the effects of the tax allowance on its R&D expenditures in 1981 and 1983. As in the United States, the information was obtained through a combination of personal interviews, correspondence, and telephone conversations. Also, a mixture of R&D executives, financial and tax executives, and chief executive officers was contacted. As in the United States, there was practically no problem of nonresponse.

The results, summarized in *Table 9-5*, indicate that company-financed R&D expenditures would decrease by about 1 percent if the tax allowance was not in existence. There seems to be very little difference in this regard between the new and old versions of the tax allowance. Nor could we detect any significant effect of the allowance on the relationship between R&D and sales (see the second section of the *Appendix* to this chapter). The weight of the evidence is that, despite the fact that the allowance has been in existence for many years, its effect is small.

As in the United States, it appears that the tax-incentive-induced increase in company-financed R&D is less than the revenue loss to the government. Based on the firms' estimates, a 95 percent confidence interval for the tax-incentive-induced increase in company-financed R&D in 1981 is 23–98 million Swedish kronor (or 0.4 to 1.6 percent), which compares with a revenue loss of about 176 million Swedish

Table 9-5

Estimated Reduction in Company-financed R&D Expenditures without R&D
Tax Allowance, Sweden, 1981 and 1983

	Year	
	1981	*1983*
Estimated reduction in company-financed R&D expenditures[a] (millions of kronor)	60	86
Total company-financed R&D expenditures (millions of kronor)	6,276	7,700
Percent reduction[b]	1.0%	1.1%

a. These are unbiased estimates based on the procedures described in note 8. For a
discussion of the sampling errors in these estimates, see the section entitled "Effects of
the Swedish R&D Tax Allowance: Survey Results."
b. If the percentage reduction for the forty firms in the sample (taken as a whole) is
computed, the result is very similar to these figures.
Source: See the Section entitled "Effects of the Swedish R&D Tax Allowance: Survey
Results."

kronor. In 1983 a 95 percent confidence interval for the tax-incentive-
induced increase in company-financed R&D is 26–145 million Swedish
kronor (or 0.3 to 1.9 percent). Although the figures in *Table 9-4* do not
extend to 1983, one would expect the revenue loss then to be at least
230 million Swedish kronor (the 1982 figure estimated by the Swedish
Ministry of Industry).[21]

Of course, the results of this survey, like those in the United States,
should be viewed with caution. However, it seems unlikely that Swedish firms deliberately underestimate the effects of the allowance, since
they have argued in favor of its effectiveness and continuation. Based
on information obtained from government officials and others, the survey results do not seem unreasonable. Many firms do not have any
income tax liability against which to apply the allowance. Even if a
firm has such liabilities, the reduction (in cents) of the after-tax price
of an extra dollar's worth of R&D to a firm that increases its R&D
expenditure (and that intends to increase its R&D expenditure for each
year in the foreseeable future) is only about 6 percent, assuming an
interest rate of 15 percent.[22]

If the price elasticity of demand for R&D is about 0.3 (which, as
indicated above, seems consistent with most of the limited evidence for
the United States), this would mean an increase in R&D of 1.8 percent
or less. But taking account of the many firms that had no income tax
liability, this is an overestimate. Thus, although it is impossible to be
precise, there is good reason to believe that, as the survey results

indicate, the effects of the Swedish R&D tax allowance have been small.

Redefinition of Activities in Sweden

The Swedish R&D tax allowance, like the U.S. R&D tax credit, seems to have caused some redefinition of activities as R&D. Since a longer period has elapsed since its introduction in Sweden than in the United States, more can be said about the extent and quantitative importance of such redefinition of activities in Sweden. Based on data from our sample of firms, reported company-financed R&D expenditures grew by about 13 percent after 1973 solely because of such redefinition of activities. However, for most firms this was a transient phenomenon, the effects being felt largely in the first few years after the allowance's introduction in 1973. During these first few years, the firms, on the average, estimated that their reported R&D expenditures grew by about 4 percent per year because of this factor. It would not be surprising if firms tended to underestimate the extent of the redefinition of activities for reasons cited in the previous section. Thus, these figures may be conservative.

The R&D Tax Credit and Special Research Allowance in Canada

Besides including the United States and Sweden, this study includes Canada, the first major nation to adopt direct R&D tax incentives. Because of space limitations, and the fact that the Canadian results will be published in detail elsewhere, a very brief summary of our Canadian results will be given. Since 1961 both current and capital expenditures on R&D in Canada have been fully deductible in the year incurred. In addition, there was both an R&D investment tax credit and a special research allowance in Canada during the early 1980s. The investment tax credit (which was taxable) was 10–25 percent of current and qualified capital expenditures on R&D, the percentage varying with the size of the firm and the location of its R&D. The special research allowance permitted corporations to deduct from their taxable income an amount equal to 50 percent of the increase in operating and capital expenditures for R&D.[23] A firm could use both the investment tax credit and the special research allowance.

To estimate the effects of the Canadian R&D investment tax credit and the special research allowance on company-financed R&D, a survey like that in the United States and Sweden was carried out. We selected a stratified random sample of fifty-five firms, which account for almost 30 percent of the company-financed R&D expenditures in Canada. Based on these firms' estimates, it appears that in 1982 the investment tax credit increased company-financed R&D expenditures (when the definition of R&D is held constant) by about 2 percent, and that the special research allowance increased them by about 1 percent. Thus the effect of these tax incentives seems to be about the same as the U.S. or Swedish tax incentives. As in the United States and Sweden, the increases in company-financed R&D expenditures seem to have been considerably less than the cost to the government in reduced tax revenue. In 1982 the Canadian government experienced a reduction in tax revenues of about $130 million ($80 million from the investment tax credit and $50 million from the special research allowance), but these two tax incentives combined stimulated at most about $87 million in extra R&D, according to a confidence interval of the sort presented in previous sections.

Each firm in the sample estimated the extent to which its reported R&D expenditures rose from the introduction of the investment tax credit and the special research allowance (in 1977)[24] to 1981 merely because of the redefinition of activities as R&D. According to the firms themselves, this redefinition resulted in about a 14 percent increase between 1977 and 1981 in their reported R&D expenditures. This rate of increase is quite close to the figure of 4 percent per year we found for the United States and Sweden (early years) in previous sections.

Because of the availability of longer time series in Canada, it was possible to do more with econometric techniques there than in the United States or Sweden. In 1980 (the last year to which the econometric results pertain), it appears that these tax incentives (the investment tax credit and the special research allowance combined) were associated with an increase in reported company-financed R&D of about $132 million, some of which was real and some of which was due to redefinition of activities. If we suppose that the 1977–1981 increase in reported R&D due to redefinition of activities occurred at a constant rate, about 9 percent of reported company-financed R&D expenditures in 1980 (that is, about $102 million) would not have been reported as R&D before the advent of these tax incentives. Deducting this amount from $132 million, we get $30 million, which is close to what the survey results estimate to have been the real effects of these tax incentives.[25] Thus, while the econometric results are subject to a variety of limitations, it is interesting that they seem quite consistent with the survey results. (Indeed, if, as some believe, the redefinition tended to occur more rapidly at the beginning than the end of 1977–1981, the figure of $30 million will be an overestimate.)

Conclusions

Our findings, while subject to many limitations, present a very consistent picture. In all of the countries we studied, R&D tax credits and allowances appear to have had only a modest effect on R&D expenditures. In the United States, Canada, and Sweden, the results are quite similar, each of these R&D tax incentives having increased R&D expenditures by about 1 percent (2 percent in the case of the Canadian investment tax credit). In large part, the similarity of the results is due to the fact that the tax-incentive-induced after-tax reduction in the price of R&D is much the same for each of these tax incentives.[26] In all of these nations, the increased R&D expenditures due to the tax incentives seem to be substantially less than the revenue lost by the government. The ratio of the tax-incentive-induced increase in R&D spending to the forgone government revenue is remarkably similar from nation to nation. For the four tax incentives studied here, this ratio ranged in 1982 (1981 in Sweden) from about 0.3 to 0.4.[27] In each country, there was substantial evidence that these tax incentives resulted in a considerable redefinition of activities as R&D, particularly in the first few years after the introduction of the tax incentive. Such a redefinition of activities is estimated to have resulted in a total increase in reported R&D expenditures of about 13–14 percent in both Canada and Sweden.

These results, based largely on carefully designed and executed surveys of business firms, seem to be some of the first reasonably systematic and comprehensive findings on this topic. As pointed out repeatedly, such surveys must nonetheless be viewed with considerable caution. However, when compared with evidence concerning the price elasticity of demand for R&D, the survey results seem reasonable. Moreover, in those cases where preliminary (and crude) econometric analyses can be carried out, the results seem consistent with the survey results. Unfortunately, there are very great difficulties in using the customary sorts of econometric analysis in this area, both because of lack of data and because many of the effects under investigation seem to be so small that it is difficult to use the available data to isolate them. Further, the real effects of these tax incentives tend to be confounded with the tax-credit-induced effects of the redefinition of activities as R&D. Unless one can obtain an independent estimate of the latter effects (from surveys or other sources), there is no very reliable way to isolate the former effects, on the basis of reported R&D expenditure data.

Based on our findings, it appears that these R&D tax incentives, in their present form, are unlikely to have a major impact on a nation's rate of innovation.[28] One possible way of increasing the effectiveness of such a tax credit is to change the computation of the base amount (specified in the 1981 U.S. tax bill as the average of the firm's R&D expenditures in the previous three years) so that there is more incentive for firms to increase R&D.[29] It is difficult to predict how much difference such a change would make without a more detailed specification of the nature of the change.[30] As long as these tax incentives result in only a modest reduction in the price of R&D, as long as they do not apply at all to a substantial proportion of firms,[31] and as long as the price elasticity of demand for R&D is rather low, their effects will continue to be modest.

Our results also provide some of the first evidence concerning the sensitivity of reported R&D expenditures to institutional changes like the introduction of R&D tax incentives. Data regarding reported R&D expenditures form the basis for a very large proportion of the empirical and econometric studies of technological change in this and other countries. Thus it is sobering to find that the introduction of an R&D tax incentive may lead to an essentially spurious increase of reported R&D expenditures of about 13–14 percent. Analysts and policy makers must be very careful to allow for distortions of this sort; otherwise, their conclusions concerning the behavior of actual R&D expenditures and the actual stock of R&D may be seriously flawed.

In conclusion, the need for additional research on this and related topics is obvious. Governments throughout the world are trying to promote technological change and innovation, and business firms must conduct their affairs within the context of the public policies that are adopted. Too frequently there is little or no attempt to estimate or analyze the quantitative effects of particular measures or programs. Despite the enormous difficulties that are encountered in this sort of research, it is important that efforts along this line be continued.

Notes

1. See Mansfield et al. (1982) and Mansfield (1983).
2. See Mansfield (1982).
3. Preliminary versions of part of this chapter were presented at the Symposium on Industrial Change and Public Policy sponsored by the Federal Reserve Bank of Kansas City in August 1983 and at the Conference on Quantitative Studies on Research and Development in Industry held by the National Bureau of Economic Research and ENSAE in Paris in September 1983.
4. See Chapoton (1983).
5. Ibid.
6. Optimum allocation rules call for the sample size in each stratum to be

proportional to the product of the standard deviation and the total number of firms in the stratum. To apply these rules, rough estimates were made of the standard deviation of x_{ij} in each stratum (see note 8 for a definition of x_{ij}). Based on chi-square tests, there was no evidence that the industrial distribution of the sample differed significantly from that of the population, or that the distribution of firms by size of R&D expenditure in the sample differed significantly from that in the population. The frame is given in *Business Week*, 5 July 1982.

7. For a summary of some early findings, see N. Jacoby and J. F. Weston (1954). Of course, many other topics have been investigated through surveys. Some of the limitations of surveys are cited in the section entitled "Evaluation of the Survey Results."

8. For the ith firm in the jth stratum in our sample, let x_{ij} be the reduction in the firm's R&D expenditures that would have occurred if the tax credit had not been introduced. If n_j and N_j are the number of firms in the jth stratum in the sample and population, respectively, our estimator of the total reduction in R&D expenditures that would have occurred under these circumstances is

$$N_1 \frac{\sum_i x_{i1}}{n_1} + N_2 \frac{\sum_i x_{i2}}{n_2} .$$

This estimator is unbiased. Its standard error equals

$$\sqrt{N_1^2 \frac{s_1^2}{n_1} + N_2^2 \frac{s_2^2}{n_2}} ,$$

where s_j^2 is the sample variance of x_{ij} in the jth stratum. (In some cases, the finite population correction factor should be—and was—added.) The 95 percent confidence interval equals the above estimator plus or minus (approximately) two of its standard errors. It is assumed that the sample size (110 firms) is large enough so that the estimator is normally distributed. Regardless of whether the normal approximation is very close, the total increase in R&D due to the R&D tax credit is very unlikely to have been as great as the revenue loss, since the latter was 11.0 standard errors above the estimate in 1981, 6.7 standard errors above the estimate in 1982, and 5.4 standard errors above the estimate in 1983. To some extent, these confidence intervals underestimate the effects of the tax credit because our frame included 91 percent, not 100 percent, of all company-financed R&D. If the firms not included in the population reacted to the credit much as those in the population did, the confidence intervals should be raised by 10 percent. If this is done, the percentage figures in the text are unaffected, and it remains true that the increase in R&D is less than the revenue loss.

9. This result is based on the data in *Business Week*, 20 June 1983, and 5 July 1982.

10. See Chapoton (1983).

11. This conclusion is arrived at by using the equation:

$$25 \left(1 - \frac{1}{3(1+i)} - \frac{1}{3(1+i)^2} - \frac{1}{3(1+i)^3} \right), \tag{7}$$

where i equals the interest rate. Thus, if $i = .15$, the actual price reduction due to the credit is 6 cents. To derive the expression in (7), note that an extra dollar of R&D this year reduces this year's tax by 25 cents but increases taxes in each of the next three years by 25/3 cents because the base amount for each of the next three years is increased by 25/3 cents. Thus, the present value of these effects is given by the expression above. For further discussion of this point, see Eisner, Albert, and Sullivan (1983).

According to the 1983 *Economic Report of the President*, the average prime rate charged by banks during 1982 was 14.86 percent. Thus, the assumption that i = .15 seems reasonable, at least as a rough approximation.

12. Ibid., 25.

13. Since R&D expenditures are deductible, the after-tax price of a dollar's worth of R&D equals 54 cents, if there is no R&D tax credit. If it is true that the effective rate of credit for firms with tax liabilities and increasing R&D is only a few percent, the effective rate of credit for all firms must be considerably lower. (In 1982, the estimated tax reduction was only about 2–3 percent of total company-financed R&D expenditures.) Thus, although it is difficult to come up with a particular figure, it seems reasonable that the reduction in the after-tax price would be less than 6 percent. However, even if it were more than 6 percent, we would expect the effect of the tax credit to be small, as long as the price elasticity of demand for R&D is low.

14. Mohnen, Nadiri, and Prucha (1983) found that the price elasticity of demand for the stock of R&D was .09 in the intermediate run and .28 in the long run. For the flow of R&D, the price elasticity was .36 in the intermediate run and .28 in the long run. (I am indebted to M. I. Nadiri for providing me with the latter, unpublished estimates.)

15. Of course, even if the price elasticity is substantially higher than 0.3, as Goldberg (1979) concludes to be the case in the long run, the tax credit's effect would be expected to be small if the price reduction is small, since there is no evidence (that I know of) that the price elasticity exceeds one.

16. This estimate contains substantial sampling error, but this is only part of the story, since there may be biases of the sort cited below.

17. Of course, the Swedish and Canadian data may also contain biases. More is said below on this score.

18. The list of firms and the data used here come from *Business Week's* annual R&D statistics for 1975–82. (Comprehensive data of this sort at the firm level were not published before 1975.) Some firms had to be excluded because the data were incomplete or not comparable over time or because the character of the firm changed due to mergers. To obtain the figures in *Table 9-3*, we summed up the actual R&D spending of the firms that could be included in each industry and divided this sum by the total expected R&D spending of these firms based on the naive forecasts.

19. This description of the Swedish tax allowance, like our description of the U.S. credit, omits many details. For the relevant provisions of Swedish tax law, see McFetridge and Warda (1983). We have relied heavily on their summary of the laws concerning R&D tax incentives in various countries. I am also grateful to many Swedish officials in industry and government who helped me understand the nature and operation of their tax allowance.

20. For these rules, see note 6.

21. These confidence intervals are constructed in the way described in note 8. It is assumed that the sample size (forty firms) is large enough so that the estimator is normally distributed. Regardless of whether the normal approximation is very close, the total increase in R&D due to the tax allowance is very unlikely to have been as great as the revenue loss, since the latter was 6.1 standard errors above the estimate in 1981 and at least 4.8 standard errors above the estimate in 1983. Because the frame includes 90 percent, not 100 percent, of all company-financed R&D, the confidence intervals underestimate the effect of the allowance. If the R&D-supporting firms not included in the

population reacted to the allowance much as the firms in the population did, the confidence intervals should be raised by about 10 percent. If this is done, it remains true that the increase in R&D is less than the revenue loss.

To calculate the percentages in this paragraph of the text, data were needed regarding total company-financed R&D expenditures in Sweden in 1981 and 1983. I am indebted to Tage Berglund of the Swedish National Central Bureau of Statistics for providing unpublished figures and estimates.

22. This conclusion is arrived at by using the expression .4 [35 − 30/(1 + i)]. If i = .15, it equals about 3–4 cents. Thus the allowance reduces the after-tax price by only about 6 percent.

To derive this expression, note that an extra dollar of R&D this year reduces this year's taxable income by 30 cents, because the difference between this year's and last year's R&D expenditure grows by one dollar. Also, this year's taxable income is reduced by 5 cents because of the one-dollar increase in R&D expenditure this year. In addition, next year's taxable income is increased by 30 cents because the difference between next year's R&D expenditure and this year's R&D expenditure is reduced by one dollar. Thus, since the marginal tax rate is 0.4, according to McFetridge and Warda (1983), the present value of these effects equals the above expression. Also, since the marginal tax rate equals 0.4, the after-tax price of a dollar's worth of R&D is 60 cents if there is no tax allowance, and the reduction of 3–4 cents amounts to a decrease of 6 percent.

23. For further details, see Mansfield and Switzer (1984) and McFetridge and Warda (1983).

24. While Canada first introduced an R&D tax incentive in 1962, it dropped it in 1966. In 1977 the investment tax credit was introduced; in 1978 the special research allowance was introduced. The fact that tax credits and other programs of this sort had existed previously in Canada probably influenced the extent of the post-1977 redefinition of activities as R&D. In 1984 further changes in these incentives were enacted by the government. See Mansfield and Switzer (1984) and the works cited therein.

25. According to the survey results, the R&D tax incentives increased R&D expenditures by about $29 million in 1980. Note that we are not saying that the increase in reported R&D due to redefinition of activities goes on indefinitely at a constant rate. On the contrary, there is evidence that it tends to peter out a few years after the introduction of a tax incentive. If it tended to be greater during the early part of 1977–81 than during the later part, the resulting estimate in the text of the real effects of these tax incentives will tend to be too high.

26. It is difficult to compare the extent of the after-tax price reduction of a dollar's worth of R&D in various countries. However, for a firm that has an income tax liability against which to apply the credit or allowance and which intends to increase its R&D expenditures in the foreseeable future, the reduction (in cents) is about 6 cents in the United States, 3 cents or 4 cents in Sweden, 6 cents for the Canadian special research allowance, and 5 cents for the Canadian R&D investment tax credit. (For the Canadian R&D investment tax credit, we assume that the firm is large.) Thus the reduction due to each of these tax credits or allowances does not vary much from case to case. Of course, what is being discussed here is the price reduction due to each tax incentive. Since Canada has two such tax incentives and the United States and Sweden have one, the total package is more generous in Canada than in the United States or Sweden. McFetridge and Warda (1983), although they base their analysis on different assumptions, also conclude that the Canadian package is more generous than the others.

27. Under simplifying assumptions, this ratio is determined by the price elasticity of demand for R&D, among other things. Thus if this price elasticity is about the same in each country, and if other conditions are met, it may not be surprising that this ratio is relatively constant from nation to nation.

28. In Sweden the government eliminated the R&D tax allowance at the beginning of 1984. Apparently, this was due in part to growing questions concerning its effectiveness. According to Swedish observers, the Parliament Committee on Taxes said that its efficiency was too low to justify its continuation.

29. If the base amount in future years is not raised by present increases in R&D expenditures, the reduction in the after-tax price of a dollar's worth of R&D will be 25 cents, rather than the expression in (7). There are many ways in which this might be carried out. For example, the base amount for a firm might depend on total industry R&D spending, not just on the firm's spending. See Eisner, Albert, and Sullivan (1983).

30. It should be noted that the Canadian investment tax credit is not incremental. Based on our results, this tax credit increased R&D by about 2 percent, which was substantially less than the revenue loss.

31. In 1980 almost one-third of the R&D in Canada was done by firms that did not have sufficient taxable income to use any of their R&D tax credits. Another third was carried out by firms that could not use all of their R&D tax credits during the year. See Mansfield and Switzer (1984).

References

Chapoton, J. Statement before the Subcommittee on Taxation and Debt Management of the Committee on Finance. U.S. Senate. 27 May 1983.

Collins, E. "An Early Assessment of Three R and D Tax Incentives Provided by the Economic Recovery Tax Act of 1981." Washington, D.C.: National Science Foundation, 1983.

Cordes, J. "Tax Policies for Encouraging Innovation: A Survey." *Technology in Society.* 1981, 87–98.

Eisner, R., S. Albert, and M. Sullivan. "Tax Incentives and R and D Expenditures." Unpublished paper, 1983.

Goldberg, L. "The Influence of Federal R and D Funding on the Demand for and Returns to Industrial R and D." Center for Naval Analysis. October 1979.

Grabowski, H. "The Determinants of Industrial Research and Development." *Journal of Political Economy,* 1968, 292–305.

Howe, J., and D. McFetridge. "The Determinants of R and D Expenditures." *Canadian Journal of Economics,* February 1976, 57–71.

Hughes, E., and D. McFetridge. "Conventional and Incremental Investment Incentives in Models of Optimal Capital Accumulation." Unpublished paper, 1983.

Jacoby, N., and J. F. Weston. "Financial Policies for Regularizing Business Investment." *Regularization of Business Investment.* New York: National Bureau of Economic Research, 1954.

McFetridge. D., and J. Warda. *Canadian R and D Incentives: Their Adequacy and Impact.* Toronto: Canadian Tax Foundation, February 1983.

Mansfield, E. "Tax Policy and Innovation," *Science* 215 (12 March 1982): 1365–76.

———. "Comments on Capital Formation, Technology, and Economic Policy,"

Industrial Change and Public Policy. Kansas City: Federal Reserve Bank of Kansas City, 1983.

Mansfield, E., A. Romeo, M. Schwartz, D. Teece, S. Wagner, and P. Brach. *Technology Transfer, Productivity, and Economic Policy.* New York: W. W. Norton, 1982.

Mansfield, E., and L. Switzer. "The Effects of R and D Tax Credits and Allowances in Canada." Unpublished paper, 1984.

Mohnen, P., M. I. Nadiri, and I. Prucha. "R and D, Production Structure, and Productivity Growth in the U.S., Japanese, and German Manufacturing Sectors." Unpublished paper, 1983.

Nadiri, I., and M. Schankerman. "The Structure of Production, Technological Change, and the Rate of Growth of Total Factor Productivity in the Bell System." *Productivity Measurement in Regulated Industries,* edited by T. Cowing and R. Stevenson. New York: Academic Press, 1981.

Switzer, L. "The Determinants of Industrial R and D: A Funds Flow Simultaneous Equations Approach," *Review of Economics and Statistics,* February 1984, 163–68.

Appendix

I. The Basic Economics of R&D Tax Credits

To aid in the interpretation of the empirical results of this study, it is worthwhile to sketch out the principal ways in which tax incentives for R&D would be expected to affect a firm's R&D expenditures. Take, for example, the case of the United States, where the R&D tax credit allows a firm to reduce its income tax liability by an amount that is proportional to the increase in its R&D expenditures (relative to a base period).[1] This R&D tax credit tends to increase the firm's R&D because it reduces the price of R&D. Suppose that the firm is considering how much R&D to carry out to support and produce a given quantity of output of a particular product (old or new) in a future period. Obviously, the firm can substitute R&D for non-R&D inputs, at least within certain limits. For example, more R&D can result in lower costs of capital or labor. Suppose that the relevant isoquant showing the combination of R&D and non-R&D inputs that will result in the desired output is as shown in *Figure A9-1* (part A).

Since this is an incremental tax credit, it applies only to R&D expenditures exceeding the amount spent by the firm on R&D in the base period (R_0 in *Figure A9-1* (part A). Thus, the isocost curve facing the firm is kinked, since the after-tax price of R&D (when account is taken of the tax credit) is lower for R&D in excess of the base amount (that is, the amount carried out in the base period) than for R&D that is less than or equal to this amount. In the case shown in *Figure A9-1* (part A) the firm will be led by the tax credit to carry out more R&D than it

Figure A9-1
Effects of R&D Tax Credit on the Optimal Input Combination of a Firm

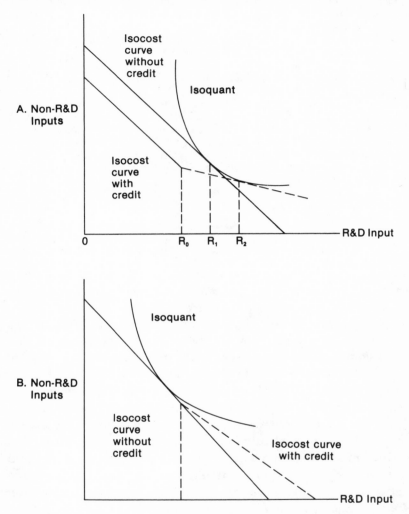

otherwise would have done. Specifically, it will increase its R&D from R_1 to R_2. However, this will not be always the case. Some firms will not find it profitable to carry out more R&D because of the tax credit. For example, this is true in the case shown in *Figure A9-1* (part B), where the firm wants to reduce its R&D expenditures to a level below the base amount. Also, if firms have no taxable profits, with the result that the credit must be carried forward, the credit's effects will be reduced.

Besides having an effect on R&D expenditures via the change in the price of R&D, tax credits may also have an effect via the change in cash flow. Suppose that a firm's R&D expenditures (R) are a linear function of its cash flow (C), in accord with a number of econometric studies (including some that are part of this project):[2]

$$R = \nu_1 + \nu_2 C + \ldots \tag{1}$$

The incremental tax credit changes the firm's cash flow in year t by:

$$\Delta C = h(R_t - R_0), \tag{2}$$

where R_t is the firm's R&D expenditure in year t, R_0 is its R&D expenditure in the base period, and h is the proportion of $(R_t - R_0)$ that can be subtracted from the firm's tax bill. Thus, the increase in the firm's R&D expenditures due to the greater cash flow is:

$$\Delta R = \nu_2 h(R_t - R_0), \tag{3}$$

and the proportional increase is

$$\frac{\Delta R}{R_t} = \nu_2 h\left(1 - \frac{R_0}{R_t}\right) \tag{4}$$

In the United States, h equals 0.25. Although relatively little is known about the value of ν_2, econometric studies have estimated that it is about 0.02 to 0.2. If these studies are at all close to the mark, this effect of the tax credit is likely to be very small. Specifically, if R_t is 25 percent above R_0, and if $\nu_2 = 0.10$,

$$\frac{\Delta R}{R_t} = .25 \times .10 \times .2 = .0050,$$

or about ½ of one percent.[3]

II. Has the Swedish R&D Tax Allowance Changed the Relationship between R&D and Sales?

Because the R&D tax incentive has been in existence much longer in Sweden than in the United States, there are more data available on which to base econometric analyses of the effects of the allowance. Although the available data are subject to a variety of limitations, an attempt was made to use these data to carry out some exploratory analyses. To keep things as simple as possible, suppose that the ith industry's reported R&D expenditures can be represented as follows:

$$R_{it} = \alpha_i + \phi_i t + \theta_i S_{it} + e_{it}, \tag{5}$$

where R_{it} equals the ith industry's reported company-financed R&D expenditures in year t (in millions of Swedish kronor), S_{it} equals the ith industry's sales in year t (in millions of kronor), t is time (measured in years from 1967), and e_{it} is a random error term. This very simple model would seem to be a natural starting point, since it is customary (as a first approximation) to relate an industry's R&D expenditures to its sales.

One way that the R&D tax allowance may have affected equation (5) is to increase α_i.[4] To test whether this was true, we divided all Swedish industries (for which R&D data are available) into five groups: (1) very low R&D industries (oil, wood, printing); (2) low R&D industries (food, textiles, metal products, pottery, shipbuilding, mining, paper); (3) medium R&D industries (industrial chemicals, metals, nonmetallic minerals); (4) high R&D industries (machinery, other transport); and (5) very high R&D industries (electrical equipment, instruments).[5]

If we pool the data within a particular group of industries, and if we allow α_i to equal $\alpha'_i + \beta\delta_t$ (where δ_t is a dummy variable that is zero prior to 1974[6] and 1 from 1974 on),

$$R_{it} = \alpha'_i + \beta\delta_t + \bar{\phi}t + \bar{\theta}S_{it} + e'_{it}, \tag{6}$$

where $\bar{\phi}$ is the mean value of ϕ_i and $\bar{\theta}$ is the mean value of θ_i for the industries within the group, and $e'_{it} = e_{it} + (\phi_i - \bar{\phi})t + (\theta_i - \bar{\theta})S_{it}$. If e'_{it} can be treated as a random error term, we can obtain a least-squares estimate of β, which is the parameter indicating whether (and if so, how) the values of α_i in this group of industries changed when the tax allowance was adopted. Using all of the data that are published by the Swedish National Central Bureau of Statistics (odd years from 1967 to 1979), we estimated the value of β in each group of industries (see *Table A9-1* for the results). In none of the five industry groups is the estimate of β even close to being statistically significant (and in two cases it is negative). Thus, there is no statistically significant evidence that the R&D tax allowance increased α_i.

Table A9-1
Estimates of β, Five Industry Groups, Sweden

Industries	*Estimate*	*Standard Error*
Very low R&D (oil, wood, printing)	1.41	1.72
Low R&D (food, textiles, metal products, pottery, shipbuilding, mining, paper)	6.86	12.91
Medium R&D (industrial chemicals, metals, nonmetallic minerals)	0.80	22.21
High R&D (machinery, other transport)	−73.72	95.83
Very high R&D (electrical equipment, instruments)	−44.05	69.69

This result is indicative of the problems involved in using the available data to obtain econometric estimates of this sort. The standard errors of the estimates of β are very large relative to the likely effects of the tax allowance, due partly to the relatively small number of years for which R&D data are available, the fact that the R&D data are not entirely comparable over time, and the crudeness of the model.[7] (Of course, the nature and quantity of data set limits on the model that can be used.) Because the standard errors are so large, this analysis can tell us little about the effects of the tax allowance. While the results are not inconsistent with our survey findings, the test is very weak. Fortunately, somewhat more precise results along this line have been obtained for Canada. (These findings were summarized in the section entitled "The R&D Tax Credit and Special Research Allowance in Canada.")

Appendix Notes

1. Although the discussion in the first section of the *Appendix* pertains to tax credits, the same considerations apply to tax allowances of the sort discussed in the section entitled "The R&D Tax Allowance in Sweden" up to the "Conclusion" section. The purpose of this section is to describe the effects of an R&D tax credit in the most basic terms. More detailed theoretical discussions are found in Hughes and McFetridge (1984). In many respects, the analysis in *Figure A9-1* is highly simplified and intended only to be illustrative.

2. For example, see Grabowski (1968), Howe and McFetridge (1976), and Switzer (1984).

3. According to Switzer (1984), v_2 is about .025 in the chemical, petroleum, electronics, and aerospace industries. Grabowski (1968) estimated that v_2 was about .02 in petroleum, but about .08 in chemicals. Other studies have resulted in estimates of about .20. Even if v_2 is as great as 0.20, $\Delta R/R_t$ only equals one percent.

4. Of course, this is not the only way in which the tax allowance could affect the equation. For example, it could alter θ_i or both α_i and θ_i. See note 7 below.

5. The industries were classified in this way on the basis of their ratios of R&D expenditures to sales. Because the drug industry's R&D expenditures as a percent of sales are so much higher than in other industries, its value of θ is likely to be much greater than in other industries. Thus, the drug industry belongs in a group by itself. But because a group of this sort would contain very few observations, this is not feasible. Consequently, the drug industry was omitted from this analysis.

6. While the R&D tax allowance was passed in 1973, it really did not have an effect until 1974, according to Swedish firms and observers.

7. Unfortunately, between 1971 and 1973, there were a considerable number of enterprises that were reclassified by industry, and a new sample of enterprises was drawn for the R&D statistics. Thus, there are problems of comparability.

Analyses were carried out to determine whether $\bar{\theta}$ was affected by the R&D tax allowance. Specifically, regressions were calculated in which $\delta_t S_{it}$ was included instead of δ_t in equation (6). This variable was never statistically significant.

Commentary
Direct Tax Incentives for R&D: Time to Cut Bait or to Fish?

Lewis M. Branscomb

Professor Mansfield's chapter on the effectiveness of research and development tax credits represents a major research effort toward better understanding of how one element of federal policy—a tax credit for incremental R&D investment—can best stimulate the private sector's all-important capacity for technological innovation and productivity growth.

Professor Mansfield's evidence fails to demonstrate a strong management response to the tax credit in the United States to date, or in Sweden and Canada over a longer period. No doubt the incentives in the current U.S. scheme can be improved. But I am nevertheless concerned about some of the apparent implications of the chapter.

The trouble is, I cannot see IBM—or even the information industry—in this report, and everyone who studies it needs to be able to bring his or her common sense business experience to bear against the analysis. We should all mistrust our common sense and our subjective judgment, especially in the face of analysis, but that is hard to do if we cannot trace the analysis back to the data.

Clearly, Professor Mansfield has collected a great deal of data that could be subjected to further analysis. In advance of its full publication and treatment, what we have here is the result of extensive surveys of companies, which have been aggregated in a fairly simple form, and a set of impressions and judgments gained from the surveys. Against that, the impressions and judgments of people in the business community may, indeed, be very relevant.

The Private Sector and Technology

Notwithstanding the importance of federal laboratories and universities, private industry is the dominant force in American science and technology.[1] About 70 percent of R&D activity in the United States, as measured by funds expended or by scientists and engineers employed in R&D, takes place in industry. Over half of all U.S. R&D funds comes from private industry.

Last year, for example, IBM spent a record $3.5 billion on research, development, and engineering, bringing its investment in these areas to more than $13 billion over the past five years.

Barely thirty years old, the U.S. information industry continues to grow at almost 15 percent a year, creating tens of thousands of new jobs annually. More important, this industry introduces new technology so rapidly that each year its products do about 25 percent more for their users in other industries, at no increase in cost.

High technology companies such as IBM differ in many ways from traditional manufacturing companies. The former compete in a tremendously dynamic marketplace and therefore *must* invest a major portion of their resources in research and product development to survive and prosper.

Among the twenty member companies of an Ad Hoc Electronics Tax Group formed in 1983 to review the effect of tax systems on U.S. electronics firms,[2] investments in R&D ranged from 6 percent to 15.8 percent of sales revenues in 1982, when R&D spending for U.S. industry as a whole was only 2.4 percent of sales.

Yet even historically more slow-paced industries (including some doomed to the designation "sunset industries") are today challenged by rapid technological change. For the new industrial technologies of automation and information management can be used—and are being used by overseas competitors—to upgrade both productivity and product at a rapid pace. Government actions can have a dramatic effect, either positively or negatively, on this process.

Federal policy areas that may have a direct impact on industrial R&D include not only overall fiscal and monetary policy but changes in patent policy and other incentives to stimulate private returns on innovation, support of research and graduate study in the institutions that train our engineers and scientists, and even government procurement criteria and practices.

Tax Policy and Innovation

One principal federal initiative, on which Professor Mansfield's chapter focuses, has been in tax policy—particularly the Economic Recovery Tax Act (ERTA) of 1981. This is a good starting point because, as noted in the National Science Board's *Science Indicators, 1982*:

To the extent that tax policy contributes to economic growth and price stability in general, it reduces investment uncertainties and thereby encourages private investment in research and development and other phases of innovative activity.

To the extent that it encourages capital investment, it influences the rate of introduction and diffusion of those technologies that are embodied in new plant and equipment.

To the extent that it provides special allowances for increased R&D expenditures, it fosters company funding of R&D, both in-house and in universities.

And to the extent that it is consistent, it reduces investment uncertainty.

The R&D tax credit section of the ERTA was enacted by the Congress to provide a significant incentive to encourage increases in R&D spending, thereby increasing the ability of U.S. companies to remain competitive with foreign corporations in developing new technology.

Perhaps it was not wholly inappropriate, however, that the tax credit benefited high technology companies in particular, for these companies typically pay the highest taxes and yet received very little relief from the 1981 tax act's Accelerated Cost Recovery System.

Consider the Alternatives

The policy question concerning the future of R&D tax credits as an instrument of federal policy has to be seen in the light of broader debate about what federal policies are appropriate for the stimulation of both productivity and innovation in American private companies.

There is a variety of important tax and financial measures, and it is appropriate that Professor Mansfield has focused his attention on one of these elements. But we should all remember that for every person who is an enthusiast about tax policy as a means of encouraging private sector investments in R&D and innovation, there are two people advocating elements of what is now called "industrial policy"—aimed at direct federal investments in technologies of, hopefully, economic importance.

A tax credit is an alternative to direct federal investment in R&D. Professor Mansfield observes that its effects across the entire economy may be relatively modest in percentage terms—for a tax credit fails the test of being a surgically specific tool for focusing lost federal revenues in the most effective possible way on specific technologies and specific industrial sectors that would most benefit the economy.

But we have to think twice about the virtues of the "hidden hand" and the shortcomings of alternative policies that are indeed aimed at having the surgical characteristic.

These alternative policies, from the Stevenson-Wydler Act to the

Advanced Technology Foundation (H.R. 4361) proposed in the spring of 1984 by Congressman LaFalce, have failings of their own. Generally, they can be characterized as having the federal government target specific industrial technologies for help.

Principles for Government Support of R&D

In deciding what R&D activities the federal government should undertake, the following principles should apply:

- Government should, of course, support the scientific and engineering research in universities that provides the knowledge base and the graduate training on which the private sector depends.
- Government should also assure the health of both the environment and the process for innovation and not substitute itself for the more effective private sector process of technology generation. Government officials are too far removed from the short-term vagaries of the marketplace to be sufficiently sensitive to these subtle and often decisive influences. The time constant for change in direction in government-directed work is much too long.
- Any proposal for federal funding of R&D aimed at benefits to employment and economic competitiveness should be subjected to the following test: Are detailed, first-hand knowledge of competitive market conditions and requirements for production and service costs necessary to make the R&D useful and competitive? If so, government should restrain its zeal to help in this manner.
- When government agencies, which don't have knowledge of the market and don't have knowledge of the economics of R&D, try to target commercial technologies of importance to the economy, they end up wasting their money; they end up distorting the competitive private marketplace, and government policy officials are driven to find a tool that does not have these deficiencies.

Delegating Judgments to the Marketplace

The incremental R&D tax credit does not have these deficiencies because it puts the responsibility for deciding what projects shall be funded in the hands of someone who is spending his own money. While the tax credit is a benefit, it's not a free ride. It still costs money to do the R&D.

But, more important, for every dollar spent on R&D, with or without a tax credit, one will spend five on manufacturing, and perhaps ten on marketing. So one needn't worry about companies being profligate about wasting R&D funds because the government is participating in the cost of the expanded R&D investment. R&D is worth nothing to anyone unless they exploit it in manufacturing and in sales, and that's where the big expenses are incurred. R&D is less than 10 percent of revenue for almost every company in America.

Professor Mansfield considers this phenomenon a reflection of a low price elasticity for R&D. I consider it the very safeguard that discourages managers from wasting the Treasury's tax collections by spending frivolously for R&D.

As we judge tax policy as it relates to the tax credit, let us remember the virtues of a tool that delegates into the markeplace the judgments on how it should be allocated. Let us not test this tax device against a hopeless challenge—which is that every dollar of revenue lost to the Treasury through this source must result in great innovative consequences within every firm that benefits from it. And, certainly, we should not subject it to the test that total R&D net spending in all firms—including the great majority who spend little or nothing on R&D—shall be stimulated by an incentive designed for innovators.

Measuring the Effect of Tax Credits

The ERTA was signed in August 1981. Since then there has only been a short time in which to evaluate the long-term effects of any tax legislation—let alone incentives for R&D—but it has been necessary to try. As early as the first quarter of 1984 Congress was considering whether to extend the R&D tax credit that is due to expire at the end of 1985. Hence the considerable attention attracted by Professor Mansfield's two-year, NSF-funded study of the effectiveness of R&D tax incentives—not only in the United States but also the established programs in Sweden and Canada.

In each country, Mansfield finds that the credits have resulted in relatively minor increases in R&D spending (on the order of 1 percent), and he finds these results compatible with previous academic work that estimates the elasticity for R&D expenditures with respect to price to be quite small—approximately -0.3. Thus he concludes: "It appears that the R&D tax credits, *in their present form* [emphasis mine], are unlikely to have a major impact on a nation's rate of innovation."

This conclusion is actually not too constructive because, for one thing, research and development is not a macroeconomic phenomenon; it is microeconomic. We are not so much interested in the country's aggregate R&D spending as in the answer to the question: Is the industrial response to the incentive one likely to lead to more competitive companies? This is an industry-by-industry issue and, sometimes, even a company-by-company issue.

In some companies, the right response to competition is *not* more R&D spending; in other industries, it emphatically is. In fact, it would be very unfortunate if the Treasury ended up subsidizing meaningless R&D in companies that have structural obstacles that prevent the R&D from being used profitably. If the tax credit meets its goal and results in getting more R&D done in the right places, we might actually end up with less R&D being done in some places where it is wasted and moving the manpower to the places where it is needed. The *net* R&D in the whole economy might not show radical growth; R&D in those companies committed to a technology-based strategy for competition might show a strong response.

In any case, in the information industry, contrary to Professor Mansfield's general conclusion, R&D spending was surprisingly strong in 1982 and 1983. The fact that some of our competitors increased their R&D even a little, in the face of sharply falling revenues, suggests that the credit may have had a fairly powerful influence. It certainly did in IBM.

Background to the Study

At the time Mansfield's U.S. survey was conducted, company funding of R&D as a percentage of firms' sales and of the national economy had been on the upswing for some time. Expenditures in constant dollars have increased annually since around 1960, with the exceptions of 1970–71 and 1975—corresponding to the two recessions of the seventies. R&D expenditures started increasing as a percent of GNP around 1977 and, in each year since, they have accounted for a larger share.

What is startling about recent R&D expenditures is that they have not shown the sensitivity to the business cycle that they did during the 1970s. Uncharacteristically, they continued to grow, both in absolute terms and as a percent of GNP during both the 1980–81 and 1982–83 recessions.

Full Impact Yet to Be Felt?

The small but growing annual increase in total R&D spending by U.S. firms cited in this report are not surprising. The tax act was only passed in mid-1981. It is difficult to believe the credits could have had any impact in that year. In 1982 and the first half of 1983, corporate profits, taxable income and hence the ability to employ the credit were relatively low.

Furthermore, research and development is a long-term investment. It is not something one casually turns on and off. In particular, as suggested earlier, one does not turn it on unless one believes one will be able to sustain an investment pattern that is compatible with the manufacturing, marketing, and other commitments that the use of R&D results places on the business.

IBM sharply increased its R&D investment, starting in 1982, partly because it is determined to be the industry leader, technologically, and partly because it was reasonably confident that it could sustain a reasonable fraction of the pace of growth if an R&D tax credit did not stay in place beyond 1985. Others who were less optimistic about the credit's permanence might well have refrained from its use.

Another reason that the full impact of the credit may not yet have been felt is that Treasury did not issue some important clarifying rules and interpretations for a year and a half after the tax credit was enacted.

For example, the Treasury Department dragged its heels on allowing R&D on computer software to be eligible. From a trade point of view, the U.S. software industry is absolutely unique. While the United States is a strong force in computer hardware, U.S. companies dominate the world in software. This is one of our most dynamic, growing, cottage industries, highly competitive, with a very high rate of new business formation. And yet, because of the way the regulations to implement the ERTA were written, this clear example of a "sunrise" industry that the American government should wish to encourage was initially excluded from the R&D tax credit benefits.

Thus, it is easy to conjecture that as firms become more aware of the advantages of the credits and have more time to adapt to them, and as the economy (and taxable income) expand in 1984 and 1985, companies will exploit the credits more extensively. In the meantime, to dismiss the credits as being inconsequential because of the experience from 1981 to 1983 is premature.

Comparability of International Data

Implicit in Professor Mansfield's chapter is the idea that he has addressed the issue of long-term impact and tested the reliability of his U.S. results by seeing if surveys in two other countries with longer tax credit experience produce similar results. They do, but there are potential inconsistencies when comparing three different national economies, three sets of government practices, and three groups of companies that may be, on average, more or less research intensive.

The results may be comparable, but without knowing more about the Swedish and Canadian firms and how they compare to the ones in the U.S. sample, it is hard to draw a conclusion. Morover, the study's survey of managements in Sweden and Canada was also made in the 1981–83 period—perhaps obscuring longer-term impact of the credits, as may have been the case in the United States.

Who Was Questioned?

Professor Mansfield wisely observes that it makes a great deal of difference *who* was questioned at the firms. Had the authors randomly chosen any number of development managers in IBM and asked their questions, they might well have received the answer that the R&D tax credit has had no discernible effect.

When I was first asked by the National Science Foundation about the tax credit's potential impact, I consulted line managers in IBM, and the general consensus was that it would not have much effect; the company would continue to spend what it had to spend. Since then, the credit has certainly helped the company's senior financial management to see more merit in a long-term strategy even more strongly based on technical leadership. But the average line development manager still has no idea what effect the credit has had on his budget.

IBM's planning system does not work that way. The "D" part of R&D (which is much larger than the "R") is simply the sum of all the development work justified by the business cases for all the products in the revenue plan. And when the development people prepare their business cases, they do not see the bottom-line tax consequences that affect the revenue and expense targets they have been given. They do see corporate guidelines for total R&D spending that may be influenced over time by tax considerations.

Tax Incentives Help Taxpayers

One disadvantage of the R&D tax credit, Mansfield points out, is that it does not help firms that have no profits. Clearly, business without profits is not a "normal" state in this country or in any capitalist society. It would have been interesting to cross-tabulate the responses by average profitability of the respondent over a several-year period, as well as by other characteristics such as size and amount spent on R&D.

If it turns out that the cost to Treasury of the credit is skewed toward firms whose growing R&D expenditures are generating growing tax revenues, the program should not be faulted for this reason.

Redefinition of Activity

Professor Mansfield is properly concerned about the possibility of substantial redefinition of activities as R&D, particularly in the first few years after the introduction of tax incentives. He estimates that such redefinition of activities has resulted in an increase in reported R&D expenditures of about 13 percent or 14 percent in both Canada and Sweden.

Redefinition of R&D activity may represent a problem for statisticians, but it does not necessarily mean that companies are taking unfair advantage of the credit. It is, in any case, a "second-order" effect. A company can only claim an increment on *equivalent* activity during the base period. Any "R&D" expenses included for the current period *must be added to the base as well.*

If you decide, for example, to include your economics research department because it is really doing R&D, you must grow that expense compared to your average cost of economics work over the past three years. The rules will not let you leverage an increase in economics research on a base of chemical engineering R&D—only on the last three years' work in economics. The Internal Revenue Service can be expected to watch this matter quite closely.

R&D versus Lost Tax Revenue

Finally, throughout the chapter, Professor Mansfield continually juxtaposes the increase in R&D spending against the lost tax revenue resulting from the R&D credit. While he does not say so, and is too good an economist to think so, one is left with the impression that the increase in R&D spending is a measure of the social gains from the credit, while the tax loss is a measure of the social loss.

Obviously, this is not true. The gains can only be measured by estimating the present value of the increase in the performance of the economy resulting from the increased R&D expenditures over time. The costs should be measured as the increase in the cost to society of financing governmental expenditures through another vehicle, such as debt, rather than through the foregone corporate tax revenue.

Comparing the increase in R&D expenditures relative to the lost tax revenue seems to have little economic content and can be misleading.

Why Favor R&D?

This brings us to a basic question that has challenged economists for years: How much should tax policy favor R&D expenditures, versus expenditures on other items?

The only reason R&D expenditures should be given differential treatment relative to other types of expenditures is that the private sector would otherwise underinvest in R&D. The main reason it would do this is because it is difficult to capture all the returns from an R&D investment, or even from the innovation it makes possible. The knowledge often quickly becomes, explicitly or implicitly, part of the public domain. Thus, the innovator is unable to capture the return on his investment.

The size of the problem is large. In earlier work,[3] Professor Mansfield and his colleagues have estimated that the social rate of return was more than twice as high as the private rate of return—56 percent versus 27 percent, across seventeen industrial innovations.

This suggests the country does benefit from increased stimulus of R&D in the private sector. But skeptics will be more readily convinced by tracking the revenue and profitabilty of specific firms who have increased their R&D consistently over at least one full product cycle of time.

Strong Response in High Tech Industry

While it is still early in the life of the R&D tax credit to prove with hard data that it has had the leverage hoped for by its advocates, there is no doubt that in the information industry the response to the credit has been strong.

From 1973 through 1981, IBM's annual increase in R&D averaged about 10 percent—well under its average 15 percent growth in revenue. In 1982, the first full year of the tax credit, IBM's increase in R&D over 1981 exceeded revenue growth by a wide margin—24 percent versus 18 percent.

The annual reports of the company's *U.S.* competitors showed that many of them, including several whose earnings were substantially down from the previous year, did the same thing. In 1983 IBM R&D growth again exceeded revenue growth, and its finance vice president has told securities analysts that this is likely to happen again in some future years.

In short, as is evident in other high tech companies, IBM has overcome a "communications lag" between its financial management and its R&D operations. Financial management has made it clear that there are incentives for increasing R&D, and that the company is now operating in a different environment and is prepared to make additional long-term commitments.

The Case for a Permanent Credit

What is needed now is the certainty that these incentives will be available in the future. The R&D tax credit can be an important element in balancing the tax burden on high tech businesses as compared with other profitable industries. So let us not bury the tax credit idea under a mountain of technical criticism; let us build on it, by making permanent some form of credit that will provide steady support on which companies can count in their long-range planning.

Expansion to Other Elements of R&D

A useful tax credit scheme can, of course, be improved. There is a variety of technical limitations embodied in the original act that deny the logically complete definition of what constitutes R&D expense.

For example, the R&D credit, as originally proposed, applied to all costs properly attributed to R&D activities under standard tax and financial accounting principles. Later, for various reasons, Congress limited the type of costs eligible for the credit to employee wage and salary costs (only to the extent subject to income tax withholding), the costs of supplies, and the costs of leased equipment.

The credit is thus not available for *purchased* equipment, yet the tax act's Accelerated Cost Recovery System does not provide an effective incentive for expenditures on short-lived R&D equipment, compared to other eligible expenses. If purchased equipment is not be credited, then it should at least be treated fairly under the depreciation rules.

New Ventures Need Help Too

Still another requirement of the current tax law that we think should be changed causes R&D expenditures incurred in the start-up phase of a new company or joint venture to be ineligible for the credit.

Currently, only expenses incurred in "carrying on" a trade or business are eligible for the R&D credit—as contrasted with the more liberal "in connection with" trade or business requirement that applies to R&D expenditures for deduction purposes.

Thus, prior to the date a company actually begins to produce products, its R&D expenditures are likely to be treated as start-up or preopening expenses and are not eligible for the R&D credit.

Of course, during the start-up phase, companies by definition do not have taxable income against which to take the credit, but its loss can still affect their tax liability in future years.

Support for University Education and Research

In contrast to these omissions, two very *fine* features of the 1981 tax act encourage industry to share its knowledge and instrumentation with universities, to their mutual benefit.

Numerous arrangements have been made in recent years to increase private industry's support of academic research and education. In the R&D tax credit, Congress sought to encourage these arrangements by allowing companies to include 65 percent of the cost of research contracted out to colleges and universities as a qualified R&D expense. That 65 percent figure was designed to approximate the ratio of wages, supplies, and leased equipment to the total cost.

In addition, another section of the ERTA encourages the donation of research equipment to universities by entitling the firm to a larger tax deduction if certain conditions are met. The gift must be new equipment that is constructed by the firm and given, without strings attached, to an institution of higher education, primarily for research purposes.

It is to be hoped that Professor Mansfield's study reveals the extent to which such cooperation between industry and academia has been fostered by these provisions of the ERTA.

Rhetoric versus Reality

Much of the current conflict over proposals to invest federal funds in R&D activities to support economic performance is a consequence of a serious mismatch between rhetoric and reality. The rhetoric typically promises much more than the reality of federal research support can possibly deliver. The result is inflated expectations, which may lead to disillusionment with the efficacy of science as a source of technology.

The rhetoric also generates opposition by those, such as myself, who do not want to see the federal agencies choosing and conducting R&D programs to develop industrial technology, for we view such activities as anticompetitive, wasteful, and in any case, likely to be a weak contributor to useful industrial capacity.

Excessive claims have been made for the immediacy and magnitude of the benefits from the R&D tax credit, just as excessive claims have been made for the benefit of targeting industries or government financing of specific commercial R&D.

We should not be captured by either of these siren songs, but there is enough evidence that the tax credit is eliciting a response that it ought, at least, to be continued for another period as the Treasury Department has proposed, if not, indeed, made permanent.

Notes

1. National Science Board, *Science Indicators, 1982* (Washington, D.C., 1983, NSB-83-1).

2. The Ad Hoc Electronics Tax Group, *High Technology Tax Policies for the 1980s* (Washington, D.C.: American Electronics Association, Computer and Business Equipment Manufacturers Association, Electronic Industries Association, Scientific Apparatus Makers Association, and Semiconductor Industry Association, 1984).

3. E. Mansfield, J. Rapaport, A. Romeo, E. Villami, S. Wagner, and F. Husic, *The Production and Application of New Industrial Technology* (New York: W. W. Norton & Co., 1977), 157.

Reply to Lewis M. Branscomb
by Edwin Mansfield

Dr. Branscomb's commentary makes a number of points about my chapter. This reply consists of a brief response to each of them.

First, he points out that, in discussing the R&D tax credit, we should bear in mind the disadvantages in alternative policies to promote civilian technology, such as the selection by the government of specific commercial projects for support. The latter approach certainly has great problems. But the sorts of heavy-handed policies Dr. Branscomb warns against are not the only alternatives to the R&D tax credit in its present form. Among other things, experiments might be carried out with forms of tax credits where there is more incentive for firms to increase R&D.

Second, he asks for more specific breakdowns by industry. I sympathize entirely with his view that the results should be broken down as finely as possible. However, when one carries out such a breakdown, the results indicate a striking, but monotonous, uniformity. I accept Dr. Branscomb's statement that in the electronics industry, "the response to the credit has been strong," but there is no evidence of this in our data. Obviously, detailed studies of this industry are needed to tell us more on this score.

Third, he points out that the U.S. data are based only on 1981–83, and that the full impact of the credit may not yet be felt. This is quite possible. However, the Canadian and Swedish tax incentives have been in place for many years, and their effects still seem to be small. Thus, although it certainly is possible that the effects will be greater in the long run, it is by no means obvious that this is the case, particularly since the credit, as it now stands, reduces the price of R&D by a very small percentage.

Fourth, he questions the comparability of the firms in the three countries that are included in the study. Put briefly, the answer is that some of the foreign firms are quite comparable to U.S. firms, and many are not. But the overwhelming fact is that, regardless of the type of firm in the Canadian or Swedish samples, there is no indication that the R&D tax incentives have had much effect. Thus, if one only includes foreign firms that are reasonably comparable with those in the United States, the results are not changed significantly.

Fifth, he points out that the answer one gets in a survey of this sort depends on who responds. This, of course, is absolutely true, and we recognized this when we designed the survey. The people who were contacted were high-level officials, frequently the chief executive officer of the firm. They could reasonably be expected to give sensible answers to the relevant questions. Sometimes they designated a high-level official to obtain and collate relevant information for us; sometimes they provided it themselves. As pointed out in the chapter, a great many of the respondents were not R&D officials. The important point is that, regardless of the type of respondent, the results were much the same.

Sixth, he suggests that it would have been better if we had looked at the impact of the credit since its inception. In fact, we did this. Our econometric work in Canada includes data going all the way back before 1962, when the first R&D tax incentive was introduced. Also, in Sweden, our econometric work extends back beyond the origin of the Swedish R&D tax incentive.

Seventh, he suggests that my chapter should have provided data for firms with profits, taken by themselves. Although there is no reason to exclude unprofitable firms, we have looked at the data for profitable firms only. The results do not indicate that the effect of the credit is large among such firms. For example, in the paper industry, the percentage increase in R&D spending due to the tax credit would be 1.3 percent, rather than 0.7 percent for all firms. In the electrical industry, it would be 0.5 percent, rather than 0.4 percent. In other industries, the pattern is essentially the same.

Eighth, Dr. Branscomb seems to believe that the paper is unduly concerned about the redefinition of activities as R&D. For analysts and policymakers who rely on R&D statistics, such a redefinition certainly can cause problems. Also, in studying the effects of the R&D tax credit, it would be a serious error not to take such redefinition into account.

Ninth, Dr. Branscomb objects to the paper's comparison of the increase in R&D expenditures with the loss in tax revenue. Such comparisons often have been made in the literature on R&D tax credits; people have been interested in how much of the tax expenditure on R&D has been devoted to R&D. However, I certainly did not say or imply that "the increase in R&D spending is a measure of the social gains from the credit, while the tax loss is a measure of the social loss."

Finally, it is important to add that I agree with a great deal of Dr. Branscomb's remarks about science and technology policy. In particular, I am as skeptical as he is of ham-handed government intervention.

10

Exploring Factors Affecting Innovation and Productivity Growth within the Business Unit

Kim B. Clark

Robert H. Hayes

Introduction

Most systematic studies of the impact that competitive rivalry has on management decisions and firm performance are based on aggregate industry data, analyzed within the classic "structure-conduct-performance" framework. That is, various characteristics of an industry's *structure* (such as the number of competitors and the size of the three or four biggest ones) are assumed to create generalized pressure on all firms. This affects their behavior (*conduct*) which, in turn, affects such *performance* measures as their average profitability.

In this chapter, however, we are primarily interested in the micro behavior of individual firms, and how specific managerial decisions are affected by—and alter—their competitive environment. We assume that competitive pressure is more the direct result of moves by specific rivals than the indirect effect of general industry characteristics. Moreover, in contrast with simple economic models that tend to assume that competition can be reduced to cost comparisons, we assume that competition is complex: There is more than one way to compete in most markets, and managers may choose from among a wide array of competitive strategies.[1] One of the implications of thinking about competitive pressure in these terms is that it focuses attention on the dynamics of competition rather than on static (or equilibrium) behavior.

The same kind of dynamic interplay characterizes technological competition. While unpredictable, discontinuous, disruptive technical change has the power to alter dramatically competitive positions and attracts most of the attention, most technical advance is evolutionary in nature:[2] The product and process technologies that underly a given market or industry change over time in roughly predictable patterns. The regularity of these patterns makes it possible to identify particular stages or phases of development and their linkages. What happens in a prior stage conditions and influences subsequent developments, but not in a wholly predictable way, since the process of development involves sequential search and learning.

In other words, history matters. At any point in time, a given firm's competitive position not only reflects the environment it currently faces, but the choices it has made in the past.[3] Among the more critical of these choices are commitments to long-lived assets (that is, investments in people, knowledge, equipment, and so forth) that are relatively irreversible. These choices reflect and shape a firm's enduring characteristics, alter its capabilities, and ultimately determine its competitive success.

Moreover, the determinants of competitive success change over time. Policies that might be effective at one stage of development may have quite different consequences at a subsequent stage. Structural characteristics, like the size of the firm, may also bear a different relationship to competitive success in different stages. As a result, the effects of specific management policies are likely to differ both over time and across industries.

Competitive jockeying over time is complicated further by the fact that it is unlikely that a firm (or a factory) can achieve a superior position, relative to its competitors, simultaneously in all competitive dimensions.[4] This is because the achievement of superiority in a given dimension—for example, delivered cost—requires policies and actions that are likely to be in conflict with the achievement of superiority in other dimensions. The trade-off of particular interest to us is the choice between flexibility and efficiency. Flexibility (the ability to accommodate changes in product or process design quickly and at low cost) can be an important source of competitive advantage when significant changes in products or processes are frequent. But retaining the flexibility to change products often forces one to forego certain actions— such as producing long runs on specialized equipment—that would allow one to lower the cost of any one particular version of the product.

Investigating these three groups of assumptions—regarding competitive dynamics, technical development, and trade-offs in managerial choice—was the motivation for the empirical analysis in this chapter. There are four parts. In the first, we describe a conceptual framework that relates managerial decisions affecting productivity and innovation to the firm's environment. Within this framework, we select certain assumptions about competition, technology, and managerial choice that appear to be testable with empirical data. The first part concludes with a brief discussion of our data set and the variables we use to measure the competitive environment, various management policies, productivity, and innovation.

In the second part we examine the influence on product innovation of managerial policies relating to R&D spending, vertical integration, and capital investment, as well as the effects of competitors, industry structure, and the technical environment. In the third part we present a similar analysis for productivity growth. The chapter concludes with a brief comment on the implications of our findings for practice and for further research.

Analytical Framework: Concepts, Hypotheses, and Data

Our attention is directed primarily at two kinds of questions. The first concerns the impact on a firm's performance of certain investment policies, such as vertical integration, research and development spending, and investment in capital equipment. Second, we are concerned with assessing the influence of its technological and competitive environment. This environment is affected both by the structure of the firm's industry and by various exogenous shocks. In organizing this analysis, we use a conceptual framework that relates both the firm's environment and its management policies to its rate of innovation and its productivity growth.

The environment is assumed to have both a competitive and a technological dimension. Within each, we distinguish between structural characteristics and dynamic changes (what we shall call "driving forces"). Structural characteristics include the number and size distribution of competitors, the maturity of existing technology, and the historical pattern of competitive interaction. The driving forces include the specific actions of competitors, major technological developments, and changes in both the size of the market and in the supply of materials or other inputs. These structural characteristics and driving forces can influence innovation and productivity both directly and, through their effects on management policies, indirectly. Moreover, the effect of a driving force (like technological change) may depend on the structural context in which it occurs. These direct and indirect effects are presented schematically in *Figure 10-1*.

Figure 10-1
Structure, Driving Forces, and Management Policy

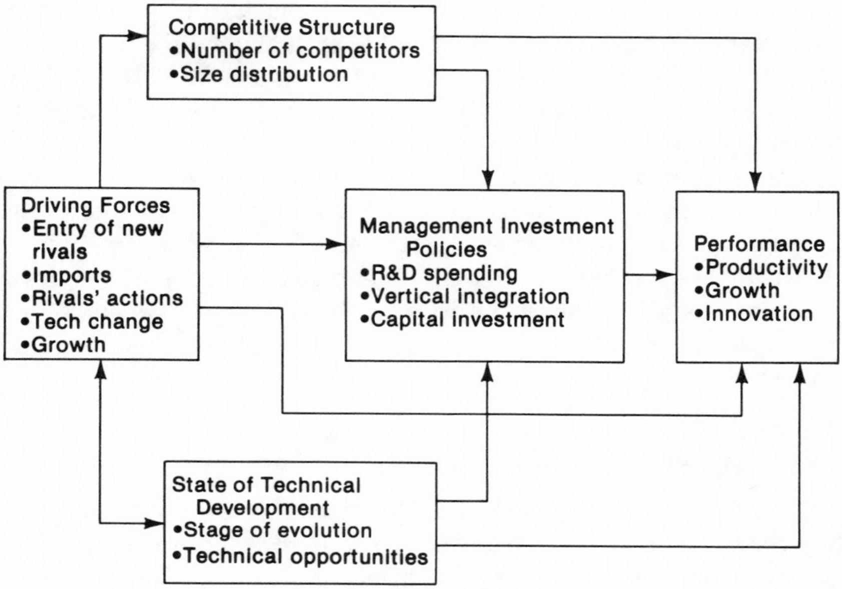

Note: Arrows indicate direction of influence.

Competitive Pressure and Technological Evolution

Using the relationships in *Figure 10-1* as a framework we focus on two hypotheses about the effect of the firm's environment on innovation and productivity growth. The first is that competitive pressure breeds vigorous competitors, and hence will lead to higher levels of new product development and faster productivity growth in most firms. Competitive pressure is affected by industry structure, the entry of new competitors both domestic and foreign, and specific actions (such as new product introductions) by existing rivals. Much of the previous empirical work on innovation and industry structure has focused on differences, across industries, in either inputs (for example, R&D spending) or outputs (for example, patents). By looking directly at such managerially relevant variables as new product introductions and total factor productivity, we hope to provide a somewhat more useful perspective.[5]

Second, our framework allows for the possibility that the intensity of new product introduction and the growth of productivity may vary with the stage of the industry's technological development. Most of the familiar models of industrial and technological evolution assert that the rate of new product introduction is high in the industry's early stages, and then declines over time as designs stabilize.[6] Productivity growth, on the other hand, is expected to peak during the industry's growth phase, as process innovation assumes major significance, and then decline as opportunities for improvement are exhausted. We examine these hypotheses using information on the age of the product. We also examine the impact of major technological discontinuities.

Management Policy

We are also interested in determining if empirical relationships can be observed between product innovativeness or productivity growth and the amount of a company's investment in research and development, new capital equipment, and vertical integration. We are particularly curious as to whether it is possible to identify a group of policies (a "policy regime") that is associated with either high innovation or high productivity, and how the former differs from the latter.

Vertical integration, for example, changes the proportion of a firm's resources that are committed to different stages of its production process and usually increases the ratio of value added to total costs. Increasing the level of integration is often expected to reduce production costs (through better information and coordination of activities, and reduced overhead costs) and/or to increase one's control over key inputs or markets.[7] However, the investments and organizational relationships that yield such advantages may also increase the cost of, and the time required for, responding to new product or process technologies. The decision to vertically integrate may thus entail a trade-off between product cost and the propensity to innovate.

Whereas relatively little empirical evidence exists about the effect of vertical integration on either productivity growth or innovation, the effect of research and development spending has been studied in some detail. Higher levels of R&D investment are generally believed to encourage higher levels of productivity growth and innovation, yet there are many open questions. How do the effects of spending on product R&D differ from spending on process R&D? How is R&D spending affected by the actions of rival firms? Under what circumstances does the development of proprietary technology create an effective source of competitive advantage?

Finally, investment in capital equipment has been the subject of a great deal of research and debate.[8] There is strong evidence that capital investment is an important source of *labor* productivity growth, but the effect of investment on the growth of *total factor* productivity is much less clear cut. While many executives and academics argue that high rates of capital spending are essential to the introduction of the new equipment and techniques that lead to growth in total factor productivity, the empirical evidence on this issue is not conclusive.[9] Nor does much evidence exist on the extent to which capital investment is related to new product development.

The Data Set

The issues we have outlined above deal with the behavior of individual firms within specific industries and therefore cannot be studied very well using the kind of industry level data that is widely available through government agencies. Previous work in this area has focused on a single industry, or a small number of firms. In an effort to explore the complex interrelationships among management policy, competition, and innovation or productivity in a much larger sample of firms, we have chosen to use data developed by the Strategic Planning Institute as part of its ongoing PIMS (Profit Impact of Market Strategies) research program. This data base contains financial, market, and strategic data for over 1,700 business units.

Although we shall refer to the business units as "firms," they are not necessarily independent companies. More often a business unit is a subdivision of a company, usually a product division or product line, that is distinguishable from other parts of the company in terms of customers served, competitors, and resources employed.[10] Our analysis focuses on the performance of over 900 North American manufacturing businesses during the period 1970–1980 (not all of which provided data for each year).

We also sought to test whether the nature of a firm's production process has an effect on the relationships between its environment, its internal policies, and its performance. Abernathy (1978), for example, suggested that the typical life cycle model of technology development (that is, transition from an early, labor-intensive stage to a mature, highly mechanized stage) applies primarily to products that are inherently differentiable. Porter (1980) also has asserted that the degree of product differentiability affects the linkage between changes in product design and changes in the production process. To capture some of these distinctions and test their importance, we divided the firms into two groups, "process" and "fabrication/assembly," based on their four-digit SIC classification.

The first group of firms is in businesses where production involves the transformation of materials from one form to another, usually under heat or pressure. The chemical industry is a prime example. In process companies, products are usually standardized (for example, defined in terms of a type of molecule) and compete in commodity markets; production processes tend to be relatively capital-intensive and automated.

The second group of businesses is much more diverse in the types of markets and customers served, and employs equally diverse manufacturing technologies. "Fabrication/assembly" involves the fabrication of parts using a variety of techniques for forming, shaping, molding, and pressing materials and for combining them into components, subassemblies, and final products. Typical industries in this category include automobiles, household appliances, and machinery. Such businesses have formed the basis for most theoretical and empirical work on technological and industrial evolution.

Table 10-1 presents definitions of the variables we use in our empirical analysis. Most of these variables are straightforward and conventional, but our measures of productivity, product innovation, and different management policies deserve some elaboration. The rate of product innovation is measured by the ratio of the sales of new products (those introduced within the last three years) to total sales. The PIMS data base distinguishes new products from "product line extensions" (defined as additions to the existing range of products that require no major R&D investment and no new technology) and "product improvements" (involving small, incremental changes to the product line). New products, on the other hand, are characterized by one or more of the following: long gestation periods, the need for new manufacturing facilities, separate promotional budgets, and separate product management.

The growth rate of productivity is measured by the rate of growth of real sales (that is, adjusted for changes in selling prices) less a weighted average of the growth rates of three inputs: total employment, purchases, and the gross book value of plant and equipment (the latter two are corrected for inflation; see the chapter's *Appendix* for further details).

The aggressiveness with which the firm pursues new technology is captured by the usual ratio of R&D expenses to total revenue. Our data allow us to distinguish between investment in new products and investment in new processes. We also use dummy variables to indicate whether or not the firm "benefits to a significant degree from patents, trade secrets, or other proprietary methods. . . ."; these reflect the firm's success in developing proprietary product and process technology.

The firm's policy regarding vertical integration can be measured in

Table 10-1
Concepts and Definitions of Basic Variables

	Variable	Definition
Measures of Performance		
NPD	Rate of product innovation	Sales of new products introduced within last three years, as a fraction of total sales
TFP	Rate of growth of total factor productivity	Rate of growth of sales (corrected for inflation) less a weighted average of the growth of employees, materials (corrected for inflation), and gross book value of plant and equipment
Industry and Competitive Characteristics		
N5; N6–10; N11–20	Competitive pressure from the number of competitors	Dummy variables indicating number of competitors (1–5; 6–10; 11–20); equals 1 if firm is in the category; 0 otherwise
IMP	Competitive pressure from foreign competitors	Share of imports in sales of firm's four-digit SIC industry in year business entered sample
ENTER	Competitive pressure from new competitors	Dummy variable equals 1 if firm's market has been entered by a significant competitor (more than 5 percent market share) in last five years; 0 otherwise
MKTGRO	Changes in demand	Rate of growth of firm's market (corrected for inflation)
NPDR	Competitive pressure from rivals' actions	Sales of new products introduced within last three years by three largest competitors as a fraction of total market sales
BIG3	Competitive pressure from major competitors	Market share of three largest competitors

Table 10-1 (*continued*)

Variable	Definition

Characteristics of the Technology

Variable		Definition
TECH	Ferment and change in technology	Dummy variable equals 1 if major technological change has occurred in products or processes in firm's industry
A31–49, 50–59, 60–69, 70	Age of industry	Dummy variables indicating epoch in which product was first introduced using current technology (1931–1949, 1950–1959, 1960–1969, 1970 +); equals 1 if in category; 0 otherwise

Management Policy

RDPRD, RDPRC	Management policy on investment in the development of technology	Expenses for product (PRD) or process (PRC) research and development as a fraction of total sales
PATPRD, PATPRC	Policy on the development of proprietary technology	Dummy variables equals 1 if firm relies to a significant extent on proprietary products (PRD) or processes (PRC); 0 otherwise
VI	Policy on the degree of vertical integration	Ratio of total manufacturing expenses (including distribution) to purchases
ICASH	Policy on reinvestment in capital equipment	New investment in plant and equipment minus after-tax cash flow, as a fraction of sales
%CH NEW	Newness of capital equipment	Percentage change in the ratio of net to gross book value of plant and equipment

several different ways. One common approach is to use the ratio of value added (defined as sales less purchases) to total revenue, but this measure is affected by one's profit margin so may not reflect accurately the relative importance of internal versus external production activities. The measure we use is the ratio of total manufacturing expenses to purchases; the larger that ratio, the greater the value added by the firm and the more vertically integrated it is.[11]

We measure the firm's policy toward capital investment by the ratio of new investment less operating cash flow (profit plus depreciation) to total revenue. A high ratio signals a high propensity to reinvest in the business, while a negative one suggests that the firm is disinvesting.

The average values and standard deviations of the variables we use are presented in *Table A10-1* of the *Appendix*. In the fab/assembly sector they indicate a somewhat higher rate of productivity growth, that imports are more important, and that new products account for a higher share of total sales. However, most of the other variables—such as industry structure, patterns of entry, number of competitors, incidence of major technical changes, and market growth—have similar values in the two sectors. The most distinctive contrasts occur in patents and vertical integration.

The businesses in the process sector rely more heavily on patents, and particularly on proprietary process development. This suggests they place greater emphasis on seeking competitive advantage through process differentiation (possibly the result of the greater product standardization in this sector). The process businesses in our sample are also much less vertically integrated, at least as indicated by the ratio of manufacturing expenses to purchases. This result is consistent with the material-intensive nature of process businesses, but may also suggest that such highly vertically integrated industries as oil and steel are not adequately represented in this sample.

New Product Development

The central issue in this chapter is how managerial policy affects innovation and productivity in different technological and competitive environments. In this section we focus on the variables that most affect the intensity of new product development. We are interested in the role that new products and processes play in competition, whether they represent an aggressive move for differentiation and competitive advantage, or an attempt to protect an existing market position. In either case, the concurrent actions of competitors are of interest.[12]

An important consideration in the firm's decisions about innovation is whether it feels it can obtain a satisfactory return from it. If introducing a new product, undertaking a certain kind of R&D, or obtaining a patent provides information to rivals that allows them to improve their capability to introduce a similar product, then the value of the innovation to the original firm—and the incentive for all firms to innovate—may be diminished. How R&D policy and other aspects of the firm's technical environment are linked to new product development may thus depend on mechanisms that facilitate the transfer of information across firms.[13]

The basic estimating equation we use relates new product intensity (that is, NPD) to variables measuring industry structure, age of the product, certain driving forces of competition and technology, and various management policies.[14] We first examine the factors affecting new product development in both process and fab/assembly firms, looking only at variables that are common to the firm and its competitors. We then estimate the specific effect that competitors' actions have on the firm's new product activity. The full estimation results are presented in *Tables A10-2* and *A10-3* in the *Appendix*; here we focus on a few selected relationships.

Product Development and the Firm's Environment

Table 10-2 examines the relationships between the intensity of a firm's new product development and various characteristics of its environment. In the case of continuous variables, like BIG3 (pressure from major competitors) or IMP (pressure from unfamiliar competitors), the coefficient represents the impact of a shift from a lower to a higher value of the characteristic. In addition to the magnitude of the coefficients, we also have indicated the degree of their statistical significance.

For example, increasing BIG3 (row 1) from 48 percent to 57 percent (that is, a shift of 20 percent, or about one-half of one standard deviation) appears to raise NPDR (the percent of competitors' sales that result from new products) in process industries by 0.6 (= 9 × .066) percentage points. This can be compared with 7.3, the share of sales generated by new product introductions in rival process firms. It is just as likely that the impact of a 1 percent change in BIG3 is greater than .066 than that it is less, and there is less than 1 chance in 200 (0.5 percent likelihood) that it is, in fact, negative.

In the case of dummy variables, such as N5 ("Does the firm have 5 or fewer competitors?"), the coefficient describes the impact of the variable having or not having a given characteristic. Thus, for process firms, the introduction of a major change in technology (TECH going from 0 to 1) has the effect of increasing the new product intensity of rival firms by 9.2 percentage points.

The estimates in *Table 10-2* suggest that the intensity of competitors' new product development is strongly affected by the age of the product, the concentration of the industry, the entry of new competitors, import pressure, and the introduction of a major technical change.

Table 10-2

New Product Development and Environmental Characteristics

Environmental Characteristics	Avg. Values for		New Product Development			
			By Competitors (NPDR)		By the Firm (NPD)	
	Proc.	Fab/A	Proc. (7.3)	Fab/A (9.1)	Proc. (8.8)	Fab/A (10.2)
Competition						
BIG3	48.0	45.5	−.066**	−.057**	.102**	−.067**
N5	.28	.26	−3.15*	[.27]	−3.96*	−2.48#
N6–10	.30	.32	−2.47#	[−.081]	−5.14**	−2.34#
N11–20	.25	.25	[−.49]	[−.74]	−3.22#	−2.88*
IMP	3.7	5.4	.174**	.191**	[.123]	.18**
ENTER	.23	.27	1.87#	3.39**	4.35**	[1.21]
Technology						
TECH	.30	.27	9.20**	4.51**	6.69**	4.10**
A31–49	.42	.40	3.16**	[−.33]	2.99#	[−.50]
A50–59	.21	.19	5.31**	3.69**	6.15**	2.14#
A60–69	.11	.14	4.61**	8.93*	[−.14]	7.73**
A70 +	.01	.01	[.03]	17.8**	[2.12]	14.9**
R^2 (for all variables)			.15	.13	.17	.23

Note: The average value of each dependent variable is in parentheses; the level of statistical significance is indicated by the following notation:
** = Highly significant (level less than 0.5 percent on a one tail test)
 * = Significant (.5–1 percent on a one tail test)
 # = Moderately significant (1–5 percent on a one tail test)
 [] = Insignificant (greater than 5 percent on a one tail test)
Index:
BIG3:   competitive pressure from major competitors
N5–20:   competitive pressure from the number of competitors
IMP: competitive pressure from foreign competitors
ENTER: competitive pressure from new competitors
TECH: ferment and change in technology
A31–70:   age of industry
For full definition of variables, see *Table 10-1*.
Source: Estimated as described in the text; complete estimation results are given in the *Appendix*.

The results for individual firms (right-hand two columns) underscore these relationships between the competitive environment and new product development. Notice that, both for competitors and the firm itself, the sales generated by new products appear to decrease continually as an industry ages in the fab/assembly group, but in the process group the largest values are found among products that emerged in the period 1950–1959.

Therefore, while the fab/assembly group appears to conform to the expectations of the familiar "product life cycle" model, process industries behave quite differently. This may reflect an atypical pattern of technical development, or extraordinary dynamism in the older industries in our sample, but it suggests that one ought to be cautious in assuming that the traditional life cycle pattern characterizes all industries.

The effect of industry structure is mixed. In the process group the competitive pressure exerted by the largest competitors (BIG3) and the entry of new competitors (ENTER) seem to bear a positive relationship to new product activity, but there is no clear pattern governing the relationship between the number of competitors and NPD.[15] In fab/ assembly firms the effect of these kinds of competitive pressure is smaller. And while the coefficients on imports and entry are positive, the market share of the three biggest competitors has a small negative effect. This effect persists even after we took into account the size of the firm; in fact, the coefficient on the firm's own market share was found to have a negative sign.[16] The implication is that the presence of rivals who have strong market positions, together with a large market share for the firm itself, discourages product innovation. Thus, in the fab/ assembly group a high innovation environment appears to be one in which a fragmented industry (low values for BIG3 and one's own market share) is subjected to pressure from imports and new competitors.

New Products and Management Policy

These results suggest that differences in technological activity, in industry structure, and in competitive pressure are linked in a direct way to differences in new product intensity. Moreover, these relationships are quite different for process and fab/assembly industries. *Table 10-3* focuses on the impact of different management policies and highlights the importance of the internal development of product technology. Product R&D spending has a positive coefficient in both groups, though the fab/assembly coefficient is larger. The estimates imply that a move from an average to a moderately high product R&D (for example, from 1.76 percent to 2.76 percent of sales) in fab/assembly businesses is associated with an increase in new product intensity of 2.54 percentage points. This can be compared with the 10.2 percent average value of NPD for these firms and represents about 15 percent of the total range of new product development activity. Although product R&D and new product intensity also have a positive relationship in the process group, product patents seem to have more effect on process firms. There does appear to be a trade-off, however, between devel-

Table 10-3
New Product Development and Management

Management Policy	Avg. Values for		New Product Development by the Firm (avg. values in parentheses)	
	Proc.	Fab/A	Proc. (8.8)	Fab/A (10.2)
RDPRD	1.40	1.76	.70**	2.54**
RDPRC	.53	.53	[−.85]	[−.57]
PATPRD	.24	.20	9.47**	2.02#
PATPRC	.28	.18	−5.00**	1.94#
VI	.64	.96	1.98**	−1.30**
ICASH	−.02	−.03	6.57#	18.5**
R^2 (for all variables)			.17	.23

Note: The level of statistical significance is indicated by the following notation:
** = Highly significant (level less than 0.5 percent on a one tail test)
 * = Significant (.5–1 percent on a one tail test)
 # = Moderately significant (1–5 percent on a one tail test)
[] = Insignificant (greater than 5 percent on a one tail test)
Index:
RDPRD: Expenses for product research and development as a fraction of total sales
RDPRC: Expenses for process research and development as a fraction of total sales
PATPRD: Extent of reliance on proprietary products
PATPRC: Extent of reliance on proprietary processes
VI: Policy on the degree of vertical integration
ICASH: Policy on investment in capital equipment
Source: Estimated as described in the text, complete results are given in the *Appendix*.

oping new products and proprietary processes (as reflected by process patents).

The analysis of the impact of vertical integration provides an interesting contrast between the process and fab/assembly results. In process businesses a high degree of integration appears to be linked to high levels of new product intensity. A possible explanation of this result lies in the nature of the product. In process firms new products are likely to involve new transformations of a given material, or new combinations of materials. The key to developing the new product may thus lie further back in the value-added chain where materials are developed or combined. Process firms with significant investments in the materials end of the business (more integrated) might thus be more likely to develop new products.

Vertical integration has the opposite effect in the fab/assembly group: Higher levels of vertical integration are associated with lower levels of new product development. This result is consistent with the notion that vertical integration requires capital investments and organizational relationships that may reduce the firm's flexibility to respond to certain kinds of changes. The degree of vertical integration may also be a proxy for a more structured, bureaucratic form of organization that inhibits the firm's willingness or ability to develop new products. Moreover, an emphasis on vertical integration may indicate that a firm is seeking to compete primarily through low cost. If so, the lower levels of new product development in highly integrated firms may reflect both bureaucratic rigidity and a desire to avoid the costly disruption to operations that new products are likely to cause.[17]

These findings further emphasize the differences in the process and fab/assembly firms. In fab/assembly firms the management policies that appear to foster a high level of new product development include intensive product R&D investment (but only supporting process R&D) and little vertical integration. Proprietary products (patents) may help but are not critical. Vertical integration appears to be particularly detrimental when technology is not stable and may therefore depend on the stage of industry development.

In process firms, policies that seem to be associated with high product innovation include an emphasis on the development of proprietary products (with supporting process R&D but little investment in proprietary processes) and greater vertical integration than in the fab/assembly group. Finally, older industries that are undergoing major changes in technology seem to benefit from vertical integration.

Technological Spillover and Competitors' Actions

The addition of the NPDR variable (the new product intensity of the three largest competitors) has a dramatic effect on these estimated relationships. Whereas all of the environmental and management policy variables in *Table 10-2* explained 17–23 percent of the variation in new product intensity, adding NDPR explains more than 50 percent (see *Table 10-4*).

This finding is all the more intriguing, and frustrating, because we were almost totally unable to identify the causes of the variation in the values of NPDR that were observed in different industries. There must be additional variables that are important—other than the industry structure variables that economists have traditionally used as a proxy for competitive pressure, and those we use here to measure differences in technological activity and industry maturity.

New product development therefore seems to be heavily influenced by the manner in which an industry has chosen to compete, but this choice is not explicable by the usual economic variables. Moreover,

Table 10-4

New Product Development, Rivalry and Technology: The Impact of
Competitor Activities

Selected Variables	Avg. Values for Proc.	Avg. Values for Fab/A	Proc. without NDPR (8.8)	Proc. with NDPR	Fab/A without NDPR (10.2)	Fab/A with NDPR
			New Product Development by the Firm (avg. values in parentheses)			
TECH	.30	.27	6.69**	−1.36#	4.10**	1.65**
RDPRD	1.4	1.8	.70**	.65**	2.54**	.80**
RDPRC	.53	.53	[−.85]	[−.88]	[−.57]	[.24]
PATPRD	.24	.20	9.47**	3.79**	2.02#	[.52]
PATPRC	.28	.18	−5.0**	[−.32]	−1.94#	[1.09]
NPDR	7.3	9.1	—	.89**	—	.71**
R² (for all variables)			.17	.57	.23	.53

Note: The level of statistical significance is indicated by the following notation:
** = Highly significant (level less than 0.5 percent on a one tail test)
 * = Significant (.5–1 percent on a one tail test)
 # = Moderately significant (1–5 percent on a one tail test)
 [] = Insignificant (greater than 5 percent on a one tail test)
Index:
TECH: Ferment and change in technology
RDPRD: Expenses for product R&D as a fraction of sales
RDPRC: Expenses for process R&D as a fraction of sales
PATPRD: Reliance on proprietary products
PATPRC: Reliance on proprietary processes
NPDR   Competitive pressure from major competitors
For full definition of variables, see *Table 10-1*.
Source: Estimated as described in the text; complete estimation results are given in the *Appendix*.

when the effect of competitors' emphasis on new product development is factored into our analysis, it changes the relationship between a company's own new product activity and the environmental characteristics and managerial policies discussed earlier. The implication is that some part of the impact of such variables as internal product R&D spending (in fab/assembly firms) and patents (process firms) is shared with—and affects the actions of—principal competitors. This effect has been referred to as "technological spillover."

In general, *external* innovations (that is, changes in technology) seem to diffuse more completely in the process group, while the spillover of *internal* developments is more substantial among fab/assembly firms. Thus, the coefficient on TECH (technological ferment) in the process group falls from 6.69 to −1.36, and its statistical significance declines markedly. In the fab/assembly group the effect of competitors' new products is somewhat less dramatic. The estimated effect of a major change in technology is reduced, but a small, statistically significant effect remains.

This is strong evidence that in both groups major changes in technology create opportunities that are widely available throughout the industry. The differences between the groups appear to reflect differences in the mechanisms by which innovations are (or are not) transferred among firms. It may be, for example, that major technological changes in process industries originate outside (for example, through university research, or by equipment or materials suppliers) and are available to all. Licensing might facilitate rapid diffusion, provided competitors are at comparable levels of technical knowledge and sophistication.

Differences in the mechanisms for transferring technology between firms are also apparent in the variables measuring internal technical development, but they seem to be more effective in the fab/assembly group. In the case of product R&D, for example, the introduction of NPDR (competitors' new product sales, as a percent of total sales) reduces the effect of internal R&D investment by a factor of three (from 2.54 to .80); in the process group, the reduction is less than 10 percent. Product patents display a similar impact. Once the actions of competitors are taken into account, therefore, it appears that investing in proprietary products (as measured by the variable PATPRD) has no significant effect in the fab/assembly group. In the process group, however, a quite sizable and statistically significant effect remains, even though adding NPDR cuts it by more than half.

Patents and other kinds of proprietary knowledge thus seem to "spill over" in both groups more than does internal research and development, particularly in fab/assembly firms. Possibly this is due to the fact that the process group in our sample is dominated by chemical firms, whose technological base is more systematic and codified than that of the average fab/assembly firm. This may make it easier to protect proprietary developments through patents and licenses.[18]

In fab/assembly industries, where products tend to be more highly differentiated, knowledge is generally more specialized and therefore less transferable. As a result, firms might be expected to be more likely to gain a competitive advantage from new products that emerge from a major change in technology. Moreover, patents play a less crucial role, and a good part of the knowledge generated through internal R&D is apparently shared (possibly through such practices as "reverse engineering") with rival firms.

This analysis of new product development suggests that certain industry/structural characteristics and driving forces in the firm's environment, as well as its management policies regarding R&D and vertical integration, play an important role in determining the level of new product intensity. To the extent that investing in new product development leads to better products, our results shed some light on the way firms achieve a competitive advantage through product innovation. We now turn to an examination of their pursuit of a competitive advantage through greater production efficiency.

Productivity Growth

Our focus in this section is on the relationship between the growth of a firm's total factor productivity and variables representing its environment and management policies. We define total factor productivity growth (TFP) as the growth rate of output (measured in real terms) less a weighted average of the growth rates of three inputs: the number of employees, the capital stock (plant and equipment), and purchased materials.[19] This difference provides a measure of the rate of improvement in the efficiency with which these inputs are transformed into output.

If competitive pressure affects how aggressively a company pursues opportunities for improved efficiency, then the degree of such pressure should influence the observed growth of productivity. There is a great deal of evidence regarding the effect that competitive pressure has on firm performance; some of the work on the relationship between a firm's market share and its growth and profitability, for example, is consistent with the notion that greater pressure results in higher performance.[20] But there has been little empirical work on the relationship between competitive pressure (including the impact of imports and other new competitors) on total factor productivity.

We were also interested in determining whether there is a relationship between the firm's technical environment and its TFP growth rate. We have already seen that new product introduction seems to be related to the age of the product and to the degree of ferment in the technology. If process improvements are affected in a similar way, we ought to see higher rates of productivity growth in those companies (such as younger ones) whose technology is changing rapidly. This is in contrast to most theoretical models, which assume that new product development is most rapid in the early years of an industry (because flexible production processes are typically employed then), and that high rates of productivity growth only emerge after designs have stabilized and volume begins to expand.

The management policies we examined reflect some of the strategic trade-offs that might be expected to influence TFP growth. Investments in R&D, for example, indicate the firm's commitment to the internal development of new products and processes. If the spillover of this internally developed knowledge to other firms is not too rapid, investment in R&D should create a competitive advantage through higher rates of TFP growth.[21] TFP growth also should be related to the aggressiveness of capital investment, to the extent that new technologies are embodied in new equipment.

In addition to the cash flow variable (ICASH) used earlier we examined the effect of the "newness" of the capital stock (reflected by %CH NEW, the change in the ratio of net to gross book value) on TFP growth. Whereas ICASH reflects a company's commitment to investment, the newness variable reflects changes in the average age of equipment and facilities.

The final management policy, vertical integration, may be linked to productivity growth in one of two ways. First, involvement in a broader span of production may provide operating efficiencies as well as technical information that is not available to less integrated firms. Second, if different segments of the production chain have different potentials for improvement, a company's productivity will be affected by those segments it chooses to perform internally. For example, if the production of a certain component is characterized by lower productivity growth, making (rather than buying) it will lead to a decrease in the firm's TFP growth rate.

These environmental characteristics and management policies are analyzed using the same variables as before, with one exception. To control for the effect of capacity utilization on productivity, we include the percentage change in utilization as an explanatory variable. The full results of our regression relating TFP (adjusted for capacity utilization) to environmental characteristics and management policies are presented in the *Appendix;* selected results are examined in *Tables 10-5* and *10-6.*

Productivity Growth and the Firm's Environment

Table 10-5 indicates strong positive relationships between productivity growth and changes in capacity utilization and market growth; moreover, these relationships are quite similar in both process and fab/assembly firms. This result is not surprising, since such important inputs as capital equipment and skilled labor are difficult to change quickly. Rapid changes in output should therefore produce changes in TFP.

Table 10-5
Productivity Growth and Environmental Characteristics

Environmental Characteristics	Avg. Values for		Productivity Growth	
	Proc.	Fab/A	Proc. (1.29)	Fab. (1.81)
BIG3	48.0	45.5	[−.013]	.042**
N5	.28	.26	−2.01#	−1.50#
N6–10	.30	.32	[.52]	−1.86**
N11–20	.25	.25	[.17]	−1.30#
MKTGRO	4.6	4.7	.29**	.24**
UTIL	2.1	2.9	.17**	.18**
TECH	.30	.27	[.60]	[.43]
R^2 (for all variables)			.307	.256

Note: The level of statistical significance is indicated by the following notation:
** = Highly significant (level less than 0.5 percent on a one tail test)
 * = Significant (.5–1 percent on a one tail test)
 # = Moderately significant (1–5 percent on a one tail test)
[] = Insignificant (greater than 5 percent on a one tail test)
Index:
BIG3: Competitive pressure from major competitors
N5–20: Competitive pressure from the number of competitors
MKTGRO: Demand growth rate
UTIL: Rate of growth of capacity utilization
TECH: Ferment and change in technology
A fuller definition of the variables is made in *Table 10-1*.
Source: Estimated as described in the text; complete estimation results are given in the *Appendix*.

The relationship between TFP and market growth may also be due to a circular causality: High rates of productivity growth permit lower prices which encourage an expansion of the market; this makes possible greater economies of scale which lead to higher TFP. Moreover, if "learning-by-doing" (the so-called "learning curve") is occurring, faster growth should lead to higher levels of TFP growth.[22]

Other aspects of the firm's environment have substantially smaller effects on productivity growth and display much greater differences between the two groups. Unlike our analysis of new product introduction, neither the age of the product nor the incidence of major changes in technology has a significant relationship with TFP growth. The number and size of competitors appears to have little influence in process firms, but does in fab/assembly firms—supporting the notion that TFP growth in such industries is encouraged by competitive pressure. Although the coefficient of BIG3 (the combined market share of the three biggest competitors) may appear small, its potential impact is quite sizable. For example, a difference of 20 points in BIG3 (for

Table 10-6
Productivity Growth and Management Polices

Management Policies	Means		Productivity Growth (means in parentheses)	
	Proc.	Fab.	Proc. (1.29)	Fab. (1.81)
RDPRD	1.61	1.85	.30**	.48**
RDPRC	.54	.56	.85*	[−.03]
PATPRD	.24	.20	−3.74**	[−.96]
PATPRC	.28	.18	[−.65]	[.48]
VI	.64	.96	2.02**	[.47]
%CH NEW	−1.74	−.56	−.11**	−.04#
ICASH	−.027	−.037	−.21**	−.21**
R^2 (for all variables)			.307	.256

Note: The level of statistical significance is indicated by the following notation:
** = Highly significant (level less than 0.5 percent on a one tail test)
 * = Significant (.5–1 percent on a one tail test)
 # = Moderately significant (1–5 percent on a one tail test)
 [] = Insignificant (greater than 5 percent on a one tail test)
Index:
RDPRD: Expenses for product R&D as fraction of sales
RDPRC: Expenses for process R&D as fraction of sales
PATPRD: Reliance on proprietary products
PATPRC: Reliance on proprietary processes
VI: Policy on degree of vertical integration
%CH NEW: Change in age of capital
ICASH: Policy on investment in capital equipment
Source: Estimated as described in the text; complete estimation results are in the *Appendix*.

example, 35 percent versus 55 percent) translates into a difference in TFP growth of about 0.8 (= 20 × .042) points in fab/assembly firms. Over ten years a difference of this magnitude translates into a TFP differential of 8.3 percent.

Perhaps the lack of any observed relationship between competitive pressure and productivity growth among process firms is due to their dependence on equipment embodying certain engineering specifications. When production flows are paced by such equipment, one might expect there would be less scope for methods improvements arising out of worker efforts, knowledge, or skill. In contrast, the positive effect of competitive pressure in fab/assembly industries—where production methods are usually less fully specified, highly engineered, and computerized than those found in the process group—suggests that managers have greater leverage over operating efficiency.

Productivity and Management Policy

The effect of management policies is presented in *Table 10-6* and provides further contrasts between process and fab/assembly firms. Looking first at research and development, we find that product R&D is important in both groups,[23] but process R&D appears to be important only in the process group (remember that the effect of product R&D is estimated while holding constant the level of process R&D, and vice versa).[24]

When product development efforts are directed toward reducing the number of components in a product, increasing the use of standardized parts, or pruning the number of processing steps, the link with productivity growth is clear. What is more intriguing is the indication that some kinds of product development actually appear to *reduce* productivity growth. An emphasis on proprietary products is associated with lower TFP growth in both groups, for example, although the effect is far more significant among process firms. High numbers of product patents may indicate that the firm has chosen to compete in other ways than product cost—and against competitors that exert less pressure to reduce costs. Alternatively, if proprietary product development is associated with frequent product changes, production efficiency may be reduced by the resulting confusion and instability. Moreover, such companies may consciously employ production technologies that permit greater flexibility—in that they are smaller and less dedicated to any specific version of the product—but are inherently less conducive to improvements in efficiency.

Table 10-6 therefore suggests that one ought to be cautious about applying the results of aggregate studies to specific firms. Although R&D (particularly product R&D) can have an important influence on a firm's TFP growth, its level and mix (product versus process) should be tailored to its production technology and competitive strategy. Similarly, the level of vertical integration has no significant influence on TFP growth among fab/assembly firms but does have a positive and significant effect in the process group. In the materials-dependent process industries, integration may improve access to information or create synergies that are not available to less integrated competitors. These results are therefore consistent with our earlier analysis of product development.

Whereas the effect of vertical integration appears to depend on the nature of the firm's production technology, the same is not true of its capital investment policies. In both groups, no matter how the data are analyzed, the coefficients on ICASH (capital investment policy) and

%CH NEW (the equipment newness variable) are negative. These effects are larger and more statistically signficant in the process group, which may reflect the fact that process firms are more capital intensive and machine driven. These negative signs are troublesome, however; interpreted literally they imply that newer capital is less productive, and that firms that aggressively invest in capital equipment experience lower TFP growth.

Part of this result may be due to the fact that inflation in plant and equipment prices can cause the newness variable to overstate the rate of increase of new capital, leading to a downward bias in the estimated coefficient. Clark and Griliches have shown, however, that while correcting for inflation does reduce this negative effect it does not eliminate it.[25] Measurement problems of this kind appear to explain about one-third of the estimated negative impact of newness. About half of the estimated effect of ICASH reported in *Table 10-6* is probably spurious as well.[26]

The remaining negative effects of equipment newness and high rates of investment may be due to the fact that introducing new equipment causes confusion and problems of "digestion." New capital equipment, particularly equipment that advances the state of the art, is likely to require changes in operating procedures, personnel skills, job assignments, material flows, and control systems.[27] Confusion increases as mistakes are made, adjustments taken, and alternate approaches developed. Such changes require time and effort, and the resources so expended do not add much to current output. For these and perhaps other reasons, the expected returns from our firms' investments in capital equipment are not visible through our measure of total factor productivity growth.

Specifying Policy Regimes That Encourage High Productivity Growth

In process firms, as we have seen, high productivity growth seems to be encouraged by high levels of spending on product and process R&D. This investment is focused on refinements and improvements rather than on major breakthroughs, and proprietary product development is not emphasized. A high degree of vertical integration is helpful. The most productive process firms are clearly those whose processes are fully "debugged," and whose capital investments have been "digested." To get there, of course, at some point one has had to assimilate new equipment. Since this reduces productivity growth, managing its introduction effectively is critical.

In the fab/assembly group, high productivity is associated with similar R&D policies, but vertical integration and capital investment appear to have different effects. As before, product R&D plays a more dominant role, and it again emphasizes product refinements. Vertical integration is only weakly related to productivity, although there is some evidence that higher levels of integration are linked to higher productivity growth in younger industries. Fab/assembly firms are not as capital dependent, so although the coefficients representing the effect of capital investment and the newness of equipment are again negative, their impact is much smaller. Like its process counterpart, a high productivity fab/assembly firm has a "debugged" process and manages new equipment introductions well. It is less affected by its capital investment policies, however.

Summary and Implications

We began this chapter with a set of loosely defined assumptions about how innovation and productivity are linked to competitive pressure, technological evolution, and various managerial policies. The empirical evidence has confirmed the general importance of these issues but has suggested a number of distinctions and refinements. We have found that dividing the sample into process and fab/assembly subgroups increases the explanatory power of our variables and illuminates a number of relationships that might otherwise be obscured. Although they sometimes displayed similar relationships, the impact of industry structure, technological spillover within the industry, product maturity, and vertical integration all appear to have quite different effects in the two groups. This is important to emphasize, because much of the conventional wisdom about industry evolution (as well as "good management practices") seems to reflect experience in fab/assembly businesses. A better understanding of the interaction between technology and competition in process industries therefore appears to be an important and fruitful area for future research.

The analysis of the relationship between product development and productivity growth has suggested a number of directions that future research (particularly in connection with fab/assembly firms) might take. One of the more important issues uncovered in our analysis was the effect of competitive pressure on product development. We found that, while certain measures of industry structure appear to affect innovation, the most powerful influence on a firm's new product activity was the way its competitors chose to compete. The fact that we can explain so little of these rivals' behavior, using conventional variables, makes this result all the more intriguing.

Competitive pressure also appears to play a small role in TFP growth among fab/assembly firms, but it has a much greater impact on new product introduction than on productivity growth. Market expansion, on the other hand, appears to have a strong effect on productivity growth. Further analysis of this relationship, as well as that between competitive rivalry and new product development, will require data that allow one to untangle cause-effect relationships.

Technological maturity also appears to have a stronger effect on new product innovation than on productivity growth. The measure we have used—the age of the product—captures the evolutionary stages of development in only a very rough way; nonetheless we have found some relatively strong evidence that the rate of new product introduction varies across those stages. That variation, however, follows the predictions of conventional models only in the fab/assembly group; in process firms the "middle-aged" products appear to be the more innovative. This finding deserves further analysis.

Technological "shocks" also seem to have a significant influence on product development but not on TFP growth. In fact, we found no evidence that TFP growth varies across stages of development, nor any significant differences between technologically stable and unstable environments. We did discover, however, that management policy was linked to productivity growth differently in process firms than in fab/assembly firms, and varied according to the age of the industry.

A comparison of *Tables 10-3* and *10-6* shows that some management policies pose no trade-off at all. For example, the firm does not have to choose between productivity growth and new products when deciding on the level of R&D spending: Both are positively linked to product R&D. The same is true for vertical integration decisions among process firms: The sign of the coefficient on TFP is the same as that on NPD.

Trade-offs are apparent, however, in decisions concerning the development of proprietary technology (as reflected in product patents) in process firms. This suggests that the kinds of capabilities required for proprietary products are different from those associated with less innovative products. A similar trade-off between cost and flexibility is apparent in capital investment policies. In both groups, firms that pursue a high rate of new product innovation support it with aggressive capital investment. This appears to create problems of "digestion"—and lower TFP growth, at least initially.

Our findings therefore support the notion that a firm in a given business cannot be all things to all customers. Choosing a competitive strategy that emphasizes product development (particularly with proprietary technology) is likely to require managerial policies that limit the firm's effectiveness in reducing cost. Other policies, like vertical integration, appear to encourage both new products and TFP growth in process firms but require trade-offs in fab/assembly firms. A more precise understanding of the technical and organizational factors affecting these trade-offs is required before we have a sufficient basis for prescribing appropriate management actions.

Notes

1. In the context of decisions about technology and production a clear statement of this idea can be found in the work of Skinner. Modern work in the economic theory of markets and competition has moved beyond the simple model to examine a range of issues connected with product characteristics and product differentiation. Papers by Spence on monopolistic competition were instrumental in this respect. See also the work of Lancaster.

2. The evolutionary nature of technical advance is a notion with a long history. The idea is closely related to Kuhn's conception of "normal" science. A more recent discussion of technological evolution can be found in Abernathy and Utterback. See also the work of Nelson and Winter, and Klein for a discussion of evolutionary economic models.

3. Kreps and Spence (1983) have recently examined the role of history in formal economic models.

4. The importance of trade-offs and their implications for manufacturing decisions is examined in Skinner's work on focus. Abernathy has examined the same issue in the context of industry evolution.

5. A survey of the literature on market structure and innovation is available in Kamien and Schwartz. As far as innovation is concerned the literature on rivalry has tended to focus on the "race to patent" phenomenon, and that work is largely theoretical. Economic analysis of productivity growth usually assumes cost minimization and full utilization of capability, and thus no scope for the competitive environment to make a difference.

6. This is clear in the Abernathy-Utterback model, and it is central to the product life cycle literature. The work of Nelson and Winter on evolutionary economic models provides a theoretical foundation for "product cycle" and "technology cycle" phenomena. See especially chapter 12.

7. The strategic issues in vertical integration decisions have been discussed in Porter (1980). See also chapter 9, "Vertical Integration and Sourcing," in Hayes and Wheelwright, and the paper by Harrigan. Buzzell has examined the link between integration and profitability.

8. There is little argument that capital plays some role in labor productivity growth, the question is how much. Further, there is controversy in the literature over definitions and measurement. See Jorgenson and Griliches, and Dennison, for a classic debate on this issue.

9. Nor do we understand well the impact on productivity growth of the embodiment of knowledge in capital equipment. See the paper by You for an empirical analysis of U.S. data.

10. The definition of a business in the PIMS data set is based on the notion of a "strategic business unit." This concept is spelled out in Abell and Hammond. The PIMS data has been widely used in studies of competition and marketing strategy and has been recently used in economic analysis of R&D and productivity growth. It provides a richness of information, but there are problems with its use. The units of observation are not representative, and the boundaries of the unit are defined by the firm itself. Further, some of the variables

(particularly the price indexes used in the productivity analysis) are likely to be measured with error. For a fuller discussion of the data set and some of its problems, see Clark and Griliches, and Clark (1984). After a careful examination of most of these problems, it is our view that they do not destroy the usefulness of the data. It is important, however, to keep in mind their limitations.

11. What we are after is a measure that captures relative commitments and involvement that firms have in different stages of the production chain. A potentially interesting measure would be the ratio of the capital stock inside the firm to that in suppliers. That information is not available, and the manufacturing to purchases ratio seemed less affected by data problems, even though it may be affected by changes in wage rates or prices rather than by changes in integration. However, in work not reported here we have estimated regressions using dummy variables for two-digit industries so that the industry level effects of wage and raw material price movements were held constant in estimating the effect of vertical integration. We found little difference in the estimates.

12. We assume that rivals are not identical. Most theoretical work in economics assumes identical rivals so that analysis can proceed in terms of symmetric equilibria. The theoretical analysis of asymmetric equilibria is far more complicated.

13. Such "spillover" has been the subject of theoretical analysis by Spence (1982), and Kreps and Spence (1983b). See also Levin and Reiss for a simple model that focuses on appropriability.

14. In the work reported here we have treated each firm-year combination as a separate observation. This ignores a possible firm component in the error term and means that the standard errors we estimate are likely to be understated. Because the design of our sample is unbalanced, the usual generalized least squares solutions to this problem are not available and the alternatives are computationally burdensome. Because of this problem we shall focus our attention on interpreting those results that are so powerful as to be little affected by this sort of adjustment.

15. It should be noted that we found no evidence of a quadratic relationship between BIG3 and NPD. This is in contrast to some of the economics literature where the relationship between concentration ratios and R&D spending is sometimes found to be quadratic (that is, either too much or too little concentration is bad for innovation). See Kamien and Schwartz for a discussion of that work. It is also of interest to note that the effect of the number of competitors seems to be consistent with the predictions of the theory of monopolistic competition, since a larger number of firms is associated with more product diversity.

16. The coefficient of the market share term was − .16 with a standard error of .023. Note that the market share variable was defined as market share at the beginning of the sample period and was not allowed to vary for any given firm over the period.

17. The effect of vertical integration on new product development varies between different subsamples of the process and fab/assembly firms. The negative effect among fab/assembly firms is largely due to younger products whose technology is changing rapidly. Vertical integration seems to have little effect, on the other hand, in situations where products are mature and the technology stable. Finally, the positive effect of vertical integration in the process group is largely due to older products' undergoing technological turmoil; where technology is stable the vertical integration variable actually appears to be slightly negatively related to new product activity.

18. Stobaugh's work on innovation in petrochemicals suggests that patents play a significant role in both product and process development.

19. See the *Appendix* for information on the definitions and method of calculating TFP. Although analysts often study the productivity of one factor of production—for example, labor—we have chosen to look at the productivity of all inputs.

20. See Shepherd for an example of empirical evidence on market share and profits that seems to imply a connection between competitive pressure and efficiency. An example of the case evidence is provided by Hayes.

21. It is traditional in the economics literature to treat R&D spending as investment that adds to the stock of knowledge. Under appropriate assumptions about the depreciation of that stock, and about competition in product and factor markets, the coefficient on the R&D-to-sales ratio in a TFP equation can be interpreted as a rate of return to R&D investment. See Griliches (1979) for a development of the theory underlying that interpretation.

22. There is little justification in traditional neoclassical economics for assuming that market expansion leads to higher rates of TFP growth. Theoretical and empirical work outside that tradition, however, suggests that the relationship is not only plausible, but quite important and pervasive. See Amsden.

23. Interpreted as rates of return, the coefficients on the R&D variables imply returns to product R&D investment of about 30 percent in the process group, and about 48 percent in the fab/assembly group.

24. In many cases it may be difficult to separate spending into "product" or "process" categories. If, when faced with that problem, the firm puts R&D spending into the product category, the product R&D data may contain a good bit of process R&D spending. This measurement problem underscores the close connection between product and process development.

25. The correction was based on the firm's reported ratio of replacement value to gross book value. See Clark and Griliches for details.

26. In the case of ICASH, a change in the capital stock appears on both sides of the estimated equation (with opposite signs), which creates the possibility of a spurious correlation. To control for this effect, we reestimated the TFP equation using labor productivity growth as the dependent variable (and the growth in the capital-labor and materials-labor ratios as independent variables). This reduced the effect of capital investment policy by 50 percent.

27. See the chapter by Hayes and Clark in Part Two of this volume for supporting evidence.

References

Abernathy, W. J., K. B. Clark, and A. M. Kantrow. *Industrial Renaissance: Producing a Competitive Future for America.* New York: Basic Books, 1983.

Abernathy, W. J. *The Productivity Dilemma: Roadblock to Innovation in the Automobile Industry.* Baltimore: Johns Hopkins University Press, 1978.

Abernathy, W. J., and J. M. Utterback. "Patterns of Industrial Innovation." *Technology Review,* June–July 1978, 40–47.

Abell, D. F., and J. S. Hammond. *Strategic Market Planning: Problems and Analytical Approaches.* Englewood Cliffs, N.J.: Prentice Hall, 1979.

Amsden, A. H. "The Division of Labor is Limited by the Rate of Growth of Market: Machine Tool Building in a Newly Industrializing Country." Harvard Business School Working Paper No. 9-784-051, 1984.

Buzzell, R. D. "Is Vertical Integration Profitable?" *Harvard Business Review,* January-February 1983, 92–102.

Clark, K. B. "Competition, Technical Diversity and Radical Innovation in the U.S. Auto Industry." In *Research on Technological Innovation, Management and Policy,* edited by R. Rosenbloom, vol. 1. London: Jai Press, Inc., 1983.

———. "Unionization and Firm Performance: The Impact on Profits, Growth, and Productivity." *American Economic Review* 74 (December 1984): 893–919.

Clark, K. B. and Z. Griliches. "Productivity Growth and R&D at the Business Level: Results from the PIMS Data Base." In *R&D, Patents and Productivity,* edited by Z. Griliches. Chicago: University of Chicago Press, 1984.

Dennison, E. F. "The Measurement of Productivity." *The Survey of Current Business* 52, pt. 2 (May 1972): 1–111.

Griliches, Z. "Issues in Assessing the Contribution of Research and Development to Economic Growth." *The Bell Journal of Economics* 10, no. 1 (Spring 1979): 92–116.

Harrigan, K. R. *Strategies for Vertical Integration.* Lexington, Mass.: Lexington Books, 1983.

Hayes, R. H., and S. W. Wheelwright. *Restoring Our Competitive Edge: Competing Through Manufacturing.* New York: John Wiliey and Sons, 1984.

Hayes, R. H. "Simpson Pump and Valve." Harvard Business School Case No. 9-683-061.

Jorgenson, D. W., and Z. Griliches. "The Explanation of Productivity Change." *Review of Economic Studies* 34 (July 1967): 249–83.

Kamien, M. I., and N. L. Schwartz. *Market Structure and Innovation.* Cambridge: Cambridge University Press, 1982.

Kendrick, J. W., and E. Grossman. *Productivity in the United States: Trends and Cycles.* Baltimore: Johns Hopkins University Press, 1980.

Klein, B. *Dynamic Economics.* Cambridge: Harvard University Press, 1977.

Kreps, D. M. and A. M. Spence. "Modeling the Role of History in Industrial Organization and Competition." Harvard Institute of Economic Research Discussion Paper No. 992, July 1983.

———. "Models of Spillovers in R&D." Unpublished paper, 1983.

Kuhn, T. S. *The Structure of Scientific Revolutions.* 2d ed. Chicago: University of Chicago Press, 1970.

Lancaster, K. "Competition and Product Variety." *Journal of Business* 53, no. 3 (1980): S79–S89.

Levin, R., and P. Reiss. "Tests of Schumpeterian Model of R&D and Market Structure." In *R&D, Patents and Productivity,* edited by Z. Griliches. Chicago: University of Chicago Press, 1984.

Nelson, R. and S. Winter. *An Evolutionary Theory of Economic Change.* Cambridge: Harvard University Press, 1982.

Norsworthy, J. R., M. J. Harper, and K. Kunze. "The Slowdown in Productivity Growth: An Analysis of Some Contributing Factors." *Brookings Papers on Economic Activity* 2 (1979): 387–421.

Porter, M. E. *Competitive Strategy: Techniques for Analyzing Industries and Competitors.* New York: The Free Press, 1980.

———. "The Technological Dimension of Competitive Strategy." In *Research on Technological Innovation Management and Policy,* edited by R. S. Rosenbloom, vol. 1. London: Jai Press, Inc., 1983.

Shepherd, W. G. "The Elements of Market Structure." *Review of Economics and Statistics* 54 (February 1972): 25–36.

Skinner, W. *Manufacturing in the Corporate Strategy.* New York: John Wiley and Sons, 1978.

Spence, A. M. "Product Selection, Fixed Costs, and Monopolistic Competition." *Review of Economic Studies,* 43 (June 1976): 217–35.

———. "Cost Reduction, Competition and Industry Performance." Harvard Business School Working Paper 82-65.

Stobaugh, R. "Creating a Monopoly." Harvard Business School Working Paper 84-21, 1984.

Strategic Planning Institute. *PIMS Data Manual.* Cambridge: Strategic Planning Institute, 1978.

You, J. K. "Embodied and Disembodied Technical Progress in the United States, 1929–1968." *Review of Economies and Statistics* 58 (February 1976): 123–27.

Appendix

Productivity Definitions and Basic Results

Conceptually, our measure of productivity growth is designed to reflect changes in the efficiency with which the firm uses three inputs—labor, capital, and materials—to produce output. To measure the growth of efficiency defined in this way we compare the growth of output to the growth of a weighted average of the inputs. The weights are chosen to reflect the relative importance of the inputs in the total cost of production. The following variables are found in the PIMS data base and reflect the rates of change (for each firm i) in:

$$\begin{aligned}
s_i &= \text{nominal sales} \\
p_i &= \text{selling price deflator} \\
k_i &= \text{gross plant and equipment, in 1972 dollars} \\
m_i &= \text{purchased materials} \\
pm_i &= \text{materials price deflator} \\
e_i &= \text{number of employees.}
\end{aligned}$$

We then define total factor productivity growth (TFP in the text) as:

$$TFP_i = (s_i - p_i) - a_m(m_i - pm_i) - a_k k_i - (1 - a_m - a_k)e_i$$

In this formulation, a_m and a_k are the shares of materials and capital in total revenue, averaged over the sample period. Because we have no data on the wage bill, we have had to assume constant returns to scale in order to use $(1 - a_m - a_k)$ as the weight for employment growth. Further detail on this calculation is contained in Clark and Griliches.

Basic Results

Means and standard deviations of the basic variables are presented in *Table A10-1. Tables A10-2* through *A10-4* present the basic regressions.

Table A10-1
Means and Standard Deviations of Basic Variables

Variable	Process		Fab/Assembly	
	Mean	Std. Dev.	Mean	Std. Dev.
NPD	8.773	18.01	10.18	18.96
TFP	1.294	14.27	1.808	13.66
BIG3	47.96	17.78	45.54	18.23
N5	.282	—	.260	—
N6–10	.304	—	.318	—
N11–20	.245	—	.252	—
IMP	3.66	6.64	5.42	7.14
ENTER	.232	—	.270	—
MKTGRO	4.62	15.27	4.67	16.82
NPDR	7.29	14.30	9.06	16.86
TECH	.295	—	.267	—
A31–49	.472	—	.402	—
A50–59	.211	—	.188	—
A60–69	.112	—	.137	—
A70+	.013	—	.013	—
RDPRD	1.400	2.32	1.755	2.22
RDPRC	.538	.94	.538	.876
PATPRD	.236	—	.199	—
PATPRC	.280	—	.177	—
VI	.643	.597	.959	.747
ICASH	−.021	.178	−.030	.095
%CH NEW	−1.73	12.7	−0.56	13.1

Source: Calculated from the PIMS data base.

Table A10-2
Basic New Product Development Regressions

Independent Variables	By Competitors (NPDR)		By the Firm (NPD)	
	Process (1)	Fab/Assembly (2)	Process (3)	Fab/Assembly (4)
IMP	.174	.191	.123	.182
	(.059)	(.043)	(.075)	(.046)
% UNION	—	—	.037	−.028
	—	—	(.017)	(.010)
BIG3	.066	−.057	.102	−.067
	(.024)	(.018)	(.031)	(.020)
MKT GRO	.054	.106	.044	.053
	(.025)	(.019)	(.032)	(.020)
YEAR	−.459	−.538	−.530	−.747
	(.187)	(.142)	(.240)	(.153)
PATPRD	—	—	9.470	2.020
	—	—	(1.321)	(0.914)
PATPRC	—	—	−4.997	−1.938
	—	—	(1.230)	(.959)
VI	—	—	1.983	−1.300
	—	—	(.846)	(0.448)
RDPRD	—	—	.701	2.541
	—	—	(.240)	(0.164)
RDPRC	—	—	−.847	−.569
	—	—	(.582)	(.385)
TECH	9.196	4.510	6.694	4.065
	(0.919)	(0.709)	(1.180)	(0.773)
ENTER	1.869	3.393	4.349	1.205
	(.932)	(0.722)	(1.190)	(.767)
N5	−3.147	0.265	−3.955	−2.478
	(1.313)	(1.039)	(1.656)	(1.115)
N6−10	−2.472	−.807	−5.136	−2.337
	(1.279)	(.993)	(1.623)	(1.060)
N11−20	−0.487	−.742	−3.226	−2.883
	(1.271)	(.986)	(1.604)	(1.050)
A31−49	3.155	−.330	2.985	−.500
	(1.106)	(.793)	(1.399)	(.846)
A50−59	5.31	3.69	6.15	2.14
	(1.30)	(.95)	(1.71)	(1.04)
A60−69	4.608	8.928	−.136	7.729
	(1.549)	(1.071)	(2.026)	(1.195)
A70+	0.031	17.79	2.122	14.85
	(2.544)	(2.76)	(4.464)	(2.97)
ICASH	—	—	6.570	18.46
	—	—	(2.753)	(3.51)
SEE	13.2	15.7	16.4	16.6
R^2	.15	.13	.17	.23
d.f	1,195	2,661	1,188	2,654

Table A10-3
New Product Development Regressions Controlling for NPDR

Independent Variables	Process	Fab/Assembly
IMP	−.086	.095
	(.054)	(.036)
% UNION	−.001	.006
	(.012)	(.008)
BIG3	.049	−.033
	(.022)	(.015)
MKTGRO	−.011	−.014
	(.023)	(.015)
YEAR	−.350	−.366
	(.173)	(.120)
PATPRD	3.79	.524
	(0.97)	(.714)
PATPRC	−.320	1.088
	(.933)	(0.751)
VI	−.505	−1.249
	(.614)	(0.349)
RD PRD	.652	.796
	(.173)	(.135)
RD PRC	−.883	.239
	(−.419)	(.302)
NPDR	.891	.711
	(.027)	(.017)
TECH	−1.361	1.652
	(0.88)	(0.605)
ENTER	3.133	−.648
	(0.858)	(.600)
N5	−1.297	−1.579
	(1.195)	(.870)
NG−10	−2.249	−.845
	(1.173)	(.827)
N11−20	−2.850	−1.971
	(1.155)	(.819)
A31−49	−0.265	.602
	(1.013)	(.660)
A50−59	0.873	.832
	(1.243)	(.807)
A60−69	−3.097	4.567
	(1.462)	(.935)
A70+	2.235	5.385
	(3.216)	(2.331)
ICASH	.046	.217
	(.020)	(.027)
SEE	11.81	12.95
R^2	.570	.533
d.f.	1,137	2,653

Table A10-4
Basic TFP Regressions

Independent	Process	Fab/Assembly
IMP	.030	.021
	(.054)	(.033)
% UNION	.037	.015
	(.012)	(.007)
BIG3	−.013	.042
	(.022)	(.014)
MKTGRO	.294	.244
	(.025)	(.015)
YEAR	−.294	−.044
	(.175)	(.108)
PATPRD	−3.741	−.957
	(.950)	(.648)
PATPRC	−.654	.482
	(.928)	(.681)
VI	2.023	.474
	(.616)	(.315)
TECH	.599	.427
	(.856)	(.548)
ENTER	−.323	−.506
	(.865)	(.544)
N5	−2.008	−1.502
	(1.202)	(0.789)
N6−10	0.515	−1.859
	(1.173)	(.750)
N11−20	0.167	−1.299
	(1.164)	(.745)
A31−49	0.588	.003
	(1.015)	(.598)
A50−59	0.230	.157
	(1.234)	(.729)
A60−69	0.952	.483
	(1.481)	(.841)
A70+	−3.018	2.370
	(3.237)	(2.132)
ICASH	−.21	−.21
	(.02)	(.03)
%CH NEW	−.105	−.035
	(.028)	(.018)
UTIL	.171	.18
	(.024)	(.01)
RDPRD	.300	.48
	(.083)	(.08)
RDPRC	.845	−.03
	(.363)	(.21)
SEE	11.9	11.8
R^2	.307	.256
d.f.	1,186	2,652

Part Three
Discussion Summary

The discussion of the chapters in this section, marked by a series of heated exchanges between participants, returned to many of the issues that were highlighted in the Overview.

Fostering "Extraordinary" Innovation

Underlying the debate on Rosenbloom's chapter about "extraordinary" innovations were two themes drawn from the historical studies of Rosenberg and Chandler, reported in Part One of this volume: the close relationship of product and process innovation, and the fact that innovations—even major ones—frequently do not flow directly from scientific research. As Dr. Lewis Branscomb (vice president and chief scientist, IBM) put it: "We find our engineers dragging our scientists into the future."

In discussing the role of corporate research and development laboratories, Branscomb reported that, unlike certain other companies (including General Electric—see the commentary by Roland Schmitt in this section), the mission of IBM's lab was not confined to producing extraordinary innovations (or "filling a corporate gap left by the rest of the organization," as one executive put it). Instead, its role was to "define the limits of critical technologies."

"The people with a revolutionary view of new products and processes are very often in the line organization," said Branscomb. He was supported by Gordon Forward (president and CEO, Chaparral Steel), who argued that it was vital that technological innovation come from all parts of an organization, not just from R&D.

Schmitt asserted, however, that GE's corporate labs were very effective at generating highly profitable innovations. Moreover, they tended to earn a higher return than GE's corporate average. But Robert Hayes (professor, Harvard Business School) pointed out that in other companies the growing distance (both physical and organizational) between corporate labs and the rest of the organization was *increasingly being recognized as unproductive: "Today, many companies are trying to figure out ways to bridge that gap."*

In line with his chapter, Ikujiro Nonaka (professor, Hitotsubashi University) argued that it was possible for large corporations to produce extraordinary innovations. Such innovations *"are not necessarily highly individualistic, as some people claim,"* he stated. Corporate cultures could (and should) be able to tolerate ambiguity for extended periods before deciding on a particular course of action. 3M's much-admired culture and organization, for example, combined *"chaos"* with rigid reward structures and other aspects of *"tightness."*

In particular, Nonaka praised 3M's system of allowing R&D staff to spend 15 percent of their time as they liked. While Schmitt claimed that applying the same rigid formula uniformly to everyone could be a *"disaster,"* Edward Roberts (professor, MIT Sloan School) said this depended on the extent of the corporation's *"underlying desire to innovate. . . . In noninnovative companies the technical staff doesn't productively spend that time even if they have it available."* In support of Nonaka, Branscomb reported that one of 3M's most successful new products of recent years, its *"Post-it"* adhesive notepads, had originated as a *"15 percent free"* project. The connection between an available technology and a potential market had been made by a researcher who used some left-over adhesive to create sticky placemarks for the hymn book he used in his church choir. 3M's approach also demonstrated the value of multiple sources of innovation within a company, suggested Branscomb.

Accelerating "Ordinary" Innovation

Achieving a better balance between the commercial and technical sides of a company was necessary if U.S. firms were to emulate the Japanese success in accelerating product development, observed Geoffrey Place (vice president, research and development, Procter & Gamble). In his opinion, U.S. corporate structures had grown very rigid in this respect and needed to become more flexible. He also emphasized the importance of the *"thinking-through"* process which a company went through before taking action. In some situations, argued Place, this prior analysis and planning took too long, while in others the lack of adequate preparation seriously prolonged implementation.

The chapter by Imai, Nonaka, and Takeuchi on Japanese new product development does not deal with this key issue, he pointed out, since all the studied companies knew their objectives from the very start. (Imai conceded, however, that on several of the sample projects, the *prior consensus-making process was more extensive than may have been suggested in their chapter).*

The Japanese chapter was also qualified by participants on other grounds. Underlining one aspect of the commentary by Hewlett-Packard's John Doyle, several participants pointed out that all the five cited development programs were "hero projects," in that they were not only successful but were unusually crucial to their companies. Hence the lessons drawn by the researchers might not be generally applicable to more normal development projects. Nor did they necessarily apply to the processes of radical innovation addressed in Rosenbloom's chapter.

Stressing that most technological development in Japan has—at least until now—been incremental, Imai replied that his findings were applicable to most of Japanese industry (although the section dealing with supplier networks applied only to fabrication-assembly companies, not to process firms). Many participants echoed Doyle's remarks about the lack of a similarly supporting network of innovative vendors in the United States. Although there are signs that a network of this sort may be developing in the auto industry, James Bakken (vice president, operations support at Ford) confirmed that such arrangements were quite rare today in the United States.

Commenting on the discrepancy between the close involvement of top management in product development within Japanese companies, and Doyle's contrary experience in the United States, Alfred Chandler (professor, Harvard Business School) suggested this could be due to differing degrees of corporate diversity. Most Japanese companies (Matsushita and a few others being notable exceptions) were still relatively nondiverse, with the result that top management involvement was more feasible and productive.

Nonaka also pointed out that in the firms he observed, issues affecting the new product's manufacturing cost were not resolved until quite late in the development cycle. This, plus the costly process of rethinking designs, might make the development process "not efficient" in conventional accounting terms (see Kaplan's chapter in Part Two for further discussion of this issue). Responding to a question by Paul Frech (vice president, operations, Lockheed Corporation) about the consequences of overlapping development phases of Fuji-Xerox (see Figure 8-4 in their chapter), Nonaka also admitted that there were dangers in having to "go to the next phase before the previous one is finished."

In general, however, most participants concurred with Place's comment that Japanese companies had shown it was possible to accelerate sharply the rate of new product introduction across a wide range of *markets. But U.S. industry was now beginning to bite back, Place asserted.*

The Role of Government Incentives

Discussing the impact of government incentives on industrial innovation, particularly that of the 1981 U.S. R&D tax credit, several participants complained that public policy continued to fail to take into account that the application of research was at least as important as its generation. This was in spite of the fact, Herbert Fusfeld (director, center for science and technology policy, New York University) recalled, that the importance of application had been stressed as recently as the late 1970s by a major federal review of innovation policy. The current U.S. tax credit did not acknowledge the "gray area" between development and manufacture, said Kenichi Imai (professor, Hitotsubashi University), although this was the focus of most Japanese R&D.

With the exception of Branscomb of IBM, most participants supported the conclusion of Mansfield's chapter that the U.S. tax credit—like its foreign counterparts—had stimulated little extra R&D. Neither as tax policy, nor as an R&D incentive, was the measure very helpful, said Nestor Terleckyj (National Planning Association). Jack Smith (vice president, manufacturing, Digital Equipment) argued that this was partly because the financial statements used by line managers tended not to include taxes. "The credit appears below the line," he said, and is thus invisible to all but the corporate center.

Place, moreover, argued that the credit was based on a misconception—that R&D was elastic to tax incentives. In fact, it was heavily people-intensive, and when skilled people were hard to come by, the credit was unlikely to have much impact on the size of R&D staffs. It would therefore only serve to inflate costs. There were better ways of achieving the desired result, he maintained, such as making scientific training more attractive through spending on education.

The Impact of Disruption on Productivity

One often observes short-term interruptions in a factory's efficiency—whether due to introducing new capital, new methods, or new processes. Long-term disruptions of the sort identified in the chapter by Clark and Hayes, which reflect an enduring conflict between innovation and productivity growth, are less widely recognized, however. Yet the participants gave almost universal support to the concept that *the introduction of any new investment is inherently confusing, and went on to add further dimensions to the chapter's analysis.*

A graphic description of the problems that can beset capital investment projects was offered by Dale Hartman (director of manufacturing technology, Hughes Aircraft). He believed that the extent of the disruption they caused was heavily dependent on management. "If you do the right things, it might be just a polite little hiccup. But it can sometimes become something approaching a belch. If you see this occurring in the long term, I suggest there is a lack of intelligent capital investment."

Operational and Structural Factors

Participants argued that disruptions caused by capital investment were exacerbated by two kinds of factors. Some are "structural" (such as choosing the wrong type or size of equipment), while others are "operational," in the sense that they affect the way manufacturing performance is measured and new investments are chosen and introduced. Together they affect the level of "confusion" and of learning in an organization, as well as the subtle interfaces between development and manufacture.

Among the many kinds of investment that have not had the desired impact on productivity, Hartman singled out some "ridiculous applications in robotics," and "white elephant" investments in flexible machining. In part, he suggested, these were due to a widespread overemphasis on capital-intensive projects—encouraged, in particular, by the Department of Defense. The payoff from noncapital-intensive investments was often higher, he asserted. The problem was compounded when automation was applied to products that had not been designed for automated manufacture, said Alvin Lehnerd (executive vice president, Sunbeam Corporation).

At the interface between operational and structural causes, Smith argued that too many firms were concentrating on direct labor-saving investment. Given the declining relative importance of manufacturing labor in most companies' cost structures, and the increase in indirect labor, it was not surprising that further investment in the former was not achieving a high return. "Everyone is talking about [investing in] robotics—what about office automation?" he asked.

Again emphasizing the importance of operational issues, Forward said that one of the reasons capital investment had an immediate impact on productivity in small steel firms was that those who made the investment decision were also responsible for implementing it.

As another approach to explaining the investment paradox, Place made an analogy with investment in research and development: When a company enters a new business, its R&D costs are generally lower than its competitors'—and below its own costs on previous products. But when it starts to achieve success in that business, it becomes much easier to justify, and secure, R&D funds. "You then go through a second phase when your R&D costs go up as a result of success," he stated. Companies then fall into the trap of having invested so much in this structural R&D that it becomes more difficult to introduce the next change.

"I have a feeling that capital is exactly the same way," Place continued. As a plant becomes more efficient, it starts "to pour concrete, just like the railroads did when they built the Cincinnati Union Terminal railroad station, or the British Empire did. Then they lost the whole thing." In other words, "the third stage of capital investment gets in the way of the next change that you have to make in order to continue to improve productivity."

The Role of Competition

Competitive rivalry played a key role in overcoming such stagnation. Not only did it stimulate efficiency and innovation, but it also energized what Place called the "inbred culture of the organization." In Joseph Schumpeter's famous words (echoed repeatedly throughout the colloquium), "creative destruction" has a key role to play: in this case, in stimulating organizational learning (of the new) and unlearning (of the old).

Underlying the ability of many companies to learn and unlearn, said Place, is the belief that their products must always be ahead of the competition whatever happens, and that "they can win." The whole Procter & Gamble organization was "built up of people who have accepted that culture; otherwise they have left." Echoing Place, Branscomb claimed that, perhaps paradoxically, companies were particularly stimulated by competition if they were already in a strong position. " 'Virtual' competition is very important," he said.

Reiterating this point—and by implication reinforcing the Clark-Hayes' chapter's conclusion about the impact of competition on productivity in certain types of firms—Jackson Grayson (chairman, American Productivity Center) reported that fully two-thirds of all the boardroom discussions he observed involved a competitive analysis of some kind. Public policy should respect—and stimulate—competition as a driving force, not restrict it by imposing competitive quotas and *like measures. While underlining the chapter's conclusion that competitive pressure is a key influence on innovation, Clark warned that it was possible for competitive pressure to become so intense (and margins so narrow) that firms were deterred from innovating.*

Several participants called for the presentation of more detailed results and the undertaking of further research. Richard Rosenbloom (professor, Harvard Business School) suggested that a more disaggregated analysis might usefully separate independent businesses from the subsidiaries of multinationals, and distinguish between related and unrelated types of businesses. Doyle pointed out that industries in different stages of development (such as domestic appliances and steel) might also show different results. And, though Clark felt that any bias caused by the short-term nature of the data would be "washed out" by the cross-sectional approach that had been used, Bakken advocated that future analyses should be based on longer-term performance measures. Others expressed concern about the measures selected and offered alternative definitions of the term "productivity."

In conclusion, all participants agreed that, while much had been learned, much still needed to be done.

Contributors

LEWIS M. BRANSCOMB is vice president and chief scientist of International Business Machines Corporation and a member of its Corporate Management Board. He joined IBM in 1972 following a distinguished career as a research physicist—and later director—for the National Bureau of Standards. He is a graduate of Duke and Harvard Universities. Dr. Branscomb is currently a member of the National Academy of Engineering, the National Academy of Sciences, and the National Academy of Public Administration. In 1979 he was appointed by President Carter to the National Science Board, and in 1980 he was elected chairman, serving until 1984.

ALFRED D. CHANDLER, JR., Isidor Straus Professor of Business History at the Harvard Business School, has written extensively on the evolution of the modern corporation. His major works include *Strategy and Structure: Chapters in the History of the Industrial Enterprise* (1962), *The Visible Hand: The Managerial Revolution in American Business* (1977), which received the Pulitzer and Bancroft prizes and the Newcomen Award, and with Stephen Salsbury, *Pierre S. Du Pont and the Making of the Modern Corporation* (1971). Professor Chandler earned his undergraduate degree and his Ph.D. in history from Harvard University. He taught at M.I.T. and Johns Hopkins before coming to the Harvard Business School in 1970.

KIM B. CLARK is an associate professor at the Harvard Business School. A member of the Harvard faculty since 1978, Mr. Clark received B.A., M.A., and Ph.D. degrees in economics from Harvard University. Professor Clark's research interests are in the areas of operations strategy, and technology and productivity. His current research focuses on management at the plant level, and the product/process development cycle. His most recent book, *Industrial Renaissance* (1983), was coauthored with William J. Abernathy and Alan M. Kantrow. He has served on the secretary's staff at the U.S. Department of Labor and was a member of the National Materials Advisory Board Committee on the Status of High-Technology Ceramics in Japan.

JOHN L. DOYLE is executive vice president of Hewlett-Packard Company with responsibility for the Information Systems and Networks sector. Doyle attended Glasgow University (Scotland) and earned his B.S. in mechanical engineering from Stanford University in 1956. He joined Hewlett-Packard in 1957 as a manufacturing engineer and participated in the H.P. honors program, earning an M.S. in engineering science in 1959. After serving in various managerial roles in the Manufacturing and Systems divisions, he became director of corporate development in 1972, and in 1976 was elected vice president of personnel. From 1981 to 1984, he served as vice president of research and development and managed H.P. Laboratories, the company's central research activity.

GORDON E. FORWARD was elected president and chief executive officer of the Chaparral Steel Company in 1982. Prior to assuming the office, he was executive vice president—production at Chaparral. He earned a B.A. from the University of British Columbia in Vancouver and a Ph.D. in metallurgy from M.I.T. Dr. Forward was general superintendent for the Lake Ontario Steel Company and senior research engineer for the Steel Company of Canada before joining Chaparral. He is a director of Co-Steel International of Toronto, Canada.

J. RICHARD HACKMAN is a professor of organizational behavior and of psychology at Yale University. He received his undergraduate degree in mathematics from MacMurray College in 1962, his Ph.D. in social psychology from the University of Illinois in 1966, and has been at Yale since then. Professor Hackman's research in social and organizational psychology includes the design of work, the task effectiveness of work groups, and social influences on individual behavior. He was the winner of the Sixth Annual AIR Creative Talent Award in the field of "Measurement and Evaluation: Individual and Group Behavior," and co-winner of the 1972 Cattell Award of the American Psychological Association (APA). He is a fellow of the APA in the divisions of Industrial and Organizational Psychology, and Personality and Social Psychology.

ROBERT H. HAYES is the William Barclay Harding Professor of Management of Technology at Harvard Business School, where he has taught courses in manufacturing strategy and production and operations management since 1966. He received his B.A. from Wesleyan University and his M.S. and Ph.D. in operations research from Stanford University. His current research is on productivity improvement and the technological development activities of companies, both in the United States and abroad. His book, *Restoring Our Competitive Edge: Competing through Manufacturing,* coauthored with Steven C. Wheelwright, won the Association of American Publishers' Award for the best book on business, management, and economics published in 1984. He is currently chairman of the production and operations management faculty at Harvard.

ANTHONY G. HOPWOOD is the Institute of Chartered Accountants Professor of Accounting and Financial Reporting at London Business School, and a visiting professor of management at the European Institute for Advanced Studies in Management, Brussels. Educated at the London School of Economics and the University of Chicago, he has served on the faculties of numerous British and American business schools. A former president of the European Accounting Association, in 1981 he served as the American Accounting Association's Distinguished International Visiting Lecturer. He is editor-in-chief of the international research journal *Accounting, Organizations and Society* and the author of numerous books and articles on the organizational and social aspects of accounting.

KEN-ICHI IMAI is dean of the Schools of Commerce, Hitotsubashi University. He received his B.A., M.A., and Ph.D. degrees in economics from Hitotsubashi University, and joined the Hitotsubashi faculty in 1964. He was a visiting research associate at Harvard University, Department of Economics, during 1978–79. Professor Imai served as chairperson of Hitotsubashi's Institute of Business Research, from 1979 to 1985. He has published several books in Japanese, including *Industrial Society of Japan: Pattern of Evolution and Change* (1983), and has been on the editorial board of *The International Journal of Industrial Organization* since 1982.

PHILIP JARYMISZYN has been a research associate at the Harvard Business School. He graduated from Harvard College with a degree in economics. His research and writing have been devoted to the impact that CEO characteristics have on firm performance.

ROBERT S. KAPLAN is the Arthur Lowes Dickinson Professor of Accounting at Harvard Business School and a professor of industrial administration at Carnegie-Melon University. He served as dean of the Graduate School of Industrial Administration at Carnegie-Melon University from 1977 to 1983. He received a B.S. and M.S. in electrical engineering from M.I.T. and a Ph.D. in operations research from Cornell University. His current research focuses on the development of new management accounting systems for measuring and motivating manufacturing performance. He received the AICPA Accounting Literature Award in 1971 and a McKinsey Award for one of the outstanding articles of 1984 in the *Harvard Business Review*. His textbook, *Advanced Management Accounting,* was published in 1982. Dr. Kaplan is currently vice president of the American Accounting Association and was selected by that organization as its Distinguished International Visiting Lecturer in 1983. He is a member of the Manufacturing Studies Board of the National Research Council.

ROBERT B. MCKERSIE is professor of industrial relations at the Sloan School of Management, Massachusetts Institute of Technology. From 1971 to 1979 he was dean of the New York State School of Industrial and Labor Relations at Cornell University. Before that, he was assistant professor (1968 to 1971), and full professor (1968 to 1971) at the Graduate School of Business, University of Chicago. Professor McKersie received his undergraduate degree from the University of Pennsylvania, and the M.B.A. and D.B.A. degrees from Harvard University. He is a member of the American Arbitration Association and an advisor to a subcommittee of the Committee for Economic Development that is studying improvement of productivity. Previously, he served as a member of the President's Advisory Committee on Federal Pay and as chairperson of the New York State Continuity of Employment Committee. McKersie is the coauthor of both *Pay, Productivity and Collective Bargaining* (1973) and *A Behavioral Theory of Labor Negotiations* (1965).

EDWIN MANSFIELD is director of the Center for Economics and Technology, and professor of economics at the University of Pennsylvania. He has taught at Carnegie-Melon, Harvard, and Yale Universities, as well as the California Institute of Technology; and has been a consultant to many government agencies, including the Executive Office of the President. Author of twenty books and over 150 papers, he has been elected a fellow of the American Academy of Arts and Sciences, the Econometric Society, and the Center for Advanced Studies in the Behavioral Sciences. He has received many awards, the most recent being the 1984 Publication Award of the Patent Law Association for the best publication on the patent system.

RICHARD R. NELSON is professor of economics and director of the Institution for Social and Policy Studies at Yale University. His research on the processes of long-range economic change has focused on technological advance and the institutions that support it. Nelson came to Yale after a long spell at the RAND Corporation. He has taught at Carnegie-Tech University and Oberlin College and has served as a senior staff member on the Council of Economic Advisors.

IKUJIRO NONAKA is a professor at the Institute of Business Research, Hitotsubashi University. Professor Nonaka received his B.S. in political science from Waseda University and his M.B.A. and Ph.D. degrees in Business Administration from the University of California, Berkeley. He taught at Nanzan University and the Japanese National Defense Academy from 1977 to 1982 and joined the Hitotsubashi faculty in 1982. He has been on the editorial board of *Organizational Science* since 1982, and has published several books. He is coauthor of *Strategic vs. Evolutionary Management: A U.S.-Japan Comparison of Strategy and Organization*, which appeared both in Japanese (1983) and in English (1985).

NATHAN ROSENBERG is chair of the department of economics at Stanford University. He received his B.A. in economics from Rutgers and his Ph.D. in economics from the University of Wisconsin. He served as editor of the *Journal of Economic History* from 1971 to 1974. His research and writing focus on the economics of technological change. His most recent book is *Inside the Black Box* (1982). Other works include *Perspectives on Technology* (1976) and *Technology and American Economic Growth* (1972).

RICHARD S. ROSENBLOOM is the David Sarnoff Professor of Business Administration at Harvard Business School where he has been a faculty member since 1960. His teaching and research activities are in the field of the management of technology. From

1976 to 1980 he was the associate dean for research and course development and before that served as director of the doctoral program.

ROLAND W. SCHMITT is senior vice president for corporate research and development at the General Electric Company and a member of its Corporate Executive Counsel. He directs the G.E. Research and Development Center at Schenectady, New York. Dr. Schmitt received his undergraduate degrees in physics and mathematics from the University of Texas and his Ph.D. in physics from Rice University. He joined the General Electric Research Laboratory in 1951 and assumed his first managerial position as head of a team of G.E. physicists and metallurgists in 1957. During 1965, he was a visiting research associate at Harvard University. Returning to G.E., Dr. Schmitt served in various leadership capacities before being named vice president of Corporate Research and Development in 1978. He assumed his present position in 1982.

WICKHAM SKINNER is the James E. Robison Professor of Business Administration at Harvard Business School. He was trained as an engineer at Yale, and after receiving an M.B.A. at Harvard in 1948, spent ten years at Honeywell in production, marketing, finance, and general management positions. He received his D.B.A. from Harvard and has been teaching at the Harvard Business School since 1960. Although he has taught courses in human resource management, his main area of interest is production management. He served three years as associate dean in charge of the M.B.A. program. He is the author of *Production Management in Developing Countries* (1968), *Manufacturing in the Corporate Strategy* (1978), and *Manufacturing: The Formidable Competitive Weapon* (1985).

LAWRENCE H. SUMMERS is professor of economics at Harvard University, where he specializes in macroeconomics and public finance. He graduated from M.I.T. with a major in economics and received his Ph.D. in economics from Harvard University. He was assistant and then associate professor at M.I.T. from 1979 to 1982. Summers is a member of the Brookings Panel on Economic Activity and is a research associate of the National Bureau of Economic Research. He has served as a consultant to the Departments of Labor and the Treasury in the United States and to the governments of Jamaica and Indonesia. Last year he served as domestic policy economist on the President's Council of Economic Advisors.

HIROTAKA TAKEUCHI is an associate professor at the Schools of Commerce, Hitotsubashi University. He received his B.A. in social sciences from International Christian University and his M.B.A. and Ph.D. in Business Administration from the University of California, Berkeley. Before joining the Hitotsubashi faculty, he taught at the University of California, Berkeley, during 1975–76, and at the Harvard Business School from 1976 to 1983. Professor Takeuchi coauthored several articles for the *Harvard Business Review* and has published articles in the *Journal of Retailing, California Management Review*, and the *International Journal of Research in Marketing*.

RICHARD E. WALTON is the Jesse Isidor Straus Professor of Business Administration at Harvard Business School. He received an M.S. in economics from Purdue University in 1954 and a D.B.A. from Harvard University in 1959. Professor Walton taught at Purdue University before joining the Harvard faculty in 1968. From 1969 until 1976 he served as the director of the Division of Research at Harvard Business School. He writes extensively in the areas of work innovations and conflict resolutions. Recently his research efforts have been devoted to the development of high commitment organizations, innovative approaches to labor-management relations, and the development of organizationally sensitive information technology.

Index

Abernathy, William, 4, 5, 6, 7, 63, 72,
  83, 93, 115, 118, 119, 121, 125,
  126, 128, 132, 151, 169, 291, 299,
  308, 337, 340, 430, 450 n. 4, 450
  n. 6
Absenteeism
  and commitment model, 248
  and TFP, 163, 173, 174, 177, 192, 193
Abu-Zayyad, Ray, 280, 285
Academic background of CEO, 132
Academic research
  and cost accounting, 149
  and extraordinary innovations, 291,
    300–301, 314, 315, 329
  and government support, 412
  and human relations, 82
  and R&D tax incentives, 420
Accounting. See Cost accounting
Adam, Everett E., Jr., 80
Administrative background of CEO,
  125, 126, 132
Agriculture
  and mass production, 71
  and science, 23, 28
  and technology, 67
Airplane industry, 29
Aizawa, Mr., 354, 355, 361
Albert, S., 389, 402 n. 29
Amsden, A.H., 452 n. 22
Appert, Nicolas, 36, 49 n. 43
Assembly line
  and commitment model, 247–248
  cost accounting study of, 201–204
  first, 196
Automobile industry, 192, 431
  and commitment model, 262
  growth of, 77
  history of, 195–196
  and steel industry, 4, 28–29

Babcock, S.M., 49 n. 41
Baranson, Jack, 83, 92
Beer, Michael, 83, 92
Bernard, J.E., 74
Blau, Peter M., 106
Bluestone, Irv, 239, 263

Bohn, Roger, 94
Branscomb, Dr. Lewis, 139, 141, 289,
  294, 295, 409–421, 459, 460, 462,
  464, 467
  answer to, 423–424
Britain
  and accountants, 233
  and Bessemer process, 32
  and commitment model, 247
  and innovation, 321
  and R&D, 14–15, 59–60, 142, 321
  and research, 24, 143
Burchell, Stuart, 231, 232
Burgelman, Robert A., 345
Burr, Don, 241
Buzzell, R.D., 450 n. 7

Camras, Marvin, 321, 322
Canada and R&D tax incentives, 294,
  383, 390, 395–396, 397, 401
  n. 24, n. 26, 402 n. 29, n. 30,
  n. 31, 413, 416, 423, 424
Canon in study of innovation and product development in Japan, 292,
  338, 340, 342–343, 344, 346, 353,
  355, 360, 367, 378
Capital investment, 2, 7, 8, 279, 290,
  450 n. 8, 462–464
  and confusion, 463
  and decision making, 427
  and labor, 281–282
  measures of, 434
  and TFP, 148, 153, 156–157, 452
    n. 26
  and vertical integration, 438
Career path
  and CEO, 115–116, 118
  and commitment model, 240
Carnegie, Andrew, 15, 26, 77, 140, 195
Cement. See Concrete technologies
Chandler, Alfred D., Jr., 14–15, 22,
  53–61, 67, 68, 70, 140, 141, 143,
  459, 461, 467
Change. See Innovation; Technological
  change
Chemical industry, 70, 72, 81, 431

Chemistry and industry, 21, 26, 28
 and by-products, 43, 51 n. 66
 in construction, 32, 47–48 n. 28
 in food processing, 37, 39–40
 in meatpacking, 40, 41–42
 in pulp and paper, 48 n. 36
 in wood, 33–34
Chief Executive Officer (CEO)
 age of, 126–128
 background of, 6, 7, 16, 17, 115–136
 and competition, 117–122, 139
 education and, 118, 128–129
 labor market for, 127
 models of, 120–122
 and performance, 140
 and production managers, 16
 tenure of, 127–128
 trends in, 124–126
Chief Executive Officer (CEO), analysis
  of, 120–136, 140
 commentary on, 137–138
 data for, 122–129
 interpretation of, 120–122
 results of, 129–134
Chinaware industry, 70
Church, A. Hamilton, 196
Cigarette industry, 72
City box-car, 338, 343, 344, 346, 347,
  353, 358, 367
Civic car, 361
Clark, Kim B., 5, 7, 16, 93, 115–136,
  140, 147, 150, 151–188, 279, 289,
  291, 299, 308, 337, 425–458, 447,
  450–451 n. 10, 462, 464, 465,
  467
 commentary on, 137–138, 189–194
Clawson, Dan, 64
Comers
 and competition, 94–95, 99–100
 as industrial lions, 101–114
 in manufacturing leadership, 16, 65,
  99–100, 111–114, 141
 survey of, 65, 101–107
Commercialization and extraordinary
  innovation, 306–309, 310
Commitment model for work force
  management, 149–150, 237–277,
  279, 284–286
 benefits from, 247–249
 and capitalism, 275
 costs and, 248
 and double-breasted strategy, 259
 evolution of, 238–242
 features of, 244–246
 managing, 267–268
 and manufacturing plants, 240
 numbers of, 150
 and power, 286
 problems of, 252, 272–276
 and sales organizations, 240

 transformation to, 150, 260–264,
  267–272, 285–286
 and work technologies, 247
Communication
 and learning, 168
 and scientific management, 74
 and self-organizing project team, 379
Compensation
 for CEO, 121
 and commitment model, 150, 241,
  244–245, 253–255, 274
 and control model, 253
 and learning, 150
 for management, 117
 and skills, 238, 242, 249, 254
 and transformation model, 249
 and transitional model, 246, 247
Competition
 and CEO experience, 117–122
 and comers, 94–95, 99–100
 and commitment model, 150, 253
 complexity of, 425–426
 and control model, 243–244
 and cost accounting, 230–231
 and decision making, 9, 63–66, 425–
  458
 economic theory of, 2, 3, 4
 and equipment policy, 297
 and extraordinary innovation, 310
 factors in, 9
 and information sharing, 359
 and innovation, 296, 448, 464–465
 and invention, 379
 and learning, 5–6, 190, 464
 and management, 2–4, 64–65, 139
 and manufacturing leadership, 66,
  83–84, 91–95
 and NPD, 8, 337–338, 342–343, 434–
  435, 437, 450 n. 1
 and patents, 450 n. 5
 and performance, 442
 and quality control, 29–30
 and R&D expenditures, 414
 and research, 1, 3
 and science, 26
 and structure, 7–8
 and technological change, 16
 and technological evolution, 428–429
 and TFP, 442
 and transformation to commitment
  model, 263
Competition, foreign, 1, 3–4, 83–84,
  97–98
 and factory as financial resource, 100
 and industrial engineering, 112–113
 and learning, 6
 and management selection, 100
 and science, 14
 and technological change, 6
 and workers, 100

Competitors, 444
  as driving force, 427
  and environment, 427
  in industrial subgroups, 449
  and NPD, 437, 441, 448, 451 n. 15,
    n. 16
  and technological evolution, 428–429
  and technological spillover, 439–442
Computer and cost accounting, 149, 222
Computer-aided design and manufac-
    turing (CAD/CAM), 66, 198, 221,
    374
Computer integrated manufacturing
    (CIM), 66
Confusion, 5, 192–193, 279–281
  and capital equipment, 463
  and commitment model, 150
  defined, 178
  and ECOs, 190
  and new equipment, 447
  and TFP, 148, 161, 169, 178–179,
    184–185
Constant, Edward, 300
Construction industry
  and concrete technologies, 73
  firm size of, 25
  and materials testing, 35
  and science, 14, 22–23, 31–34, 46–47
    n. 17, 47 n. 23, n. 26, 47–48
    n. 28, 48 n. 34, n. 36
  and steel industry, 29, 30–31
Control model for work force manage-
    ment, 9, 149, 150, 242–244, 284–
    286
  transition from, 243–244
  and work technologies, 247
Cook, Randall L., 169
Corcoran, John E., 72
Cost accounting
  and control, 232–233
  origin of, 196
  research and, 227–228
  roles of, 231–232
Cost accounting systems and manufac-
    turing innovations, 147, 197–218
  changing, 208, 212–213, 283
  computer-based, 222
  and early factory system, 68
  historical perspective of, 195–197
  innovations in, 221–222, 225 n. 3
  and labor, 282
  lag of, 8, 199–200, 200–201, 207–
    208, 218–225, 225–226 n. 4, 226
    n. 5, 230, 279, 282–284
  and management, 67, 227–235
  as organizational tool, 232
  and process innovation, 225–226 n. 4
  and scientific management, 74, 199
  and social control, 233–234
  study of, 200–220

Davidson, William H., 97, 155
Dennison, Edward, 1, 450 n. 8
Distribution
  and cost accounting systems, 199
  and extraordinary innovation, 307,
    311
  and innovation, 309
Divisia method and TFP, 186 n. 1
Division of labor
  and supplier network, 364–365
  and overlapping phase management,
    350–351
Division of labor, shared, 366–367
Dolby, Ray, 322
Douglass, Elisha P., 67
Doyle, John, 141, 281, 284, 285, 289,
    293, 294, 377–381, 461, 465, 467
Dudley, Charles B., 46 n. 16
Dyer, Davis, 94, 337, 354, 360

Economic Recovery Tax Act (ERTA),
    384, 410, 413, 415, 420
Edison, Thomas, 305, 306, 313
Edmondson, Harold, 140, 282, 283
Education, 2
  and CEO performance, 118, 128–129,
    132, 133, 137–138
  and cost accounting, 223–224, 230
  and function, 141–142
  and industrial lions, 141
  and R&D tax incentives, 420
  of worker, 174
Efficiency
  and competition, 452 n. 20
  and cost accounting systems, 203,
    209, 211
  defined, 4
  and the Depression, 81
  and factory system, 77
  and flexibility, 426
  and innovation, 3, 4–9, 289, 290, 337,
    462–463
  and manufacturing process, 196
  measuring, 79
  and performance, 64
  and product development, 461
  and production management, 80
Eisenhower, [Dwight], 83
Eisner, R., 389, 402 n. 29
Electrical equipment industry
  comers in, survey of, 101–107
  and commitment model, 262
Electronics industry
  comers in, survey of, 101–107
  and R&D, 410
  and R&D tax incentives, 423
Emerson, Harrington, 196
Employee. *See* Work force
Employee involvement (EI), 239, 246,
    261

Employment assurance
  and commitment model, 150, 245,
    252–253, 273–274, 276, 285
  and control model, 253
  in transformation model, 246
  See also Job security
Employment, long-term in Japan, 356–
  357, 373
Engineering Change Orders (ECOs)
  and confusion, 5, 190, 279, 280
  and learning curve, 192
  and production process, 189–190
  and TFP, 5, 148, 161, 162, 163, 180–
    183
Engineers
  and commitment model, 240
  and ECOs, 183
  and industry, 53, 142
  and information sharing, 370
  and innovation, 293
  and mass production, 196
  and product development, 355, 378
  as science, 24, 46 n. 9
Environment
  dimensions of, 427
  driving forces and, 427
  and NPD, 435–437, 442
  and production process, 430
  and technological evolution, 450 n. 2
  and TFP, 443–445
Ephlin, Don, 239, 240, 263
Equipment policy, 7, 191, 290
  and commitment model, 238
  and competition, 6, 197
  and confusion, 5, 161, 178
  and innovation, 290
  and learning curve, 192
  and mass production, 71
  and NPD, 447, 452 n. 25
  and performance, 427, 463–464
  and R&D tax incentives, 419
  and TFP, 147, 152, 162–163, 168–
    169, 183–184, 429–430, 443,
    446–447, 448, 449, 450 n. 9
Extraordinary innovation. *See* Innovation, extraordinary

Fab/assembly plants, 193
  defined, 431
  and learning, 281
  and innovation, 101 n. 2, 296
  in study of innovation and productiv-
    ity factors, 430–431, 434, 436–
    437, 438–439, 440, 441, 444, 445,
    446, 447, 451 n. 17, 448, 449, 452
    n. 23
  in study of TFP, 152, 155, 156, 164,
    165, 169, 170–171, 173, 175,
    177–178, 179, 180, 183–184

Factory
  as financial resource, 64, 65, 77
  history of, 95–99
  as human resource, 114
  as laboratory, 113
  perception of, 15, 16, 98
  as productivity machine, 90–91
Factory system
  and foreign competition, 91–95
  management of, 75
  and mass production, 70–72
Factory system, history of, 5, 66–101
  from 1780–1850, 67
  from 1850–1890, 70–72, 75
  from 1890–1920, 73–77
  from 1920–1960, 78–83
  from 1960–1980, 83–84
  from 1980s and beyond, 91–95
  significance of, 95–99
Faraday, [Michael], 20
Farnham, Dwight, 96
Financial measures, 282–284
Financial reporting, 223, 230
Flaherty, M.T., 94
Fisher, Franklin M., 120
Flexibility
  and competition, 338
  and decision making, 449
  defined, 426
  and efficiency, 426
  factors supporting, 340–362
  in Japan, 338, 361, 362–371
  and multilearning, 354
  and product development, 353,
    360
  and supplier network, 369
  and vertical integration, 439
Flexible manufacturing, 193, 198, 221,
  229, 230, 231
Fong, Hsien-T'ing, 70
Food processing industry
  and mass production, 72
  and quality control, 50 n. 51
  and science, 14, 23, 36–44, 49 n. 41,
    50 n. 55
Ford, [Henry], 77
Foreman
  evolution of role of, 16, 96, 111
  and labor relations, 113
  and mass production, 71–72, 73
  and scientific management, 74, 75,
    76, 85
Forward, Gordon E., 111–114, 140, 285,
  459, 463, 467
Frasch, Herman, 51 n. 66
Frech, Paul, 461
Fricke, Dr., 26
Fuller, Steve, 239
Fusfeld, Herbert, 462

Gain sharing, 255, 275, 276
Galvani, [Luigi], 20
Gantt, Henry, 196
Garvin, David, 94
Germany, 317, 322, 383
   and academic research, 143
   competition of, 83
   factory system of, 140
   R&D and, 14, 15, 56, 59
Gilbreth, [Frank Bunker], 75
Gilchrist-Thomas, Sidney, 27
Ginsberg, Charles, 322, 323
Glass industry, 70, 81
Glover, John G., 71, 73
Goheille, Kenneth R., 192
Goldberg, L., 400 n. 15
Goldmark, Peter, 303
Government
   and competition, 464–465
   and innovation, 289
   and R&D, 10, 142–143, 294–295,
      409–410, 411–415, 423
   See also Tax incentives and R&D
Government background of CEO, 132
Granstrand, Ove, 393
Grayson, Jackson, 92, 464
Grievances, 173–174, 177, 190, 192
Griliches, Z., 447, 450 n. 7, n. 8, 450–
      451 n. 10, 452 n. 21
Growth accounting, 117
Gutman, Herbert J., 68

Hackman, J. Richard, 267–277, 285,
      468
Hammond, John Winthrop, 40, 72
Hartman, Dale, 141, 280, 282, 463
Harvard Business School, 140, 141,
      147, 148, 149, 196, 282, 283, 285,
      289, 459, 461, 465
Hawthorne experiments, 82
Hayes, Robert H., 5, 6, 7, 83, 84, 92,
      115, 118, 119, 121, 125, 126, 128,
      132, 140, 147, 150, 151–188, 279,
      282, 284, 286, 289, 425–458, 459,
      462, 464, 468
   commentary on, 189–194
Heavy defense industries, 65, 101–107
Herzberg, Frederick, 114
High tech industry, 192, 193
   and confusion, 279–280
   and R&D tax incentives, 418–419
   in TFP study, 152, 154, 155, 156–
      157, 164, 165–168, 169–170,
      172, 174, 175, 177, 178, 179,
      180–181
Hirschman, Albert, 152
Hirschmeier, Johannes, 60
History, significance of, 9, 11–143
   and CEO, 115–136

   and competition, 426, 427
   and extraordinary innovation, 300–
      301
   of firm, 3
   and industrial lions, 63–110
   and science, 13–17, 19–51
Holley, Alexander Lyman, 77
Hopwood, Anthony, 227–235, 468
Horovitz, Jacques H., 233
Hounsfield, Geoffrey, 331
Household appliance industry, 431
Howard, A.W., 50 n. 51
Howe, Henry, 49 n. 40
Human resource management
   and commitment model, 276
   history of, 82
   in Japan, 355–357
   and multilearning, 368
   and overlapping phase management,
      350

Ibuka, Masaro, 318
Ichniowski, Bernard E. ("Casey"), 173,
      174, 183, 189
Imai, Ken-ichi, 6, 142, 289, 290, 292,
      337–375, 460, 461, 462, 468
   commentary on, 377–381
Industrial engineering
   and foreign competition, 112–113
   goals of, 96–97
   history of, 75–76, 79
Information
   and management, 2–3
   and NPD, 435
   and supplier network, 365, 366
Information industry, 410, 414
Information sharing, 369–370
   and overlapping phase management,
      350
   and product development, 351
   and self-organizing project teams,
      348
   and subtle control, 358–359
   and supplier network, 369–370
Information systems and cost account-
      ing systems, 200, 229
Innovation, 4–5, 295–296
   and competition, 337, 425–458, 464–
      465
   and cost accounting systems, 200–
      220
   development phase of, 293
   and efficiency, 4–9, 337
   entrenching effects of, 291, 299
   and environment, 427
   exploitation phase of, 291, 292
   exploratory phase of, 292
   and extraordinary innovation, 329
   and learning, 359–362

Innovation (*continued*)
  limitations of, 373–374
  and multilearning, 353–357
  overlapping phase management in, 347–353
  process of, 340
  and self-organizing project teams, 345–347
  speed of, 362–371
  and supplier network, 362–371
  and top management, 342–345
Innovation and product development in Japan, study of, 337–375
  conclusion of, 371–373
  descriptive model of, 340
  methodology of, 338
  need for, 337–338
Innovation and productivity growth, factors in, study of, 425–458, 462–463
  data set for, 430–434, 450–451 n. 10
  firms in, 430–431
  and management policy, 429–430
  results of, 454–458
Innovation, extraordinary, 289, 291–292
  characteristics of, 299–300
  commentary on, 329–335
  commercialization of, 310–311
  and decision making, 299, 302, 310, 311–314, 329–331
  an experimentation, 304–306, 330–331
  exploitation phase of, 309–311, 330, 331
  formulation phase of, 291, 302–306, 330, 331
  fostering, 459–460
  gestation phase of, 291, 292, 300, 302, 306–309, 331
  and invention, 330–331
  and ordinary innovation, 329, 333–335
  and organization, 329, 331–333
  phases of, 330–331
  problem-solving mode of, 307–309, 310
  process of, 310–311
  and R&D, 332–335
  research needed for, 314–315
  risks of, 297–299
  speculative mode of, 305, 310, 323–324
  and technical development, 308
  video recording as, 317–327
Innovation, factors in, study of, 425–458
  framework for, 427–434
  implications of, 448–450
  interpretation of, 451 n. 14

Innovation, incremental, 289, 290, 292–294, 300
  subtle controls of, 293
Innovation, technological, 1–10, 87–88, 90. *See also* Technological change
Invention
  and extraordinary innovation, 292, 307, 316 n. 20, 330–331
  and innovation, 381
  and subtle control, 379
Inventory
  and cost accounting systems, 208
  and manufacturing leadership, 101 n. 3, 198
  as measure, 282
  and TFP, 147
Inventory, WIP, 192, 280
  and cost accounting systems, 199
  and TFP, 148, 170–172, 180, 181, 184–185
Iron and steel industry
  and mass production, 70
  and science, 14, 27–31

Jaikumar, Ramchandran, 94
Japan
  and academic research, 143
  and breakthrough projects, 373
  competition of, 15, 83, 84, 92, 139, 142–143
  and corporate culture, 373
  cost accounting systems in, 221, 283
  ECOs and, 280
  and employment assurance, 252, 356–357, 373
  factory system of, 101 n. 3, 140
  and financial measures, 283
  human resource management in, 355–357
  and innovation, 292, 295
  and inventory management, 101 n. 3, 171, 184
  and learning, 281
  managers in, 195
  manufacturing process in, 204–205
  organization structure in, 8
  and process development, 290
  and product development, 8, 289, 290, 292–294, 322, 460, 461
  and R&D, 60, 142, 462
  strategy of, 199
  and tax incentives, 383
  technological development in, 461
  and transformation to commitment model, 263
  and VTRs, 321, 324, 325
  and WIP inventory, 171, 184
  and worker, 8, 284
  See also Innovation and product de-

velopment in Japan, study of;
Supplier network and product development in Japan
Jarymiszyn, Philip, 7, 16, 115–136,
140, 468
commentary on, 137–138
Job design
and commitment model, 244, 252
in control model, 242
and transformation model, 261
in transition model, 247
Job enrichment, 250, 276
Job evaluation, 253–254
Job security
in commitment model, 248
in control model, 242
See also Employment assurance
Jorgenson, D.W., 450 n. 8
Just-In-Time inventory system (JIT),
205, 206, 207, 208, 209, 218

Kamien, M.I., 450 n. 5
Kanban systems, 84, 192
Kanter, Rosabeth Moss, 93, 337, 351
Kantrow, Alan, 93, 151, 169, 337
Kaplan, Robert S., 8, 94, 141, 148, 149,
195–226, 282, 461, 468
commentary on, 227–235
Katz, Harry C., 173, 192
Kawamoto, Mr., 345, 346, 353, 357,
360, 361, 371, 378, 380
Kawashima, Mr., 346
Kearney, A.T., 92
Keihin Seiki, 362
Kendrick, John W., 153
Klein, B., 450 n. 2, 453
Kobayashi, Mr., 345, 351, 378
Kochan, Thomas A., 192
Korea, 83, 93
Kreps, D.M., 451 n. 13
Kropper, Jon, 284
Kuhn, T.S., 450 n. 2
Kuznets, Simon, 20

Labor, 97, 207
as cost, 90–91, 243, 281–282
and cost accounting systems, 148,
210, 211, 212
in early factory system, 69
importance of, 463
and production process, 51 n. 63
and TFP, 153, 154, 166–167
See also Work force
Labor-management committees, 276
Labor-management relations, 8, 15, 198
in control model, 243
future of, 113
history of, 69, 81–82, 95
and production management, 85
and TFP, 177–178

See also Work force management
Laboratory
establishment of, 53
and extraordinary innovation, 332–
335
factory as, 113
in industry, 28, 33
See also Research and development
(R&D) laboratory
Laboratory, testing
evolution of, 50 n. 51
and food processing industry, 39
and R&D, 26, 28
LaFalce, John J., 412
Laspeyres approach, 153–154
Lawrence, Paul R., 94, 337, 354, 360
Layoffs, 191
and TFP, 174, 177
and transition model, 246
Leadership, manufacturing
as architects, 70–72
comers in, 65, 94–95, 99–100, 101–
107, 111–114
and early factory system, 67–70
evolution of, 7, 63–110, 113
and extraordinary innovation, 312
and foreign competition, 91–95
and mass production, 70–71, 76–77
new breed of, 94, 100
and new technology, 66
from 1920–1960, 78–83
from 1960–1980, 83–84, 95–99
in 1990s, 99
and production management, 77, 84–
91
requirements for, 197–198
and scientific management, 73–77
as technological capitalists, 66–70
and top management, 81, 98–99
traditional characteristics of, 64
and transformation to commitment
model, 263
Learning, 279
and capital equipment, 463
and commitment model, 150
and compensation, 150
and competition, 5–6, 190, 464
and confusion, 281
and experience, 165–168
and high tech industry, 279–280
and innovation, 290–291, 293, 294
institutionalization of, 360, 373
and management, 65, 272
and NPD, 6
organizational transfer of, 359–362
and product development, 342, 372,
381
and production process, 368
and self-organizing project team, 381
and standard costs, 154

Learning (*continued*)
  and supplier network, 368–369
  and TFP, 165–179
  value of, 281
  See also Multilearning; Unlearning
Learning-by-doing, 340, 365, 372, 444
Learning curve, 79, 165, 191, 192, 368
Learning, shared, 167–168, 193
Lehnerd, Alvin, 463
Leonard, Frank, 94
Levitt, Theodore, 362
Lions, industrial
  history of, 9, 16, 63–101
  need for, 139
  source of, 101–110, 140–141
Location of factory, 9, 152
Lodge, George, 98
Lowell, Francis Cabot, 67

McCaskey, Michael B., 95, 103
McFetridge, D., 400 n. 19, 400–401
  n. 21, 401 n. 26
McGowan, John, 120
McGregor, Douglas, 114
McKersie, Robert B., 189–194, 285, 469
Magnetic video recording. *See*
  Videotape recorders (VTRs)
Management, 6, 7, 9, 160, 193, 429–
  430
  as architect, 15, 65, 99, 111, 113
  as caretaker, 16, 139
  in commitment model, 150, 240, 244,
    245, 252
  and company history, 3
  and competition, 4, 63–66
  and confusion, 5, 463
  in control model, 242, 243
  as coordinator, 64
  and cost accounting systems, 222–
    223
  as custodian, 15, 64, 65, 111, 113
  evolution of, 66–91
  by exception, 193
  and extraordinary innovation, 291–
    292, 293, 300–302, 304–306
  history of, 1920–1960, 78–83
  and incremental innovation, 292–293
  and information, 2–3
  and innovation, 298, 299, 310, 429–
    430
  as labor input, 117
  and learning, 272
  and mass production, 71–72, 73, 76–
    77
  "modern," 4
  and NPD, 65, 289, 437–439
  by the numbers, 4, 6, 283
  by objectives, 250
  and overlapping phase development,
    350

  by portfolio, 4
  of process development, 289
  and production process, 190
  research and, 1, 2–4
  and subtle control, 357–359
  and tax incentives, 409
  and TFP, 147, 152–153, 159–160,
    160–184, 447–448
  and transformation model, 261, 268–
    269
  and transition model, 247
  See also Labor-management rela-
    tions; Scientific management;
    Union-management relations
Management, middle
  as architects, 139
  and commitment model, 285
  evolution of role of, 16
  history of, 74–75, 75–76
  and product development, 373
  and top management, 111
Management, participative, 113–114,
  193
Management, production
  and competition, 83–84
  history of, 7, 16, 75–76, 80, 84–91,
    96–99
  as housekeepers, 95
  and manufacturing leadership, 77
Management, professional, 78–83, 118,
  129
Management, top
  as architects, 15, 16, 139
  as caretakers, 16
  and commitment model, 240–241
  and control, 78
  and cost accounting systems, 224–
    225
  and early factory system, 75
  evolution of role of, 13, 15, 16
  and factory, 16, 77
  and middle management, 111
  and product development, 342–345,
    372, 378, 461
  and production managers, 16
  and project teams, 375 n. 13
  and work force, 64
  See also Chief Executive Officer (CEO);
    Leadership, manufacturing
Management selection, 7
  and commitment model, 241
  and competition, 100
  evolution of, 15
Managers. *See* Management
Mansfield, Edwin, 289, 294–295, 383–
    407, 423–424, 462, 469
  commentary on, 409–421
Manufacturing leadership. *See* Leader-
    ship, manufacturing
Marconi, [Guglielmo], 20

Market
  and competition, 343–344
  and control, 379
  as driving force, 427
  and extraordinary innovation, 299
  and innovation, 291, 332, 450 n. 5
  and R&D, 412–413
  and scientific applications, 22, 25, 27,
    39, 41
  and size of firm, 46 n. 10
Marketing
  and extraordinary innovation, 300,
    301–302, 325
  and R&D expenditures, 412–413
Marketing background of CEO, 7, 125–
    126, 131, 137
Marsland, Stephen, 83, 92
Marx, Karl, 43, 51 n. 64
Marzocchi, Luigi, 321
Maslow, Abraham H., 114
Mass production, 15, 96
  and cost accounting systems, 197
  and early factory system, 70
  evolution of, 196
  and management, 73, 76–77
  and process technology, 70–72
  and science, 35
  and strategy, 15
Massachusetts Institute of Technology
    (MIT), 143, 189, 285, 460
Masterson, Earl, 321
Materials management, 190, 280
  and commitment model, 240
  and TFP, 152, 153, 154–156
Materials Requirements Planning
    (MRP), 79, 80, 96
Materials testing, 34–36, 46 n. 16, 49
    n. 40, n. 41
Maxwell, [James C.], 20
Mayo, Elton, 82
Metallurgy
  and concrete, 47 n. 25, 48 n. 29
  evolution of, 27–31
  first laboratory for, 28
  industrial payoff of, 31
  and markets, 27
  and materials testing, 34–35
  and production processes, 25
  and science, 22, 23, 30
  See also Iron and steel industry;
    Steel industry
Metalworking industry
  comers in, survey of, 101–107
  and early factory system, 67–68
  growth of, 70
  and mass production, 71
  and NC, 81
  and technology, 67
Methods and procedures department,
    75

Miller, Jeffrey, 141, 280, 284
Miya, Mr., 355
Mogenson, Alan, 79
Mohnen, P., 389, 400 n. 14
Morale
  and cost accounting systems, 199
  and TFP, 163, 173, 174
Morita, Akio, 318
Mowery, David, 54
Multilearning
  defined, 354
  and group evaluation in Japan, 359
  and human resources management,
    368
  and innovation, 293
  and product development, 353–357,
    373, 378–379

Nadiri, M.I., 389, 400 n. 14
Nakamura, Mr., 355
Natural resources and science, 26–27,
    38–40
Nelson, Richard R., 67, 69, 71, 75, 117,
    137–138, 151, 301, 450 n. 2, n. 6,
    469
Network, supplier. *See* Supplier net-
    work
New breed of manufacturing managers,
    94, 100, 112, 139, 140
New product development (NPD), 7, 30,
    428–429
  and competition, 437, 448, 451 n. 12
  and decision making, 427, 434–435
  defined, 431
  in environment, 435–437
  estimating, 435, 448
  factors in, 434–442
  and learning, 6
  and management, 437–439
  measures of, 431
  and product maturity, 435, 442
  and technological change, 442
  and technological maturity, 449
  and TFP growth, 446, 448
  and vertical integration, 451 n. 17
  See also Product innovation
Nonaka, Ikujiro, 6, 281, 289, 290, 292,
    337–375, 460, 461, 469
  commentary on, 377–381

Olofsson, C., 231
Operations background of CEO, 125–
    126, 131, 132, 133, 140
Organization
  and extraordinary innovation, 315,
    329, 331–333
  and product development, 372–373
Organizational structure, 147
  and competition, 7, 9
  and environment, 427

Organizational structure (*continued*)
  and industry subgroups, 448
  and NPD, 435, 437
  and scientific management, 74–77
  and TFP, 152
Ouchi, William, 378
Overlapping development phase, 461
  management of, 347–353, 378
Overreaching and transformation
    model, 249–250, 268
Overtime, 173, 174, 190

Paasche approach, 154
Participative management, 113–114,
    193
Pasteur, [Louis], 37
Patents
  and NPD, 434, 437, 438, 440, 441,
    449, 450 n. 5, 452 n. 18
  and TFP growth, 446
Performance
  and CEOs, 129–134
  and commitment model, 241, 244,
    269–270
  and compensation, 275
  and competition, 442
  in control model, 242
  and cost accounting systems, 213–
    216
  of firm, defined, 119
  measurement of, 64, 119–120, 135
    n. 6, 463–464
  and production process, 430
Perkin, William H., 59
Personnel. *See* Staff
Personnel department, history of, 74–
    75
Pestillo, Pete, 239
Peters, Thomas J., 95, 119, 378
Phased Program Planning (PPP) sys-
    tem, 349, 351, 355, 372
Pilkington, Alistair, 302
PIMS data set, 431, 450–451 n. 10
Pipp, Frank, 140, 141, 285
Place, Geoffrey, 142, 281, 284, 460, 464
Planning
  and commitment model, 150, 245
  and innovation, 293
  and management, 113
  and transformation model, 249–250
Pollard, Sidney, 74
Poniatoff, Alexander M., 317, 318
Porter, Michael, 312, 430, 450 n. 7
Poulsen, Valdemar, 317
Problem solving
  in commitment model, 150, 245
  and extraordinary innovation, 307–
    309, 310, 313
  and invention, 316 n. 20

  and overlapping phase management,
    350
  and supplier network, 365
  in transitional model, 246
Process industries, 193
  and learning, 218
  and innovation, 101 n. 2, 296
  in study of innovation and productiv-
    ity factors, 430, 431, 434, 437,
    438, 439, 440, 444, 445, 446, 447,
    448, 449, 451 n. 17, 452 n. 23
  in TFP study, 152, 156, 164, 168,
    169, 170, 171–172, 177, 178, 179
  See also Food processing industry
Process innovation, 290, 431
Process technology
  and automation, early, 80–81
  and commitment model, 247
  and food processing industries, 36–44
  and management, 64
  and mass production, 70–72
Product design, 56, 306–309, 310–311
Product development, 10, 198, 289
  accelerating, 460–462
  and competition, 428, 450 n. 1
  and cost accounting systems, 199
  definition of, U.S., 377
  factors supporting, 340–362
  overlapping phase management of,
    347–353
  and performance, 120
  and science, 41–44, 54
  sequential phase management and,
    349–350
  in United States, 371–373, 374
  and waste products, 51 n. 64
  See also Innovation and product de-
    velopment in Japan, study of;
    New product development; Prod-
    uct innovation; Project team,
    self-organizing
Product development, speed of
  and competition, 338
  factors supporting, 340–362
  in Japan, 289, 362–371
  and multilearning, 354
  and overlapping phase management,
    350
Product innovation, 289–290
  and by-products, 44
  and competition, 8
  history of, 13
  and process innovation, 290
  and science, 20
  and TFP, 296
  See also New product development
Product life cycle, 436–437
Product maturity
  and industry subgroups, 448

and NPD, 435
and technological maturity, 449
and TFP growth, 444
Production department, 16, 75–77, 101
   n. 2
Production management. *See* Management, production
Production process
   and cost accounting systems, 199
   and ECOs, 189–190
   effects of, 430
   and history of, 13
   and labor, 51 n. 63
   and learning, 368
   and management, 190
   and science, 25, 30
   and scientific applications, 54
Production technology and natural resources, 38–40, 270
Production throughput rate, 170
Productivity, 145–286
   and anticipation, 191
   and capital equipment, 464
   and CEO background, 115–136
   and comers, 112
   and commitment model, 150
   and competition, 1–10, 425–458,
     464
   and cost accounting, 148–149
   decline of, 1–2, 5, 6–8, 91–95, 193
   definitions of, 465
   and environment, 427
   factors in, 151–188
   and foreign competition, 97–98
   improvement of, 9–10, 14
   and industrial engineering, 96–97
   and innovation, 4–5
   and labor, 207
   and learning, 5–6
   and managerial factor, 152
   measurement of, 2, 160, 431
   and organizational structure, 152
   and product innovation, 8
   and production management, 80, 90–
     91
   and R&D, 53–61
   and research, 2
   and science, 19–51
   and technological innovation,
     1–10
   variance of, 147
Productivity growth
   and capital, 450 n. 8
   and capital equipment, 450 n. 9
   and competition, 428
   and innovation, 290, 428, 429, 462–
     463
   measures of, 2, 431
   and R&D, 429

and technological development, 428–
   429
   See also Innovation and productivity
     growth, factors in, study of
Productivity, partial factor, 153, 154
Productivity, total factor (TFP)
   and capital equipment, 429–430
   defined, 442, 454
   and environment, 442, 443–445
   factors in, 147–148
   growth of, 442–450
   and innovation, 296, 428
   and management, 152–153, 159–160,
     160–161, 442
   and market growth, 444, 452 n. 22
   measuring, 152, 153, 186 n. 4
   and NPD, 448
   and R&D, 452 n. 21
   and standard costs, 153–154
   and technological spillover, 443
   and vertical integration, 443
Productivity, total factor (TFP), growth
   of, 442–450, 452 n. 22
Productivity, total factor (TFP), study
   of, 151–188
   calculation in, 157, 452 n. 19
   data analysis of, 161–184
   data collected for, 153–161
   input of, 154–157
   and learning, 165
   methodology for, 159–160, 186–187
   output of, 153–154, 179
   summary of, 184–187
Profit sharing, 241, 255, 275
Profitability
   and CEO background, 115–136
   as measure, 199
   and performance, 120
   and R&D tax incentives, 416–417
   and vertical integration, 450 n. 7
Project team, self-organizing
   backgrounds of, 347, 348, 378
   and division of labor, 351
   at Hewlett-Packard, 380
   and innovation, 345–347
   in Japan, 345–347, 351–353, 373
   and learning, 360–361
   and multilearning, 354–357
   and overlapping phase management,
     347–353
   phases of, 347–353
   and subtle control, 357–359, 379
   and tension, 344–345
Prucha, I., 389, 400 n. 14
Pullman, George, 77

Quality circles, 246, 250–251, 261, 276
Quality control
   and competition, 14, 29–30, 84

Quality control (*continued*)
　and cost accounting systems, 199
　and food processing industry, 50
　　n. 51
　and JIT, 206
　and product development, 61
　as scientific application, 53, 54
　and steel industry, 29–30
　and TFP, 147–148
Quality output, 197, 248
Quality of Work Life (QWL), 261, 263,
　264 n. 7
　and commitment model, 239, 248
　and unions, 259, 260

Reed, Rex, 239
Reject rate and TFP, 169–170, 184–185
Research, 1, 2–4, 23, 24
　application of, 462
　and by-products, 43
　evolution of, 23–24
　and extraordinary innovation, 292,
　　314–315
　and innovation, 459
　public sector and, 23
　and science, 23–24
　social payoffs of, 23
Research and development (R&D), 429,
　447
　as CEO background, 115, 123, 126,
　　132, 133, 137, 140
　and competition, 6, 7, 440, 441
　and confusion, 280
　distribution of, 45
　and extraordinary innovation, 332–
　　335, 459–460
　function of, 141–142
　and government, 10, 409–410, 411–
　　412, 423
　and innovation, 429
　in Japan, 362–363, 462
　and JIT, 207
　managing, 289, 290
　and national welfare, 59
　need for, 139
　and NPD, 437, 439, 442
　and organization, 60
　relationship between, 61
　and science, 44–45
　and TFP growth, 443, 446, 452 n. 21
　trends in, 15
　See also Tax incentives and R&D
Research and development (R&D) ex-
　penditures, 464
　and competition, 414
　cost of, 417–418
　and decision making, 427
　and economy, 414
　and marketing, 412–413
　and NPD, 452 n. 23, n. 24

　and performance, 427
　and technological change, 398
Research and development (R&D) labo-
　ratory, 198
　evolution of, 14, 15, 21, 25–26
　factory as, 113
　and testing laboratories, 26, 28
Return on investment (ROI)
　and efficiency, 148, 196–197
　and management, 4, 77
　as performance measurement, 64
Robbins, Owen, 283
Roberts, Edward, 460
Robotics, 66, 198, 221
Roethlisberger, Fritz, 82
Rosenberg, Nathan, 13–14, 19–51, 70,
　141, 142, 143, 301, 459, 469
　commentary on, 53–61
Rosenbloom, Richard S., 68, 289, 290,
　291–292, 297–327, 459, 461, 465,
　469–470
　commentary on, 329–335

Sabotage and early factory system, 68,
　69
Salaries. *See* Compensation
Sarnoff, David, 303, 306, 321
Sasser, W. Earl, 94
Scanlon Plan, 82, 255
Scanners and VTRs, 319–322
Schankerman, M., 389
Schlemmer, Carl, 279, 280
Schmenner, Roger W., 169
Schmitt, Dr. Roland, 289, 313, 329–
　335, 459, 470
Schonberger, Richard J., 83, 92, 362
Schumpeter, Joseph, 4, 293, 295, 297,
　361, 464
Schwartz, N.L., 450 n. 5
Science, 13–15, 19–51, 53–61
　and construction industry, 31–34, 47
　　n. 26
　and food processing industry, 36–44,
　　49 n. 41, n. 45
　and meatpacking industry, 40–44, 50
　　n. 55
　and natural resources, 26–27, 38–40
　and personnel, 24
　and product development, 54
　and product life, 31
　and R&D, 44–45
　and steel industry, 27–31
　and technology, 20, 45, 56
Science, applications of, 13, 20–27, 45–
　46 n. 1
　and by-products industry, 42–44
　and construction industry, 31–34,
　　46–47 n. 17, 47 n. 19, n. 23, 48
　　n. 34, n. 36
　and food processing industry, 36–44

and markets, 22–23
and meatpacking industry, 40–42
in metallurgy, 27–31
and production process, 54
and pulp and paper industry, 48
   n. 36
and society, 20
and steel industry, 28–31
Science Indicators, 1982, 410–411
Scientific management, 78, 80, 196
  and cost accounting systems, 148,
   199, 222, 223
  and factory system, 73–77
Segmentalism, 351, 375 n. 11
Semiconductor manufacturer, cost accounting study of, 213–218
Shepherd, W.G., 452 n. 20
Siemens, Werner von, 59
Singer, Isaac, 15
Size of firm, 14, 15
  and CEO background, 132–134
  and management, 73–77, 132
  and market, 46
  and mass production, 71
  and production processes, 25
  and science, 25, 49 n. 45
  and scientific applications, 22–23
  and TFP, 152
Skills and compensation, 274–275
  in commitment model, 238, 254
  in control model, 253
  in transformation model, 249
  in transitional model, 246, 247
Skills development, 2, 354
Skinner, Wickham, 5, 7, 15, 63–110,
   141, 178, 450 n. 1, n. 4, 470
  commentary on, 111–114
Slade, Bob, 142, 279, 281
Slater, Samuel, 67
Smith, Jack, 67, 462, 463
Software and cost accounting systems,
   199–200
Spence, A.M., 450 n. 1, 451 n. 13
Staff
  and commitment model, 248
  and mass production, 71–72
  in R&D, 55–56
  and science, 24
  and scientific management, 74
Staff specialists, history of, 75–77, 85,
   111, 113
Standardization
  and early factory system, 14, 67–
   68
  and foreign competition, 84
  and product development, 61
  as scientific application, 53, 54
Standards, work, 79, 150
Steel industry, 112, 434, 463
  and commitment model, 262, 263

and construction industry, 31–32,
   46–47 n. 17, 47 n. 19, n. 23
history of, 196
and quality control, 29–30
and science, 22, 27–31
  See also Iron and steel industry;
   Metallurgy
Steinmueller, W. Edward, 301
Stevenson-Wydler Act, 411
Stobaugh, R., 452 n. 18
"Strategic business unit," 450–451
   n. 10
Strategy, 191
  and extraordinary innovation, 312–
   314
  and foreign competition, 3
  and innovation, 294, 377
  and mass production, 15
  and research, 23–24
Structure. *See* Organizational structure
Subtle control, 357–359, 379, 392
Success. *See* Performance
Sugar industry, 70
Sullivan, M., 389, 402 n. 29
Summers, Lawrence, 7, 16, 115–136,
   140, 470
  commentary on, 137–138
Supervisor
  and commitment model, 238, 241,
   257–258
  and early factory system, 67
  and transformation model, 249
Supplier network
  defined, 362
  and shared division of labor, 351
  in United States, 375 n. 17, 379–380
Supplier network and product development in Japan, 338, 351, 362–
   371, 373, 379, 461
  and information sharing, 369–370
  and innovation, 290, 293
  norms, shared of, 371
  and reciprocity, 370–371
  self-organization of, 365–366
  speed and, 338
Suzuki, Mr., 358
Svalander, P.A., 231
Sweden and R&D tax allowance, 294,
   383, 390, 391–395, 397, 400–401
   n. 19, 401 n. 21, n. 26, 402 n. 28,
   405–407, 407 n. 1, n. 4, n. 6, 413,
   416, 423, 424
Switzer, L., 402 n. 29
Switzerland, 83

Taiwan, 83
Takeuchi, Hirotaka, 6, 289, 290, 292,
   337–375, 377, 460, 470

Tax incentives, 424
and innovation, 410–411, 462
and new equipment, 419
and start-up companies, 419–420
in Sweden, 395
in United States, 390–391, 417
Tax incentives and R&D, 289, 294–295,
412–415, 462
benefits of, 418, 420–421
cost of, 424
permanence of, 419
in United States, 384–391
Tax incentives and R&D, effects of,
397–398, 403–407, 413–415, 416
in Canada, 395–396, 401 n. 26, 423,
424
redefinition of R&D as, 390–391,
395, 417, 424
in Sweden, 392–395, 400 n. 17, 423,
424
in United States, 387–390, 400 n. 13,
n. 14, n. 15, n. 16, 423
Tax incentives and R&D, survey of,
383–407, 407 n. 3, n. 4
Canada in, 395–396, 401 n. 24, 402
n. 29, n. 30, n. 31, 413, 416
companies included in, 385–386
conclusions of, 397–398, 402 n. 27,
n. 29
methodology of, 386–387, 398–399
n. 6, 399 n. 7
results of, 387–388, 399–400 n. 11
Sweden in, 391–395, 396, 400 n. 18,
n. 19, 401 n. 26, 402 n. 28, 405–
407, 407 n. 1, n. 4, n. 6, 413, 416
United States in, 393, 394, 395, 396,
397, 401 n. 26, 403, 405
Taylor Frederick, 16, 74, 75, 79, 96,
101 n. 1, 196, 243
Taylor, R.W.C., 69, 70, 75
Technical environment
and NPD, 434–435, 451 n. 13
and TFP growth, 442
Technological change, 2, 3, 425–426,
435
and competition, 6, 9–10
and confusion, 5
and cost accounting system, 198–199
and decision making, 63–66
defined, 300
as driving force, 427
and innovation, 151–188
and learning, 279–280
and management, 5, 65, 297–327
and NPD, 442
and R&D expenditures, 398
and science, 22–23, 36–44
and tax incentives, 383–407
and vertical integration, 439, 451
n. 17

See also Innovation and product development in Japan
Technological constraints, 66–67, 70–
72
Technological discontinuities, 425–426,
429
Technological evolution, 428–429, 450
n. 2
Technological innovation, 1–10, 87–88
Technological maturity, 427, 449
Technological revolutions, 300–302
Technological spillover, 451 n. 13
and competition, 65, 439–442
defined, 440
and industrial subgroups, 448
and manufacturing leadership, 66,
198
and NPD, 435
and R&D, 443
Technology, managing, 287–465
Terleckyj, Nestor, 462
Testing
and food processing industry, 37–38
materials, 34–36, 46 n. 16, 49 n. 40,
n. 41
and product development, 61
and railroad industry, 46 n. 15
as scientific application, 14, 53, 54
Textile industry, 67, 72
Thompson, E.P., 68
Time study, 79, 196
Tobin's q, 119–120, 121, 129, 131, 132
Toffler, Alvin, 113
Total Quality Control (TQC) movement, 354–355
and multilearning, 378
Towne, Henry, 196
Toynbee, Arnold, 66, 69
Training, 191, 193
and commitment model, 241
and ECOs, 183
and learning curve, 192
and overlapping phase management,
350
and product development, 355
and TFP, 162–163, 173, 175
Transformation model for work force
management, 246–247, 249–252
and power, 268–269
problems of, 267–272
rate of, 260–264, 285–286
Transilience, 291, 299–300
Trist, Eric, 193, 264 n. 7, n. 11

Union
and commitment model, 237, 238,
248
and computer-based technology, 256
and control model, 243
and early factory system, 68, 69

and EI, 239, 240
and employee voice, 245
history of, 82
and QWL, 259, 260
and TFP, 149, 152, 177–178
Union-management relations
and commitment model, 150, 239,
240, 245, 258–260
and computer-based technology, 257
and transformation model, 245, 246,
263
United Kingdom. *See* Britain
United States and tax incentives, 384–
391, 393, 394, 395, 396, 397, 400
n. 13, n. 14, n. 15, n. 16, 401
n. 26, 403, 405, 417, 423
Unlearning, 291, 361–362, 373
Ure, Andrew, 68
Utterback, James, 143, 450 n. 6

Vaccara, Beatrice N., 153
Van Sant, William, 284
Variety amplification
and product development, 340
and self-organizing project teams,
347, 366
Variety reduction, 341, 342
and overlapping phase management,
372
and PPP approach, 372
and product development, 340
and self-organizing project teams,
349
and supplier network, 365, 366
Veblen, [Thorstein], 4
Veller, Gerhard, 280
Vertical integration, 7, 196
and decision making, 427, 450 n. 7
and industry subgroups, 448
and innovation, 296
measures of, 431, 433, 434, 451 n. 11
and NPD, 438–439, 449–450, 451
n. 17
and performance, 427
and profitability, 450 n. 7
and technological change, 439
and TFP growth, 442, 443, 446, 447,
448, 449–450
and trade-offs, 429
Video cassette recorder (VCR), 292,
317–327
Videodisc, 298, 316 n. 19
Videoplayer, home, 291, 298, 301, 303
Videotape recorders (VTRs), 303, 312,
325–326
design of, 319–327
origin of, 317–318
Videotex, 297, 315 n. 1

Walton, Richard E., 8, 9, 149, 150,
237–265, 284, 285, 286, 470
commentary on, 267–277
Warda, J., 400 n. 19, 400–401 n. 21,
401 n. 26
Waste products
and product development, 51 n. 64
and scientific research, 53
Waste rates, 169–170, 184–185, 248
Watanabe, Mr., 343, 346, 353, 361
Waterman, Robert H., Jr., 95, 119, 378
Weick, Karl E., 340
Welch, Jack, 334
Wells, David A., 75
Wheelwright, S.C., 92, 152, 450 n. 7
Willey, Stephen, 283
Wingard, Donald, 143
Winter, Sidney G., 301, 450 n. 2, n. 6
Wood. *See* Construction industry
Work environment
and early factory conditions, 68–69
and subtle control, 358
Work force
age of, and TFP, 174
in commitment model, 150, 241, 248
as cost, 64
and early factory system, 67, 68, 69
education of, 174
and innovation, 293
as managers, 241
and mass production, 71–72
perceptions of, 15, 64, 65, 100
and product development, 354
and TFP, 149–150
See also Labor; Labor-management
relations
Work force, blue-collar, 198, 258, 262
Work force, clerical, 262
Work force management
paradigms for, 264 n. 11
policies for, 7, 8, 148, 152, 173–178,
198
See also Commitment model for work
force management; Control
model for work force management; Transformation model for
work force management
Work-in-process (WIP), 280. *See also*
Inventory, WIP
Work technologies, 247, 255–257
Worker. *See* Work force

Yachiyo Kogyo, 362
Yoshino, Mr., 358
You, J.K., 450 n. 9
Yui, Tsunehiko, 60

This book was set in a Century Schoolbook typeface created by the Linotype Company for digitized photo composition. This version follows closely an 1894 revival by T. L. DeVinne of Century Expanded, but retains the modern look and improvements for legibility added by a Mr. Van Sayre for the Monotype Corporation in 1932. The book was printed by offset lithography on acid free paper.